Integrating Multiculturalism into the Curriculum

COUNTERPOINTS

Studies in the Postmodern Theory of Education

Shirley R. Steinberg
General Editor

Vol. 391

The Counterpoints series is part of the Peter Lang Education list.
Every volume is peer reviewed and meets
the highest quality standards for content and production.

PETER LANG
New York • Washington, D.C./Baltimore • Bern
Frankfurt • Berlin • Brussels • Vienna • Oxford

Integrating Multiculturalism into the Curriculum

From the Liberal Arts to the Sciences

Edited by Sandra Mayo & Patricia J. Larke

PETER LANG
New York • Washington, D.C./Baltimore • Bern
Frankfurt • Berlin • Brussels • Vienna • Oxford

Library of Congress Cataloging-in-Publication Data

Integrating multiculturalism into the curriculum: from the liberal arts to the sciences / edited by Sandra Mayo, Patricia J. Larke.
pages cm. —
(Counterpoints: studies in the postmodern theory of education; v. 391)
Includes bibliographical references.
1. Universities and colleges—Curricula—United States.
2. Multicultural education—United States. 3. Multiculturalism.
4. Critical pedagogy. I. Title. II. Mayo, Sandra. II. Larke, Patricia J.
LB2361.5.M384 378'.010973—dc23 2012036413
ISBN 978-1-4331-0978-2 (hardcover)
ISBN 978-1-4331-0977-5 (paperback)
ISBN 978-1-4539-0841-9 (e-book)
ISSN 1058-1634

Bibliographic information published by **Die Deutsche Nationalbibliothek**.
Die Deutsche Nationalbibliothek lists this publication in the "Deutsche Nationalbibliografie"; detailed bibliographic data is available on the Internet at http://dnb.d-nb.de/.

The paper in this book meets the guidelines for permanence and durability of the Committee on Production Guidelines for Book Longevity of the Council of Library Resources.

29 Broadway, 18th floor, New York, NY 10006
www.peterlang.com

Printed in the United States of America

CONTENTS

SECTION IV. GUIDES TO SYLLABI CHANGE

McCoy College of Business

Fine Arts and Communications

College of Science and Engineering

College of Applied Arts

Liberal Arts

University College

PREFACE

Integrating Multiculturalism into the Curriculum: From the Liberal Arts to the Sciences models a multicultural curriculum paradigm that has been a success at Texas State University–San Marcos; it is a universal model involving content and pedagogy that educators from other regions of the United States and even outside the United States will find useful. The strategies have been successfully presented at two northeast colleges and at a university in South Africa. In addition, the strategies were successfully used by multiculturalist Margie Kitano at San Diego State University in California. Theories from multicultural scholars around the country inspire the model. It is applicable to a diverse field of content disciplines taught throughout the United States and abroad, including teacher education, social work, music education, mathematics, and freshman seminar. The pedagogical strategies include culturally responsive teaching, communicating across differences, incorporating women and gender issues, and writing as a tool for infusing multicultural issues.

Integrating multiculturalism into the curriculum has been on the radar of colleges and universities around the United States for the last fifty or more years. The Civil Rights Movement led to a greater emphasis on inclusiveness throughout our society. Educational scholars, researchers, and practitioners have moved the multicultural curriculum initiative forward. They have been supported by a marketplace that is demanding a more culturally sensitive, multiculturally literate workforce.

Multicultural literacy is the ability to understand and appreciate the similarities and differences in the customs, values, and beliefs of one's own culture and the cultures of others (NCREL, 2003). According to the Institute for Educational Leadership Report (2005), to be culturally competent, our educational leaders need:

- an understanding of critical theories about how people learn, and the impact of race, power, legitimacy, cultural capital, poverty, disability, ethnicity, gender, age, language, and other factors on learning;
- an understanding of patterns of discrimination, inequality, and injustice, and the benefits and liabilities associated with individual groups; and
- an ability to articulate one's own philosophy of education and to use it to maintain the status quo or to empower others' active participation in their own transformations. (IEL, 2005)

In addition, our leaders need to know culturally relevant curricula and instructional strategies, and to possess a global perspective, all in support of student achievement. They have to be "cultural brokers," creating safe spaces where they effectively manage pressure, tension, stress, and turbulence. All of this must be done with empathy, commitment, high expectations, role modeling, and openness (IEL, 2005).

The Multicultural Curriculum Transformation and Research Institute at Texas State University–San Marcos (Texas State) seeks to help faculty review the theory and best practices relevant to becoming culturally competent facilitators of learning. This book will help readers to understand the Texas State paradigm for success in making courses more multicultural.

Section I consists of two chapters. Chapter 1 shares the history of the Multicultural Curriculum Transformation and Research Institute, including its goals, institutional support, pedagogical strategies, and faculty recruitment. Chapter 2 includes discussion of seven years of data, including faculty feedback and student survey responses.

Section II includes representative articles from faculty presenters/facilitators at the Institute. The five chapters give the readers a sampling of the content presented at the Institute.

Section III includes seven chapters by Texas State faculty who attended the Institute and then altered their courses. Each chapter describes how their courses were transformed, with course information from before and after changes. The chapters also discuss sample lectures, student projects, and other materials that assisted in the transformation process.

Section IV includes twelve course transformation samples from six colleges of Texas State: the College of Business Administration, College of Fine Arts and Communication, College of Science and Engineering, College of Applied Arts, College of Liberal Arts, and University College. Each sample includes an assessment instrument discussing the transformation strategies and the transformed syllabus. The assessment instrument is the multicultural course identification instrument used as a standard form for all faculty members seeking a multicultural designation for their courses.

The Multicultural Curriculum Transformation and Research Institute is a university-wide initiative with input and participation at all levels. The president reports on the progress of the initiative in reports to the university and the board of regents. The provost sends a recruiting letter each year to the deans to forward to the faculty, and sends congratulatory letters to the faculty after completing the Institute. The deans, in consultation with the department chairs and the director of the Institute, select the participants and recognize them at opening semester convocations. The faculty members serve as consultants, hold sessions for their colleagues, and encourage participation each year. This process denotes a real commitment for diversity, for it is truly a community effort. This book, with participation from faculty presenters and faculty participants, reflects the village that makes the Institute a success.

In conclusion, *Integrating Multiculturalism into the Curriculum: From the Liberal Arts to the Sciences* presents a model created in the diverse state of Texas; Texas State University's demographics, with 35,000 students, reflect the diversity of the state and the nation. This book provides ideas for a cross-section of university and college disciplines—history, English, psychology, anthropology, art history, sociology, education, mathematics, and others—across the country and abroad. It provides tools that can be used to positively impact a diverse group of university students preparing themselves for work and citizenship in the twenty-first century.

We would like to thank the following individuals who provided valuable support, from editing to reviewing manuscripts, in preparing this book for publication: Stacey Wilson, Luann Walker, Geneva Gay, Evangeline Castle, Alan J. Singer, Robert Ellison, Alex Colvin, Brenda T. Walker, Deneese Jones, Valerie Pang, Ronald Rochon, Pamela Melcher, Gwendolyn Webb-Hasan, Jamaal Young, Gail Taylor, and Patricia Marshall.

References

Institute for Educational Leadership (IEL). (2005). *Preparing and supporting diverse, culturally competent leaders: Practice and policy considerations.* Washington, DC: Author. Retrieved from http://www.iel.org/pubs/diverseleaders.pdf

North Central Regional Educational Laboratory (NCREL). (2003). *EnGauge twenty-first century skills: Literacy in the digital age.* Naperville, IL: Learning Point Associates, North Central Regional Educational Laboratory and the Metiri Group. Retrieved from http://pict.sdsu.edu/engauge21st.pdf

SECTION I.

History of the Institute and Institute Research

This section includes two chapters—one on the history of the Multicultural Curriculum Transformation Institute, and the other on research from the Institute. Chapter 1 covers the goals, institutional support, pedagogical strategies, and faculty recruitment. Chapter 2 covers seven years of data from the Institute, including faculty feedback and student survey responses.

1

Multicultural Curriculum Transformation at Texas State University–San Marcos

Sandra Mayo

Historical Overview

> We are in a search of what John Dewey called "The Great Community," but, at once, we are challenged as never before to confront plurality and multiplicity.
> —Green, M., The passions of pluralism: Multiculturalism expanding community

Introduction

In 1984 Texas State University–San Marcos (Texas State, or the University) began a significant commitment to diversity by establishing the Center for Multicultural and Gender Studies (the Center, or MCGS) to manage a minor in ethnic studies (now diversity studies) and women's studies. As the country rallied to the call for an inclusive curriculum for K-12, Texas State took additional steps to ensure student exposure to diversity issues. In 1999 the President's Task Force on Diversity recommended a five-point strategy for enhancing diversity at Texas State University (at that time, Southwest Texas State University) that included a curriculum proposal. The proposal articulated the following goals:

- By fall 2000, students in Freshman Seminar will have two sessions that deal with diversity issues, led by specially trained Freshman Seminar instructors.
- By fall 2004, graduation requirements for all incoming freshmen will include two courses (a minimum of 6 hours) that carry a "MC" designation indicating multicultural emphasis.

However, their recommendations remained in the proposal stage until 2001, when a new director of the Center began her tenure with the mission to study the multicultural curriculum environment and move the initiative forward. Fortunately, the University was beginning the development of the new strategic plan with an extensive diversity component that included recruitment of faculty, staff, and students, as well as increasing the use of HUB (historically underrepresented businesses) vendors and diversifying the curriculum. The new MCGS director worked with the Equity and Access Committee, which led development of the diversity component of the plan that included the multicultural curriculum component. The University's 2004–2009 Strategic Plan (updated to 2012, then 2017) states that "...the curriculum will reflect a multicultural perspective...[and] annually, two courses in each college will be modified to reflect multicultural content and/or perspectives."

Shortly after the approval of the 2004–2009 University Strategic Plan, the Center director proposed the Multicultural Curriculum Transformation Institute (the Institute) as a way to accomplish the goal annually. Immediate approval of this plan by the provost led to the pilot year in 2004 and the establishment of the Multicultural Curriculum Transformation Institute at Texas State in 2005 (renamed Multicultural Curriculum Transformation and Research Institute in 2008).

This chapter will introduce Texas State and the Center for Multicultural and Gender Studies. It will then focus on the Institute's goals, organizational history, pedagogical strategies, and recruitment of faculty.

Texas State University–San Marcos and the Center for Multicultural and Gender Studies

Texas State University–San Marcos is a doctoral granting university located between Austin and San Antonio, Texas on the Interstate 35 corridor. In Fall 2012 Texas State had approximately 34,000 students enrolled in ninety-seven bachelor's, eighty-nine master's, and nine doctoral degree programs offered by the following colleges: College of Applied Arts, McCoy College of Business Administration, College of Education, College of Fine Arts and Communication, College of Health Professions, College of Liberal Arts, College of Science and Engineering, University College, and the Graduate College.

Texas State's campus is the largest one in the Texas State University system, and the sixth largest university in the state of Texas. Today it consists of a 457-acre main campus and 5,038 additional acres in recreational, instructional, and farm and ranch land. More than 35% of the students are students of color. *Hispanic Outlook* ranks Texas State fourteenth in the nation for the number of bachelor's degrees awarded to Latino students. The University is one of the top twenty producers of Hispanic baccalaureate graduates in the nation and is among the largest producers of new K-12 educators in the state each year.

As part of the College of Liberal Arts, the Center for Multicultural and Gender Studies, in addition to managing the annual Multicultural Curriculum Transformation and Research Institute, houses and administers the undergraduate diversity studies minor (renamed from ethnic studies in 2009) and the graduate and undergraduate women's studies minor. The Center sponsors the Women and Gender Research Collaborative and the peer-reviewed online *Journal of Research on Women and Gender*. The Center also houses a resource library to assist faculty and students with content related to diversity issues. In addition, the Center sponsors and co-sponsors a variety of co-curricular activities including symposiums, exhibits, book and film discussions, and workshops. Through private donations, MCGS offers annual scholarships to students. The director of MCGS works in collaboration with an advisory council of faculty and staff representing Texas State colleges and departments.

The Multicultural Curriculum Transformation and Research Institute Organizational History

The director of the Center manages the Institute with two associate directors, an administrative assistant, and a student worker. A team of faculty members, including national known guest scholars and Texas State faculty and staff consultants facilitate the delivery of the content via lectures, small group sessions, and one-on-one consultations. In collaboration with the chairs and deans, the Center director selects two faculty members from each college to participate each year, based on their applications. After completing the Institute, faculty members submit a transformed syllabus and an assessment instrument describing the transformation. The transformation documents are reviewed by the MCGS advisory council for a recommendation, and then forwarded to the chair and dean for final approval of the multicultural designation.

In the 2006 spring semester, the second year of the Institute, systemic change came to Texas State in the area of multicultural curriculum. The provost, with the sanction of the Council of Deans, announced a university-wide procedure for identifying and classifying multicultural courses. Thus began the Texas State process for courses to receive University-approved multicultural designations.

In 2011, the Center for Multicultural Cultural and Gender Studies held its seventh annual Multicultural Curriculum Transformation and Research Institute (MCTRI or the Institute) to help the colleges of the University achieve the goal of transforming courses to reflect multicultural content and perspectives. In 2004 the two-month summer pilot program began, with four faculty members working on research and implementation of multicultural curriculum infusion best practices. Two faculty members represented the College of Science and Engineering, one represented the College of Education, and one the McCoy College of Business Administration. Their work produced not only transformed courses but also a collection of resources for faculty in their departments and colleges. The

Institute ran as a two-week session for the first three years (2005, 2006, and 2007), and then it was revised to a one-week session in 2008, 2009, 2010, and 2011.

Since 2005, 102 Texas State faculty members—representing all of the colleges—have completed the Institute (including one guest). Many of the faculty members who transformed a course during the Institute also transformed their other courses after their participation in the Institute. Several faculty members have led sessions on multicultural curriculum best practices for their departments, and officially serve as multicultural curriculum consultants for their colleges. In addition, throughout the year, the director of the Center (and the Institute) engages in one-on-one mentoring of faculty members who have not completed the Institute but wish to transform their courses in order to receive a multicultural designation.

Diversity studies, international studies, and women's studies are the key multicultural content areas identified for multicultural designations. To receive a multicultural content designation, the course must have a minimum of 60% multicultural content; to receive a multicultural perspectives designation, the course must include multicultural approaches to teaching strategies, assessment, and classroom dynamics. Courses with the multicultural perspectives designation (without the multicultural content designation) have less than 60% multicultural content. Most of the transformed courses have received both multicultural content and multicultural perspectives designations. To date, nine core curriculum courses have received multicultural designations:

- Communication 1310 (Fundamentals of Human Communication);
- English 1310 and English 1320 (Freshman English);
- History 1310 and History 1320 (History of the United States);
- TH 2313 Introduction to Fine Arts: Theatre;
- MUSI 2313 Introduction to Fine Arts: Music;
- ARTS 2313 Introduction to Fine Arts: Art; and
- DANC 2313 Introduction to Fine Arts: Dance.

Through this work, Texas State achieved and surpassed the goal recommended in 1999 by the President's Diversity Task Force to include at least six or more required hours with multicultural content or perspectives for all students; in 2012 we had a total of eighteen hours required in the core. (Students choose one of the four fine arts courses.)

Once a course receives the multicultural designation, the information is communicated in the comment section of the course schedule by section. The department may seek a multicultural designation for all sections, as in the core courses mentioned above. Unless the designation was sought and approved for all sections of the course, only the section taught by the faculty member who completed the transformation will show the multicultural designation. If all sections of the course are multicultural, as in the freshman English writing courses, then the catalog also notes the multicultural designation. The Center website includes an annually updated inventory of courses with multicultural designations. Deans, chairs, and college advising offices receive a listing each semester of the courses in the semester schedule that have multicultural designations. This list is also posted on the Center website. Students, upon request, may have the multicultural courses identified on their transcripts.

Rationale and Objectives

The Institute works to help Texas State to recruit and retain a diverse population of students. The purpose is to enhance faculty excellence in serving the students. The focus is on positive outcomes for students, including helping them (1) to enhance their multicultural understanding and sensitivity, (2) to manage effectively in the multicultural marketplace at home and abroad, and (3) to operate effectively at all levels of a democratic pluralistic society.

The annual Institute goals support the multicultural curriculum initiative at Texas State. The Institute goals are as follows:

- To enhance understanding of best practice multicultural curriculum teaching strategies;
- To assist faculty with multicultural curriculum transformation;
- To provide networking opportunities;
- To help faculty improve course evaluations;
- To develop department leaders in multicultural curriculum transformation;
- To promote research and publication in multicultural curriculum; and
- To help the colleges of Texas State achieve the multicultural curriculum strategic plan goals.

Expected outcomes from the Institute are:

- Greater understanding of multicultural teaching content and pedagogy;
- Greater awareness of resources available to assist with multicultural curriculum transformation;
- A completed multicultural course assessment instrument for at least one course;
- A transformed syllabus for at least one course; and
- A transformed course that can receive a multicultural designation.

Pedagogical Foundation

The pedagogical foundation of the Institute is aligned with Texas State's Multicultural Policy Statement, which has been included in the catalog since 1984. It states:

> [The University] believes that freedom of thought, innovation, and creativity are fundamental characteristics of a community of scholars. To promote such a learning environment, the university has a special responsibility to seek diversity, to instill a global perspective in its students, and to nurture sensitivity, tolerance, and mutual respect. Discrimination against or harassment of individuals on the basis of race, color, national origin, religion, sex, sexual orientation, age, or disability are inconsistent with the purpose of the university. (Texas State University–San Marcos, 2010)

The definition of multicultural education that guides the work of the Institute comes from Margie Kitano's "Rationale and Framework for Course Change" (1997a):

> Multicultural education is the development of citizens for a more democratic society through provision of more accurate and comprehensive disciplinary knowledge and through enhancement of students' academic achievement and critical thinking applied to social problems. The promotion of the values of diversity and equal opportunity for all people through understanding of the contributions and perspectives of people of differing race, ethnicity, culture, language, religion, gender, sexual orientation, and physical abilities and disabilities. (p. 12)

In addition, James Banks's five dimensions of multicultural education undergird the multicultural pedagogy at Texas State. They are: (1) content integration, (2) [enhanced awareness of] knowledge construction, (3) prejudice reduction, (4) equity pedagogy, and (5) an empowering school culture (Banks, 2004). Introducing Texas State's Multicultural Policy Statement, and highlighting its resemblance to definitions and dimensions clarified by Kitano and Banks, helps highlight for faculty the rationale and significant goals and pedagogical strategies of multicultural education, but also the wide net of potential benefits.

Margie Kitano's article "What a Course Will Look Like After Multicultural Change" (1997b) is the inspiration for the multicultural curriculum paradigm at Texas State. This paradigm includes a course description that identifies the multicultural elements, and multicultural goal statements related to four basic elements for change: content, teaching strategies, assessment, classroom dynamics. Drawing on the scholarship of multicultural educators over the past twenty-five years, Kitano recommends classifying the transformation elements into three levels: (1) the traditional curriculum (noninclusive), (2) the addition of different perspectives (inclusive), and (3) critical thinking, examination of the construction of knowledge, and synthesis of old and new perspectives. Many other scholarly books and articles also inform the Institute's work.

For example, the Institute's activities relating to understanding the culture of self and others are influenced by Kenneth Cushner's *Human Diversity in Action* (2006); its strategies for inclusiveness and teaching students of color by Geneva Gay's *Culturally Responsive Teaching* (2000); communicating in conflict as articulated in Mitchell Hammer's *Intercultural Conflict Style Inventory* (2005); assessing student learning in a multicultural environment in Rena Lewis's "Assessment of Student Learning" (1997); and strategies for assessing diversity courses in Jack Meacham "Assessing Diversity Courses" (2000).

Snapshot of the Weekly Institute Schedule

This section will provide a snapshot of the one-week program of professional development for faculty in the Institute. The activities expose faculty to the elements (theory and practice) of Texas State's course infusion paradigm.

The Activities. Variety was the goal in the day-to-day activities of the Institute. Thus, the week included formal presentations with interactions, individual reflection, small group discussions and brainstorming, independent research, and networking. Each day ran from 8:30 a.m. until 4:30 p.m. with an hour break for lunch. Lunch was provided so that participants would be encouraged to stay and network during the lunch hour. Each morning began with debriefing and reflections from the previous day. During the two-week Institute, there was more time allotted for individual research and reflection, so many of the faculty completed their transformations before they left the Institute. Nevertheless, faculty welcomed the sacrifice of independent time because they found it easier to take one week, rather than two weeks, to devote to the Institute between the spring semester and summer sessions.

The Process. Transforming the course involves analyzing it to determine multicultural infusion in four major areas (content, teaching strategies, assessment, and class interactions), identifying the level of infusion, identifying the percentage of multicultural content, and identifying the focus as U.S., international, women's studies, or a combination of these. The activities and content of the Institute aid faculty members in rethinking all of these areas.

The Elements.

- Course Description: rethinking and rewording, and/or including an overview statement;
- Goals: rethinking, including revising and adding;
- Content: rethinking content and determining the level of infusion;

- Teaching Strategies: rethinking instruction, with an awareness of learning styles and of the need for variety in pedagogical strategies;
- Assessment: rethinking assessment to meet the needs of the course, but also with an awareness of the diversity in learning styles;
- Interactions: rethinking faculty-to-student and student-to-student interactions, with student engagement as a significant goal; and
- Evaluation/Outcomes: documenting the effectiveness of multicultural goals.

The Topics. Some of the key topics during the week of the Institute include:

1. reflecting on your teaching style,
2. cultural self-assessment,
3. Texas State student diversity,
4. cross-cultural communication and intercultural conflict,
5. culturally responsive teaching in theory, and content-specific strategies,
6. multicultural resources and research strategies,
7. learning styles and culturally responsive assessment practices,
8. infusing multiculturalism into the curriculum through writing,
9. infusing a global perspective,
10. infusing images and realities of women,
11. multicultural strategies in large, small, and online classes, and
12. research initiatives: documenting the effectiveness of multicultural goals.

In addition, previous participants led a few sessions in which they discuss their transformations—from Institute to transformation and implementation, and student feedback.

Recruitment of Faculty. The keys to success in getting faculty to "buy in"—that is, to participate in multicultural curriculum transformation projects with the Institute—have involved six factors, which I discuss below.

Institutional Support. The most significant strategy for success was getting the multicultural initiative detailed in the 2004–2009 University Strategic Plan (updated to 2012, then 2017), with specific outcomes measures. In addition to a clearly articulated strategic plan, ongoing financial support for the Institute encourages faculty involvement. The financial support assists with management, instruction, faculty participation, stipends, and supplies. Two faculty members from each college may receive funds to attend each year, with some flexibility as needed.

Compensation. With demands on faculty time coming from other workshops, research projects, teaching, service, and summer vacation, compensation in the form of a substantial financial stipend encourages faculty to dedicate one or two weeks to earn a multicultural designation for a specified course. Moreover, tenure-track faculty members and senior faculty members are inspired by the opportunity to enrich their teaching, review best-practice teaching strategies, and network with their colleagues. Faculty compensation includes incentives to turn in outcome measures reports for transformed courses, and to make conference presentations or publish articles related to the transformation.

Emphasis on Benefits. The Institute's promotional materials emphasize the benefits of attending, including stipends, networking, improved student responses, research opportunities and incentives, and consultant opportunities.

Consultant Opportunities. An official board of consultants made up of former Institute participants now exists for each college. Participants have welcomed the honor and the opportunity to serve as leaders in multicultural education in their colleges and departments. Beginning in 2008, the Institute's recruitment brochure personalized the call to enroll by including testimonials from previous participants representing all of the colleges of the University. In addition, former participants have had the opportunity to serve on an ad hoc committee to give input for revision of future Institutes.

Well-Planned, Relevant Instruction. The week of activities is a combination of theory and practice. A participant handbook with information and activities and an online resource site supplements and complements the Institute's presentations and activities. The daily activities include opportunities for self-reflection, growth, and change. Faculty participants get ideas from the diverse group of presenters and each other. Many find the opportunity to network with other faculty from their disciplines and other disciplines at the University productive and inspiring.

Conclusion

Having a multicultural curriculum transformation institute can assist all stakeholders, faculty, students, and the university as a whole with preparing a workforce for living and working in a global society. No longer can institutions rely on mere rhetoric in their missions regarding diversity; they must begin to strategically address the issues to enhance the ability of faculty to utilize multicultural course transformation to prepare multiculturally literate students who will, more than any previous generation, live and work in the global society.

> We require a curriculum that can help provoke persons to reach past themselves and to become. We want to see them in their multiplicity linking arms, becoming recognized. We want them in their ongoing quests for what it means to be human to be free to move. (Greene, 1993a, p. 220)

References

Banks, J. (2004). Multicultural education: Historical development, dimensions and practice. In J. Banks & C. Banks, *Handbook of research on multicultural education* (2nd ed.) (pp. 3–29). San Francisco, CA: Jossey-Bass.

Banks, J., & Banks, C. (2004). *Handbook of research on multicultural education* (2nd ed.). San Francisco, CA: Jossey-Bass.

Cushner, K. (2006). *Human diversity in action: Developing multicultural competencies for the classroom* (3rd ed.). Boston, MA: McGraw-Hill.

Gardner, H. (1993). *Frames of mind: Theory* of *multiple intelligences*. New York, NY: Basic Books.

Gay, G. (2000). *Culturally responsive teaching: Theory, research and practice*. New York, NY: Teachers College Press.

Greene, M. (1993a). Diversity and inclusion: Toward a curriculum for human beings. *Teachers College Record, 95* (2), 211–221.

Greene, M. (1993b). The passions of pluralism: Multiculturalism expanding community. *Educational Researcher, 22* (1), 13–18.

Hammer, M. R. (2005). The intercultural conflict style inventory: A conceptual framework and measure of intercultural conflict approaches. *International Journal of Intercultural Research, 29*, 675–695.

Kitano, M. (1997a). Rationale and framework for course change. In I. A. Morey & M. Kitano (Eds.), *Multicultural curriculum transformation in higher education: A broader truth* (pp. 1–17). New York, NY: Allyn & Bacon.

Kitano, M. (1997b). What a course will look like after multicultural change. In I. A. Morey & M. Kitano (Eds.), *Multicultural curriculum transformation in higher education: A broader truth* (pp. 18–34). New York, NY: Allyn & Bacon.

Lewis, R. B. (1997). Assessment of student learning. In I. A. Morey & M. Kitano (Eds.), *Multicultural curriculum transformation in higher education: A broader truth* (pp. 71–88). New York, NY: Allyn & Bacon.

Meacham, Jack. (2000). Assessing diversity courses. *Diversity Digest* (spring/summer). Retrieved from http://www.diversityweb.org/digest/sp.sm00/courses.html

Morey, I. A., & Kitano, M. (1997). *Multicultural curriculum transformation in higher education: A broader truth*. New York, NY: Allyn & Bacon.

Texas State University–San Marcos. (1999). *President's task force on diversity*. San Antonio, TX (university archives).

———. (2004). Strategic plan 2004–2009. Retrieved from http://www.upa.txstate.edu/University-Plans/University-Plans-/contentParagraph/0/content_files/file4/2004-2009%20University%20Plan.pdf

———. (2010). Multicultural policy statement. *Undergraduate Catalog 2010–2012*. Retrieved from http://www.txstate.edu/curriculumservices/catalogs/undergraduate/catalogs/10-12.html

2

Program Evaluation: The Multicultural Curriculum Transformation and Research Institute

Patricia Larke

Program evaluations are necessary when sharing results regarding the effectiveness and impact of a program. As such, the Multicultural Curriculum Transformation and Research Institute (the Institute) has had ongoing program evaluation since 2005 (Mayo & Larke, 2010). The Institute's program evaluation aligns with Potter's (2006) research about critical and emancipatory program evaluation that is based on action research. The Institute program was designed for social transformation of multicultural education content and activities in college courses. Under Potter's model, "the purpose of evaluation is to develop the critical awareness of those involved in program—not only about their own practices, but also about the social issues and the power relationships implicit in the social contexts in which they work" (pp. 421–422). The work is based on Friere's (1972) critical evaluation research that involves understanding forms of structural oppression (relating to race, gender, SES) and empowering program participants to mobilize against them. The program evaluation involves documenting stories, teaching materials, and examples of classroom work, and a self-evaluation process to denote development and improvement.

There were three research questions that guided the evaluation process: (1) What were faculty perceptions about the Institute?; (2) How did faculty transform their courses?; and (3)What were faculty and students perceptions about the transformed courses? Data were collected at three points, via Institute evaluation surveys, completed every year at the end of the Institute; faculty-submitted outcome measures reports of the transformed courses; and student evaluations of transformed courses. This chapter will discuss the results of the Institute evaluation surveys for the past seven years; a summary of three outcomes measures reports; and selected faculty and student responses to transformed courses and faculty testimonials.

Results of Institute Evaluation Survey, 2005–2011

Faculty Participants

The total number of faculty participants in the Multicultural Curriculum Transformation and Research Institute in the years 2005–2011 was 102. The greatest number of participants was in 2008, with 17 participants, and the least number was in 2007, with 12 participants. Over seven years, participants attended the Institute from all of the colleges in the University (see Table 1). Applied Arts had a total of 15 participants, Fine Art had 16 participants, Business had 13 participants, and Health and Education each had 12 participants. Liberal Arts had the most, with 20 participants, and Science had the least, with 5 participants. Science, University College, Health, and Applied Arts were the only colleges that did not have participants every year. During 2007, one faculty member was sent from her college in Boston, Massachusetts to experience the Institute and make a recommendation for further work in this area. (Thereafter, the college in Boston invited the Institute director to lead workshops for them and to help train several faculty members to conduct similar workshops at their institution.)

Table 1. Institute Participants, 2005–2011

	2005	2006	2007	2008	2009	2010	2011	Total
Applied Arts	2	2	0	2	5	2	2	15
Business	1	3	1	2	2	2	2	13
Education	2	2	1	2	1	2	2	12
Fine Arts	3	2	3	3	2	1	2	16
Health	2	1	2	2	0	2	3	12
Liberal Arts	3	3	3	3	4	2	2	20
Science	1	1	0	1	0	1	1	5
University College	0	1	2	1	1	2	1	8
Other University	0	0	0	1	0	0	0	1
Total	14	15	12	17	15	14	15	102

Table 2. Completed Evaluations, 2005–2011

Year	%	# Com	Total #
2005	92	13	14
2006	73	11	15
2007	100	12	12
2008	94	16	17
2009	100	15	15
2010	92	13	14
2011	100	15	15
Total		95	102

Conference Evaluation Instrument

After each year, the director conducted an evaluation. The evaluation instrument consisted of seven questions about the Institute materials, information from facilitators, communication, hospitality, sharing with colleagues, administration of program, and overall Institute evaluation. Participants responded with ratings the were given numerical values of: 1 = poor, 2 = fair, 3 = good, and 4 = excellent. From 2005 to 2009, the evaluation instrument had eight questions; one question was eliminated in 2010. For the purpose of this research, only seven questions were examined because all participants had the same seven questions on their evaluation instrument for the years 2005–2011. In addition, there were three open-ended questions.

Completed Evaluations

In 2005, 92% (N= 13 of 14) completed the evaluations; in 2006, 73% (N= 11/15) were completed; in 2008, 94% (N= 16/17) were completed; in 2010, 92% (N=13/14) were completed (see Table 2). There was a 100% completion rate in 2007 (12/12), 2009 (15/15), and 2011 (15/15). The overall completion rate between 2005 and 2011 was 94% (N=95/102).

Table 3 shares the mean scores of the 95 participants who completed the conference evaluation instrument. The administration of the program had the highest mean (M=3.90); sharing information with colleagues was second (M=3.88); hospitality (M=3.86) was third. Communication had a mean of 3.83 and the Institute materials mean was 3.82.

Table 3. Mean Scores of Evaluation Instrument, 2005–2011

Stem	Mean
Institute Materials	3.82
Information from Facilitators	3.77
Communication	3.83
Hospitality	3.86
Sharing with Colleagues	3.88
Administration of Program	3.90
Overall Institute Evaluation	3.84

The Institute had more than ten guest speakers, from various departments in the University as well as other invited national speakers. Participants felt that the speakers provided valuable information, as indicated by the 3.77 of 4.0 mean score. The speakers' topics were:

1. cultural self-assessment;
2. cross-cultural communication;
3. intercultural conflict;
4. culturally responsive teaching and content enrichment;
5. multicultural curriculum resources and research strategies;
6. learning styles and culturally responsive assessment practices;
7. infusing multiculturalism into the curriculum through writing;
8. enriching the curriculum with images and realities of women;
9. transformation strategies for large, small, and online classes;
10. review of multicultural assessment instruments; and
11. documenting effectiveness of multicultural goals.

Overall, the participants felt that the Institute was informative, they learned much from the speakers, the hospitality was impressive, and the program's leadership was commendable, as evidenced by the Institute's overall evaluation of 3.84.

Analysis of Open-Ended Questions. Three open-ended questions were included on the survey. A content analysis of the three questions revealed three themes: faculty networking, instructional materials, and strategies and empowerment.

Faculty Networking. Faculty found the collaboration and interactions with other faculty members a valuable part of the experience. They felt that getting to meet and network with other faculty members was the highlight of the Institute. For example, one respondent wrote:

> I was delighted by this experience. I was able to successfully transform my syllabus, and the session I attended also let me interact with teachers from various disciplines. On any issue I was able to hear a variety of perspectives, and I came away from my session convinced there are plenty of committed teachers at [the institution]. (Professor A)

Instructional Materials and Strategies. Faculty comments about the instructional materials indicated that they enjoyed the opportunity to share instructional materials, exchange ideas, and learn new pedagogy and content. One faculty member stated:

> The Institute reminded me about many of the goals I'd had when I became a university professor, and it introduced me to new strategies for realizing those goals. It was also taught in the way I want to teach: openly, welcoming alternate views, and championing differences. (Professor B)

Additionally, faculty commented on how they were rethinking their syllabi and incorporating culturally responsive teaching and other information into their courses. One faculty member stated: "I thought a lot about the way I teach and how I learn and how they're not aligned." Faculty acknowledged the effectiveness of the speakers in providing useful information and multiple perspectives about issues. One participant stated: "I was enriched by the plethora of approaches presented by the facilitators and participants."

Several faculty members noted that participating in the Institute had boosted their self-confidence. For example, one wrote, "I felt empowered and justified in my ways of thinking about how courses should be taught...I knew that I was a good teacher before, but now I feel I can be a great teacher!" Another faculty captured it further by noting "...the validation that I do already teach in a culturally responsive way, and now I have the resources to take it even further!"

When asked how the Institute can be improved, the suggestions included adding information on Latino students, gender issues, and differently-abled students. In addition, the participants wanted more hands-on information, and suggested including previous graduates as speakers and providing more time with speakers.

Summary of Three Outcomes Measures Reports

Participants from the Institute prepare outcome measures reports as a part of the program evaluation after teaching the transformed course. Upon completion, usually at the end of the semester, the outcome measures report is submitted to the director for review. The report includes background about the course, information related to the course transformation, and student responses to the evaluation instrument used to assess the success of the multicultural goals. The three courses selected for the analysis here are: English 1310 and 1320 (fall 2010 report), English 3385 (fall 2008), and History 1310 (fall 2008). Each is represented in Tables 4, 5, and 6.

English 1310 and 1320

English 1310 and 1320 are freshman English courses. These courses were taught with thirteen sections, and this outcome measures report is based on 235 student evaluations that accounted for 7% of fall 2010 enrollment (see Table 5). The faculty met and agreed that the evaluation items should be expressed as statements rather than questions. The three statements were:

1. This course introduced texts and writers from a variety of cultural groups;
2. This course taught me to keep my readers in mind as I draft and revise my work; and
3. The instructor used a variety of class activities and types of assessment (for example, small-group activities, peer review, multiple drafts of papers, self-assessment).

The rates of positive responses (yes, agree, or true) to the statements were: 98% for statement 1, 89% for statement 2, and 99% for statement 3. A summary of students' comments indicates that they enjoyed reading a wide variety of authors that included Lao Tzu, Machiavelli, and Martin Luther King Jr., and that they felt that the class activities were very helpful.

English 3385 Children's Literature

This course involved a total of forty-eight students from two sections (see Table 5). This outcome measures report used two open-ended questions that were specific to multicultural aspects of teaching. These questions were: (1) What are the best features of the course?; and (2) Do you feel that this course has increased your cultural awareness, or your appreciation of diversity, or your understanding of the forces that shape culture or identity, and if so, how? While only eleven students responded in written statements to question 1, the summary of their statements revealed that they enjoyed learning about different cultures and different perspectives in reading, and that reading about different perspectives can affect others' outlooks on life. For question 2, 98% (N=42) of the students responded. They felt that the course challenged their Eurocentric thinking, and that the class highlighted the importance of accepting others. In this report, the instructor provided comments about students' evaluations, stating, for example, that students gained not only academic knowledge but also knowledge that will influence their way of thinking. This supports the notion that multicultural education is a philosophy and process, a way of thinking and a way of doing (Larke, 1991).

History 1310

This is a first-semester freshman American History course. The outcome measures report for this class included an online survey that 217 of the 350 students volunteered to complete. Thus, the response rate was 62%. The survey consisted of five statements to which students responded using a Likert-type scale (responses range from strongly agree to strongly disagree). The five statements were:

1. This course has helped me to understand myself and others in ways that go beyond stereotyped groups and categories;
2. I now have an increased awareness of the causes and effects of structural inequalities and prejudice;
3. This course introduced ideas I had not previously encountered;
4. I have been able to see connections between the material in this course and society today; and
5. I am now more convinced of the importance of the material in this course than when I began the course.

An analysis of the statements revealed that 70% agreed of strongly agreed with statement 1, and 89% felt the same about statement 2, while 84.5 to 85% either strongly agreed or agreed with statements 3 and 5, and 81.5% had the same level of agreement with statement 4. The report also provided a summary of comments for each of the statements. The comments ranged from an appreciation of the benefits of cultural diversity to an acknowledgment of the connection between the materials in the course and issues in society today. The summary report noted that students gained greater knowledge of diverse groups in American history and an appreciation of both the historical significance of cultural diversity and the significance of historical events for society today, and that students learned to see events or issues from others' perspectives.

Table 4. Selected Course Transformation Outcome Measures Report—English 1310 and 1320

Course Transformation Assessment for English 1310 & 1320 Fall 2010	Background: In August 2006 the Multicultural and Gender Studies Advisory Council endorsed multicultural content (MC) and multicultural perspectives (MP) designations for all sections of both first-year English courses (ENG 1310 and ENG 1320). The designation was discussed with English faculty during fall 2006 and first communicated in the catalog and schedule of classes for spring 2007.As reported at the end of the spring 2007 semester, a pilot assessment was less than satisfactory. The single broad evaluation question used at that time proved to be unclear to a number of students. As a result, the evaluation form was revised to include three specific questions designed to assess the multicultural content and perspective of those courses. The three questions were phrased as declarative statements (see below) and were placed on the standard departmental evaluation form. This revised form was first administered at the end of fall 2007 and is still being used.		
MC/MP Assessment Results/ Student Responses	Q1. This course introduced texts and writers from a variety of cultural groups.	Q2. This course taught me to keep my readers in mind as I draft and revise my work.	Q3. The instructor used a variety of class activities and types of assessment (for example, small-group activities, peer review, multiple drafts of papers, self-assessment).
1. Results from 235 student evaluations (representing 7% of the total fall 2010 enrollment in ENG 1310 and 1320) were examined. **2. The 235 students represent 13 sections of ENG 1310 and 1320, taught by 13 different instructors.**	**98% responded yes, agree, or true to statements.** **Summary of Statements** • "We read many different authors with various views and beliefs" • "We studied a very diverse group of authors" • "I enjoyed reading from such a wide range of authors" • "I would have never read some assigned things" • "[Reading the World] included Lao Tzu, Machiavelli, and Martin Luther King"	**89% responded yes, agree, or true to statements.** **Summary of Statements** • "It was harder than expected" • "I had trouble with this at the beginning, but as I planned other essays I remembered who I was writing to" • "I kept reminding myself about the peer critique" • "In all our prompts it says to consider our audience, and that helps" • "The outlines and rough drafts allowed me to keep this in mind"	**99% responded yes, agree, or true to statements.** **Summary of Statements** • "Involved the class a lot" • "Did many creative group activities that got every student involved" • "I liked when we put our desks in a circle to do class discussion; very helpful" • "Lots of activities that were very helpful" • "Extremely beneficial" • "Helped me understand my mistakes" • "Made the class more interesting"

Table 5. Selected Course Transformation Outcome Measures Report—English 3385 Children's Literature

Course Transformation Assessment for English 3385—Children's Literature Fall 2008	Background: In fall 2008 this course was transformed in respect to Multicultural Content and Perspective. In addition to the standard departmental student evaluation form, an additional evaluation question form was provided to students. The purpose of this two-pronged approach was to enable a distinction to be made between prompted and unprompted responses. The supplementary question sheet was designed to directly prompt students to reflect on their experience of the multicultural content and perspectives in the course. However, in designing and implementing this instrument, it was also expected that if the multicultural aspects of the course had indeed been genuinely effective, students should be able to offer positive feedback on these aspects without having to be prompted for it. In administering the instrument, the standard form was given to students first.		
MC/MP Assessment Results/ Student Responses	Q1. What are the best features of the course?	Q2. Do you feel that this course has increased your cultural awareness, or your appreciation of diversity, or your understanding of the forces that shape culture or identity? If so, how?	Q3. What was the instructor's Assessment of Course after student evaluations?
1. The course was taught to two sections of ENG 3385 with a total enrolment of 48. **2. 43 students completed evaluations when two sections were combined.**	**11 students responded.** **Summary of Statements** • "The diversity of the works studied" • "[Using] examples not just from American culture and history" • "Learning about different cultures" • "[Going] beyond the texts and discuss[ing] real world issues" • "Different perspectives of reading" • "[Reading] diverse children's stories" and "learning how reading [these] can affect people's outlook on life"	**98% (n=42) responded affirmatively to the questions.** **Summary of Statements** • "I have learned to think about things in not such an ethnocentric manner." • "I feel like I will leave this course with a mindset more open to various cultures and beliefs." • "I feel that I have gained the ability to analyze texts from different cultures and relate them to identity." • "This class has helped me to understand the importance of accepting others. Not everyone is the same, and getting out of one's comfort zone is crucial to the betterment of one's life."	**Summary of Statements** • Apparent that the majority of students enjoyed and benefited from the multicultural content and perspectives introduced by the course • Students recognized that the multicultural content was meant not only to be understood only in terms of intellectual knowledge, but also to address issues of perspective, and to shape the way they think and the way they approach issues of diversity in their own lives.

Table 6. Selected Course Transformation Outcomes Measures Report—History 1310

Course Transformation Assessment for History 1310 Fall 2008	Background: In summer 2008 the Multicultural and Gender Studies Advisory Council approved the multicultural content (MC) designation for all sections of the first-semester freshman survey course in American History, History 1310. Sections taught by Professor M, who completed the Multicultural Course Transformation Institute in May 2008, receive the MC and MP (multicultural perspectives) designation. Professor M designed an assessment survey for her teaching theater section of History 1310 in fall 2008. The survey was posted on the course's TRACS website at the end of the semester, and students were urged to complete it on a voluntary basis.						
MC/MP Assessment Results/ Student Responses	**Q1. This course has helped me to understand others and myself in ways that go beyond stereotyped groups and categories.**	**Q2. I now have an increased awareness of the causes and effects of structural inequalities and prejudice.**	**Q3. This course introduced ideas I had not previously encountered.**	**Q4. I have been able to see connections between the material in this course and society today.**	**Q5. I am now more convinced of the importance of the material in this course than when I began the course.**	**Q6. What was the summary of open-ended responses?**	**Q7. What was the instructor's Assessment of Course after student evaluations?**
1. Out of the approximately 350 students enrolled in the course, 217 completed the survey. **2. It consisted of five statements to which students could respond "strongly agree," "agree," "neutral," "disagree," and**	**70% students agreed or strongly agreed with this statement** **Summary of Statements** • Need to be more open-minded • Expressed an enhanced appreciation for the benefits and significance of cultural diversity.	**89% students agreed or strongly agreed with this statement** **Summary of Statements** • Three groups most commonly mentioned in relation to inequality and prejudice were women, African Americans, and Native Americans.	**84% responded agreed or strongly agreed with this statement** **Summary of Statements** • Social history component of the course. • Course's emphasis on the correlation between geographical and cultural differences.	**81.5% responded agreed or strongly agreed with the statements.** **Summary of Statements** • Expressed a greater understanding of how past prejudices and inequalities have structured today's society.	**84.5% responded agreed or strongly agreed with the statements.** **Summary of Statements** • Better able to relate to a history centered on multicultural social perspectives.	• Gained a greater knowledge of diverse groups in American history • Learned to see events or issues from others' perspectives. • Gained an appreciation for the historical significance of cultural diversity.	• Student answers reflect the success of one of the central objectives of the course, which is to provide students with a more accurate and complete understanding of American history. • Answers reflect a good grasp of the key themes of the course:

"strongly disagree," as well as an open-response question.		Students explained that while they knew something about the history of women, the theft of Indian land, and the issues of slavery and race discrimination, they felt that in the past they had gotten a "white-washed" version of these topics that did not allow them to fully understand the larger implications for society and the groups involved.	• Course's more in-depth coverage of Indian and slave cultures. Lecture material and readings on the evolution of attitudes towards gender and sexuality.	• Spoke more generally of gaining a greater appreciation of the extent to which the past shapes the present.	• Better able to understand the relevance of early national history for society today	• Gained an appreciation for the significance of historical events for society today.	1. How liberty for European Americans came at the expense of freedom for Native Americans and African Americans; 2. How liberty for men came at the expense of freedom for women; and 3. How subordinate groups have constantly tried to widen concepts of freedom and liberty to realize their radical democratic potential. • Overall, survey results suggest that the basic content and structure of the course are effective in achieving the goals of a multicultural curriculum.

Additional Responses From Faculty and Students About Transformed Course and Institute

Faculty participants completed follow-up surveys at the end of the semester and sent responses after teaching the transformed course. One faculty member stated:

> I have noticed a steady increase in the number of students who mention diversity and multicultural teaching in their comments on my course instructor evaluations, as well as those who give positive feedback regarding the "transformed" areas of my courses. (Professor C)

A second faculty member remarked:

> I get even more of these comments verbally. I feel I have always emphasized multiculturalism in my courses, but whereas the amount of emphasis has been constant, the institute help me change how I approach integrated multiculturalism in my teaching. (Professor D)

One faculty member noted, "I have also noticed that faculty now comment on multiculturalism within my T&P [tenure and promotion] materials" (Professor E).

One education faculty member added a question to her student survey, to which all students (100%) responded that the professor addressed relevant issues regarding diversity. One student captured the essence of the professor with the following statement:

> One of the most amazing characteristics of Professor F's teaching is her ability to create a space that is safe and comfortable for every one of her students. Her class encompasses such a great variety of experiences that help promote diversity and establish an environment in which all the voices are welcome, regardless of race, class, sexuality, gender, ethnicity, etc. Being an international student, I truly appreciated the classroom community that accepted and encouraged my cultural differences. (Student A)

Faculty Testimonials About the Institute

One faculty member remarked:

> My research interests include language issues in multicultural/multilinguistic populations and the courses I teach have a natural tendency toward topics in this area. However, while attending the MC Institute, I found that I can infuse multiculturalism into an entire course instead of brief section.... I benefited most from the MC Institute through expanding my views on how to present information to students in the most effective ways, particularly by acknowledg-

ing and allowing for different learning styles, as well as through widening my perception of multiculturalism.

Another faculty member stated that he was surprised at how easy it was to make his courses more diverse, and he has continued to use many of the ideas from the Institute in his teaching, including in a quantum mechanics class. One faculty member made comments about how she was able to manage cultural conflicts: "Participating in the Institute allowed me to see many more cultural connections in my research and teaching life." These comments were similar to others made by Institute participants over the years.

Summary

It is evident from the evaluation data that the Institute has made a change in the way faculty teach at Texas State University–San Marcos. Across the years, there is consistency in the evaluation instrument mean scores about the effectiveness of the Institute. The overall evaluation of the Institute was 3.8 points out of 4, with 94% of the participants completing the survey. Most of the participants ranked the Institute as excellent (4). The faculty and student comments were positive about the course changes. In course evaluations, according to the outcome measures report, student and faculty comments revealed that they learned valuable information about multicultural education issues. In addition, 78% of freshman surveyed volunteered to complete an evaluation that had questions specifically aligned with multicultural content. Faculty testimonials revealed that they learned much from the Institute to apply to their teaching as well as to their professional lives. More details of similar responses can be read in later chapters in this book that are authored by faculty participants. There is no doubt that the Institute is making changes in the way faculty are teaching about multiculturalism. Results from the Institute's evaluations can serve as a model for other universities that are serious about making systemic changes to integrate multiculturalism into their courses across college campuses.

References

Freire, P. (1972). *Cultural action for freedom*. Harmondsworth, UK: Penguin.

Larke, P. J. (1991). Multicultural education: A vital investment strategy for culturally diverse youth groups. *Journal of the Southeastern Association of Educational Opportunity Personnel, 10* (1), 11–22.

Mayo, S., & Larke, P. J. (2010). Multicultural education transformation in higher education: Getting faculty to "buy in." *Journal of Case Studies in Education, 1*, 1–9.

Potter, C. (2006). Program evaluation. In M. Terre Blanche, K. Durrheim, & D. Painter (Eds.), *Research in practice: Applied methods for the social sciences* (2nd ed.) (pp. 410–428). Cape Town, South Africa: UCT Press.

SECTION II.

Selected Content Presentations by Facilitators

This section includes representative presentations from four faculty facilitators at the Institute. The chapters give readers a sampling of the content presented during the Institute. The presenters' topics ranged from managing communication to culturally responsive teaching, introducing global perspectives, and incorporating the female voice.

3

Managing Communication and Disputes: The Multicultural Classroom

Walter Wright

Professors who want to encourage dynamic classroom discussions while maintaining respectful and supportive classroom environments can benefit from acquiring some basic communication and dispute-resolution skills and imparting those skills to students by discussing and modeling them in their classrooms. When students are from diverse cultural backgrounds, or when a course emphasizes multicultural content, professors can also benefit from becoming aware of the different approaches to communication and dispute resolution that people from different cultural backgrounds may bring into a classroom. This chapter is a guide to acquiring the necessary information and skills and using them effectively with students.

Without becoming experts in communication or dispute resolution, professors and students can acquire some basic skills in both areas and use the skills effectively in the classroom. This chapter provides references to some skills-building books to which professors and students may refer. Keeping in mind that time frames and budgets may both be limited, and that neither communication nor dispute resolution may be the primary subject of a multicultural course, this chapter also provides references to websites to which professors and students may refer for quick, inexpensive information and skills-building advice.

Defining and Acquiring Basic Communication and Dispute-Resolution Skills

This section will discuss three basic communication skills and three basic dispute-resolution skills. The basic communication skills are active listening, effective questioning, and summarizing or restating with neutral language. The basic dispute-resolution skills are discussing issues in a criticism-free zone, controlling defensive reactions, and considering other perspectives. These six skills are not the only communication or dispute-resolution skills professors and students might find useful in a classroom, but they are some of the most helpful, and classroom participants can learn to use them effectively in combination.

Basic Communication Skills

Active listening requires a listener to focus carefully on a speaker's words and body language in an effort to capture the speaker's entire message. An active listener seeks to understand the message before responding to it. Several books demonstrate active listening skills and help the reader acquire them (e.g., Brown & Smith, 2006; Burley-Allen, 1995). Because active listening is a popular subject among communication, negotiation, and mediation professionals, numerous websites provide basic, easy-to-understand information (e.g., Mind Tools, Ltd., 1996–2011). After reviewing the basic information, one should understand the importance of limiting "external distractions" (e.g., cell phones, other electronic devices, loud noises) and "internal distractions" (e.g., one's personal issues or concerns); focusing on the speaker's words, tone of voice, and body language; suspending judgment about the speaker's opinions or motives; and allowing the speaker to express an idea or opinion without interruption.

Effective questioning empowers a listener to use questions, rather than declarative statements, to maximize the information a speaker is willing to share and to clarify the speaker's meaning. Rather than convey an attitude of superiority or judgment, an effective questioner conveys an attitude of genuine interest in a speaker's message. Effective questioning in classroom discussions is motivated by a desire to understand the speaker's beliefs, ideas, and intentions. For such purposes, a professor might refer to Honolulu Community College's online *Teaching Tips Index*, particularly the section on "Using Questions Effectively in Teaching" (Honolulu Community College, 2011). Students as well as professors could benefit from reading about the types of questions and the strengths and weaknesses of each type (e.g., Binder, Bergman, & Price, 1996). After reviewing the basics, one should understand that the most useful types of questions include (a) "open" questions, which request a narrative response and allow the speaker to choose much of the response's content; (b) "clarifying" questions, which help the listener determine the speaker's meaning or intent; and (c) "closed" questions, which encourage a speaker to fill narrow, specific gaps in a listener's understanding. One also should understand the importance of avoiding or cautiously using "leading" questions, which suggest desired answers and sometimes contain outright declarations that may cause the speaker to respond defensively.

Summarizing or restating with neutral language permits a listener to demonstrate understanding of a speaker's message without expressing agreement or disagreement with the message. A listener who summarizes or restates a message with neutral language neither supports nor threatens the speaker or any other participant in a classroom discussion. Participants in classroom discussions summarize or restate in order to demonstrate their understanding of each other's messages. They can refer to some of the basic online information about this subject (e.g., Department of Veterans Affairs, 2004); the same is true for using neutral language. After reviewing the basics, one should understand that summarizing or restating with neutral language involves the use of nonjudgmental, descriptive language that accurately captures the speaker's entire message, including any emotional content.

Basic Dispute-Resolution Skills

The Harvard Negotiation Project inspired several popular dispute-resolution resources, including *Getting to Yes* (Fisher, Ury, & Patton, 1991) and *Getting Past No* (Ury, 1993), which negotiators often use when they engage in interest-based bargaining (sometimes called "win-win negotiation"). Mediators and facilitators have used ideas from the same books as a basis for many of their mediation models. Likewise, professors can use ideas from *Getting to Yes* and *Getting Past No* when structuring respectful and productive classroom discussions. These two books are inexpensive and easy to read, but information about interest-based bargaining is also available online and in other books. Three ideas for the classroom derived from these books are discussed below.

The idea of *discussing issues in a criticism-free zone* is derived from an important principle of interest-based bargaining expounded in *Getting to Yes*: "inventing options for mutual gain." Interest-based bargainers believe they achieve better negotiation outcomes by devoting a portion of each negotiation to a brainstorming session, during which each party in turn generates options while the other party or parties consider the options; no criticism of an option occurs until each party clearly understands the option, its purpose, and its potential effects. In a similar vein, discussing issues in a criticism-free zone permits a participant in a classroom discussion to express an opinion or idea without encountering immediate criticism.

Because *Getting to Yes* has been a popular book for decades, abundant information about this principle is available online (e.g., Glaser, 2003–2010). After reading the basic information in the book or online, a professor should appreciate the potential benefits of a criticism-free zone for a classroom discussion. A professor can specifically demarcate and protect a time during a classroom discussion when any student can express an idea or opinion without fear of criticism. After engaging in a criticism-free discussion of the opinion or idea, the other participants in the discussion may evaluate it with their own support or criticism, and a discussion of the opinion or idea ensues.

The idea of *controlling defensive reactions* during a classroom discussion is derived from the principle of "going to the balcony" in *Getting Past No*. When an interest-based bargainer is disturbed by a counterpart's negotiation position or tactic, an immediate emotional reaction is one possible response. Emotional reactions are often defensive, involving either an attack on, a flight from, or a submission to the position or tactic. Instead of reacting defensively, an interest-based bargainer "goes to the balcony" and takes time to consider the effect of a defensive response. After also considering alternative responses that could be more productive for the negotiation, the interest-based bargainer tends to choose one of the alternative responses. In a similar vein, a classroom discussion can be more productive when participants control their defensive reactions and work to maintain a productive atmosphere.

Basic information about *Getting Past No*, including the concept of "going to the balcony," is widely available online (e.g., Conflict Resolution Consortium, 2003–2010). As an additional resource, another book, *Taking the War Out of Our Words: The Art of Powerful Non-Defensive Communication* (Ellison, 2009), expands on the idea of "going to the balcony" and provides a step-by-step guide to using nondefensive language. After reading the basic information about nondefensive reactions and communication, professors should understand the importance of controlling their own defensive reactions in the classroom and encouraging students to do the same. Instead of responding immediately to an opinion or idea with which the listener disagrees, the listener pauses, asks questions, and considers the possible consequences of a defensive reaction. After such reflection, the listener may decide to respond in a nondefensive manner, which should strengthen the classroom discussion.

The idea of *considering other perspectives* is derived from *Getting Past No*'s concept of "stepping to their side" (i.e., stepping to a negotiation counterpart's side) and viewing the negotiation from that perspective. Interest-based bargainers anticipate two primary benefits from "stepping to their side." First, they hope to obtain a better understanding of the interests that underlie a counterpart's bargaining position. Second, they hope to convince their counterpart of their good faith, and to build trust by making proposals that may satisfy the counterpart's underlying interests. Similarly, participants in classroom discussions who consider the other participants' perspectives can better understand the others' underlying concerns, and build goodwill by demonstrating their understanding of those concerns.

Because of *Getting Past No*'s popularity, numerous websites devote space to explaining the basics of "stepping to their side" (e.g., Conflict Resolution Consortium, 2003–2010). After reading the information, a professor will understand the importance of considering students' perspectives and encouraging students to do the same as an integral part of classroom discussions. Discussion participants may choose to adjust their personal perspectives, or at least view other participants' perspectives less judgmentally.

Imparting Basic Communication and Dispute-Resolution Skills in the Classroom

The Importance of Modeling the Skills

A professor who wants students to use productive communication and dispute-resolution skills must do more than acquire knowledge about the skills and impart them to students; the professor must also model the skills. The ground rules proposed in the next section are for professor behavior as well as student behavior.

Discussing the Concepts and Creating Ground Rules

To the extent time constraints and budgets permit, it may be useful to discuss basic communication and dispute-resolution concepts at the beginning of a course. Reading assignments, even if limited to online sources, can be useful. A list of ground rules containing the following bullet points may also help professors and students engage in respectful and productive discussion.

- A mind is like a parachute; it works best when it is open. Open your mind to others' ideas and opinions during class discussions.
- Actively listen to others as they speak.
    - ✓ Listen carefully to what speakers say; words are important.
    - ✓ In addition to listening to the words, observe speakers' body language and tone of voice for clues about the words' meaning and importance to the speakers.
    - ✓ Reduce your "external" distractions. Turn off your cell phone and other electronic devices.
    - ✓ Reduce your "internal" distractions. When another person is speaking, it is about the other person, not about you, your ideas, your opinions, or your problems.

- ✓ Listen to understand the other person, not to respond to what the other person says.
- ✓ Do not interrupt while another person speaks.
- Live in the question.
- ✓ Start by asking open-ended questions that allow a speaker to answer with a narrative response, and control the response's content (e.g., "What do you think about . . .?," "Can you tell me more about . . .?," "What happened?").
- ✓ Follow up with clarifying questions that increase your understanding of the speaker's meaning (e.g., "When you used the word 'discrimination,' what did you mean?," "When you said 'that's just the way they are,' what did you mean?").
- ✓ Use closed-ended questions to fill in details (e.g., "Was the light red or green?," "What time was it?").
- ✓ Avoid leading questions, especially if they contain veiled accusations (e.g., "Don't you think the rest of the world should get on board with capitalism?," "Don't you think I'm right?," "Weren't you the one who started the argument?").

- When listening to others speak, consider how their life experiences have contributed to their perspectives. Try to determine their underlying interests and concerns, and frame your responses to reflect your understanding of those interests and concerns.
- Summarize what you hear with a degree of humility (e.g., "Correct me if I'm wrong, but you seem to be saying you approve the president's foreign policy but not his domestic economic policy. Am I getting it right?").
- Respect the "criticism-free zone." Don't express disagreement with the ideas and opinions of others until the professor indicates it is time for reflections, evaluations, and responses.
- Voice agreement or disagreement with a speaker's idea or opinion only after you are sure you understand it. When you disagree, use the same respectful language and tone you hope others will use when they disagree with you.
- "Go to the balcony" if you sense a strong, immediate, emotional reaction to someone's idea or opinion. Before you respond, consider the possible consequences if you attack, give in to, or run away from the idea or opinion. Try to frame a nondefensive response that encourages continued conversation and exploration of different points of view.

Cross-Cultural Aspects of Communication and Dispute Resolution

Professors should be aware that communication and dispute-resolution concepts are grounded in each society's culture. The information and suggestions imparted in this chapter reflect a North American perspective on appropriate communication and dispute-resolution techniques in a classroom. Professors and students from other cultures may arrive in a classroom with different perspectives. This section provides professors with basic information about one set of cross-cultural differences that may arise in a classroom, and resources for working with the differences. The differences discussed in this section certainly are not the only cross-cultural differences that may affect communication and dispute resolution, but they illustrate the additional layer of complexity involved when cross-cultural differences appear in the classroom.

Different Communication Styles that Affect Dispute Resolution

Cultural perspectives about disputes affect the ways people communicate about them. Two major communication differences involve the direct or indirect approach people take to resolving disputes and the emotional restraint or expressiveness they use when communicating about them (Hammer, 2003). In the United States, most people approach disputes directly and with emotional restraint, an approach called the *discussion* style. Discussers are most comfortable when they can address disputes in a straightforward and calm environment. They may become lost or confused if the other party approaches a dispute indirectly, and they may feel uncomfortable if the other party addresses the dispute with significant emotion. While the discussion style prevails in the United States, it is not the exclusive dispute-resolution style. Three other styles exist:

- *Engagement*, which values a direct approach to conflict and emphasizes emotional expressiveness. Engagers, like discussers, prefer a straightforward approach to disputes, and they use emotion to demonstrate their genuine concern about the subject matter of a dispute. They may perceive someone who fails to express emotion during a dispute as a "cold fish," and they may miss important clues from parties who deal with disputes indirectly.
- *Accommodation*, which values an indirect approach to conflict and emphasizes emotional restraint. Accommodators often attempt to "save face" (their own or the other party's) by seeking calm environments to ask questions, tell stories, or use metaphors in face-to-face discussions with the other party. As an alternative to face-to-face communication, they may use third-party intermediaries to address a dispute privately with the other party. Accommodators may perceive direct or emotionally charged communication about a dispute as rude or a loss of face.
- *Dynamic*, which values an indirect approach to conflict and emphasizes emotional expressiveness. Dynamics, like accommodators, value face-saving devices such as questions, stories, metaphors, and third-party intermediaries. Like engagers, they employ emotional expression to demonstrate an appropriate level of concern about a dispute. Discussers, with their direct and emotionally restrained approach to disputes, may baffle dynamics, and discussers may feel the same way about dynamics.

The engagement, accommodation, and dynamic styles exist not only in the United States; they also often dominate in other societies. When professors and students with different dispute-resolution backgrounds participate in discussions, possibilities for misunderstandings abound.

Resources for Working with Different Communication Styles

Two important resources exist to increase understanding of the four different dispute-resolution styles and to provide tools for working with each style. Both resources could prove useful to professors and students, but time constraints and budgets may permit only professors to take advantage of them.

The first resource is Dr. Mitchell Hammer's *Intercultural Conflict Style Inventory* (Hammer, 2003), which provides a short testing instrument to help people determine their own dispute-resolution styles. The inventory includes an interpretive guide to assist in understanding the patterns of each style, and it explains the strengths and weaknesses of each style. Taking the test and reading the interpretive guide provide the reader with valuable information about all four styles. With this information, a professor should be able to work more effectively with each style.

The second resource is a video, *A Different Place: The Intercultural Classroom* (Intercultural Resources Collaborative, 1993). For professors, this video is especially helpful because it illustrates each of the dispute-resolution styles and demonstrates how people with different styles can misunderstand and fail to communicate effectively with each other when they speak about important, controversial subjects. The visual representations of the various styles should also help professors identify them when they appear in the classroom.

Conclusion

Teaching in a modern university classroom is challenging, and it can be especially challenging when a course contains multicultural content; possibilities for communication errors and disputes abound. Because of the challenges, the thought of teaching multicultural curriculum may be intimidating. However, professors can acquire basic communication and dispute-resolution information and skills. When they use the information and skills effectively in the classroom, the environment should be suitable for respectful, engaging discussions during which genuine education occurs.

References

Binder, D. A., Bergman, P., & Price, S. C. (1996). Questioning. In E.W. Trachte-Huber & S. Huber (Eds.), *Mediation and negotiation: Reaching agreement in law and business* (pp. 42–49). Cincinnati, OH: Anderson.

Brown, S., & Smith, D. (2006). *Active listening* (2nd ed.). New York, NY: Cambridge University Press.

Burley-Allen, M. (1995). *Listening: The forgotten skill: A self-teaching guide* (2nd ed.). Hoboken, NJ: John Wiley & Sons.

Conflict Resolution Consortium. (2003–2010). Book summary of getting past no. Retrieved from http://www.beyondintractability.org/bksum/ury-gettingpast

Department of Veterans Affairs. (2004). Active listening for mediators. Retrieved from http://www.au.af.mil/au/awc/awcgate/va/mediation/medskills.htm

Ellison, S. S. (2009). *Taking the war out of our words: The art of powerful non-defensive communication*. Deadwood, OR: Wyatt-MacKenzie.

Fisher, R., Ury W., & Patton, B. (1991). *Getting to yes: Negotiating agreement without giving in* (2nd ed.). New York, NY: Penguin Books.

Glaser, T. (2003–2010). Book summary of getting to yes. Retrieved from http://www.beyondintractability.org/bksum/fisher-getting

Hammer, M. R. (2003). *Intercultural conflict style inventory: Interpretive guide*. Ocean Pines, MD: Hammer Consulting.

Honolulu Community College. (2011). Teaching tips index: Using questions effectively in teaching. *Faculty Guidebook*. Retrieved from http://honolulu.hawaii.edu/intranet/committees/FacDevCom/guidebk/teachtip/teachtip.htm#questions

Intercultural Resources Collaborative. (1993). *A different place: The intercultural classroom* [Video]. (Available from Intercultural Resources Collaborative, http://www.irc-international.com/).

Mind Tools, Ltd. (1996–2011). Active listening: Hear what people are really saying. Retrieved from http://www.mindtools.com/

Ury, W. (1993). *Getting past no: Negotiating your way from confrontation to cooperation*. New York, NY: Bantam Books.

4

Culturally Responsive Teaching in Higher Education: What Professors Need to Know

Patricia Larke

While culturally responsive teaching (CRT) was meant from its inception to address the needs of students at the elementary and secondary school levels, it has great potential for use in higher education, too. The underlying premise of culturally responsive teaching is to provide equitable educational outcomes for all students. Like elementary and secondary schools, higher education classes are becoming more and more culturally, linguistically, economically, and ethnically diverse (CLEED), according to Larke and Larke (2009). And as higher education classes become more diverse, professors must develop more teaching strategies that are inclusive of the changing student populations on their campuses, in order to deliver their courses more effectively. Therefore, this chapter discusses several topics of the culturally responsive teaching presentations that were presented at the Multicultural Curriculum Transformation and Research Institute. More specifically, the chapter will address:

1. the need for culturally responsive teaching in higher education;
2. culturally responsive teaching itself;
3. D2 and E2 approaches to implementing culturally responsive teaching; and
4. understanding the so-called C's of implementing culturally responsive teaching.

Need for Culturally Responsive Teaching in Higher Education

The need for CRT in higher education has been impacted by three areas. These areas are demographic changes, historic tradition, and global society.

Demographic Changes

There has been an increase in college enrollment over the past thirty years. In fact, during the years 1999 to 2009, the enrollment increased 38%, from 14.8 million college students to 20.4 million (NCES, 2011). This increase is a direct result of a rise in the numbers of students of color and females. Since 1976 the number of Hispanic/Latinos, African Americans, and Asian Pacific Islanders has increased. During the same period, 1976–2009, the percentage of Hispanic/Latino students increased from 3% to 12%, while both Asian/Pacific Islanders and African Americans increased 5%. At the same time, enrollment of White students fell from 83% to 62% (NCES, 2011). According to Pollard (2011), there is a gender gap in college enrollment and graduation. Pollard notes a "feminization" in higher education, in that "women are more likely to enroll in, and graduate from college than men."

Historic Traditions and Global Society

The delivery of instruction in higher education has been and continues to be predominately in the lecture-style format. While this may be the norm, many professors are using more technology to enhance their instruction (Jakee, 2011). Yet, the fact remains that teaching in academia cannot remain in a one-size-fits-all model grounded in Western ideology. Educating students to live and work in a global society is the vision of higher education institutions. With the advancement of technology, learning about other countries and people is no longer regulated to a page in a textbook; instead, with online web resources such as Google Earth, Facebook, Twitter, and YouTube, students have access to information about people on any continent within seconds, 24 hours a day. As a result, the workforce is comprised of people who are able to communicate in several languages, are technologically skilled, and can engage in culturally appropriate practices that enhance the quality of the business product.

Culturally Responsive Teaching

Culturally responsive teaching (CRT) is an instructional pedagogical strategy whose main purpose is to address the needs of all students. It was first introduced by Ladson-Billings in 1992 and further expounded in her 1994 work, *The Dreamkeepers*. Gay's book, *Culturally Responsive Teaching* (2000), provided deeper insights to helping educators understand and apply tenets of culturally responsive teaching in their respective classrooms and schools. Gay (2000) and Ladson-Billings (1995) state that culturally responsive pedagogy rests on three criteria or propositions: (a) Students must experience academic success; (b) Students must develop and/or maintain cultural competence; and (c) Students must develop a critical consciousness through which they "challenge the status quo of the current social order" (Gay, 2000, p.160).

Gay (2000; 2011) states that using the cultural characteristics, experiences, and perspectives of ethnically diverse students as conduits of teaching enhances their learning. To endorse CRT, educators must develop a cultural diversity knowledge base, design culturally relevant curricula, demonstrate cultural caring while building learning communities, develop cross-cultural communication skills, and be able to develop cultural congruity in classroom instruction. She further states that these components are not optional, nor can they be done in isolation. It is within this conceptual framework that CRT can be applied to teaching in higher education. Three components of CRT that are most applicable to higher education are: cultural competence, critical consciousness, and academic success. Cultural competence uses cultural characteristics, experiences, and perspectives of ethnically diverse students as conduits of teaching. Critical consciousness helps students develop a broader perspective of the sociopolitical consciousness in order to critically analyze societal relationships. Academic success entails improving the academic achievement of ethnically diverse students by teaching them through their own cultural and experimental filters (Gay, 2000; Ladson-Billings, 1995).

Implementing CRT is a complex process that involves both teaching skills and professional practices. Teaching involves assembling a set of specific practices, activities, resources, and materials during a designated allocation of time for one or several educational purposes. CRT professional practices are shown in behaviors such as thoughts, interpretations, choices, values, and commitments of specific instruction.

D2 and E2 Approach to Implementing CRT

To teach culturally responsively in higher education requires a so-called D2 and E2 approach. First, instructors should develop a multicultural education knowledge base (D1) before they are able to design a course (D2) to incorporate the tenets of culturally responsive teaching. Second, professors should engage students (E1) and evaluate their course content and student progress (E2). Each of the D2 and E2 components will be discussed in the next section.

Develop a Knowledge Base

First, instructors must develop a knowledge base and become aware of the issues of diversity. Diversity is more than race, gender, or religious differences. Culturally responsive teaching and diversity issues are integral components of the discipline of multicultural education.

Multicultural Education (ME)

What is multicultural education? Multicultural education is a field of study whose major aim is to create equitable educational opportunities for students from diverse racial/ethnic, social class, cultural, and religious groups (Banks & Banks, 2004). Multicultural education is a philosophical concept and an educational process. It is a concept built upon the philosophical ideals of freedom, justice, equality, equity, and human dignity that are contained in, for example, the Declaration of Independence. It recognizes, however, that equality and equity are not the same thing: Equal access does not necessarily guarantee fairness (Grant, 1994). Sonia Nieto (2000) identifies seven components of multicultural education. Understanding these components is important when discussing diversity in education. She says that multicultural education is:

- Antiracist education—paying attention to all discriminatory practices (in the curriculum, educational choices, relationships, etc.);
- Basic education—central to the curriculum;
- Important for all students—not just for students of color, but for everyone;
- Pervasive—permeating the entire curriculum, not just a subject, a month-long project, or merely an item to be covered;
- Education for social justice—learning how to think and behave in ways that ensure fairness, and that people have the power to make changes;
- A process—ongoing and dynamic; no one stops becoming; and
- Critical pedagogy—a transformative process to think in multiple ways that leads to action.

There are theories that undergird the discipline of multicultural education as well as *-isms* that are essential in understanding CRT. A few are discussed below.

Cultural Pluralism Theory

Cultural pluralism theory states that no one chooses their ancestry, that each person has something valuable to contribute to society, and that people should be viewed in an egalitarian mode rather than an inferior or superior mode (Kallen, 1956). First of all, when viewing students of color, or any students in your class, realize that they cannot choose their ancestors; students who come to your class did not choose their race or culture. The theory also states that each person has something of value to contribute to society, and that everyone should be viewed in an egalitarian mode rather than an inferior or superior mode. Therefore, when students come to your program/course, they come seeking the knowledge that instructors have to offer. When instructors value students, they accept their language, culture, history, and ancestors.

Empowerment Theory

Paulo Freire's concept of empowerment aligns well with CRT. According to Freire (1974 as cited in 2000) empowerment is knowledge gained that enhances one's strength, competence, creativity, and thus freedom of action, and knowledge of social relations that dignifies one's own history, language, and culture to enable people to act, grow, and become. Providing students with knowledge to empower them is essential to CRT.

ME-Isms and Levels of Prejudice

Within multicultural education is embedded an understanding of the *-isms* (Larke, 2010). These *-isms* are racism, sexism, classism, ageism, and religionism. Also, providing information about Allport's levels of prejudice is beneficial both to students and instructors.

Wineberg's definition of racism fits well with CRT. According to Wineberg, racism is a system of privilege and penalty based on one's race. It consists of two facets: (1) a belief in the inherent superiority of some people and in the inherent inferiority of others; and (2) the acceptance of the way goods and services are distributed in accordance to these judgments (Wineberg cited in Nieto, 2000). The definition expands racism to include both privilege and penalty, which are often overlooked when the term is used or implied.

The other *-isms* of sexism, classism, ageism, and religionism are self-explanatory. For example, sexism is discrimination based on sex, classism is discrimination based on class, ageism is discrimination based on age, and religionism is discrimination based on religion.

Gordon Allport (1954) introduced levels of prejudice in his seminal work in the 1950s, and this theory is still prevalent today. While most people do not perceive themselves as prejudiced, Allport defines behaviors such as ethnic jokes and avoidance of specific people as prejudice. What follows is a brief discussion of Allport's five levels of prejudice.

The first is antilocution, or participating in ethnic jokes. Often, negative things are said in the privacy between friends. This supports social positionality: People see themselves as better than others by making such statement as "those people" or "our group." This supports the notion that "I don't like those people, either...so I am like you." Therefore, people justify participating in ethnic jokes, even when the joke is about their own ethnic group. The second level is avoidance—when people avoid others because they do not want to be associated with a particular group. For example, parents will say to their children, "I don't want you to talk to those children," or people will say that you should avoid a certain type of group. The third level is discrimination, and perhaps this level is most familiar to students. Discrimination is prejudice plus action. Many legal actions have been filed because of discrimination in housing, education, and employment. There are also some other areas such as colorism; that is, discrimination based on skin phenotype—someone who has a lighter complexion against someone who is darker.

Figure 3. Allport's Levels of Prejudice

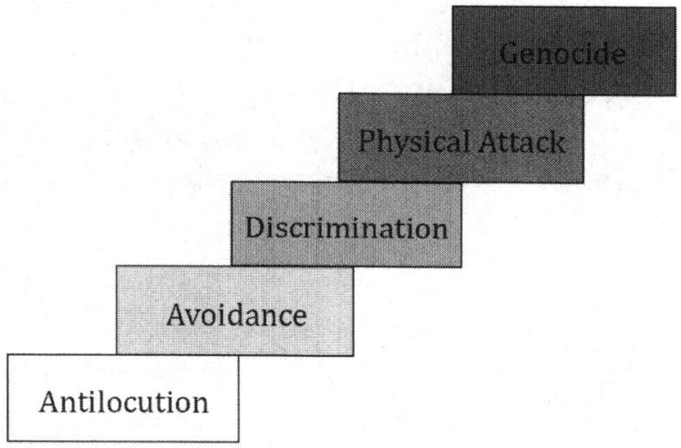

The fourth level is physical attack. People are attacked because of who they are and who they represent; for example, gay bashing, and attacks on Middle Easterners after 9/11. The fifth and final level is genocide. This is the most extreme level of prejudice. Examples of this are the Klu Klux Klan's activities in the United States during the 1900s, the Holocaust during World War II, and today, incidents in Darfur, Sudan.

Levels of ME Awareness

As indicated from the definition of multicultural education and *-isms*, ME and CRT are more than food, fashion, and fun. There are levels of diversity awareness, according to Banks (2004). The first level is the contributions approach. In this approach, teachers introduce heroes and "sheroes," food, fashion, and fun, folklore, or a list of people of note. For example, the math and science classes may introduce a picture of a female of color mathematician or scientist. The second level is the additive approach. With this approach, the course, the instructor gives extra credit to students for diversity information. but the information is not a part of the "canon" or tested information. The third level is transformation. In this level, knowledge is inclusive and presented from multiple viewpoints. The last level is social action, in which the knowledge that is presented changes the views of society. For example, engineering courses help students to design buildings that are structurally sound, environmentally safe, culturally affirming, and economically feasible to reflect the culture of the community.

Develop and/or Revise Courses

Instructors should develop course materials to enhance the three tenets of CRT: cultural competence, critical consciousness, and academic success. Modifying their syllabi, developing lectures, and changing required readings are necessary. Revision of the syllabus is a place to start. Culturally responsive teaching is professional work that involves taking action intentionally and skillfully, in a timely manner, under conditions that are changeable and problematic. CRT involves taking actions to structure the setting in which learning occurs.

Syllabus Development and/Revision

A syllabus is required for teaching a course on college campuses, and it must include information that meets the guidelines of the institution. This section will detail how to incorporate CRT components into a syllabus. Section 1 of a syllabus contains course information such as course name and number, date/time/location of the course, course credit hours, and instructor's contact information. In section 2 there is course catalogue information. Changing course catalog information often requires completing paperwork and following the guidelines according to the institution's course revision committee—any changes in course description must be approved by the institution's course committees. Section 3 includes information about objectives and learning outcomes for the course. This is an opportunity to provide specific learning outcomes that integrate culturally responsive teaching and multicultural education issues. Section 4 is critical for making CRT changes, for it includes the list of reading materials for the course. Within the last decade, new texts, articles, and audiovisual materials that are inclusive of diversity issues have been developed in many disciplines, from the sciences to the liberal arts. Instructors should check with the institution's librarian for any new listings in this area. Sections 5, 6, and 7 contain logistical information on courses; the weighting of assignments is particularly important when determining grades. Instructors should give considerable thought in section 9 regarding what to include about CRT and MEI (multicultural education issues). This section can be developed once instructors complete their e-research activity (see Table 1). The last section includes information about an institution's policies and federal and state policies, if applicable.

Table 1. Developing a CRT/MEI Course Syllabus

Syllabus Section	**Syllabus Information**	**Culturally Responsive Teaching (CRT) and Multicultural Education Issues (MEI)**
1. Course Information	Course Number, Section, Date/Time/Location, Credit, Professor Name/Contact Information	
2. Course Description	**Use information in college catalogue;** **make sure any changes are approved by respective committees**	**Add any MEI or CRT changes to course description**
3. Course Objectives/ Learning Outcomes	What should students learn from the course?	Add MEI or CRT to learning outcomes and objectives
4. Required Texts/ Readings	Select texts and readings that support CRT and MEI issues	Add new readings and texts that incorporate CRT and MEI
5. Course Expectancies	How will the students be assessed? List exams, e-folios, papers, etc.	Will any CRT and MEI be included in the assessments?
6. Assignments, Grading Scale, and Due Dates	Find out the college/university's policies regarding letter and numeric grades; decide the weight of CRT and MEI assignments	CRT and MEI should never be an extra credit assignment, but an equally weighted assignment
7. Due Dates and Assignment Information	Be explicit about class requirements	
8. Lecture Topics, Reading Assignments	Identify topics, readings, resources for the course	Highlight CRT and MEI issues
9. University/ Department Policies	Always include policies such as diversity policies, plagiarism, American Disabilities Act, etc.	

CRT Lesson

To design a CRT lesson, begin first with a topic that responds to an issue of diversity. Look at your class syllabus and identify any topic that is applicable to a diversity issue. After identifying the topic, conduct a literature search on the topic. Look for readings and other materials to support your topic. Once the topic has been identified, develop a lecture to support the topic, and write objectives and other appropriate information for the lesson such as reading list, guiding questions, etc. Three critical questions to think about are:

1. What are the objectives and learning outcomes?;
2. What is the delivery system?; and
3. Is the information accurate and authentic?

Design a class project to support the topic with the appropriate grading rubrics. In designing your project develop ways to enhance student engagement. Select projects that are "life-changing" and projects that involve the use of technology and support reflective practices (getting students to think and write about their learning).

Table 2. Designing CRT Lessons

Using E-Research to Identify Culturally Responsive Teaching Activities to Transform Courses			
Issues	**Websites**	**Lecture**	**CRT Projects**
Identify three CRT issues that you would include in your course. Issue A Issue B Issue C	Find two websites to support each of the CRT issues. Website A Website B Website C	Identify a lecture topic and write outline. • Objective/Learning Outcomes • Readings • Outline of Lecture	Develop one CRT project for your course. Write a paragraph description. Include a grading rubric.

Engaging students

Student engagement is vital to the implementation of CRT. This engagement is critical to their learning process. The development of projects, papers, and other class projects that require students to reflect and use their cultural frames of reference is essential. Studies support that when students are engaged in the learning process, the quality of their work increases. CRT understands the pedagogy of place (POP), as noted by Raymer (2001). POP states that learning occurs when students connect subject matter to their own lives and surroundings, and critically reflect upon both the connection and the new materials being studied. In other words, assignments are connected to students' lives. POP notes that learners come to understand themselves as inheritors, inquirers, and contributors of knowledge in overlapping webs of social, cultural, natural, scientific, and technical understanding. Students see themselves as contributing, not just absorbing. Like CRT, POP helps learners understand themselves as both products of and creators of interconnections among people and places. These learners see themselves as connecting with others in the world, while weaving critical reflection, active engagement, and real-world application into the learning process and educational environment. Students see the connection to the real world. Part 3 of this book contains several examples in which faculty share their teaching experiences with courses that they developed or revised.

Evaluation

Evaluation is integral to the CRT process. CRT projects and assignments must be included in class evaluation and grading. The evaluation of CRT projects should not be rewarded as extra credit. In section there are explanations about the effects of evaluation and how it is used to improve course ratings and student achievement. This section discusses how an action plan can be a useful evaluation tool.

An action plan is a list of goals and activities that can enhance culturally responsive teaching. This involves three components: goals for the instructor, goals for the students, and goals for the department or program. The goals should involve activities that can be done immediately, short-term goals and activities that can be done over time, or long-term goals. One way to provide an incentive to keep the long-term goals and reflect upon the short-term goals is to make two copies of the completed action plan. Take one copy and place where it can be seen often as a reminder, and place the second copy in a stamped self-addressed envelope and ask a colleague to mail the envelope after six months. This process will help to keep instructors accountable to their goals for culturally responsive teaching. See Table 3 for an example of an action plan.

Table 3. CRT Action Plan

Culturally Responsive Teaching It Is Not by LUCK, but by Design Action Plan			
Goals	Yourself	Students	Program/Department
Short-Term Goals	1. 2. 3.	1. 2. 3.	1. 2. 3.
Long-Term Goals	1. 2. 3.	1. 2. 3.	1. 2. 3.

Understanding the C's of Implementing Culturally Responsive Teaching

For CRT to be implemented in higher education, instructors should respond to critical questions in the following six C's. They are: commitment, co-responsibility, communication, cultural understanding, courage, and change.

Commitment

What level of commitment do you bring? Is it lip service, just talk? What action plans do you have to change your courses? Do you foster a caring commitment? Caring means to know, to act, and to respond in ways to enhance personal development and academic achievement for all students. Being thoughtful, kind, and compassionate in your actions will ensure that programs and projects are responsive to class, race, gender, and religious inequalities.

Co-Responsibility

This means professors, students, and departments working together. All must share the responsibility of making it safe to discuss controversial topics and making the activities academically enriching for students. Class evaluations provide vital information.

Communication

What messages do you send to your students about diversity? How do culturally, linguistically, economically, ethnically diverse (CLEED) students know that you want them in your classes or programs? What do you know about students other than their names?

Cultural Understanding

Is your knowledge of cultural issues accurate and up to date? What have you read lately about diversity in your discipline? What do you know about rural students and students of color, or international students? Do you believe in the color-blind deficit mentality that "I don't see color, and I treat all my students the same?"

Courage

How do you find the strength to make efforts? The reality is that many classrooms support classism, racism, and sexism in subtle but powerful ways because many of these issues have been part of the fabric of life in many countries. Note that, for some discipline such as science, math and even education engaging in culturally responsive teaching is not rewarded with tenure and promotion. Sometimes, engaging these issues can produce lower student evaluations, which are used for tenure and promotion and merit decisions.

Change

How do you alter, adjust, and transform your courses and programs to accommodate differences (e.g., racial, sexual, religious)? Change requires moving out of one's comfort zone.

Conclusion

Historically, instructional delivery on college campuses has been—and continues to be—via the lecture. The premise of this chapter has been not to debate the quality of the lecture style, but to share how CRT can enhance the quality of college teaching. CRT is an effective pedagogical tool that can enhance teaching in college courses. CRT includes three areas: cultural competence and understanding, critical consciousness, and academic success. These are the same areas that embody teaching and optimal student learning outcomes. Note that if CRT is to work effectively, instructors will have to develop, implement, and evaluate its effectiveness.

References

Allport, G. W. (1954). *The nature of prejudice.* Cambridge, MA: Addison-Wesley.

Banks, J. A., & Banks, C. (Eds.). (2004). *Handbook of research on multicultural education.* San Franciso, CA: Jossey-Bass.

Banks, J. (2004). Multicultural education: Historical development, dimensions, and practice. In J. Banks & C. Banks (Eds). Handbook of research on multicultural education, (pp. 3-49). San Francisco, CA: Jossey-Bass.

Freire, P. (2000). *Pedagogy of the oppressed* (Rev. 30th anniv. ed.). New York, NY: Continuum.

Gay, G. (2000; 2011). *Culturally responsive teaching* (1st, 2nd eds.). New York, NY: Teachers College Press.

Grant, C. (1994). Challenging the myths about multicultural education. *Multicultural Education, 2* (2), 4–9.

Jakee, K. (2011). Overhauling technical handouts for active student participation: A model for improving lecture efficiency and increasing attendance. *International Journal of Teaching and Learning in Higher Education, 23* (1), 98–108. Retrieved from http://www.isetl.org/ijtlhe/pdf/IJTLHE864.pdf

Kallen, H. (1956). *Cultural pluralism and the American idea.* Philadelphia, PA: University of Pennsylvania Press.

Ladson-Billings, G. (1992). Reading between the lines and beyond the pages: A culturally relevant approach to literacy teaching. *Theory into Practice, 31* (4), 312–320.

———. (1994). *The dreamkeepers: Successful teachers for African-American children.* San Francisco, CA: Jossey-Bass.

———. (1995). But that's just good teaching! The case for culturally relevant pedagogy. *Theory into Practice, 34* (3), 159–165.

Larke, P. J. (2010). The future of multicultural education research. *National Forum of Multicultural Issues Journal, 7* (2) 3–6.

Larke, P. J., & Larke, A. (2009). Teaching diversity/multicultural education courses in the academy: Voices of six professors. *Journal of Higher Education, 3,* 1–8.

National Center for Education Statistics (NCES). (2011). Fast facts. In *Digest of Education Statistics, 2010* (NCES 2011-015) (pp. 281–535). Washington, DC: U.S. Department of Education.

Nieto, S. (2000). *Affirming diversity: The sociopolitical context of multicultural education* (3rd ed.). New York, NY: Longman.

Pollard, K. (2011). The gender gap in college enrollment and graduation. Population Reference Bureau website. Retrieved from http://www.prb.org/Articles/2011/gender-gap-in-education.aspx

Raymer, A. (2001). *Pedagogy of place facilitation guide: Cultivating and promoting place-based education.* Lexington, KY: Appalachian Rural Education Network and University of Kentucky Appalachian Center.

5

Infusing Global Perspectives into the Curriculum

Ani Yazedjian

The challenges of the new millennium are unquestionably global in nature. This reality imposes a new and urgent demand on Americans, one this country has been all too quick to ignore: international knowledge and skills are imperative for the future security and competitiveness of the United States. The rhetoric of a decade attests to the widespread recognition of this fundamental truth, yet concrete steps to fulfill this need have been few. Strong leadership and a coherent policy are still lacking, and the cost of inaction grows ever greater (NAFSA, n.d.). Even prior to September 11, 2001, the American Council on Education (1998) issued a report articulating the need to have globally competent workers and arguing that waiting until after a crisis erupts to develop this expertise would be too late. We saw the impact of this lack of preparation in the aftermath of September 11th and the ensuing U.S. involvement in Iraq and Afghanistan. Yet, many of these issues persist, and are even more pressing today.

The content of these aforementioned reports highlights the challenges faced by institutions of higher education. Although colleges and universities have for decades lauded the value of a global perspective, few have taken purposeful and intentional steps to ensure they are graduating globally competent workers. Infusing a global perspective into courses across the curriculum is one effective strategy for accomplishing this objective. However, a report by Green (2005) indicates even at institutions characterized by the American Council on Education as "highly active" in internationalization efforts, only 25% of students say their instructors frequently relate course material to larger global issues, and only 15% are encouraged by instructors to participate in international activities. These figures indicate that many more faculty members, across institutions, can take steps to infuse a global perspective into the courses they teach. These topics should not be relegated to certain social science and humanities courses, but should be incorporated into courses across the institution. The purpose of this chapter is therefore to highlight the importance of preparing globally competent graduates, to identify the relevance of a global perspective to courses in various disciplines, and to provide some strategies by which a global perspective can be infused.

Why Is a Global Perspective Important?

There are a number of reasons why infusing a global perspective into courses across the curriculum is important. First, enabling students to develop a global perspective assists them in attaining future employment. Recent research shows that due to their engagement in business abroad, more corporations, both small and large, are looking for potential employees who possess foreign language skills and cross-cultural awareness (Hudzik, 2011). These skills and attitudes will be important even for employees who never leave the country, as more of them will interact with colleagues around the world despite their U.S.-based positions. Yet, beyond the practical benefits of developing a global-ready workforce, a global perspective can enable students to develop a better understanding of the interconnected world in which they live. and assist them in making more informed and responsible decisions.

Infusing a global perspective into courses across the curriculum is particularly important as research has found that "American students lack even basic geographic knowledge, not to mention exposure to world regions, languages and cultures. Given our increasingly global economy, this lack leaves U.S. students educationally and economically handicapped" (Willard, n.d., p. 2). Yet, many students might not even be aware of these deficits, and even less aware of the impact these might have on their future employment prospects as these exact competencies are being sought by employers today. To illustrate, the 2005–2006 Michigan State Recruiting Trends report identified "geographic awareness and a global understanding or perspective on events" as the primary new competencies sought in job seekers (p. 19). The report noted "as businesses become realigned globally, having employees with an awareness of space (where countries, cities, are located on one level), social and cultural geographic movement, as well as dominant physical assets of a region will be critical to a company's vitality" (p. 19).

In light of these demands, scholars have significant concerns that institutions are not sufficiently preparing graduates to become globally competent citizens and workers (Hunter, White, & Godbey, 2006). For example, few college graduates in the United States can speak another language, or have a deep understanding of, or interest in, the rest of the world (some would argue that they have little understanding of even the

U.S.). As previously stated, although many schools include verbiage related to internationalization in their missions, visions, and goals, few have developed systematic strategies for accomplishing their objectives, or measure the outcomes associated with these ideals. Therefore, although most higher education officials agree in theory that preparing global-ready graduates is an important goal, few of their institutions take the steps necessary to make this happen. Although some disciplines might give students this exposure, many argue that in order for these goals to be reached, a comprehensive internationalization plan would need to be instituted. In other words, students need to be exposed to a global perspective in classes across the curriculum, not just in certain classes in the humanities or social sciences.

What Makes a Globally Competent Worker?

Interestingly, although a common assumption is that study abroad and language learning are the most important aspects of becoming globally competent, Hunter and colleagues' (2006) findings did not support this assumption. Based on the responses of a diverse sample of participants ranging from human resource managers at transnational corporations to United Nations officials and senior international educators, the authors found that the critical step toward becoming globally competent was to develop an understanding of one's own cultural norms, expectations, motivations, and biases. They asserted it is from developing an understanding of the self that one can explore the rest of the world with a nonjudgmental attitude. However, it is not sufficient to develop only a sense of cultural self-awareness. Globally competent individuals understand their impact on the world and the impact the world has on them. Based on research by Wilson and Dalton (1997), Hunter and colleagues (2006) argue that globally competent workers need to develop both perceptual knowledge (e.g., open-mindedness, resistance to stereotyping) and substantive knowledge (e.g., of other cultures, languages, and global issues).

Various scholars have identified specific characteristics of globally competent workers (Bremer, 2006; Hunter et al., 2006; Wilson-Oyelaran, 2011). Some of these typologies include concrete attributes and represent characteristics specific to global issues (e.g., fluency in another language, knowledge of political history of another country) (Bremer, 2011). Other typologies are more abstract, and represent characteristics of college graduates more generally (e.g., the capacity to respect difference, ability to see an issue from multiple perspectives) (Wilson-Oyelaran, 2011). These scholars believe it is more critical to possess skills such as open-mindedness and cultural awareness. They believe these "soft skills" will predispose individuals to a willingness to develop more specific global knowledge when the need arises. However, in order to most adequately prepare students, institutions of higher education should provide students the opportunity to develop both these "soft skills" and the content knowledge necessary to be successful in today's global economy.

What Can Faculty Do?

There is little argument that the most effective programs for preparing global ready graduates are comprehensive in nature (Hudzik, 2011). Although these kinds of programs require support from upper levels of institutional administration, faculty also play a critical role in globalizing an institution, as they are on the front lines with students, exposing them to new information and ways of thinking. Faculty have a wide range of choices regarding the degree to which they wish to infuse a global perspective into the courses they teach. Some faculty may wish to completely transform existing courses, while others might incorporate activities, assignments, and examples with a global focus into their existing course plans. For faculty already transforming their courses to include a multicultural perspective, integrating examples related to global issues can be easily incorporated as part of that perspective. However, these activities, assignments, and examples should be integrated purposefully, and these purposes should be clearly communicated to students.

To begin, instructors can develop their own awareness by exploring how their course content relates to global topics. One way this can be done is by consulting the "Global Issues on the United Nations Agenda" for guidance. Once faculty have established this foundation, they can consider adding a course objective related to globalization on their syllabus. Then, instructors could structure activities that allow students to accomplish that objective. These activities could be ongoing throughout the semester (e.g., having students in a journalism class read and report on an article from an international newspaper on a weekly basis), and they could be individual assignments (e.g., having students in a family studies course complete a paper examining their own cultural values, norms, and biases) or group activities (e.g., having students in a health class brainstorm strategies for dealing with a possible pandemic). In addition, given the lack of empirical research regarding the effectiveness of globalizing the curriculum for student learning outcomes, it is important to measure the effectiveness of these activities and the accomplishment of these objectives in order to add to the body of literature on this topic.

After developing a globalization-related objective, faculty should encourage self-reflection among their students. They should develop activities designed to make students aware of their own values and become more open-minded. They should then provide students the opportunity to apply this growing awareness (see Appendix for resources). One way this can be done is to encourage students to learn about the world around them and consider the similarities and differences they encounter. Faculty can do this by linking current events around the world to topics discussed in their classes. These linkages should be made frequently in order for students to move beyond considering these events as isolated examples that might be irrelevant to their lives and instead understand the global world in which they live.

Faculty members could also share their own travel experiences in the classroom. Faculty with limited travel experiences could apply for a semester-long Fulbright award or participate in a shorter-term Fulbright-Hays Seminar Abroad. Alternatively, faculty members could ask domestic and international students in their courses to share with classmates their own experiences. However, particularly for international students, faculty should point out that these students are speaking as individuals and do not represent the experiences of entire groups.

Finally, faculty can encourage discussion about responsible behaviors associated with global citizenship. They can encourage students to consider how their behaviors impact the rest of the world and how the behaviors of the rest of the world have an impact on them. For example, faculty can teach students about the practice of exporting U.S. electronic waste to developing countries (Claiborne, 2009). In countries such as Ghana, children scour these dump sites looking for copper. They light fires to melt the plastic and then inhale toxic fumes as they retrieve the copper, which can earn them up to $2 a day. Faculty can then ask students to discuss the ethical implications of these practices, and encourage them to consider their own practices from a more globally informed position.

Additionally, faculty could take steps to become what Merryfield (2002) calls global educators. Although Merryfield's target is K-12 educators, her thesis is relevant for university instructors as well. For example, Merryfield states that global educators address stereotypes and challenge misperceptions. They teach about cultures and global issues from multiple, often conflicting perspectives, relying on primary sources from the culture of interest. They ask students to read literature, history, news, or websites from other parts of the world. They try to set up direct contact with others from different parts of the world, either by tapping local resources or by using technology to connect with others from across the globe. One way a faculty member could do this is by creating a collaborative online project site with a colleague abroad and having their students contribute to discussions or activities throughout the semester. After that, students could be given the opportunity to reflect on their learning experience. These activities should be mutually beneficial, putting students on an equal footing, and ideally, should last long enough for meaningful relationships to develop and true learning to take place. Alternatively, faculty could have students follow a Twitter feed or Facebook group related to a course topic. Purposeful steps such as those mentioned above can empower students to develop the skills and knowledge to become globally competent workers and socially responsible citizens.

Examples of Activities

This section highlights some activities relevant to different courses. Although not an exhaustive list, it provides some examples for faculty to consider (see Appendix for a list of websites). In a class about the cultural diversity in families, I asked students to examine how popular media covered issues related to a selected course topic. Students were asked to find a current event from a news source and create a 5-minute PowerPoint presentation summarizing the event, explaining how it related to the course topic, and incorporating course material. These presentations occurred throughout the semester, usually on the day the topic was being covered in class.

In the same course, I invited a group of Central American teachers who were in the U.S. for a one-year teacher-training program at a local community college to come and talk about life in their respective countries. The teachers formed groups and discussed various topics such as education, family life, and their experiences in the U.S., and students moved in groups from one presentation to the next. Students then completed a paper reflecting on the common themes they heard (since the panelists were from different countries), relating the information back to course readings, and comparing the experiences of the teachers with those of their own families of origin. Over the years I used this activity, the panel was frequently mentioned as a course highlight in end-of-semester evaluations.

On another occasion, a faculty member from a Russian university was visiting our campus. The local host asked if I wanted the professor to give a guest lecture in my adolescence course. I was not given much advance notice about the opportunity, and initially I was reticent because the visit would impact the course schedule. Nevertheless, I invited the professor, and the students were so interested in the presentation they continued to ask questions even after the allotted time had ended. Again, the students commented on how valuable and eye-opening the experience had been, and I was happy to have made that decision. I share this example as it demonstrates the flexibility we need to demonstrate if we choose to infuse a global perspective into the classes we teach. In some instances, we will have the luxury of planning ahead and integrating relevant experiences into our course outlines. In other instances, we will face unexpected opportunities to add to our courses a layer of authenticity that we might otherwise be unable to provide.

Although these examples could be integrated most appropriately into social science classes, there are opportunities to infuse a global perspective into classes in other disciplines as well. For example, regardless of discipline, another possibility would be to bring Fulbright Visiting Scholars to campus through the Occasional Lecturer Fund. The program provides funding for institutions to invite scholars to campus for a two- to three-day period. During their visits, scholars can engage in a number of different activities, such as participating in department events, giving guest lectures in classes, and delivering special presentations to various audiences. Alternatively, faculty members could arrange guest lectures by individuals affiliated with local agencies or businesses that maintain global interests. These presentations, too, would expose students to the local perspectives of those currently working in today's global economy.

A global perspective can be infused even into programs that are more focused on professional preparation. For example, Charlson and Vouchilas (2010) describe the transformation of a basic construction course in an interior design program. First, one international learning objective and two new outcomes were added to the course. Then, the final student project was revised so that students had to complete designs for an international "green" resort rather than a residential dwelling. Students selected countries on different continents and learned about the local geography, climate, materials, and design practice. They then applied the construction techniques to the unique demands of their particular contexts. In addition to learning traditional concepts, students had the opportunity to learn about other cultures and apply new interpretations of traditional concepts in an international setting.

Similarly, a global perspective could be infused into science courses. Many scientific discoveries have been made in other parts of the world, and the people responsible for them could be mentioned when these discoveries are discussed in a class. For example, the ancient civilization of Angkor, Cambodia developed a complex system of waterways to irrigate their rice fields as early as the tenth century. Discussing the elements of these innovations and comparing them to current practices can enable students to see similarities in centuries-old practices and identify changes over time. With respect to modern science, many of today's global issues such as climate change, pandemics, or environmental sustainability will need to be managed by future scientists who have the technical knowledge to deal with the scientific issues, but also the skills to apply this knowledge in a global context.

Alternatively, in a math education course, students can receive instruction regarding how concepts are taught in U.S. classrooms, and then watch videos or read articles about strategies employed to teach these same concepts in other countries. Students can then compare and contrast these forms of instruction and discuss the implications of these differences. In addition to providing students with knowledge of other parts of the world, these kinds of exercises can better prepare students to more effectively teach the diverse students they will encounter in their future classrooms.

An issue that could be addressed in fashion merchandising classes would be the experiences of low-wage laborers in garment factories in developing countries. Students could be pressed to explore topics related to whether profit-driven motives and socially responsible business practices have to be mutually exclusive, or whether U.S.-based corporations should change their business strategies to align with the practices of the country in which they will be working, or how female labor-force participation can impact the quality of life for an entire family system and contribute to the local economy.

In a business class, faculty members could inform students that China is now the world's largest market for cars, and discuss how that impacts the price of gas for American consumers. The recent financial crisis provides a good illustration of that relationship. During the recession, American demand for oil decreased, but the price of gas did not experience a corresponding drop because of the increasing demand for oil in China. After explaining these occurrences, faculty could ask students to discuss how these changes impact the global economy more broadly, and their local economies more specifically. These examples illustrate how, with some careful thought, a global perspective can be infused into existing course structures.

Conclusion

This chapter has highlighted the importance of preparing globally competent graduates, identified the relevance of a global perspective to courses in various disciplines, and provided some strategies by which a global perspective can be infused. Although these classroom strategies are a critical first step in preparing graduates for the global economy, they will be most effective when implemented as part of a comprehensive institutional plan. However, more research is needed regarding the most effective methods for infusing a global perspective into the curriculum. These data are critical not only for faculty who are considering transforming their courses, but also for colleges and universities as they consider systematic ways to internationalize their institutions.

Appendix

The following list includes some examples of websites which provide instructors resources related to global topics, media (e.g., photos, videos), class activities, and assignments. Although some of the activities and assignments are geared toward K-12 teachers, they can be modified for a college classroom.

- Foreignaffairs.com – Classroom section: http://www.foreignaffairs.com/classroom
- Fulbright Scholar Program – Occasional Lecturer Fund: http://www.cies.org/olf/
- Globalization 101: http://www.globalization101.org/globalization/
- Oxfam International: http://www.oxfam.org/
- Peace Corps: http://www.peacecorps.gov/wws/educators/lessonplans/
- Teach Global Ed: http://teachglobaled.net/
- TED – Ideas Worth Spreading: http://www.ted.com/
- United Nations – Global issues page: http://www.un.org/en/globalissues/
- UNICEF: http://www.unicef.org/
- UNESCO – Media Center:
- http://www.unesco.org/new/en/unesco/resources/multimedia/
- WHO – Millennium Development Goals:
- http://www.who.int/topics/millennium_development_goals/en/
- World Press: http://www.worldpress.org/gateway.htm
- YouTube – Carnegie Council Channel: http://www.youtube.com/user/carnegie council

References

American Council on Education. (1998). Educating for global competence: America's passport to the future [Opinion paper]. Washington, DC: Author. Retrieved from http://www.eric.ed.gov/PDFS/ED421940.pdf

Bremer, D. (2006). Wanted: Global workers. *International Educator,* (May/June), 40–45.

Charlson, J., & Vouchilas, G. (2010). Internationalizing an interior design course: A model for global FCS curricula. *Journal of Family and Consumer Sciences, 102* (4), 43–48.

Claiborne, R. (2009). U.S. electronic waste gets sent to Africa. *ABC Good Morning America,* August 2. Retrieved from http://abcnews.go.com/GMA/Weekend/story?id=8215714&page=1

Green, M. F. (2005). *Internationalization of U.S. higher education: A student perspective.* Washington, DC: American Council on Education.

Hudzik, J. K. (2011). *Comprehensive internationalization: From concept to action.* Retrieved from http://www.nafsa.org/resourcelibrary/default.aspx?id=24045

Hunter, B., White, G. P., & Godbey, G. C. (2006). What does it mean to be globally competent? *Journal of Studies in International Education, 10* (3), 267–285.

Merryfield, M. (2002). The difference a global educator can make. *Educational Leadership, 60* (2), 18–21.

Michigan State University. (2005). 2005–2006 recruiting trends. Retrieved from http://www.ceri.msu.edu/wp-content/uploads/2010/03/2005-06-report-final-PDF.pdf

National Association of State Facilities Administrators (NASFA). (n.d). Strategic task force on education abroad. Retrieved from http://www.nafsa.org/publicpolicy/default.aspx?id=6662

Willard, J. (n.d.). Global competency. LanguageCorps. Retrieved from http://www.nafsa.org/_/File/_/global_competency_2.pdf

Wilson-Oyelaran, E. B. (2011). Diversity in education abroad: A plan for our campuses. *IIE Networker,* (spring), 30–33.

6

Notes on Infusion and the "Female Voice": A Philosopher's Unfinished Journey*

Audrey McKinney

The call for infusing women's voices into the canons and courses of the Western European academic tradition has its own significant history and tradition. Some disciplines have responded to the call with notable suppleness. As a result, instructors creating and shaping their syllabi in these fields need not wrestle with questions of how to incorporate works of, by, and about women; those works are front and center, and easily and unselfconsciously drawn upon when crafting a course. But not all academic fields have been so responsive. My own field of philosophy has been a "stubborn beast," and a quick survey of syllabi for introductory philosophy courses shows why it is all too easy for students to come away from the course believing that there are few if any female philosophers.

I have tackled the task of infusion in both my introductory and advanced courses, sometimes successfully, sometimes not, and I offer here some guiding principles that have emerged from and shaped my journey. Though the examples discussed are drawn from philosophy, readers are encouraged to discover ones appropriate to their own disciplines. And, though my focus is on the voices of women, the guiding principles can be adapted to the multiple tasks of infusion involved in the construction of culturally sensitive courses. Infusion is a creative act to which we will each lend our distinctive voices.

Enriching Courses and Disciplines with Women's Writings

Infusion should be a "win-win" proposition for both the instructor and the students. Philosophy, in the Western European tradition, has been positioned as the quest for universal truths and disinterested knowledge. But the call to recover and recognize women's voices in philosophic discourse has given rise to a sustained critique of the conception of "disembodied reason" presupposed in the works of Plato, Descartes, and other major philosophers.

A common (albeit unjustly facile) way that some students dismiss material in historically oriented survey courses is the "dead White male" critique. (Let us ignore for the moment the sweeping assumption that the authors—if not identified by ethnicity or race—are best categorized as "White.") Consider interweaving the texts of "dead White males" with the writings of females (living or dead) that draw upon or call into question the "canonical" texts. In my introductory course in philosophy, I sometimes have students read John Stuart Mill's *Utilitarianism* along with Carol Gilligan's *In a Different Voice*; the pairing allows for a more nuanced understanding of Mill's position, and also helps to highlight the strengths and weaknesses of Gilligan's "ethics of care." Another fruitful pairing is the ethical writings of Jean-Paul Sartre and selections from Simone de Beauvoir's *The Ethics of Ambiguity.*

Going Beyond Canonical Sources

Though women do not figure among the canonical contributors to the development of modern philosophy, there are wonderful examples of lively and challenging correspondence between the "major figures" (Kant, Descartes, Hobbes) and women who read and think critically about their texts. Indeed, in a number of cases, the women point directly to the most problematic features of the major thinker's work. Princess Elisabeth of Bohemia, in a letter to René Descartes, raises *the* central question for a dualist understanding of the mind: How can a nonphysical "stuff" causally interact with the physical realm? And in an exchange of letters between Immanuel Kant and Maria von Herbert, we see Kant in the role of philosophical counselor bringing his moral theory to bear when advising von Herbert on whether or not she should reveal her past to her present lover. The value of including these exchanges goes well beyond illustrating that women have been part of the discourse of philosophy. In addition to displaying the "humanity" of the canonical philosophers (Kant as a philosophical counselor, indeed!), the exchanges model respectful critique and show that philosophy isn't simply a set of static doctrines, but an activity among engaged thinkers. With philosophy construed as a conversation across centuries in which the students too can participate, there is room for the recognition that philosophic discourse arises from "situated voices," rather than the "view from nowhere." A wonderful way to explore the situated nature of voice is to pair selections from Gloria Anzaldúa's *Borderlands* or Toi Derricotte's *The Black Notebooks* with Descartes' depiction of disembodied subjectivity.

Emphasizing Critical Reasoning

Much social science research in the mid-twentieth century—and much clinical research—was conducted by male researchers, and sampled exclusively male (and often, exclusively White middle-class college student) populations. Using the standard "tools" of critical analysis, students are quick to point out the limitations of the research and can consider how to construct more inclusive studies or how to rework the overly generalized conclusions drawn from the research. And students can be encouraged to use their critical faculties to see when claims or studies purporting to be about *all* women are really claims about only *some* women—usually, "straight" women or White women or middle-class women or women of power.

Recognizing Past Exclusion or Marginalization

Positioning women simply as "victims" or as "the historically excluded" unintentionally perpetuates that marginalization. In effect, women—including the female students in the classroom—remain the "outsiders" awaiting permission for entry. (A corollary is that positioning women exclusively as victims positions men exclusively as powerful oppressors or aggressors—both historically and conceptually false.) Certainly, students should learn that Aristotle regarded women as only defectively rational—he really did mean *man* is a rational animal—and that Hobbes, when writing about the state of nature, refers to women and children as the possessions of the males engaged in the solitary, nasty, and brutal competition characteristic of a world without sovereign authority. But by moving beyond the mere observation of exclusion and looking more deeply at these theorists, students can see that in Aristotle's case, not all males are regarded as fully rational—slaves (both male and female) are less rational than the wives of the male citizens—and an understanding of a complex social ordering justified by "natural facts" emerges. And just how "solitary" is the life of the man in the Hobbesian state of nature if he is surrounded by a household including a wife, children, and slaves?

Simply including a "woman module"—that is, inserting into your course a brief selection "on women" (or the "place of women")—very often does not do justice to the contributions women can make and have made to a discipline. The module approach simply continues the marginalization of women's voices. Let the term *infusion* be your guide here. By including attention to and works by women throughout the course, you "normalize" the place of women within the discipline. To borrow bell hooks' phrase, women move from "margin to center" (though this is often best accomplished by shifting the center; that is, by reconsidering the place and importance of traditional, canonical texts). Linda Martín Alcoff's "The Problem of Speaking For Others," when read in tandem with John Stuart Mill's defense of freedom of speech, generates a rich discussion of the power and responsibility inherent in speech. If the article is presented as a "stand alone," especially if placed in a "woman's voice module," students might well miss the way in which it both contests and extends Mill's views.

Recognizing the Complexity of Women's Voices

The infusion of women's voices is *not* a project separate from multicultural infusion. There is no such thing as "*the* women's point of view": Make the effort to have readings by women from a variety of cultural and racial perspectives. Thinking about the empath Lauren Olamina, a fictional character in Octavia E. Butler's *Parable of the Sower*, helps students to recognize the individualism and autonomy "built into" accounts of ethical egoism (and other "standard" moral theories as well). When discussing John Stuart Mill's *On Liberty* and his insights about the "tyranny of the majority," I've made use of *Ramadan*, a "graphic short" by Jennifer Camper: The main character is a Muslim-American lesbian who daily negotiates the "demands" that she mute or conceal one or another of her multiple identities. In addition, assumptions about race and subjectivity that are embedded in continental philosophy are nicely explored in works by Donna-Dale Marcano and Ofelia Schutte.

In the early 1980s, teachers of feminist theory and women's studies courses were called to task not for failing to include the voices of women— obviously, women's voices abounded in their courses—but rather for overemphasizing the writings and situation of White women. Soon, the writings of Toni Morrison, almost always *Sula*, appeared regularly in the syllabi of women's studies courses—*Sula* became *the* canonical "women of color" text, and students encountered the text in course after course after course. In introductory philosophy texts of that era, the "woman's voice" was often represented by Shulamith Firestone, who called for the liberation of women from the "tyranny of childbirth"; though wonderfully prickly, Firestone's work, especially when presented outside of the context from which it emerged, was all too easy for students to dismiss. More recently in introductory texts, the selections emphasizing "a" or "the" "woman's voice" are often focused on the ethics of care—worthy inclusions, to be sure, but hardly sufficient in themselves.

Leave space for contrarian voices and for texts in which women don't "write *as* women"—that is, explicitly from or about the perspective of women. Not all female philosophers engage in "me-search," and indeed, some specifically eschew it. Hazel Barnes' existentialist critique of Ayn Rand's ethical egoism illustrates disagreement between two female theorists about ethical issues that are not (in any immediate sense) "gendered." Jacqueline Scott's "Nietzsche and Decadence: The Revaluation of Morality" provides a thoughtful platform from which to discuss both Nietzsche's conception of values and the nature of philosophy more generally. And a selection from any female thinker critical of feminist philosophy (Susan Haack comes to mind) will provide a breath of contrarian air, and will alert students that there is no "party line" of female voice and that even the critiques of the traditional canon embedded in the course can themselves be subject to thoughtful challenge.

Going Beyond the Textbook

Most introductory philosophy readers still contain about forty articles, only two or three of which are by women (and typically, only women of Western European ancestry). Infusion, then, requires that you look beyond the textbook to enrich your selections. Google and other search engines can be invaluable in helping you broaden your appreciation of possible readings and topics. You can often find syllabi from courses similar to your own; perusing them can jump-start your thinking about how to shape your own selections. Going beyond the textbook likely will also mean going beyond traditional academic resources: Blogs, cartoons, graphic novels, autobiographical essays, YouTube selections, and online discussion groups are just a few of resources available to twine into your course. And, you can enlist your students in the task of finding new materials. In my introductory class, a few times each semester, I have students bring "Internet finds" on a given topic to class. In addition to positioning the students as co-investigators on the topic, the assignment almost always brings to my attention a helpful article or site of which I was unaware. I have found that many students do particularly creative and insightful work when they elect the semester-long blog assignment: Their "web intelligence" and unconfined thinking takes them across disciplinary boundaries and allows them to make connections that would simply never occur to me—and which do, then, find their way into later versions of my courses.

A "Thought Experiment"

Before constructing your "real" syllabus, challenge yourself to devise a syllabus exclusively with women authors and/or centered on issues or case studies in which women play an especially important role. This can be very helpful for pushing you beyond the usual canonical boundaries (and beyond the works most frequently drawn upon when seeking inclusion). Do works or themes that you might otherwise have overlooked suggest themselves? Let these new "angles of vision" inform the actual syllabus you produce for your course.

Don't be surprised to find that the inclusion of new readings and topics has a ripple effect on the way in which you come to approach other selections in the course. The works included in a course will inevitably be in dialogue with each other. Inclusion creates the possibility for further, sometimes even more fertile, inclusion. But also, don't be surprised if some of the new readings you introduce into the course do not work as well as you had anticipated. *You* can't do it all; one course will not transform an entire discipline. Your successful efforts toward inclusion, however, might well spur colleagues to transform their courses as well.

I shall continue to craft my syllabi—adding here, deleting there, pairing and uncoupling readings—hoping both to honor the past of my discipline and to point to its future. The next generation of scholars is taking our courses now; let us provide them with the tools and encouragement for the ongoing task of the mindful reshaping of their disciplines.

Note

* I wish to thank Professor Sandra Mayo for inviting me to speak on the topic of "infusing women's voices" at the Multicultural Curriculum Transformation and Research Institute sessions held at Texas State University–San Marcos in May 2005. My thinking has been sharpened by the insightful questions and commentary from Institute participants both then and in every succeeding year. I wish also to thank Nancy Riley for reviewing this manuscript with a keen eye and a wise heart.

References

Anzaldúa, G. (1987). *Borderlands/la frontera: The new mestizo.* San Francisco, CA: Spinsters/Aunt Lute Press.

Barnes, H. (1967). *An existentialist ethics.* Chicago, IL: University of Chicago Press.

Beauvoir, S. de. (1948). *The ethics of ambiguity.* New York, NY: Philosophical Library.

Butler, O. E. (1993). *The parable of the sower.* New York, NY: Four Walls Eight Windows.

Camper, J. (1994). Ramadan. In *Rude girls and dangerous women.* Bala Cynwyd, PA: Laugh Lines Press.

Correspondence between Descartes and Princess Elisabeth. (2010). (Jonathan Bennett, Trans.). Retrieved from http://www.earlymoderntexts.com/pdf/descelis.pdf

Derricotte, Toi. (1999). *The black notebooks: An interior journey.* New York, NY: W. W. Norton & Company.

Gilligan, C. (1982). *In a different voice: Psychological theory and women's development.* Cambridge, MA: Harvard University Press.

Haack, S. (2000). *Manifesto of a passionate moderate: Unfashionable essays.* Chicago, IL: University of Chicago Press.

Lopez McAlister, L. (1996). *Hypatia's daughters: 1500 years of women philosophers.* Bloomington, IN: Indiana University Press.

Marcano, D. (2003). Sartre and the social construction of race. In R. Bernasconi (Ed.), *Race and racism in continental philosophy* (pp. 214–226). Bloomington, IN: Indiana University Press.

Martín Alcoff, L. (1991–1992). The problem of speaking for others. *Critical Inquiry, 20* (winter), 5–32.

Nuccetelli, S., Schutte, O., & Bueno, O. (2009). *A companion to Latin American philosophy.* Hoboken, NJ: Wiley-Blackwell.

Rand, Ayn. (1961). The objectivist ethics. In *The virtue of selfishness* (pp. 13–39). New York, NY: Penguin Books.

Schutte, Ofelia. (2000). Continental philosophy and post-colonial subjects. *Philosophy Today, 44* (SPEP Supplement), 8–17.

Scott, Jacqueline. (1998). Nietzsche and decadence: The revaluation of morality. *Continental Philosophy Review, 31* (1), 59–78.

Waithe, M. E. (1987–2004). *A history of women philosophers, vols. I–IV.* New York, NY: Springer.

Zweig, A. (Ed.). (1968). *Philosophical correspondence, 1759–1799: Immanuel Kant.* Chicago, IL: University of Chicago Press.

Section III.

Course Transformation Implementation: From Concept to Student Feedback

This section includes seven chapters by Texas State faculty who have attended the Multicultural Curriculum Transformation and Research Institute and transformed their courses. Each chapter provides information about how courses were transformed in disciplines such as social work, family and consumer sciences, curriculum and instruction, music, and mathematics, and in University Seminar. The chapters include course information from before and after the transformations, from the perspectives of the authors. The chapters also discuss sample lectures, student projects, and other materials that assisted in their transformation process, as well as some personal stories about the process.

7

COLLEGE OF APPLIED ARTS

Multiculturalism in Social Work Education

Christine Norton, Raphael Travis, Catherine Hawkins, and Mary Tijerina

Introduction: History of Multiculturalism in Social Work

> Dignity and worth of the individual, person-in-environment, social justice, starting where the client is...

These and other tenets of the social work profession suggest a natural affinity with the ideals of diversity, inclusiveness, and multiculturalism. Nevertheless, the extent to which the profession of social work has come to embody these ideals can best be described as a developmental process. This chapter highlights the history and progression of multiculturalism in social work practice and education, especially within the current context of the Council on Social Work Education's new Educational Policies and Standards. A global framework is utilized in order to consider international as well as national and local multicultural issues in social work education. This chapter builds on the dual educational pedagogies of multicultural education and experiential learning in social work, and expounds on the Kitano model of multicultural curriculum transformation. Case examples of transformed social work courses from the Multicultural Curriculum Transformation and Research Institute at Texas State University–San Marcos are presented, as well as qualitative and quantitative research studies documenting the efficacy of such approaches.

Social Work as a Profession

Social work emerged as a professional activity in the United States during the late nineteenth century, and was rooted in religious efforts directed at helping the poor. Volunteer "friendly visitors" initially sought to raise the moral status of the poor. By the 1890s the volunteer visitors had become social workers, attending training programs to update their skills and accepting paid leadership positions in social welfare agencies. Gradually, these early social workers extended the application of their skills to include other types of charity work, including practice in child welfare institutions and juvenile courts.

A milestone in the development of children's services in the U.S. was the founding in 1853 of the Children's Aid Society of New York (CAS). Established by Charles Loring Brace and a group of social reformers at a time when orphan asylums and almshouses were the only "services" available for poor and homeless children, CAS became one of the most influential, far-reaching, and controversial programs in the child-saving movement of the nineteenth century. Educated as a minister, Brace sought to give children an alternative to life in the slums and teeming city streets. Grounded in the conviction that institutional care stunted and destroyed children, Brace envisioned and implemented an emigration program, the mission of which was to remove as many poor children from the negative influence of their situations to "good Christian homes" in the Midwest U.S., where they could be transformed into self-reliant members of society through gainful work, education, and a wholesome family atmosphere (Gish, 1999). Although the motives behind Brace's approach and its implications on the family structure continue to be debated, the emigration program laid a foundation for the modern conception of foster care, as well as many organization and administrative methods still employed by social service agencies today (Gish).

Patterned after a similar movement in England, the settlement movement that emerged in the U.S. in the late 1880s focused more on the *causes* of poverty than the moral flaws of the poor, and often it offered residence, education. and social services to those in need. Instead of directing their efforts at changing the individual behaviors and values of the poor, settlement workers tried to change the neighborhoods and expand opportunities for working-class people who were poor but not indigent, bringing new attitudes and perspectives to the charity field. The most famous American settlement, Hull House, was established in Chicago in 1889 by Jane Addams and Ellen Gates Starr. The social reformer Grace Abbott resided there from 1908 to 1917, and served as director of the League for Immigrant Protection, a program designed to help immigrants adjust to their new lives and protect them from mistreatment (Kirkland, 1989). Abbott eventually became known for her leadership in prompting the federal government's intervention into social problems, and particularly for her role as head of the Children's Bureau, a major center of social investigation and change (Costin, 1983). Abbott's concern for the welfare of children fueled her work toward passage in 1921 of the Sheppard-Towner Act, which allowed for government aid for mothers and children and provided the first federal grants to aid the social welfare of children (Popple & Leighninger, 2011).

The problems of urbanization and poverty in the U.S. were complicated by the dynamics of mass immigration from a variety of different countries, as well as by the internal migration to northern cities by some 400,000 Black southerners following World War I (Platt & Chandler, 2001). Immigrants and internal migrants alike were drawn to America's largest cities by the promise of jobs in thousands of flourishing new industries, but they were met by overcrowding, unemployment, sanitation problems, segregation, and discrimination in employment and other aspects of daily life. These unique and overwhelming problems drew the attention of those concerned about the nation's general welfare, and fueled the settlement approach that focused on improving the immigrants' circumstances.

Two important contextual factors helped to increase the diversity perspective of the settlement movement in the U.S. First was the emergence of the first contingent of college-educated women. In a society where career opportunities for women with a university education were very restricted, large numbers of women found themselves drawn to the new roles offered by the settlements. Thus, while men played key roles in English settlement work, in the U.S., settlements were dominated by young, college-educated women. A second factor was religious tolerance. While early U.S. settlement workers were strongly motivated by their religious, Protestant beliefs, most came to accept that their work in the predominantly immigrant—and Catholic—neighborhoods would be seriously compromised by a strong religious emphasis. Consequently, the settlement movement was largely nonsectarian. Settlement workers concentrated on changing the general situations they uncovered in their neighborhood surveys. Public education, juvenile courts, citizenship, labor issues, civil rights, daycare, and cultural awareness programs are just a few examples of the reform-minded activities carried out by settlement workers (Popple & Leighninger, 2011).

Despite the influences of gender diversity and religious tolerance, the settlements were far from perfect. While a few leaders such as Lillian Wald and Jane Addams rose above the common biases of the times, most settlement workers accepted the racial stereotypes that were then so prevalent even among the educated. Social welfare organizations and social work agencies of the day were not eager to have African-American clients, and in many cases, had explicit policies or time-honored customs that excluded them (Carlton-LaNey & Alexander, 2001). The majority of settlements ignored the issues of the urban African American, and the few settlements that did try to address the problems faced by African Americans were segregated and forced to create a closed network within the larger settlement movement. The first and second Black settlement houses in the U.S. were founded by Sara A. Collins Fernandis in

Washington, D.C. and Rhode Island, respectively (Crouse, Battle, McFeaters, & Glazer, n.d.). Janie Porter Barrett, an African American social work pioneer and race activist, started Georgia's Locust Street Settlement in her home with a weekly sewing class for girls; it quickly grew into an array of clubs and activities. Barrett's commitment to child well-being led to the establishment of a child welfare department in this settlement, and later to the establishment of the Virginia Industrial School of Colored Girls (Carlton-LaNey). Birdye Henrietta Haynes, the first Black to graduate from the Chicago School of Civics and Philanthropy, and a trained settlement worker, held leadership roles at Chicago's Wendell Phillips Settlement and New York's Lincoln House. In addition to the inadequate housing and lack of employment opportunities facing the Black community, Haynes focused on the social and recreational needs of the community, especially young boys and men (Carlton-LaNey, 1994).

The segregation of the social welfare system at the turn of the century notwithstanding, some White settlement leaders did play an important role in combating racism. In 1908, following race riots in Springfield, Illinois, concerned citizens organized a conference on race. Led by settlement workers including William Walling and Mary Ovington, the conference was attended by a large number of prominent White and Black people. Plans were made at this conference for the creation of a permanent organization, which then evolved into the National Association for the Advancement of Colored People (NAACP). This and other multicultural contributions came directly from the social work profession.

Social Work Education: Past

Early social work leaders were quick to realize that education would inevitably play a key role in attainment of true professional status. The early charity organizations took the lead in education; in the early 1890s, Mary Richmond, then director of the Baltimore Charity Organization, began developing training programs, which were widely copied by other charity organizations. In 1898 the New York Charity Organization started the first school for social workers, consisting of a six-week set of summer classes and including formal lectures and fieldwork. By 1919 this program had grown and changed its name to the New York School of Social Work, later to become the Columbia University School of Social Work. The settlements were not far behind. In 1901 the Chicago Commons Settlement cooperated with the University of Chicago to offer extension courses on social work. By 1907 the program had grown into a full curriculum known as the Chicago School of Civics and Philanthropy. In 1920 it officially became the University of Chicago School of Social Work. By 1920 there were seventeen schools of social work that formed the Association of Training Schools of Professional Schools of Social Work. The Atlanta University, the first school of social work for African Americans, was established in the early 1920s by E. Franklin Frazier (Platt & Chandler, 1988). Although Frazier's writings regarding race and prejudice engendered considerable controversy, he contributed significantly to social work education through his original research on the economic, political, and attitudinal factors that shape the systems of social relationships. His writing on the Black family was among the first sociological works on African Americans researched and written by an African American.

In 1932 the Association of Professional Schools of Social Work responded to the challenge posed by the rapid expansion of public agencies, adopting a minimum curriculum that required a year of full-time study. In 1934 the Association required that all schools seeking accreditation must be affiliated with a college or university. In 1939 accreditation requirements were increased to include a two-year curriculum.

Since its creation in 1952 by a merger of the American Association of Schools of Social Work and the National Association of Schools of Social Administration, the Council on Social Work Education (CSWE) has been sanctioned by the Council on Higher Education Accreditation as the sole accreditor of social work educational programs in the United States (Austin, 1997). CSWE is authorized to establish educational requirements for social work education, assess a program's ability to meet these standards, and award accreditation if the standards are met. State licensing laws all agree that only graduates from a CSWE accredited program are eligible to apply for a social work license and, thus, practice social work (Colby, 2009). Social work education for practice involves two levels. Bachelor-level social work education provides the entry-level degree to the profession; commonly referred to as BSWs (Bachelor of Social Work), bachelor-level practitioners provide direct front-line services utilizing generalist social work practice as their practice model. Master-level social workers, commonly referred to as MSWs (Master of Social Work), are prepared for advanced and specialized models of practice.

Social Work Education: Present

Over the last decade, there has been a general transitioning by postsecondary education in the U.S. toward a competency-based model of education. Competency-based education aims to prepare a student to perform a work role that meets a clearly defined standard. Educational programs identify competencies, gear curriculum toward students' performance, and evaluate students on their ability to perform the specific competency with its necessary knowledge and values. In 2008 CSWE adopted the competency-based model, revising its educational policies and accreditation standards (EPAS) toward assessment of educational outcomes and student achievement of practice competencies. Rather than prescribe particular content areas (e.g., human behavior, research, policy, practice, and diversity), social work programs identify what their students are capable of doing upon graduation as a consequence of the educational experience (Holloway 2008). By focusing on building competency in specific practice behaviors, students can professionally engage clients and colleagues based on skills they've acquired in their coursework. The CSWE competency-based model identifies ten minimum core competencies that the curriculum must address in all bachelor and master programs. For each of the ten core competencies, a set of practice behaviors is delineated (CSWE, 2010). The competencies and practice behaviors most clearly associated with multicultural competencies are listed in Table 1.

Table 1. CSWE Educational Policy and Accreditation Standards Relating to Cultural Competency

Competency	Practice Behaviors—Social Workers:
2.1.4. Engage diversity and difference in practice	• Recognize the extent to which a culture's structures and values may oppress, marginalize, alienate, or create, or enhance privilege and power • Gain sufficient self-awareness to eliminate the influence of personal biases and values in working with diverse groups • Recognize and communicate understanding of the importance of difference in shaping life experiences • View themselves as learners and engage those with whom they work as informants
2.1.5 Advance human rights and social and economic justice	• Understand the forms and mechanisms of oppression and discrimination • Advocate for human rights and social and economic justice • Engage in practices that advance social and economic justice
2.1.7. Apply knowledge of human behavior and the social environment.	• Utilize conceptual frameworks to guide the processes of assessment, intervention, and evaluation • Critique and apply knowledge to understand person and environment

Note. Adapted from Council on Social Work Education Educational Policy and Accreditation Standards, which seek to establish thresholds for professional competence.

Competency 2.1.4: Engage diversity and difference in practice

By building awareness and minimizing biases, students are prepared to fully embrace their professional roles free of unnecessary hindrances to effectiveness. Students become skilled at identifying their own personal and environmental influences upon diverse populations. Student ability to effectively engage clients free of bias increases the potential for respectful inquiry and learning to take place. Each of these competencies is invaluable at the professional level.

Competency 2.1.5: Advance human rights and social and economic justice

When students have a strong grasp of the pathways to optimal human rights and justice, they can better identify intervention strategies to facilitate positive change. These particular skills of understanding, advocacy, and action have added value at both the local and the international level, where themes of oppression and justice are prominent in many countries.

Competency 2.1.7: Apply knowledge of human behavior and the social environment

The interrelatedness of person, environment, and culture make knowledge of human behavior and the social environment essential for social workers. Students' ability to use this knowledge in guiding the helping process prepares them for core professional responsibilities. This knowledge guides professional social work assessments, interventions strategies, and evaluations.

Social Work Education: Future Directions

Prior to the revision in the educational standards, teaching diversity in social work education generally followed a multicultural approach that emphasized either cultural sensitivity or cultural competence. This former approach stressed tolerance for diverse persons, understanding of cultural norms, and cross-cultural strategies, but it often fell short due to cultural encapsulation, in which social work continued to practice from a Euro-American ethnocentric point of view (Sue, 2006). Though the emphasis was on preparing the emerging practitioners to be able to adjust to client needs in order to meet those needs (Sisneros, Stakeman, Loyner, & Schmitz, 2008), there was a genuine lack of understanding of others' worldviews. While social work education has tried to augment awareness and appreciation of differences, it has been criticized for its failure to address the interrelatedness and interconnectedness of oppressions such as those based on race, class, and gender (Schriver, 2000). This is a valid concern, given that victims of oppression are the very persons that social workers and social work educators encounter and deal with on a regular basis.

In order to address this concern, a broader view of cultural competence is needed. Sue (2006) provides a multidimensional model of cultural competence in social work that is

> ...characterized by the use of universal and cultural specific strategies that are consistent with the lived-experience and cultural values of the client. This approach is predicated on the acknowledgement of a three-dimensional human existence (i.e. individual, group, and universal) that is balanced between individualism and collectivism in a socio-cultural context. Therefore, in addition to focusing on the client, the role of the [worker] also focuses on the client's systems and when necessary, acts on these systems to produce change in the spirit of social justice. (Sifford & Ng, 2010)

Multicultural social work should therefore focus on various competencies. According to Sue & Sue (2003), these competencies include three primary domains: (a) awareness of one's own values, beliefs, and biases; (b) knowledge about the culture of various ethnic groups; and (c) culturally relevant interventions. These are the areas in which CSWE has begun to shift.

Parallel to the competency-based shift in social work education was the revision of the National Association of Social Workers (NASW) Code of Ethics, a document that provides general guidance in the practice of social work. The 2008 revision specifically addresses the issue of cultural competence, stating that "social workers should obtain education and seek to understand the nature of social diversity and oppression with respect to race, ethnicity, national origin, color, sex, sexual orientation, gender identity or expression, age, marital status, political belief, religion, immigration status, and mental or physical disability" (p. 34). The Code of Ethics also highlights issues of respect for others' differences and prohibits any kind of discrimination based on these differences. Finally, the NASW Code of Ethics urges social workers to engage in social and political action on behalf of those who may be marginalized in society because of their differences.

These revisions, along with the revised social work educational standards and competencies, provide a significant impetus to study of the nature of oppression in society and within social work education in general. In this way, social work, both as a profession and as an academic discipline, supports the idea of multicultural education and course transformation. Therefore, as social work educators we were compelled to take advantage of the Multicultural Curriculum Transformation and Research Institute (MCTRI) at Texas State University–San Marcos, which highlights multicultural education pedagogy, practice, and research. First, however, we felt it was important to clarify how multicultural education fits with social work education.

International Social Work and Universal Human Rights

The first way in which multiculturalism seems to fit well with social work education is the commitment to instill a global perspective in our students, in order to better prepare them for leadership in the twenty-first century. A global or international perspective is a required component of social work education in the U.S. The Council on Social Work Education mandates inclusion of content on the "global interconnectedness of oppression" and "international issues of social welfare policy and social service delivery" (CSWE, 2001). The International Federation of Social Workers states that "Principles of human rights and social justice are fundamental to social work" (IFSW, 2010). Yet, this massive amount of cross-discipline content must be organized in some systematic way if students are to gain a sufficient understanding the vast and perplexing array of problems facing the global community today. Universal human rights provide a useful organizing framework that advocates an activist orientation and encourages students to pursue an ethical stance toward equality, especially for the most poor, oppressed, and vulnerable people.

Human rights are at the very heart of social work, a uniquely value-based and action-oriented profession focused on empowerment and enhancement of well-being. Human rights are linked to social and economic power. Reichert (2006) connects human rights principles to social work practice through six primary interventions: challenging oppression, empowerment, strengths perspective, ethnic-sensitive practice, feminist practice, and cultural competence. These interventions are core elements of multicultural education as well and should be the focus of experiential learning in all social work courses.

Parallels between Multicultural Education and Experiential Learning

When people hear the phrase *multicultural education*, they often do not know what to think. Certain critics believe that multicultural education can actually narrow the curriculum and take away from current educational policies and standards; however, the purpose of multicultural education is to create a "broader truth" and to enhance student learning through multiple perspectives (Morey & Kitano, 1997). In order to help social work students and faculty understand the pedagogy of multicultural education, we found it useful to draw parallels between multicultural education and experiential education, which incorporates experiential learning theory as a core learning process. Experiential Learning Theory (ELT) emphasizes the central role that experience plays in the learning process, and is an accepted and well-known pedagogy in social work education. Much like multicultural education, experiential education can transform higher education in a way that engages students and facilitates a greater level of participation in the learning environment. ELT is built on the philosophical foundation of experiential education, and has its roots in the theories and philosophies of John Dewey (1938), educator, psychologist, and pragmatist philosopher. The Association for Experiential Education defines experiential education as "a process through which a learner constructs knowledge, skill, and value from direct experiences" (AEE, 2002, p. 5). Three core principles that are most related to multicultural education in social work are: (1) experiential learning occurs when carefully chosen experiences are supported by reflection, critical analysis, and synthesis; (2) the results of the learning are personal, and form the basis for future experience and learning; and (3) opportunities are nurtured for learners and educators to explore and examine their own values (AEE, 2002, p. 5).

Likewise, experiential learning focuses on both the content and process of student learning. According to the Association for Experiential Education (2010), which promotes the use of experiential learning in education, the mission of experiential education is to create a more just and compassionate world by transforming education. Social justice goals of experiential education include decreasing ethnocentrism and increasing conflict resolution. Luckmann (1996) defines experiential education as a "process through which a learner constructs knowledge, skill and value from direct experience" (p. 7). This new knowledge is then applied and tested in new situations. Experiential learning is the cornerstone of social work's "signature pedagogy," field education, in which students work in social services agencies and apply the knowledge they have gained in the classroom in a real-world setting (CSWE, 2010).

Multicultural education builds on the core principles of ELT by developing citizens for a more democratic society through comprehensive disciplinary knowledge; educational strategies that promote achievement *and* engagement; critical thinking *applied* to social problems; and the promotion of the values of diversity and equal opportunity (Morey &

Kitano, 1997). Multicultural education seeks to include the contributions and ideas of people of differing races, ethnicities, cultures, languages, religions, genders, sexual orientations, physical abilities and disabilities, etc. Multicultural education also uses various instructional strategies, assessment, evaluation, and feedback, and promotes more equitable classroom and community interactions.

While a full explanation of the two educational pedagogies is beyond the scope of this chapter, Table 2 highlights the parallels between ELT and multicultural education. Understanding the parallels between these two pedagogies enabled us to transform our courses into multicultural courses in such a way that empowered students to actively participate in the learning environment. Through the Multicultural Curriculum Transformation and Research Institute, we gained valuable knowledge on best practices for broadening and enriching the curriculum by re-envisioning goals, content, teaching strategies, assessment, and classroom interactions with a multicultural lens.

Table 2. Finding the Parallels Between Multicultural Education and ELT

Multicultural Education	**Experiential Education (ELT)**
Contributes to the development of citizens for a more democratic society	Contributes to the development of citizens for a more democratic society (Dewey)
Employs critical thinking	Employs critical thinking
Focus on action and reflection* (in working toward social justice) *Often uses writing to promote self-awareness	Focus on action and reflection (in working toward creative problem solving on micro, mezzo, and macro levels)
Inclusive, community building	Inclusive, community building
Learning from our own and others' experiences (exposure to a broader truth)	Learning from experience: often *our own* experiences of the world are challenged by others in the group
Addresses conflict; promotes equity in relationships (educator as facilitator)	Addresses conflict; promotes equity in relationships (educator as facilitator)
Seeks to improve knowledge, awareness, and skills	Seeks to improve knowledge, awareness, and skills

Multicultural Curriculum Transformation and Research Institute (MCTRI)

The Multicultural Curriculum Transformation and Research Institute (MCTRI) at Texas State University–San Marcos is a week-long seminar sponsored by the Center for Multicultural and Gender Studies (MCGS) in the College of Liberal Arts that assists faculty with resources and professional development activities to encourage the infusion of multiculturalism in the curriculum. This opportunity for training for skills in the infusion of multicultural content and process was intriguing to us as instructors because we all wanted and continue to want to stay at the forefront of culturally sound pedagogy. What we experienced and learned during the MCTRI profoundly expanded our notion of how multicultural infusion could benefit social work education.

The Kitano Model and Social Work Courses

During the MCTRI, we were immersed in the *Kitano model* of multicultural education, which provided clarity about how to transform existing courses into multicultural courses. Multicultural course transformation refers to the "modification of a given course to appropriately incorporate multicultural content, perspectives, and strategies (Kitano, 1997a, p. 2). Such change meets the following three objectives: provide a more comprehensive, accurate, and intellectually honest view of reality; prepare all students to function in a multicultural society; and better meet the learning needs of all students, including those who are diverse (p. 2).

Kitano argues that the importance of multicultural course transformation goes far beyond the curriculum. Ethnic minority students have lower rates of graduation and take longer to complete their degrees. There continue to be instances of overt discrimination and debates about "preference." Although faculty diversity is improving, there are insufficient ethnic minority doctoral graduates to meet increasing demand. Research supports the effectiveness of multicultural education across all levels, but there is little evidence that institutions of higher education are monitoring progress. She addresses several assumptions underlying her model (pp. 12–16), such as the following:

1. Multicultural education is for all, not just for members of marginalized groups. It is a quality education that enables all students to interact more effectively.
2. Transformative scholarship offers students a more comprehensive truth because it challenges, expands, and revises established mainstream scholarship.

3. While all groups have the same underlying abilities, they may have different cognitive and learning styles. Therefore, competent instructors should use a wide variety of teaching methods.
4. Academic achievement is a critical factor in promoting equal opportunity. While some students from some groups may be underprepared, this should not be confused with lower potential.
5. Academic achievement alone does not eliminate structural barriers to career attainment and social integration.
6. Higher education faculty can play a significant role in developing a more equitable society. Faculty engage in multiple spheres of influence in pursuing change, including self, classroom, organization (department, college, school, institution), and community (local, regional, national, international).

Finally, Kitano identifies six principles and practices of multicultural education (p. 16). First, diversity should permeate the total campus environment. Second, content and materials should present and analyze diverse perspectives. Third, instructional strategies should promote excellence, build on strengths, and include opportunities for growth. Fourth, objectives should include fostering skills for informed citizenship and cooperation. Fifth, assessment procedures should accommodate students' expression of accumulated knowledge and skills. Sixth, evaluation should be ongoing and systematic.

Once a course is altered, it can fall under one of the following levels of potential course change: exclusive, inclusive, or transformed. Kitano emphasizes that change is an ongoing process (not an outcome) and will require several semesters of planning, experimentation, and revision. In an exclusive course, content is traditional and mainstream, instruction is didactic, student assessment is through written exams, and classroom dynamics are controlled by the instructor. In the inclusive course, the content includes both traditional and alternative perspectives, instruction relies on a range of teaching methods focused on active learning, assessment involves several strategies to allow individual differences in expression, and dynamics support participation by all students. In a transformed course, content challenges traditional perspectives and encourages new ways of thinking and knowing, instruction is based on shared power to the greatest extent feasible, and encourages personal as well as academic growth, assessment includes self-evaluation and projects, and dynamics lead to real-life change.

Social Work Course Transformation

As social work faculty, we were able to deeply reflect upon where and how our courses could be completely transformed. We went into the Institute ready to change course content only, but left the Institute embracing the Kitano (1997) model for multicultural course transformation, with plans to change: (1) course goals, (2) course content, (3) course instruction, (4) assessment and evaluation characteristics, and (5) classroom interactions. A thorough inventory of our courses and focused attention to all aspects of the teaching and learning environment allowed us to substantially improve our courses across many more dimensions than we could have imagined. Before looking at several case studies of course transformation, we will briefly highlight some of the major ideas within each domain of change. There were substantially more ideas for each domain of change than we could possibly integrate in our first iteration of course transformation; however, our preliminary ideas are highlighted below across the five domains of change.

Course Goals. For the overall course goals, it became apparent that it wasn't simply the delivery of current, meaningful, and evidence-based course content that was important. There were different types of goals that we needed to address. For example, we needed to help convey to students the type of learning environment that we were committed to providing, particularly in terms of equal opportunities for all types of students to learn—free of bias. We needed to consistently prevent domains of exclusion, and create classroom environments where students felt they mattered.

Course Content. We expected that improvements to course content would be the biggest area of change. Course content includes classroom/lecture content as well as assigned instructional material (e.g., books, journal articless and videos). We anticipated that we would identify areas of content that were insufficiently descriptive about cultural norms, dynamics and strengths. Again, preconceived notions were broadened, and our ideas expanded. Ideas for change also included improved contextualization of content. For example, we saw value in better situating content within historical and future contexts, in using full names to clearly distinguish gender and ethnicity of researchers/theorists, in better identifying major social work pioneers and leaders by gender and ethnicity, and in introducing innovative and new perspectives that may contest dominant views.

Course Instruction. The next area of transformation was course instruction. We felt that course instruction had a narrower range of associations with multiculturalism, aside from language and general experiences. What became apparent through the Institute was that the unique social realities of students had many implications beyond language. For example, not only would students have unique histories and experiences that could contribute to and enrich the classroom learning environment, but they may also have substantial differences in learning styles and preferred learning modalities.

Student and Course Assessment. Conceptualizing what should be assessed in our courses allowed for the consideration of a more robust evaluation plan. The expanded notion of what is important meant not only that multicultural knowledge and attitudes could be assessed among students (outcomes), but also that the multicultural atmosphere could be assessed as well (process). These process considerations included *how* students were assessed, such as potentially allowing students to choose how they were assessed (e.g., examinations, papers, presentations) or to choose self-assessment. Equally important for students was making the grading process more transparent, with, for example, grading rubrics.

Course Interactions. Course interactions differed from course instruction in that course content dealt more with overall perceived course value, while course interactions dealt with specific interpersonal dynamics and experiential activities within the classroom. For example, after assignments were submitted, was feedback specific and unambiguous? Were assignment expectations clear? How were issues of race/ethnicity handled within the classroom? Consideration was given even to the inclusiveness of fixed office hours.

This holistic process of course transformation led to significant changes in several social work courses taught by various faculty members, as well as the creation of a new course that focuses on international social work and human rights. The following section provides case studies and research conducted on the impact of multicultural course transformation in social work education.

Case Studies of Course Development and Transformation in Social Work Education

International Social Work & Universal Human Rights (Catherine Hawkins)

Because of the importance of promoting a global perspective in social work education, my participation in the MCTRI led me to create a new elective course in the social work curriculum. Though the relevant scholarly literature has grown in the past decade (e.g., Healy, 2008; Ife, 2001; Mapp, 2008; Payne & Askeland, 2008; Reichert, 2003, 2007), Dominelli (2007) reports a lack of articles on human rights in major social work journals. Thus, this course was created to expand students' professional boundaries beyond American-centric social work, while at the same time recognizing that global problems also manifest at the local level. The course focused on the need for international social work to be culturally sensitive (Ahmadi, 2003; Gray & Fook, 2004; Skegg, 2005), as well as on universal human rights.

All elements of the newly created course met the guidelines of the Multicultural Curriculum Transformation and Research Institute (MCTRI). The course fulfilled the definition of multicultural education, which specifies the promotion of the values of diversity and equal opportunity for all people through understanding of the contributions and perspectives of people of differing races, ethnicities, cultures, languages, religions, genders, sexual orientations, and physical abilities (Kitano, 1997a). Each of the guidelines discussed below are based on Kitano's model, and refer to both the level of the course and the revised syllabus.

First, the course description in the syllabus made specific reference to multicultural content, in terms of both examining cultural factors that impact universal human rights and encouraging students to engage in critical cultural inquiry. Second, the course objectives in the syllabus explicitly addressed multicultural aspects, including cognitive, affective, and behavioral components. For example, students were expected to articulate current debates, such as universalism vs. cultural relativism (cognitive). They were required to explore significant contemporary human rights issues and engage in personal and cultural self-reflection (affective). They were guided to integrate knowledge, values, and skills through pursuing advocacy and action for change (behavioral).

Third, the content of the entire course was at the transformed level of course change, based on Kitano's (1997b) model. International social work and universal human rights are inherently multicultural; thus, this content was infused throughout the course. Diverse perspectives were incorporated into each class session through an ongoing examination of underlying themes (e.g., American exceptionalism vs. globalism, imperialism vs. nativism, etc.). According to the MCTRI guidelines, this approach constituted a level-three course design in which a new framework synthesizes old and new perspectives. That is, the course moved beyond level one (supporting traditional views) and level two (studying diverse groups) to engage in critical analysis of U.S. and world societies. This included the ability to value diversity, exhibit an informed sensitivity, and actively engage with other cultures.

Social realities and conflict in the U.S. and world societies were critically analyzed. The required text (Mapp, 2008) identified three major interrelated barriers to human freedom (poverty, discrimination, and lack of education) and examined five global problems: forced labor, child welfare, war and conflict, AIDS, and women's issues. Resources came from human rights organizations such as Human Rights Watch, Amnesty International, and United for Human Rights. Websites displaying photographs and videos and excerpts from books or movies helped to generate an imperative to care for all people, and to see our connections to all people.

Fourth, I employed a wide variety of instructional strategies that were student-centered, experiential, and focused on creating a community of learners. This qualified as a level-three approach, as compared to level one (instructor-centered) or level two (combined instructor- and student-centered). Teaching methods included group discussion, classroom activities, field-based experiences, audio/visual aids, Internet-based resources, formal and informal written assignments, required readings, scholarly research, personal self-reflection journals, individual presentations, and interactive guest speakers. I built on the preexisting strengths-based perspective of social work education and practice.

An often overlooked component of current pedagogy in higher education is the affective component of learning. I helped students to process emotionally painful content as well as to overcome a pervasive sense of pessimism regarding the enormity of human problems. Several strategies were useful in this regard. Throughout the course, students maintained informal (nongraded) journals, which were a rich source of material for classroom discussion as students shared their challenges and changes with each other. In facilitating this discussion, I role-modeled how they should express themselves appropriately, as well as how to create a support system. I presented evidence of progress toward achieving universal human rights, such as the Millennium Development Goals, which document substantial progress in poverty reduction, access to primary education, reduced child mortality, HIV and malaria control, and some aspects of environmental sustainability, and which are closely connected to the professional mission of social work, especially its call for advocacy and action toward universal social and economic justice (UNDP, 2010). I required them to identify examples of successful programs as part of weekly activity assignments and a semester-long project. I counseled students that it is empathy that bridges knowledge and action. This empathy requires a delicate balance between recognizing our similarities with others and respecting our differences.

Fifth, student learning, which accommodates students' strengths and maintains high standards of expectation, was assessed through multiple methods. The assessment strategies employed focus on growth, action-oriented projects, self-assessment and reflection, meaning making, synthesis, and application. This moved beyond level one (which relies on a single method) and level two (which uses multiple methods that accommodate student strengths but fall short of growth-oriented strategies). In an autobiography assignment at the beginning of the semester, students looked at their individual and cultural development and reflected upon how their background has influenced their attitudes and behavior. In a self-reflection paper at the end of the semester, students considered how they had grown and changed throughout the course, and speculated on their future directions. This allowed for authentic self-evaluation and change.

The course was very action-oriented. Experiential learning strategies were employed through action and reflection, and students engaged in a weekly activity, sometimes assigned by me and sometimes of their choice. Each week they had to pursue an out-of-class experience to gain a broader perspective of human rights and then write a brief reaction paper. They also had to conduct two interviews: one with a professional working in the field of human rights, and one with an individual who had experienced a human rights violation. The interview assignments were particularly powerful in generating empathy for people of diverse backgrounds and experiences. Students were required to select and read an additional book that gave them an alternative cultural perspective from a different group within or beyond the U.S.

Finally, students conducted a semester-long project that entailed pursuing specific action steps to redress a human rights problem. In this assignment, they conducted an in-depth analysis of a specific problem and identified proposed or actual solutions. Then, they were required to apply the knowledge, values, and skills gained in the course toward at least one specific action step. This helped students to see themselves as active and effective advocates for human rights. I explicitly note that the benefits of rights come with responsibilities to help others achieve them (Ife & Fiske, 2006).

Sixth, classroom interactions represented a systematic process that promotes equality, addresses oppression, and supports cultural competence. In addition, there were planned opportunities for cross-group interactions, with a common goal of making connections. This level-three multicultural infusion is in contrast to level one, in which there is little attention paid to cultural variables, and level two, in which efforts are made in this regard but fail to fully integrate cultural variables. A major aspect of the course was unstructured, open-ended discussions in each class session that encouraged students to value diversity and equity, to accept themselves and others, and to work actively toward social change. These discussions were arranged in both large group and small group formats to accommodate different comfort levels and styles of communication. Thus, we mutually created a classroom community that was respectful and inclusive, that shared power, and that capitalized on strength, choice, and personal growth. I pointed out to students their privilege, not only in achieving a higher education, but also in being able to freely express their opinions and engage in an open discussion of human rights. One of the most rewarding aspects of teaching this course for me was to watch the evolution of a cohesive group with a shared goal, as students became teachers to each other and envisioned themselves as competent change agents at the local, national, and global levels.

Seventh, course evaluation gave students the opportunity to comment on the multicultural aspects of the course. The evaluation used by the academic unit contained both quantitative and qualitative questions, although no item asked specifically about multicultural content or process; this is an area that will be targeted for future improvement. Nevertheless, the narrative feedback (collected anonymously and shared with the instructor only after grades were submitted) overwhelmingly suggested that the intentional development of a new multicultural course was thorough and effective. See Table 3 below for a sampling of some of the narrative feedback.

Table 3. Narrative Evaluation, International Social Work, and Universal Human Rights

How was this course particularly effective?	How will this course affect your education and/or your future?	How are you different having taken this course?
It took my existing passions and implemented them. It was cool to see a group together who was united in thoughts of human rights.	It led me further in my path of future activism and how to effectively help others.	I have a better understanding of cultures, oppressed humans, their oppressors, and my role as a human on this earth.
This course especially helped me to develop a holistic perspective and to be a more aware individual.	It was extremely effective in opening my eyes to the world and what I learned in this class will stay with me forever and help me to make a difference.	Now I know how to "take action" against human rights violations and I feel empowered to do so!
The material of this course, human rights and violations throughout the world are very tender subjects. The instructor led the class in a discussion-based manner that was particularly effective because we were able to express our emotions as well as to learn from others.	I learned a lot about myself and I am now surer of my future in international social work and the fight for human rights.	I used to not even know about human rights and now I am educated enough to educate others and how we can protect others from being violated in the world.

How was this course particularly effective?	How will this course affect your education and/or your future?	How are you different having taken this course?
It raised my awareness to issues that I had no idea were occurring across the globe.	This was the most beneficial class that I have ever taken throughout my college career! I have learned not to be silent and to act.	I have a more holistic view of what is actually going on in the world rather than just the facts and statistics you learn about in other classes.
This class was particularly effective in broadening my empathy and awareness of global human rights violations.	This course actually opened my eyes to new possibilities in the future. I can actually see myself as working for an international human rights organization after graduation.	I am much more grateful for what I have—my family, my education, even my own personal safety. I am much more aware of violations globally. I am a better person for having taken this course, and I have a stronger desire to create a tangible difference in the world.
The discussions helped me to learn not only from the instructor, but from peers as well. Guest speakers were very informative about their human rights work.	I will value my education much more knowing that there are people all over the world fighting and dying for what I too often take for granted.	I am thinking in broad, worldly terms now.
It allowed me to think critically about issues that affect human beings, and taught me to think of solutions. I learned about things we don't usually hear in the media and was motivated me to work for the prevention of human rights violations.	It has made me realize that I am a global citizen.	I feel that I am much more aware of world issues and effective solutions.
I learned a lot through the open discussions, and feel I have improved my social work skills.	It helped me understand problems that affect today's world, and how to handle an issue. It has taught me to be more tolerant and this will allow me to effectively communicate with people from different cultural backgrounds and to work with them on a common cause.	It has increased my empathy toward others, and helped me to have an open mind about everything I encounter.

In sum, developing a multicultural course with a focus on universal human rights provided a useful and manageable framework for helping social work students to build a truly global perspective. This is particularly valuable in the U.S., where students may tend toward xenophobia and a pervasive sense of entitlement. This potential national bias must be weighed against the ongoing reality of social, economic, and political inequity within the U.S. In this global era, students must be assisted to engage in an informed discussion of the universal aspects of human rights, to gain awareness about the pressing problems of inequality around the world (especially for children), to identify proposed and workable solutions, and to develop a manageable framework for understanding local, national and global connections. The ultimate goal is to empower students to work toward creating a world that is just, fair, and humane for all people.

Foundation Social Work Practice I (Raphael Travis)

The course I chose to transform was an introductory social work practice course for MSW students. This course looks at social work practice from a generalist perspective, with an emphasis on the micro and mezzo levels including data collection, assessment, intervention planning, and evaluation. Students study social work theory and practice methodology applied to problem solving with individuals, families, and groups. In this course, I wanted to ensure that the future social work professionals that matriculate through the course recognize the magnitude of their responsibility to be culturally responsive in practice (NASW, 2007).

Though many change ideas were considered, only a few could be implemented in the available time. Examples of some of the changes made in this course are provided below, including amendments to the syllabus, classroom/lecture content, student assessment, and course evaluation. First, sample changes to the syllabus, classroom content, and student assessment are highlighted, followed by a review of course evaluation results.

Changes to Syllabus: Instructor Aims and Student Participation

One of the clear implications for me upon conclusion of the Institute was that the implicit objectives for the course were more refined, and thus my role as the instructor had to change to a certain degree. I felt that these modifications should be made explicit to students. This notion of explicit attention to what we seek to achieve multiculturally in a given course is described in great detail by Kitano (1997b, p.19). I developed *instructor aims* that captured the spirit of these intentions:

1. Create a community of learners where students interact with each other and the instructor;
2. Create learning experiences that consider diverse starting points and diverse backgrounds;
3. Support diverse students' acquisition of subject matter knowledge and skills;
4. Support students' acquisition of a comprehensive knowledge of the helping process; and
5. Support students' understanding of how one's own background, experiences, beliefs, and values may influence the theory and strategies selected for direct practice.

My expectations of students also needed a richer, more explicit articulation in the syllabus. Students were then alerted to their role in creating a more multiculturally sound environment. It wasn't simply me, the facilitator, trying to create an atmosphere; it was identified as a two-way dynamic between the instructor and students. Students could see these expectations on paper, they were verbally introduced to them by me in the classroom, and then I worked to help these expectations manifest in partnership with students in the classroom throughout the course. Student participation was defined as follows:

1. Students will actively engage in creating knowledge and meaning by integrating old and new concepts from their own experiences;
2. Students will analyze prior experiences in light of new course frameworks;
3. Students will critically analyze course material and current beliefs;
4. Students will participate in assignments at a level that is personally challenging;
5. Students will work through concepts that are problematic, conflicting, or confusing through reading, discussion, reflection, and writing;
6. Students will share knowledge with each other and the instructor;
7. Students will listen openly and respectfully to the views of others.

Changes to Classroom/Lecture Content

The Institute also fostered clarity around the many potential changes to classroom/lecture content. I will highlight one segment of one lecture to illustrate how content was modified throughout the course. One area that stood out as profoundly important and worth greater sustained emphasis was *the inclusion of a global perspective* in all aspects of the course. I chose to introduce this notion early to help frame the course. To enhance student engagement in these discussions, video news clips and footage accompanied discussion as often as possible.

Students were introduced to the principle that local dynamics are international dynamics, and that most course concepts that are discussed have local and international examples. Furthermore, our attention to culturally specific realities does not preclude common and shared issues, but it shows how common issues may manifest in culturally specific ways.

For example, I described similarities between xenophobia in South Africa toward immigrants from neighboring Zimbabwe, and anti-immigration sentiment in the United States toward immigrants from neighboring Mexico. Importantly, social workers may be involved in issues of immigration from many different perspectives. They may find themselves working with a person who feels threatened by the immigration situation (e.g., a worker recently laid off, a business owner with economic interests); a person coping with anti-immigrant sentiment directed at him (as a documented or undocumented immigrant); a person coping with declining opportunities to provide for her family in her country of origin; a person coping with being separated from family back home; a person coping with peers or family members who express heavy anti-immigrant sentiments; or a family trying to negotiate acculturation dynamics among its members. The issue for emerging social workers is how to be deeply empathic, effective, and culturally appropriate in all these instances.

I also discussed one of social work's roles as improving the responsiveness institutions to human needs. I included an example of how differences exist in perceived government responsiveness to similar situations, using examples of three incidents: (1) the 2008 China earthquake, (2) the Myanmar/Burma cyclone Nargis in 2008, and (3) the United States' Hurricane Katrina in 2005. Next, I introduced how non-governmental organizations advocate for and help sustain efforts to improve responsiveness of institutions to individuals and families in need. I compared domestic efforts of the United Way to international efforts of InterAction. Students were informed how many helping professionals, often social workers with CBOs or NGOs, are often involved when governments are overwhelmed, in the same way that social workers may respond or be called upon when families or other systems are overwhelmed and insufficiently responsive to individual or family needs.

A second major principle that I introduced during week one was that global issues often have local implications. The military involvement of the United States in Iraq has direct implications for family systems and psychological/mental health, which are core aspects of the course. I introduced the myriad manifestations of how social workers might end up working with someone impacted by this international issue. They might work with a returning veteran (with challenges of PTSD, finding work, interpersonal dynamics, existential issues, or mood instability); a parent of a veteran, or a wife and child coping with a soldier overseas; family members coping with loss from a soldier's death; or family members dealing with the dynamics of a person whose behavior changed after military service.

Changes to Student Assessment: The Immersion Project

The "Immersion Project" had two basic goals. The first was to allow students to strengthen their understanding of the need for lifelong attention to cultural competencies and sensitivity. The second goal was to increase understanding of how cultural knowledge is shaped from multiple perspectives. Students were asked to seek out three types of information sources to help increase their understanding of a group that is of greatest interest (and unfamiliar) to them. The broad parameters of the project were adapted from Juliet Rothman's (2008) "knowledge acquisition" projects designed for her social work students prior to their assessment of community-based agency/program/service cultural competence.

The suggested three culture-specific information sources were a book or article, a film, and an event or an interview with an individual that represents that group. The broader rationales were to move away from simple book knowledge and increase experiential knowledge, to increase interpersonal comfort in unfamiliar circumstances, and to expand their notions of culture and subcultures beyond the familiar race and ethnicity. Students were asked to describe the subject population, their interest in the group, and their initial understanding (i.e., preconceived notions) of the population. Next, students were asked to describe the immersion experiences with a general overview, an explanation of why the source was chosen, and at least two major conclusions drawn from each experience. Then, students were asked to briefly highlight similarities and differences in the information across the sources. To conclude, students were asked to share any new understandings that emerged for them. They were also asked to consider how this information might be applicable to their current or future professional practice in the areas of engagement, trust, and rapport building, and how it was applicable to assessment and problem definition.

Some of the topics that students pursued were substance users, gang culture, Hispanics/Latinos including the indigenous Latino Diaspora, interracial relationships, prisoner reentry into the mainstream population, Mormon culture, foster care alumni, organ donors, polyamorists, deaf culture, and the LGBTQ community.

Changes to Course Evaluation

The course evaluation strategy was to examine the multicultural infusion *process* according to students, as opposed to examining specific student outcomes across multicultural knowledge, attitudes, or behavior. Though the School of Social Work still conducted its traditional, competency-based evaluation, I felt that these early waves of course transformation should be dedicated to ensuring that the *process* was unfolding as desired; the outcomes related to this process could be assessed later. The core domains of content, instruction, assessment, and classroom interactions were based on the Kitano model (1997a). The measurement tool was not a previously validated instrument, but it was research-informed and adapted from principles of the Kitano model. Each domain included several indicators closely linked to the literature. Five-point Likert-type response categories (i.e., strongly disagree to strongly agree) were used for a total of twenty-five questions. Results are provided from data from the second iteration of the course, in fall semester 2009. Scores ranged from a low of 0 to a high of 5.

Course Content. Content questions included five prompts examining the extent to which: content was inclusive of multiple perspectives; content dealt with how race, class, and gender can influence knowledge construction; and content promoted critical analysis of different social realities. The mean score was 4.62.

Course Instruction. Instruction questions included six prompts examining classroom instruction, such as: how connected course content was to real world situations (e.g., in the workplace, the family, or community); how well concepts were linked to students' prior and current experiences; and how well the classroom instruction encouraged high-quality oral and written presentations. The mean score was 4.58.

Student Assessment. Assessment questions included six prompts examining the nature of student assessments. such as the extent to which: students were offered choice in how to assess their understanding of material; assignments encouraged meaningful self-reflection; rigorous standards were perceived to have been maintained; and support was sufficient for helping meet course standards. The mean score was 4.15.

Classroom Interactions. Classroom interaction questions included eight prompts examining actual dynamics of the classroom and the atmosphere fostered by the instructor, such as the extent to which: ground rules of respect were understood; cooperation among diverse individuals was encouraged; biased statements were addressed promptly; and the ability to develop cross-cultural competencies was provided. The mean was 4.15.

Limitations

Limitations of this evaluation include being a cross-sectional and process-related assessment. Thus, it was neither a comprehensive outcome assessment nor an assessment of change over time. Findings are also limited in their generalizability due to the small sample size. Yet, although statistically it is not possible to link these outcomes to the class, some limited positive-outcome findings (e.g., "I see connections between course content and situations I'll face at work, in my family, or as a citizen") helped convey that a solid proportion of students demonstrated favorable multicultural outcomes at the conclusion of the class. More importantly, process-related results were a reflection of the atmosphere that was created after specific and deliberate steps were taken to integrate the multicultural model proposed by Kitano.

Advanced Social Work Practice with Groups (Christine Norton)

As a social worker, I have been immersed in the world of human diversity in a variety of settings. My social work education, training, direct practice, and code of ethics have all set a high standard for cultural competence, ownership of privilege, and respect for the dignity and worth of every individual. In its focus on cultural competence and social diversity, the National Association of Social Workers Code of Ethics (2008) states that:

- Social workers should understand culture and its function in human behavior and society, recognizing the strengths that exist in all cultures.
- Social workers should have a knowledge base of their clients' cultures and be able to demonstrate competence in the provision of services that are sensitive to clients' cultures and to differences among people and cultural groups.
- Social workers should obtain education about and seek to understand the nature of social diversity and oppression with respect to race, ethnicity, national origin, color, sex, sexual orientation, gender identity or expression, age, marital status, political belief, religion, immigration status, and mental or physical disability. (para. 27)

Because of this strong focus on diversity, when I became a social work educator, I assumed that multicultural issues were inherently interwoven throughout the curriculum through a focus on oppression, social justice, and diverse and marginalized groups of people; however, when I examined the direct practice curriculum more closely, I realized that diversity issues were still somewhat compartmentalized into several class sessions instead of being infused throughout the courses I was teaching.

When I participated in the Multicultural Curriculum Transformation and Research Institute (MCTRI) at Texas State University–San Marcos, I chose to transform a graduate-level social work course in advanced practice with groups. Having taught the course previously, I knew that several class sessions were already devoted to cultural competence; however, it seemed that the multicultural content of the course needed to be expanded.

The course is a required advanced practice course that students take in either their second year of the MSW program or the second semester of the Advanced Standing MSW program. As such, there are certain educational standards for teaching social work with groups that must be followed. When I transformed the course into a designated multicultural course, several faculty who helped create the course were concerned that I not stray too far from the original content of the course so that students still developed the basic competencies required by the Council on Social Work Education's Educational Policies and Accreditation Standards (2010).

In order to maintain the disciplinary integrity of the course, I did not change any of the readings or assignments, but instead *added* diversity content to the course through additional readings, experiential activities, and guest speakers, and I made sure that this content was infused throughout the syllabus. I also worked to create a highly participatory environment that encouraged experiential learning, with the goal of increasing students' multicultural awareness, knowledge, and skills in social work practice with groups.

I found that this course was the perfect course to transform because social work practice often brings together heterogeneous groups of people, and it is critical that group work facilitators are culturally competent when running these groups. The Association for the Advancement of Social Work with Groups (2010) states that it is essential that the group workers have "an appreciation and understanding of such differences as those due to culture, ethnicity, gender, age, physical and mental abilities and sexual orientation among members that may influence practice" (p. 4). In order to enhance students' levels of cultural competence, I decided to transform my course into a multicultural course and assess whether or not this transformation led to greater multicultural awareness, knowledge, and skills. In order to transform the course, I had to infuse my course with regards to both multicultural content and process.

Diversity, Dialogue, and Doing

In the case of my course, Advanced Social Work Practice with Groups, I focused on three areas to transform and then assess. The first was *diversity*. In multicultural education, it is important to include diversity content, so I made sure that I included journal articles about multicultural group work, cultural competence, and even intercultural conflict styles (Hammer, 2004). I was also very intentional about defining diversity as an interwoven fabric inclusive of all people. I taught students about the cultural issues in group work, utilizing the iceberg definition of culture (SAMHSA, 2005), and encouraged them to think critically about diversity issues that are "below the surface" when facilitating groups. I also role-modeled a deep appreciation and respect for differences, and elicited each student's personal experiences of the world through journal writing and reflection and observation activities.

The second component I focused on in my course transformation was intergroup *dialogue*. Intergroup dialogue is a process in which people of different backgrounds come together to discuss their differences in a safe, supportive, and facilitated setting. The goals of intergroup dialogue are "to encourage self-reflective conversation and inquiry that break through the surface tension created by difference; clarify and address issues of potential conflict (e.g., interracial/interfaith relationships, affirmative action, social integration on campus); and challenge students to rethink many of their attitudes, assumptions, and political and social understandings through sharing of feelings and experiences, critical analysis of historical and sociological material, and consideration of alternative perspectives" (Zuniga, 2010, para. 6).

Not only did students learn about intergroup dialogue, they also had the opportunity to engage in dialogue in an actual group. In order to learn by *doing*, students participated in a group work lab in which they were placed in heterogeneous groups and given the task of creating support and mutual aid among group members by using intergroup dialogue and other advanced social work practice group skills. The class was divided into two groups, and each group met for ten weeks. The group members took turns cofacilitating the groups, participating in the groups, and observing the groups. In this way, the process of *diversity, dialogue,* and *doing* allowed for the course readings, lectures, and activities to be applied in an actual group setting.

Students were informed about the process of multicultural course transformation and were aware of the new course content, pedagogy, and process. At the beginning of the course, I invited them to be a part of a participatory action research study in which they would help me assess the impact of transforming the course on their multicultural awareness, knowledge, and skills.

Outcomes: Increasing Multicultural Awareness, Knowledge, and Skills

In order to assess the impact of multicultural course transformation on students' levels of multicultural awareness, knowledge, and skills, I designed a mixed-methods participatory action research study that utilized standardized quantitative measurements alongside active, qualitative processes of data collection and analysis. In participatory action research, researchers engage in experimental actions with the goal of finding new ideas or solutions to a particular problem or area of concern, while empowering the participants (Hult & Lennung, 1980; Reason & Bradbury, 2001; Stringer, 1999). In the case of my research, the goal was to utilize experiential learning and multicultural course transformation to increase students' multicultural awareness, knowledge, and skills in order to prepare them for advanced direct social work practice with groups.

The study consisted of twenty-two graduate social work students (N=22) with a mean age of twenty-seven. The sample was 95% female, 63% Caucasian, 28% Hispanic, and 9% African American. At the beginning of the course, students were given an adapted version of the Multicultural Awareness, Knowledge, and Skills Survey (MAKSS) (Corey, 2010). This assessment tool reports items on three subscales:

- Knowledge (e.g., "At the present time, how would you rate your understanding of the following term? 'Ethnicity'")
- Skills (e.g., "How would you rate your ability to effectively secure information and resources to better serve culturally different clients?")
- Awareness (e.g., "In general, how would you rate your level of awareness regarding different cultural institutions and systems?"). (Dunn, Smith, & Montoya, 2006, p. 472)

Students then participated in several multicultural "interventions" as a part of the course transformation, and then completed the adapted version of the MAKSS again at the end of the course. Students also presented their own qualitative findings at the end of the semester in a final group presentation, which consisted of their subjective assessments of the impact the course had on them. Table 4 highlights the interventions and assessments used as a part of the multicultural course transformation.

Table 4. Multicultural Interventions and Assessments

Multicultural Interventions	Multicultural Assessments
Diversity content (additional readings, activities, guest speakers)	Quantitative data: MAKSS (pre-to-post)
Intergroup *Dialogue*	Qualitative data: Final group presentation
Doing: Group work lab	

Data collected from the MAKSS were analyzed statistically; however, due to the small sample size and a lack of a control group, data was analyzed not via statistical significance, but rather through effect sizes. According to Neil (2008),

> when examining effects using small sample sizes, significance testing can be misleading because it's subject to Type II errors. Contrary to popular opinion, statistical significance is not a direct indicator of size of effect, but rather it is a function of sample size, effect size and *p* level. In these situations, effect sizes and confidence intervals are more informative than significance testing. (para. 8)

Effect sizes basically answer the questions "Did we get an effect?" and "How much of an effect did we get?" (Neil, 2008). When examining the quantitative results of the MAKSS, we can see that the multicultural course transformation *did* in fact have a positive effect on students' multicultural awareness, knowledge, and skills. Table 5 highlights the effect sizes broken down by each various construct of the MAKSS, and shows that students' multicultural awareness increased the most, with knowledge and skills following slightly behind.

Table 5. Effect Sizes from the MAKSS (Adapted) Pre-to-Post Scores

Construct	Pre-Test Mean	Post-Test Mean	Effect Size
Awareness	3.1	3.7	Cohen's d = -0.96 Large
Knowledge	3.2	3.5	Cohen's d = -0.63 Moderate
Skills	2.9	3.4	Cohen's d= -0.69 Moderate

These positive quantitative findings were reconfirmed by the qualitative data that students provided in their final group presentations. Students repeatedly reported on the benefits of the course and the impact it had on increasing their awareness of and sensitivity to others. Students commented that the course provided them with a "deeper understanding and respect for diversity among group members." They also reported that the course helped "group members to learn about the complexities of a multicultural society" and "become more empathic and caring" towards others who are different. Along those lines, students reflected that the course helped them to develop an "appreciation of difference, reduced bias, and enhanced empathy." Students said that practicing intergroup dialogue in the group work lab allowed them to "challenge misconceptions and biases in a safe environment," and that it "created a sense of belonging and empowerment through our commonalities." In summary, students said that by participating in this course they gained "new perspectives on life." All of these statements reflect huge shifts in students' awareness and knowledge of others as unique, diverse human beings.

In the area of multicultural skills development, which showed moderate effect sizes but lagged behind both awareness and knowledge on the pre-to-post changes in the MAKSS scores, student *did* report during their final group presentations that they "developed conflict resolution skills" by participating in the group work lab. This finding certainly deserves more exploration in future research, but it is not an unusual outcome for students participating in group work activities, and it is a key skill to have as a social worker.

Certainly, there are limitations to this study. The small sample size and lack of experimental design limit the ability to generalize these findings to other courses; however, students' active participation in the process and evaluation of the multicultural interventions implemented in this course provided both quantitative and qualitative evidence of an increase in multicultural awareness, knowledge, and skills resulting from the intentional process of multicultural course transformation.

Conclusion

Reflecting back on these case studies, we learned that the Multicultural Curriculum Transformation Institute transformed not only the content of our courses, but also the way we taught. As we clarified our educational pedagogy to combine multicultural education and experiential learning, we saw a positive impact on the process and outcomes of student learning. Transforming our courses led to the inclusion of a broader truth that included a global perspective, intergroup dialogue, and a focus on human rights.

The Kitano model has been shown to be a meaningful structure within which to develop and evaluate classroom multicultural improvement strategies. Further, the steps that were taken to improve course goals, course content, course instruction, assessment and evaluation characteristics, and classroom interactions were successful in improving the overall multicultural atmosphere, process, and outcomes.

Regarding the integration of multiculturalism in general, findings suggest that multicultural course infusion is a true transformation of the course. It requires extensive research, reflection, and planning. The process can be helped considerably with a model to draw upon, such as the Kitano model. Specific to social work, findings highlight how important it is to move beyond course content focused on culturally competent practice to think expansively about multiculturalism infused throughout the entire course. We are extremely grateful for the opportunity to transform our social work courses into multiculturally designated courses, and we will continue to solidify our multicultural change objectives, with consistent reflection upon the strengths and challenges of the multicultural classroom environment.

Multicultural Resources in Social Work Education

Websites

Association for Experiential Education: http://www.aee.org

Council on Social Work Education's Educational Policies and Standards: http://www.cswe.org/File.aspx?id=13780

EdChange Multicultural Awareness Activities: http://www.edchange.org/multicultural/activityarch.html

Intergroup Dialogue, Education and Action (IDEA) Center: http://socialwork.uw.edu/research/research-centers#IDEA

NASW Code of Ethics: http://www.naswdc.org/pubs/code/code.asp

Journals

Journal of Ethnic and Cultural Diversity in Social Work

Journal of Social Work Education

Journal of Teaching in Social Work

Books

Critical Multicultural Social Work (2008) by Jose Sisneros, Catherine Stakemn, Mildred C. Joyner, and Catheryne L. Schmitz. Chicago, IL: Lyceum Books.

Education for Multicultural Social Work Practice: Critical Viewpoints and Future Directions (2004) by Lorraine Gutiérrez, Maria Zuñiga, and Doman Lum. Alexandria, VA: Council on Social Work Education.

Multicultural Social Work Practice (2005) by Debra Wing Sue. Hoboken, NJ: Wiley.

References

Ahmadi, N. (2003). Globalization of consciousness and new challenges for international social work. *International Journal of Social Welfare, 1* (1), 14–23.

Association for the Advancement of Social Work with Groups. (2010). *Standards for social work practice with groups* (2nd ed.). Retrieved from http://www.aaswg.org/files/AASWG_Standards_for_Social_Work_Practice_with_Groups.pdf

Association for Experiential Education (AEE). (2002). *What is the definition of experiential education?* Boulder, CO: Author.

———. (2010). Experiential education works...for social justice practitioners. Retrieved from http://www.aee.org/applications/socialjustice

Austin, D. (1997). The institutional development of social work. *Journal of Social Work Education, 33*, 599–607.

Carlton-LaNey, I. (1994). The career of Birdye Henrietta Haynes, a pioneer settlement house worker. *Social Service Review* (June), 254–273.

Carlton-LaNey, I., & Alexander, S. C. (2001). Early African American social welfare pioneer women: Working to empower the race and the community. *Journal of Ethnic & Cultural Diversity in Social Work, 10* (2), 678–684.

Colby, I. (2009). An overview of social work education in the United States: New directions and new opportunities. *China Journal of Social Work, 2* (2), 119–130.

Corey, M. S., & Corey, G. (2010). *Groups: Process and practice*. Belmont, CA: Brooks/Cole.

Costin, L. B. (1983). *Two sisters for social justice: A biography of Grace and Edith Abbott.* Chicago, IL: University of Illinois Press.

Council on Social Work Education (CSWE). (2001). Educational policy and accreditation standards. Retrieved from http://CSWE.org

———. (2010). Educational policy and accreditation standards. Retrieved fromhttp://www.cswe.org/Accreditation/41865.aspx

Crouse, M., Battle, M., McFeaters, S., & Glazer, E. (n.d.). *Pioneers in professionalism: Ten who made a significant difference, 1880–1930.* National Association of Social Workers Maryland Chapter website. Retrieved from http://nasw-md.org/display common.cfm?an=1&subarticlenbr=12#Fernandis

Dewey, J. (1938) *Experience and Education*. New York: Collier Books.

Dominelli, L. (2007). Human rights in social work practice: An invisible part of the social work curriculum? In E. Reichert (Ed.), *Challenges in human rights: Social work perspective* (pp. 16–43). New York, NY: Columbia University Press.

Dunn, T. W., Smith, T. B., & Montoya, J. A. (2006). Multicultural competency instrumentation: A review of reliability generalization. *Journal of Counseling and Development, 84*, 471-482.

Gish, C. (1999). Rescuing the "waifs and strays" of the city: The western emigration program of the Children's Aid Society. *Journal of Social History, 33* (1), 121–141.

Gray, M., & Fook, J. (2004). The quest for universal social work: Some issues and implications. *Social Work Education, 23* (5), 625–644.

Hammer, M. (2004). The intercultural conflict style inventory: A conceptual framework and measure of intercultural conflict approaches. Paper presented at the 17th annual conference of the International Association for Conflict Management, June 6–9, Pittsburgh, PA. Retrieved from http://papers.ssrn.com/sol3/papers.cfm?abstract_id=601981

Healy, L. M. (2008). *International social work: Professional action in an interdependent world* (2nd ed.). New York, NY: Oxford University Press.

Holloway, S. (2008). *Council on Social Work Education, Commission on Accreditation: Some suggestions on educational program assessment and continuous improvement.* Washington, DC: Council on Social Work Education.

Hult, M., & Lennung, S. (1980). Towards a definition of action research: A note and bibliography. *Journal of Management Studies, 17* (2), 242–250.

Ife, J. (2001). *Human rights and social work: Towards right-based practice.* Cambridge, MA: Cambridge University Press.

Ife, J., & Fiske, L. (2006). Human rights and community work: Complementary theories and practice. *International Social Work, 49* (3), 297–308.

International Federation of Social Workers (IFSW). (2000). Definition of social work. Retrieved from http://www.ifsw.org/f38000138.html

Kellogg, C. (1917). *NAACP: A history of the National Association for the Advancement of Colored People: Vol. I.* Baltimore, MD: Johns Hopkins University Press.

Kirkland, W. (1989). *The many faces of the Hull House.* Chicago, IL: University of IllinoisPress.

Kitano, M. K. (1997a). A rationale and framework for course change. In A. I. Morey &M. K. Kitano (Eds.), *Multicultural course transformation in higher education: A broader truth* (pp. 1–17). Boston, MA: Allyn & Bacon.

———. (1997b). What a course will look like after multicultural change. In A. I. Morey & M. K. Kitano (Eds.), *Multicultural course transformation in higher education: A broader truth* (pp. 16–34). Boston, MA: Allyn & Bacon.

Leiby, J. (1979). *A history of social welfare and social work in the United States.* New York, NY: Columbia University Press.

Luckmann, C. (1996). Defining experiential education. *Journal of Experiential Education, 19*, 6–7.

Mapp, S. (2008). *Human rights and social justice in a global perspective: An introduction to international social work.* New York, NY: Oxford University Press.

Morey, A. I., & Kitano, M. K. (Eds.). (1997). *Multicultural course transformation in higher education: A broader truth.* Boston, MA: Allyn & Bacon.

National Association of Social Workers (NASW). (2007). *Indicators for the achievement of NASW standards for cross-cultural competence in social work practice.* Washington, DC: Author.

———. (2008). Code of ethics of the National Association of Social Workers. Retrieved from http://www.naswdc.org/pubs/code/code.asp

Neill, J. (2008). Why use effect sizes instead of significance testing in program evaluation? Retrieved from http://wilderdom.com/research/effectsizes.html

Payne, M., & Askeland, G. A. (2008). *Globalization and international social work: Postmodern change and challenge.* Burlington, VT: Ashgate.

Platt, T., & Chandler, S. (1998). Constant struggle: E. Franklin Frazier and black social work in the 1920s. *Social Work, 33*, (July/August), 293–297.

Popple, P. R., & Leighninger, L. (2011). *Social work, social welfare and American society* (8th ed.). Boston, MA: Allyn & Bacon.

Reason, P., & Bradbury, H. (Eds.). (2001). *Handbook of action research: Participative inquiry and practice.* Thousand Oaks, CA: Sage.

Reichert, E. (2003). *Social work and human rights.* New York, NY: Columbia University Press.

———. (2006). *Understanding human rights: An exercise book.* Thousand Oaks, CA: Sage.

———. (Ed.). (2007). *Challenges in human rights: A social work perspective.* New York, NY: Columbia University Press.

Rothman, Juliet. 2008. *Cultural competence in process and practice: Building bridges.* San Francisco, CA: Pearson Education.

Schriver, J. (2000). *Human behavior and the social environment: Shifting paradigms in essential knowledge for social work practice* (3rd ed.). Boston, MA: Allyn & Bacon.

Seitzinger Hepburn, K., & Kaufmann, R. K. (2005). A training guide for the early childhood services community: "The cultural iceberg." United States Department of Health and Human Services—Substance Abuse and Mental Health Services Administration (SAMHSA). Retrieved from http://store.samhsa.gov/shin/content/SVP07-0152/SVP07-0152.pdf

Sifford, A. & Ng, K. (2010). Book review of *Leadership in diverse and multicultural environment.* Retrieved from http://www.leadingtoday.org/weleadinlearning/bookreviewrev2.htm

Sisneros, J., Stakeman, C., Joyner, M. C., & Schmitz, C. L. (2008). *Critical multicultural social work.* Chicago, IL: Lyceum.

Skegg, A. (2005). Human rights and social work: A Western imposition or empowerment to the people? *International Social Work, 48* (5), 667–672.

Stringer, E. T. (1999). *Action research* (2nd ed.). Thousand Oaks, CA: Sage.

Sue, D.W. (2006). *Multicultural social work practice.* Hoboken, NJ: John Wiley & Sons.

Sue, D. W., & Sue, D. (2003). *Counseling the culturally diverse: Theory and practice.* New York, NY: John Wiley & Sons.

United National Development Programme (UNDP). (2010). *The millennium development goals report 2010.* Retrieved from http://www.un.org/en/development/desa/news/statistics/mdg-2010.shtml

Zuniga, X. (2010). Fostering intergroup dialogue on campus: Essential ingredients. *Diversity Digest.* Retrieved from http://www.diversityweb.org/Digest/w98/fostering.html

8

COLLEGE OF APPLIED ARTS

Family and Consumer Sciences

Andrew Nance and Keila Tyner

The broad discipline of family and consumer sciences has a long history as an applied field with roots in home economics. This original tie to home economics uniquely situates the interdisciplinary field within a human ecology perspective, where a focus is placed upon human interactions with their environment. Within human ecology, "emphasis is given to the creation, use, and management of resources for creative adaption, human development, and sustainability of environments" (Bubolz & Sontag, 1993, p. 419). As such, the family and its near environment provide the unifying basis for the academic disciplines within family and consumer sciences, which include family and child development, nutrition, family and consumer science education, interior design, and fashion merchandising.

Because family and consumer sciences places emphasis on families and their well-being, the development of academic curriculum that incorporates and elucidates principles of multiculturalism and diversity is of much importance. Specifically, the family is viewed as an ecosystem that is dependent upon the natural environment and the social environment that serves to enhance the quality and meaning of life (Paolucci, Hall, & Axinn, 1977). The family ecosystem functions within broader society, and as such, is rife with variety in structure and constitution. Therefore, academic curriculum within the field of family and consumer sciences has a theoretical basis, in addition to an ethical obligation, in providing students with content that emphasizes multiculturalism and diversity.

The purpose of this chapter is to highlight the multicultural curriculum transformations of two courses within the Department of Family and Consumer Sciences at Texas State University–San Marcos, a course in interior design and a course in fashion merchandising. Professors for both courses attended the Multicultural Curriculum and Research Institute (the Institute) in May 2009 at Texas State University–San Marcos.

Interior Design

The practice of interior design is concerned with not only interior environments, but also the occupants of those environments. According to the National Council for Interior Design Qualification (NCIDQ), "Interior design is a multifaceted profession in which creative and technical solutions are applied within a structure to achieve a built interior environment. These solutions are functional, enhance the quality of life and culture of the occupants, and are aesthetically attractive" (NCIDQ, 2011, p. 1). The occupants may be a family or a group of unrelated individuals; in either case, understanding the needs of the occupants becomes the quintessential problem for which interior design attempts to provide an environmental solution. A basic premise in teaching interior design is that gaining insight to the occupants of a place will likely result in a more successful solution to the "problem" of a particular environment. To this end, perceptions and experiences outside of one's own cultural milieu become integral to the process of learning how to design environments for the habitation of others. Inherently multicultural, interior design must acknowledge and provide for people of all backgrounds, cultures, personal interests, and socioeconomic status.

The traditional interior design curriculum is comprised of lecture-based courses and studio-based learning courses. Studio-based learning is characterized by the identification of a problem, followed by a period of design development augmented by lectures, desk critiques (professor-student consultations), and formal presentations (Lackney, 1999). Both lecture and studio courses have potential to focus on multiculturalism. This section of the chapter will focus on the curriculum transformation of Contemporary Issues in Interior Design, a studio-based learning course within the interior design program at Texas State University–San Marcos.

Multicultural Curriculum Transformation: Contemporary Issues Studio

I attended the Institute in May 2009 and proposed a transformed course curriculum as well as instruction, with the intent of providing a broader cultural experience for my students. My interest in participating in the Institute stemmed from discussions with colleagues who had attended the Institute in prior years, as well as my interest in continued development of teaching strategies.

Upon completion of the Institute, I found myself integrating new policies and teaching strategies in order to augment learning in all of my classes. The Institute provided me with language and techniques to understand not only my own biases and habits, but also those of my students. This understanding has allowed me to provide a more inclusive learning environment for my students.

Syllabus Transformation

Contemporary Issues in Interior Design, a capstone course offered in both fall and spring semesters, is the last in a series of four design studios. As the title suggests, students are asked to consider contemporary issues concerning interior design such as the needs of the aging and elderly, affordable housing, sustainability, healthcare and healthcare outreach, and education for nontraditional students, to name a few. As exemplified by the topics listed, contemporary issues in interior design deal with multicultural issues (e.g., age, gender, and ethnic issues); therefore, they warrant focus on multicultural content and perspective. Once a contemporary issue is identified, students research the topic, identify a potential client (or representative population), and develop a design solution over the course of the semester. Multicultural transformation for this course was attained by implementing various course changes as exhibited in the syllabus, and includes modification of course objectives, evaluation descriptions, scheduling of assignments, and course policies. Details of the course, which are included in the syllabus, are provided below.

Course description. Specialized research in interior design to include design issues such as barrier-free environments, medical facilities, historic preservation/adaptive reuse, international interiors, energy issues, sustainable design, and design for special needs.

Course objectives.

1. Identify students' own personal cultural perspective.
2. Research and identify specific contextual and cultural responses to the contemporary issue.
3. Implement a culturally responsive methodology for researching the issue.
4. Create a preliminary presentation of research and initial proposals to the studio and allow response to feedback from their peers with intergroup dialogue and culturally educated questioning.
5. Demonstrate an ability to present the complete design solution in a culturally appropriate format.

The objectives were modified to include self-reflected cultural perspective awareness in the students; increased emphasis on culturally responsive research methodologies, and peer dialogue.

Having taught this course for four years, I had observed that with little exposure to events and conditions outside of their own personal experiences, most students selected familiar topics, operating largely within their socioeconomic comfort zone. With the intent of increasing the opportunities for exposure to contemporary issues affecting people with a broader multicultural perspective, I encouraged the students to begin their research with international design competitions. Design competitions are always driven by a particular problem of a particular place, dealing with specific needs of specific occupants. An affordable housing competition set in San Antonio, Texas, for example, is geared particularly towards the ethnic, socioeconomic, and cultural conditions of San Antonio. It would be rather naïve to assume that a solution for San Antonio is the correct solution for similar projects in Los Angeles, Albuquerque, or New York City, or much less urban or rural locales of other countries. The students were asked to focus on competitions that involved multicultural issues such as affordable housing, aging in place, education and schools, and cultural centers, to name a few. Usually sponsored by government grants, housing coalitions, outreach firms, or in the case of many of the international competitions, social development programs, participation in these competitions provides exposure to a variety of multicultural perspectives. When each student is encouraged to select a different project and competition, multicultural topics discussed in group reviews are in-depth, varied, and interesting, to say the least. In addition, providing a multicultural content focus for students helps to prepare them to address such civic-based and quality-of-life issues to meet the diverse needs of occupants. In addition, exposure to such multiculturalism provides students the opportunity to reach beyond their usual comfort zone in considering the built environment. Some websites to reference for international design competitions include:

1. American Institute of Architecture Students, http://www.aias.org
2. American Society of Interior Designers, http://www.asid.org
3. Death by Architecture, http://www.deathbyarchitecture.com
4. International Interior Design Association, http://www.iida.org

Scheduling. Semester grading previously had consisted of three or four major grades throughout the semester. The nature of design projects is inherently accumulative: Step one leads to step two, etc. It was observed that with so few deadlines, students oftentimes had difficulty accumulating and developing the appropriate amount of work for each submission. In the transformed curriculum, the semester grades were divided into the basic design phases of a design project: pre-design, schematic design, design development, and construction documents/ presentation. Each phase was broken into three to five subcategories, yielding incremental assignment deadlines occurring approximately once a week. Working within a regular schedule of submission deadlines, students were better able to stay "on track" with their research and design development.

Policies. With the goal of accommodating heuristic learning in project development, a new resubmittal policy was incorporated to encourage students to refine incomplete or missing work. Extra credit and financial assistance (from the university) was offered to those motivated to enter their projects in the design competition.

Instructional strategies. During the initial two weeks of the course, the students were exposed to several of the worksheets and exercises used in the Institute seminar. Open discussions on self-assessment were facilitated by the instructor to touch upon the various biases that we reflect due to our own cultural experiences. These discussions were intended to provide a "platform of understanding" from which to help each student identify his or her own culturally influenced design biases. Throughout the semester, group discussions, desk critiques, individual review via consultation with the instructor, lectures, and demonstrations were utilized to great extent to facilitate individual learning.

Assessment of student knowledge. Students submit weekly assignments. Each assignment is intended to both expose students to "industry standard" contract documentation and allow for an instrument for reflection upon the level of completion of each phase of a project.

- A preliminary presentation is given at mid-semester to the class and a local professional, potential client, or subject expert.
- Students engage in self, peer, and instructor critique of their research, client, and group skills.
- A final end-of-semester presentation is given to the class. Again, local professionals, future clients, and industry experts are invited to attend and participate.

Classroom interactions. As the student enrollment for this course is small (on average, fewer than fifteen students), the instructor is able to give personalized attention to each student individually, as well as work with the cohesive group.

Department acceptance. Both students and faculty were interested in the notion of a multicultural transformation. Students responded favorably to the various self-assessment exercises conducted at the beginning of the course, and openly engaged in discussions about multiculturalism, perceptions, and design.

Research Results

The spring 2010 semester was used as a case study for the implementation of the transformed course. Here are some of the results of the transformed course.

Sample Projects

Topics of the final projects included affordable housing; housing for homeless adults and children; community centers; cultural centers; a school for girls (in Iraq); and affects of interior design on mental health and rehabilitation. Two projects of note are the Grand Concourse Beyond 100 competition: Civic Micro-Centers, by Emily Siegel, located in the Bronx, New York, and the USGBC 2009 Natural Talent Design Competition: Maverick Place, an affordable multifamily housing by Cheryl D'Sa in San Antonio, Texas.

The Civic Micro-Centers project focused on the fact that the primary ethnic background of the community adjacent to this particular site (building location) in the Bronx is of Caribbean descent. The competition was "open" in terms of programmatic requirements; however, the proposal was required to contribute to the revitalization of the Grand Concourse in the Bronx. Caribbean music was an important source for inspiration. The concept was inspired by the Plena y Bomba and characterized by simplicity and repetition, and the improvised movement of the "call and response" structure in traditional Caribbean music. This concept was applied to the programmatic use of the building incorporating a cultural art gallery to showcase Caribbean artworks, and an open-air market accessible from the concourse. Providing spaces for impromptu social interactions and high visibility throughout were key aspects of the Ms. Siegel's design, and they were achieved in part through large window-walls opening the interior gallery spaces to the bustling streetscape of the Grand Concourse. The building acts as the metaphoric 'response' to the 'call' of this student's interpretation of the manner in which the Caribbean community utilizes urban spaces.

Maverick Place, an affordable housing community proposed for an area in San Antonio known as the River North Project, was a comprehensive plan to create a livable, pedestrian-friendly community and business development northeast of the downtown area. According to the U.S. Census Bureau (2008), approximately 14% of families in San Antonio, Texas live below the poverty line; San Antonio residents are in great need of affordable housing options. The focus of this project was to explore ways of creating positive social environments for the residents of the proposed housing complex. Ms. D'Sa proposed four key elements to achieve a sustainable, affordable community: (1) use of great design aesthetics to make the complex indistinguishable from market-rate housing, (2) integrity in materials, (3) sense of belonging, with individualized units rather than repetitive floor plans, and (4) ties to the community including public social gathering spaces, encouraging interactions between residents. Derived from the importance of community interactions, Ms. D'Sa's conceptual solution was focused on the idea of connections. The design proposal included literal connections to the community through public gathering areas (courtyards, parks, and gardens) that link to surrounding neighborhoods, as well as connections of indoors to outdoors, providing outdoor living spaces for each resident, fostering relationships between the various occupants. The proposed vibrant color scheme of yellows, greens, and reds—a symbolic connection to the Mexican heritage of San Antonio—further reinforces the proposal of a solution tied to a place and its people.

Each of these student project examples showcases the multicultural and diverse approaches to creating habitable interior environments tailored to the potential end-users or occupants of the space. With a keen eye on significant cultural characteristics, an interior designer can create layers of symbolic meaning for inhabitants. Through increased focus on multiculturalism, student projects not only are more diverse, but also exhibit higher levels of creativity because students are encouraged to reach beyond their own cultural perspectives.

Student Perceptions. A brief survey was issued, and completed by six of the ten students enrolled in the course. Survey items were assessed using a four-point Likert-type scale with the following possible answers: 4 = absolutely, 3 = somewhat, 2 = minimal impact, and 1 = not really.

1. This course exposed me to the idea that I should keep in mind my own cultural background as a lens through which I examine architecture and interior design from other cultures. Mean=3.17/4.
2. I was encouraged to explore contemporary issues in design using international design competitions as a vehicle to research the needs and problems of other cultures. Mean=3.67/4.
3. This course introduced perspectives from a variety of cultural groups. Mean=3.0/4
4. I feel that I successfully explored a contemporary issue and developed a culturally sensitive solution to the program or needs of the community. Mean = 3.5/4.
5. The instructor used a variety of class activities and types of assessment (for example: peer review, multiple submittals, resubmittals, self-assessment exercises). Mean=3.67/4.
6. This course introduced texts, readings, and perspectives from a variety of cultural groups. Mean=2.83/4.0
7. I entered my design into the selected competition. (50% indicated that they would have if the competition entry deadline had not already passed.)
8. I selected an existing competition to create my project around. Mean=2.5/4.0.

Results from this survey indicate that students gained a level of cultural exposure and enhanced their knowledge and understanding of contemporary issues in interior design from a multicultural perspective. Basing the major design project on an international design competition allowed students to engage with current, real-world topics relevant to the discipline.

Instructor Observations. The final outcome of the efforts of the semester yielded interesting results. Due to the seasonal and sequential nature of competition schedules, no students were able to officially enter their respective competitions; yet, almost all students were successful in integrating their referenced competitions into their final projects. In the cases where students could not enter the competitions, they were encouraged to find local/regional representative communities and conditions similar to those in the competitions in order to continue their research (where possible). Located in Central Texas, Texas State University–San Marcos draws students from all across the state. In most cases, the students have no understanding of the cultural history of this area. Thus, identifying a local area in which to conduct project research provided the students with exposure to issues, communities, and cultures in their near environs that otherwise would have been overlooked, or misunderstood.

Strategies for Faculty

Key strategies for faculty interested in incorporating multicultural curriculum transformation include:

1. Use competitions to model project research and program development. This provides an excellent basis for informed, current, culturally targeted discussion.
2. Use self-reflection exercises and open discussions to help students identify their own perceptions and preconceived notions before proceeding with project research. This step is integral to the understanding of a multicultural perspective of program needs.
3. Pursue and investigate local resources with which to expose students to other cultures and issues. As students often are not from the same area where they attend university, it is conceivable that a multicultural experience can be achieved within local or regional communities.

Conclusions

The multicultural transformation of Contemporary Issues in Interior Design has been an excellent learning process for this instructor. All of the changes made in the course have provided the students with a better learning environment, rudimentary tools to begin the process of understanding themselves as well as others, the opportunity to investigate issues that are outside of their current experiences, and the challenge of incorporating the design process into this understanding and research.

Fashion Merchandising

Within the curriculum of fashion merchandising, students take a variety of courses that cover the relevant content needed for careers in the fashion industry. The fashion industry is a global trade comprised of three main levels (with auxiliary services that support each level), which include: (1) the producers of raw materials and textiles, (2) the producers of finished textile and apparel products, and (3) the retail distributors of finished goods to the ultimate consumer. Fashion merchandising programs across the country generally offer a variety of courses that provide students with a foundation of industry specifics and operations, and also highlight the overall concept of fashion as a sociocultural phenomenon and fashion consumption as a symbolic means of expressing the self. As such, a multicultural approach to courses rooted in historical, cultural, social, and psychological perspectives of fashion, dress, and appearance and the study of fashion consumption would be important in shaping student knowledge and understanding of the global fashion industry. Such courses seek to engage students in critical thinking and broader abstract thought related to contexts in which fashion and appearance management occurs. While multiculturalism may be infused in any fashion-merchandising course, these types of courses in particular offer opportunity and linkage to explore diverse and multicultural aspects of fashion. This section of the chapter will focus specifically on the curriculum transformation of the course Culture and Consumer Behavior in the fashion-merchandising program at Texas State University–San Marcos.

Multicultural Curriculum Transformation: Culture and Consumer Behavior

I attended the Institute in May 2009 after having been appointed assistant professor of fashion merchandising the previous fall semester. My past experiences with multiculturalism prior to the Institute included both master's and doctoral certifications in women's studies, teaching an introductory course discussion section of women's studies, and teaching a social psychology of dress and appearance course in the textiles and clothing program, which fulfilled an undergraduate diversity course requirement at my doctoral granting institution.

My interest in attending the Institute stemmed from my own desire to improve my skills in the classroom. My expectations were to expand not only my understanding of possible multicultural course content, but also, and more importantly, my approach as a professor in creating a tolerant and diverse presentation of that content in the classroom. I believe that diversity—in students, content, evaluation, and perspective—is critical to student learning. Therefore, I felt that by gaining knowledge of multicultural teaching strategies, I could in turn become better at teaching in general.

After completing the Institute, I found that my expectations were not just met but exceeded. Completing the program took time and dedication, but I am confident that my course change was positive and that my teaching skills overall were improved. This unique program could be modeled at other higher education institutions to infuse the much needed content and perspective of multiculturalism and diversity across academic curriculum.

Syllabus Transformation

The course Culture and Consumer Behavior is a sophomore-level course focused on providing students with a basic understanding of social and psychological aspects of fashion and fashion consumption. The course evaluates a number of theoretical perspectives related to the semiotic aspects of fashion consumption, primarily from a consumer standpoint (as opposed to a marketing perspective). This course is required for fashion merchandising majors but appeals to other family and consumer science majors as well. Details of the course, which are included on the syllabus, are provided below.

Course description. The study of theories related to culture and appearance that influence fashion and fashion product consumption.

Course objectives.

1. Examine theories related to the cultural and consumer aspects of fashion.
2. Explore the many facets of popular culture as an impact on consumer behavior, specifically as it relates to fashion.
3. Define terms associated with the study of appearance, adornment, and dress.
4. Investigate social, ethical, and environmental issues related to human consumption and the role of government and business in consumer protection.
5. Examine secondary sources of data and collect primary sources of data related to a specific market segment within U.S. culture.

Course overview. This course will investigate the role of dress and appearance in nonverbal communication, development of the self, and social interaction of individuals, with particular emphasis on diverse appearances by various cultures and subcultures found across the globe.

The study of theoretical examinations of dress, particularly those rooted in sociology, will be inspected. Also, the course will explore dress as a collective behavior and a social process, with critical examination of the fashion industry's impact on dress and the body. Students will think critically about how culture shapes ideas, notions about appearances, and the interrelationship of factors influencing the dress and appearance choices of diverse individuals as well as subsequent purchasing behaviors. Students also will critically reflect on the individual and collective, and symbolic and communicative nature of dress, adornment, and consumption. A multitude of theoretical approaches will be applied.[1]

The description and course objectives were not changed during the transformation, but the addition of the course overview was aimed at highlighting in greater depth the overall aspects of multiculturalism infused within the course. Beyond the addition of the course overview, the course transformation centered on (1) expanding multicultural content within course topics covered during lecture, (2) incorporating more discussion with the lecture, and (3) enhancing assignments to have more multicultural focus.

Course content. Originally, the course topics dealt with general aspects of consumer behavior, with basic concepts of culture touched upon. After the transformation, key multicultural topics were explored in greater depth to provide students with more exposure to such topics. Some examples of the multicultural focus included deeper exploration of culture using various cultural examples and the processes of acculturation; discussion of gender and sexuality as key components to one's sense of self and identity; examination of body image and other body-related aspects that contribute to identity, such as stigmatized bodies and bodies with disabilities; investigation of the role stereotypes and prejudices play in shaping our perceptions of others; and exploration of various religiously motivated appearances. Each of these topics highlighted the diverse array of appearance management choices that individuals could use to highlight, communicate, or express their sense of self and identity.

Discussion. Discussion was viewed as a key means for exploring topics in class in more depth, allowing students to examine and challenge their own thoughts on topics through constructive dialogue with the instructor and classmates. A course policy was added to the syllabus: "Class discussion and reflection are key tools in building knowledge and as such, will be utilized regularly during class. It is important to respect others and their opinions, even if those opinions differ from your own.

The professor will maintain an open and inclusive environment that students may feel safe expressing themselves." The policy was added to ensure that students respected one another's differences and felt the class environment was open and inclusive of various student perspectives.

Discussions infused in the course centered on course topics and generally recent and relevant real-life based subjects. For example, one discussion related to ethnicity included the subject of President Obama and the First Family. The class was prompted with the question: "How do you think having the first African-American president and First Family of the U.S. will affect the portrayal of African Americans in the media?" Students wrote down their own thoughts and then formed small groups to discuss the topic further. Finally, the groups shared their overall thoughts with the entire class and the instructor facilitated discussion.

Assignments. For this transformation, methods of student evaluation were altered to focus less on exams and more on including a greater variety of assignments to accommodate different learning styles. Exams make up a portion of the course grade, but after the transformation, a major course project, in-class activities, and class discussion and participation comprise a portion of the grade as well. The major course project, the Consumer Research Project, was transformed to include a higher level of multiculturalism and focus on diversity.

Specifically, the project is designed for students to research a target consumer group that represents a unique subculture or niche market segment within the U.S. Students collect both primary and secondary sources of data, which includes a database search, consumer observations, media analysis, and consumer interviews.[2] The key multicultural element of the project is the selecting of an appropriate consumer group to research. Students are required to choose a consumer group that has demographic characteristics different from their own, such as a different ethnicity, gender, income range, or age. In addition, the consumer group must be one that is somewhat underrepresented in mainstream U.S. culture; that is, one that represents a unique subculture or niche market segment.

According to McKeachie and Svinicki (2006), cognitive learning strategies are "goal-directed approaches and methods of thought that help students to build bridges between what they already know or have experienced and what they are trying to learn" (p. 308). This type of learning strategy becomes integrated into the students' knowledge base, and can be recalled for application and problem solving to enhance critical thinking skills (p. 308). By collecting primary and secondary data about a particular consumer group, students can connect their own consumer experiences to those of another market segment in a tangible way that highlights the diverse, multifaceted cultures represented within the U.S.

Overall, student feedback on the course since the transformation has been positive. In regular course evaluations, students comment that the project is interesting and engaging while challenging them to explore consumer groups that they may have known little about before the project. Students also comment that the course content highlights information about various groups of consumers and diverse appearances within the U.S., and that this information will enable them to be better equipped for future interactions with the global fashion industry. Some students have commented that through the project, lecture, and discussions, they came to appreciate diversity of other people and cultures, and that the course encouraged them to be more open and tolerant of people who differed from themselves. A multicultural approach not only can broaden a student's perspective, but also has the ability to create a higher level of tolerance for others.

Strategies for Faculty

There are other strategies to incorporate multiculturalism into the fashion merchandising curriculum, and numerous opportunities to better prepare students for a diverse global society. In particular, course content could focus on international dynamics related to production and consumption that play out within the fashion industry, especially topics about sustainability. Sustainability is a concept deeply rooted in the human ecology perspective, and it would provide a fruitful platform from which to expand multicultural concepts. Moreover, any course within the fashion merchandising curriculum has the potential for multicultural infusion, as the discipline is well suited for examination of diversity and multiculturalism.

Additionally, other course assignments may be employed to augment the level of multicultural perspective. While class size may play a role in utilizing certain types of written assignments, journaling is one such strategy that provides critical reflection and reflective discourse, a crucial element in transformative learning (Merriam, 2004). As such, journaling provides a forum through which students can actively engage and personally relate to course content.

Conclusions

The Multicultural Curriculum Transformation and Research Institute at Texas State University–San Marcos was an integral resource for me in transforming my course to provide students with knowledge, skills, and understanding to be positive, open, and tolerant citizens. The Institute enhanced my teaching skills, and this transformation certainly would not have been possible without the guidance and resources provided.

Finally, the Institute provides a systematic means for faculty to infuse multicultural and diverse perspectives within the curriculum. Providing multicultural content and perspectives to students is increasingly imperative in a global society, and the mission of higher education is to provide students with the knowledge and tools necessary for success in such a society. Therefore, the model set forth by the Multicultural Curriculum Transformation and Research Institute is a valuable resource to build and expand upon at other colleges and universities.

Notes

1 Some content from the course overview was derived from another course, TC165 Appearance in Society, taught by Mary Lynn Damhorst at Iowa State University.

2 Portions of the Consumer Research Project have been used and modified from the Trend Forecasting Notebook assignment developed by Mary Lynn Damhorst at Iowa State University for TC165. Project materials are also found in the instructor's guide from *The Meanings of Dress* (Damhorst, Miller-Spillman, & Michelman, 2005).

References

Bubolz, M. M., & Sontag, M. S. (1993). Human ecology theory. In P. G. Boss, W. J. Doherty, R. LaRossa, W. R. Schumm, & S. K. Steinmetz (Eds.), *Sourcebook of family theories and methods: A contextual approach* (pp. 419–448). New York, NY: Springer.

Cushner, K. (2006). *Human diversity in action: Developing multicultural competencies for the classroom* (3rd ed.). Boston, MA: McGraw-Hill Higher Education.

Damhorst, M. L., Miller-Spillman, K. A., & Michelman, S. O. (2005). *The meanings of dress* (2nd ed.). New York, NY: Fairchild.

Hammer, M. R. (n.d.). *Intercultural conflict style inventory, interpretive guide and facilitator's manual.* Retrieved from http://www.hammerconsulting.org

Kitano, M. K., & Morey, A. I. (1997). *Multicultural course transformation in higher education: A broader truth.* Boston, MA: Allyn & Bacon.

Lackney, J. A. (1999). *A history of the studio-based learning model.* Retrieved from http://www.edi.msstate.edu/work/pdf/history_studio_based_learning.pdf

McKeachie, W. J., & Svinicki, M. (2006). *McKeachie's teaching tips: Strategies, research, and theory for college and university teachers.* New York, NY: Houghton Mifflin.

Merriam, S. B. (2004).The role of cognitive development in Mezirow's transformation learning theory. *Adult Education Quarterly, 55*, 60–68.

National Council for Interior Design Qualification. (2011). Definition of interior design. Retrieved from http://www.ncidq.org/AboutUs/AboutInteriorDesign/DefinitionofInteriorDesign.aspx

Paolucci, B. Hall, O. A., & Axinn, N. (1977). *Family decision making: An ecosystem approach.* New York, NY: Wiley.

U.S. Census Bureau. (2008). San Antonio City, Texas—ACS selected economic characteristics. American FactFinder website. Retrieved from http://www.factfinder2.census.gov

9

COLLEGE OF EDUCATION

Multicultural Curriculum Transformation in Two Teacher Education Courses

Maria De la Colina and Barbara Davis

This chapter describes the experiences of two College of Education faculty members who participated in the multicultural transformation at a public university in the southwestern United States. The research conducted by the first author in spring 2004 facilitated curriculum changes in an undergraduate reading education course in the way the multicultural content was delivered. This was done through an array of different multicultural teaching strategies. The curriculum changes implemented by the second author in fall 2009 in a graduate elementary education course for initial teacher certification resulted in a more systematic and intentional focus on diversity issues and multicultural perspectives. In both cases, the curriculum transformation translated into positive student outcomes and facilitated students' learning of diversity in a safe learning environment without the typical resistance.

Rationale

During the last decade, our nation has had a significant increase in immigration. Thus, higher education faces a tremendous challenge as colleges of education strive to better prepare teacher candidates for an increasingly diverse public school population. The number of public school students who do not speak English as their primary language is increasing as well. In 1979, an estimated 9% of all five- to seventeen-year-olds in the U.S. were language minorities; by 2006 that number had increased to 20.3% (National Center for Educational Statistics, 2006). In Texas, the number of English language learners (ELLs) attending public school increased 29%. In 2009, more than 137 languages were taught in Texas schools, and ELLs comprised 15% of the total population; and of that population, 90% were Hispanics (Texas Education Agency, 2009). With these drastic demographic changes, teachers are faced with teaching a population of students with cultures and languages that are unfamiliar to many teachers. Furthermore, these teachers often lack the preparation to provide their multicultural students with the culturally sensitive environment needed to foster their learning (Gregorian, 2001; Scarcella, 1990).

Moreover, this increase in diversity brings a number of challenges for a predominately White, female, middle-class teacher workforce (Ball & Tyson, 2011; Garmon, 2004; Howard, 2010). According to the 2007–2008 *Schools and Staffing Survey*, approximately 83% of teachers in the United States are non-Hispanic White, and 75% are female (Coopersmith, 2009). Thus, there is a "demographic divide," a term coined by Gay and Howard (2000), "wherein many [preservice] teachers face the reality that they are most likely to come into contact with students from cultural, ethnic, linguistic, racial, and social class backgrounds different from their own" (Howard, 2010, p. 40). Therefore, it is imperative that teacher preparation programs focus on issues of diversity (Ball & Tyson, 2011; Darling-Hammond & Bransford, 2005; Irvine, 2003; Ladson-Billings, 1999; Little & Bartlett, 2010; Nieto, 2004). Teacher educators must do more to help preservice teachers develop the skills needed to confront and resolve these issues (Darling-Hammond, Wise, & Klein, 2001). If we want to really change practice in a meaningful and long lasting way, teachers must alter their beliefs and conceptions of practice, their theories of practice, and their theories of actions, in addition to learning a new subject (Gay, 2010). The development of knowledge in multicultural education, in particular, has become a primary theme in contemporary university-based teacher education as well (Cochran-Smith, 2004; Cockrell, Placier, Cockrell, & Middleton, 1999).

According to Villegas and Lucas (2002), in order to shift teacher education beyond "the fragmented and superficial treatment of diversity," teacher educators must express a vision of teaching and learning in a diverse society, and use that vision in a systematic way to guide the infusion of multicultural issues throughout the preservice curriculum. These researchers also highlight several important points about the vision that culturally responsive teachers should consider. The authors point out that culturally responsive teachers: (a) are socioculturally conscious, (b) have affirming views of students from diverse backgrounds, (c) see themselves as responsible for and capable of bringing about changes to make schools more equitable, (d) understand how learners construct knowledge, and are capable of promoting knowledge construction, (e) know about the lives of their students, and (f) design instruction that builds on what their students already know, while stretching them beyond the familiar (Villegas & Lucas, 2002).

During the 2004–2005 academic year, a university located in the southwestern United States established a Multicultural Institute that was designed to include all of the above recommendations, in addition to other issues of interest. The next few sections provide a recollection of my (refers to first author) involvement with the Center for Multicultural and Gender Studies (MCGS) at this university during the first year of my tenure-track position, just a year before the Multicultural Institute's inception.

Background

In spring 2004 the MCGS started a project to implement a university-wide multicultural curriculum transformation. The ambitious goals of this project were to infuse multicultural and gender issues into existing curricula. For this purpose, a representative of the College of Education, as well as two other representatives—one each from the College of Business Administration and the College of Science—were contracted as consultants and assigned to:

1. assist the director of the Center for Multicultural and Gender Studies with researching best practices in multicultural/diversity curriculum design,
2. assist the director with one-on-one or small group consultations with faculty to share relevant research and resource materials,
3. assist in the development of a resource notebook, and
4. redesign with a multicultural perspective one required class.

I was the representative from the College of Education, and Literacy Education for Culturally and Linguistically Diverse Children (RDG4320) was the required course I chose to redesign. The reason I chose this course, which already had a multicultural content, was that I had not been very successful with the course outcomes. Specifically, I had been unsuccessful with the classroom interaction, and I had been unsuccessful in lessening the students' poor attitudes and biases towards the curriculum on issues such as racism, prejudice, discrimination, and gender, among others. Some of my students, to my amazement, were very disrespectful, critical, and judgmental about all of these issues. The fact that I am a Latina person of color was another issue of discontent for some of the students in this class, and it had been reflected in my end-of-course evaluations. I remember some of the comments that I read: "She needs to go back to Mexico. . ."; "I am not going to teach any of 'these' type of students"; "I don't know why I need to take this class. . . "; "I believe that gays and lesbians are going to hell, why should I affirm or even respect these people. I did not like the content of this class." Fortunately, not all the evaluations were like this, but in my opinion, one evaluation of this type was one too many. The fact that the enrollment for this course was over 100 did not help, either. Thus, for me, this was a great opportunity that I gladly embraced. I started my research for best practices in multicultural/diversity curriculum, and what follows are the completed goals after the review of literature was finished.

Goals Completed

1. Current research articles and sample syllabi were located and reviewed. A resource notebook for the College of Education was developed, comprised of (a) professional articles focusing on best practices in multicultural/diversity curriculum design, (b) multicultural education college syllabi from across the nation, and (c) multicultural education resources and World Wide Web sites.
2. A plan was generated for sharing the bibliography of research and resource materials with other faculty in one-on-one or small group consultations.
3. The required curriculum and instruction course Literacy Education for Culturally and Linguistically Diverse Children (RDG4320) was redesigned based on best practices in multicultural/diversity curriculum design research findings.
4. The transformed curriculum was implemented in fall 2004.

Best Practices in Multicultural/Diversity Curriculum Design Summary

I searched the literature for best practices. The next section contains a summary of the best practices that were infused in my course during the pilot year (2004) of the Multicultural Institute.

According to research regarding best practices in multicultural education in higher education in the United States, colleges of education need to prepare future teachers to infuse multiculturalism in the curriculum (Gay, 2010; Villegas & Lucas, 2002). The article "Program Ownership and the 'Transformative Agenda' in Colleges of Education: Teachers of Teachers Working Towards a More Equitable Society" (MacDonald, Colville-Hall, & Smolen, 2004) was based on research conducted in fall 1998. Four Midwestern, state-assisted, metropolitan universities were surveyed. The focus of the surveys was to look further into faculty members' perceptions of the preparation of teachers in their institutions to work with diverse student populations in a culturally pluralistic society. Faculty members listed various practices needed to achieve a more equitable society:

- Provide extensive exposure to diverse situations in schools and communities for undergraduate students to understand the increasingly diverse needs and experiences of K-12 students (add more field practice experiences over a longer period of time in a more controlled environment).
- Assist students and educators in seeing themselves as part of a diverse global community.
- Instruct students about best practices, politics, and related issues.
- Assist students to be aware of the dramatic changes in the demographics of students and communities.
- Do not use poorly credentialed faculty or part-timers to teach multicultural classes. The fact that an instructor is a person of color or liberal does not automatically qualify him/her as having expert knowledge of the field.

- Do not force the issues when students have not had the opportunity to interact with those of another culture.
- Do not preach.
- Avoid having an excessive quantity of material for the time frame.
- Include guest speakers with multicultural backgrounds or experiences.
- Teach students to view events, concepts, and facts through various lenses such as African American history, women's history, Asian American history, Latino American history, and all other previously differentiated fields of knowledge.
- Address important social issues including racism, sexism, and classism in the curriculum.
- Teach preservice teachers to understand and appreciate parental involvement.
- Prepare them to work with parents in a sensitive and responsive manner.
- Expand efforts towards all groups, not just one.
- Incorporate diversity into other courses that faculty teach.

Tatum (1994) also recommends that teacher educators invite practicing teachers and administrators as guest speakers to their classes to share their multicultural experiences and dilemmas. It is important to have "White allies" or models of European American women supporting equality and working towards multicultural education.

In "Challenges in Multicultural Teacher Education," Amber Carpenter-LaGattuta (2004) offers the following recommendations regarding promising practices in multicultural education. She stated that the purpose of a multicultural teacher education course must be clarified and justified to the students enrolled:

- The issues related to reforming school practices should be presented as controversies that derive from competing ideological viewpoints;
- The students should be prepared for "real-life" teaching situations by learning about teaching experiences and concerns receiving training in methodological guidance;
- The students' own diversity should be recognized and incorporated into their teacher education course;
- Guest speakers who are currently teaching and administering in urban schools should serve as models; and
- Creating a safe classroom environment can promote more in-depth and honest discussion of taboo topics.

Researchers studying multicultural practices agree with the idea that multicultural "infusion" in teacher education requires that some of the existing ideologies, values, assumptions, and instructional practices guiding the preparation of teachers change (Gay, 2000; Nieto, 2004; Banks, 2001). Several researchers recommend establishing a safe environment for discussing and learning about multiculturalism (Krashen, 1992; Cummings, 1986).

Piquemal and Kouritzin (2003) developed a table of guidelines for establishing a safe environment for discussing and learning about culturally sensitive issues:

1. Each person can and should contribute to developing a high level of *trust.*
2. We must all practice *respect* for ourselves and [others].
3. We must agree to participate in *open* and *honest* discussion and debate.
4. Everyone should respect the views of others even if we do not agree with them.
5. We should practice positive and productive ways in which we can convey our perspectives, feelings or disagreements.
6. Everyone should be willing to make comments or contribute to discussions that will promote cross-cultural learning.
7. We must *listen* to others, as well as *listen to ourselves* to continue to support strong and healthy communication.
8. Everyone should feel comfortable and safe about asking questions of others.
9. We all need to take time to think and question our own assumptions of others.
10. It is critical that we all practice being accepting and *nonjudgmental* and *open-minded.*
11. We must remember that no one is an expert on all cultures, but we should all be consistently learning new things about others.
12. It is imperative that we understand that no one person speaks as a representative of the entire ethnic, cultural, or social groups to which they belong.
13. We can help turn around misinterpretations or misunderstandings.
14. We recognize that we are all here to learn and one of the most valuable ways to learn is from each other.

—Piquemal & Kouritzin, 2003, p. 23

In order to successfully prepare preservice teachers, it is necessary that they understand that there is an incredible ethnic, cultural, racial, and linguistic diversity within the United States. Thus, an integral part of preparation for teaching diverse students should be extensive field practice involving multicultural schools.

Curriculum Transformation in an Undergraduate Teacher Education Course

The required curriculum and instruction course Literacy Education for Culturally and Linguistically Diverse Children (RDG4320) was redesigned based on best practices in multicultural/diversity curriculum design research findings. The redesigned curriculum included the following additions and deletions.

Additions

The purpose of a multicultural teacher education course was clarified and justified to the students enrolled based on the course goals and objectives at the beginning of the semester. The text assigned for this course was *Affirming Diversity: The Sociopolitical Context of Multicultural*

Education (4th ed., 2004) by Sonia Nieto. The text's case studies regarding students of color were an integral part of the class discussions. This was also clarified at the beginning of the semester. There was also clarification about the sensitivity of the issues for class discussion, such as discrimination, prejudice, and sexual orientation.

According to Carpenter-LaGattuta (2004), students should be prepared for "real-life" teaching situations by learning about teaching experiences. Students should also be taught to view events, concepts, and facts through various lenses such as African American history, women's history, Asian American history, and Latino American history. Thus, in addition to sending the students to local schools to conduct guided observations, I added to the syllabus two documentary videos that discussed in depth the issues mentioned above. *I Am a Promise* (1993), produced by Alan and Susan Raymond, was shown first. *I Am a Promise* was filmed at Stanton Elementary School, an inner-city school in North Philadelphia where 90% of the students live below the poverty line and come from single-parent homes. The school becomes the anchor and primary stabilizing influence in the children's lives. The film includes dramatic profiles of young children succeeding despite their many family difficulties, including drug addiction, foster care, and homelessness. *I Am a Promise* recounts the saga of a devoted principal determined to bring equality in education to impoverished urban children.

The second video, *The Color of Fear* (Mun Wah, 1994), was shown at the middle of the semester. This is the internationally acclaimed film about eight men of various ethnicities who spend a weekend in Ukiah, California, engaging in an intimate and honest dialogue about race and the effects of racism on their lives and families. What makes *The Color of Fear* unique is the authenticity of the participants' stories and the intensity of their anguish and pain. Each one of them shares how racism has affected their lives and how the stereotypes restrict and diminish their opportunities and relationships. *The Color of Fear* is a film about fear and the consequences if it is not handled and discussed. But it is also about hope, and the importance of each of the participants staying in the project until the end and getting to know each other *because* of their differences and not despite them. I watched the first documentary on TV. Watching this video gave me a different perspective about what happens in some urban schools, and helped me to understand issues of poverty, drug addiction, homelessness, and prejudice at a deeper level. I had no firsthand experience with these issues. Being a Latina, I have a lot of experiences dealing with Hispanic students. The population depicted in this documentary, however, was mainly African American. For this reason, I decided to show it to my students. It impacted them as well. I came across the second documentary when I was reviewing literature for this project. The title intrigued me, so I decided to watch it to see if it was appropriate for my students. I knew at this point that just lecturing about racism and its consequences was not enough. This video impacted me as well as my students. I did not lecture about racism anymore; I showed the video to cover this topic. Two class periods were used to watch the two documentary videos. One of the videos was shown at the beginning of the semester, and the other one towards the end. The guidelines for establishing a safe environment for discussing and learning about culturally sensitive issues were first established (Piquemal & Kouritzin, 2004). Then, after watching each one of the videos and holding a class discussion, the students were asked to write a reflection on the first video. For the second video, the students were asked to answer a questionnaire.

Early in the semester, a guest speaker visit was added to the syllabus to conduct sensitivity training and talk about cross-cultural communication. The presenter spoke about the different communication traits of specific cultural groups. More emphasis was given to "hands-on experience" than to lecture. Thus, extensive field practice in multicultural schools was assigned to the students over a longer period of time, in a more controlled environment. This offered exposure to diverse situations in schools and communities so that students could understand the increasingly diverse needs and experiences of K-12 students. The students were given a set of specific questions dealing with learning issues in the multicultural classroom. I assigned three professional journal articles for the students to read before conducting field practice, in order to understand how diverse students learn. The students were required to interact and observe multicultural students, and to keep a journal to answer directed questions posed for the observations. Students were asked to reflect, look at the facts, and form an opinion, rather than simply memorize information. The instructor served more as a facilitator than as a lecturer.

Deletions

There was no preaching. There was no emphasis on memorization, quizzes, or busy work. Excess material was trimmed from the original syllabus to fit the time frame. For this purpose, chapter highlights and topics were offered to students in PowerPoint presentation format and posted on the electronic blackboard.

Closing Remarks

The purpose of this project was to infuse multicultural and gender issues into an existing curricula. The changes did not appear to be too drastic on paper. Once the new curriculum was implemented, however, the difference observed was more drastic than predicted.

The first notable positive difference was the classroom climate. Piquemal and Kouritzin's (2004) guidelines for establishing a safe environment were shared with the students on the first day of classes, and this made a big difference. The climate in the classroom was now respectful, trusting, nonjudgmental, and open-minded. This new climate enhanced discussion about very sensitive issues such as discrimination, prejudice, and sexual orientation.

The second surprise appeared in the students' reflections after watching the first video documentary, *I Am a Promise*. Most of the students had never been exposed to the experiences depicted in this documentary, such as homelessness (among children), drug addiction, and prostitution. This documentary was very powerful in stirring the students' emotions. Many of the reflections included comments such as, "I had no idea that students could come to school with so many problems"; "How can students concentrate in school when they don't have anything to eat at home?"; and "How can one cater to *all* students' needs?" These comments were very interesting because all of these experiences had been communicated to the students before showing this video. It was after watching the video that these experiences made sense to the students, and they understood them as one more "reality" of a diverse America.

The third surprise was the improvement in grades on the first exam. The overall distribution improved to a mean score of 87.93% for this class, compared to 80.5% for a previous class. The exam was a multiple choice test covering the first four chapters of Sonia Nieto's (2004) text and the topics covered in class. The improvement in the first exam scores of this class may be attributed to the addition of the videos, which contextualized the book's content.

I received the last surprise on the final day of classes. The students presented me with a multicultural children's book, *Sumi's First Day of School Ever* (2003) by Soyung Pak, which many had autographed. Some of the comments included:

> "Your class has educated all of us in ways we never could have thought! I have truly enjoyed your class and look forward to the future."
>
> "I enjoyed your class and you made me think about cultural diversity in a whole new way."
>
> "Thank you for all your time and support. I really enjoyed and looked forward to your class every day. I have learned so much this semester. I really enjoyed learn-

ing about cultural education and bilingual education. Congratulations on all your hard work! Keep it up and thank you for being such a GREAT role model."

All in all, after these changes were implemented, in terms of content, social realities and conflict were critically analyzed through field practice and through the documentaries. In regards to construction of knowledge (Morrey & Kitano, 1997), the results agree with the literature: There was a systematic creation of community of learners. Students were not lectured to as much; instead, they were required to discuss and reflect upon the course topics. This change impacted assessment as well, because the students were engaged in authentic forms of self-reflection that were used as a means of evaluation. Classroom interaction, which was a problem before these changes were made, was changed by systematically planning strategies that promoted equity and opportunities with cross-group interactions with a common goal that included Piquemal and Kouritzin's (2004) guidelines for establishing a safe environment. This semester was one of the most rewarding semesters of my career. I understood better than ever how carefully planning a curriculum based on researched best practices can make all the difference for the students and the instructor.

Table 1. Original/Transformed Syllabus Course Objectives

A. Original Course Objectives	B. Transformed Course Objectives
1. To identify and internalize the content and organization of the elementary and middle school curriculum	1. To identify and internalize the content and organization of the elementary and middle school curriculum
2. To relate the practical applications of curriculum organization to instructional programs and student learning	2. To relate the practical applications of curriculum organization to instructional programs and student learning
3. To develop lessons and an instructional unit	3. To develop lessons and an instructional unit using culturally responsive teaching strategies
4. To explore and analyze the issues of curriculum development	4. To explore and critically analyze the issues of curriculum development and diversity
5. To analyze and evaluate the Texas Essential Knowledge and Skills and how they relate to curriculum	5. To analyze and evaluate the Texas Essential Knowledge and Skills and how they relate to curriculum
6. To explore methods of classroom organization and management in the K-8 classrooms	6. To explore methods of classroom organization and management in the K-6 classrooms that promote culturally responsive teaching
	7. To infuse knowledge of English as a Second Language (ESL) education and factors that contribute to an effective multicultural and multilingual learning environment (ESL Standard II)

In the next section, another professor in the College of Education describes her experience transforming a graduate-level curriculum and instruction course. This professor attended the Multicultural Institute in spring 2009.

Curriculum Transformation in a Graduate Teacher Education Course

In response to the need to better prepare teacher candidates for a diverse student population, beginning in fall 2009 the College of Education at this public university in the southwestern United States incorporated bilingual and English as a Second Language (ESL) standards throughout its initial teacher certification program. To become more proficient in these standards, I (refers to second author) attended numerous professional development opportunities, including the Institute in spring 2009. As a result, I transformed my syllabus in a graduate curriculum and instruction course for students who are seeking initial teacher certification and a master's degree. This course deals with principles of elementary through middle school curriculum development and classroom management. The transformed goals of this course included infusing multicultural content as well as multicultural perspectives. In particular, the goals included developing a community of learners who (a) construct knowledge through social interaction; (b) critically examine diversity issues in education; (c) apply knowledge gained about teaching and learning in field-based settings; and (d) become effective, culturally responsive teachers who continually reflect on their practices. (See Table 1, above, for a comparison between the original and the transformed syllabus course objectives.)

In fall 2009, the first semester that I implemented the transformed syllabus, I collected both quantitative and qualitative data to determine what influence the changes had on the students' attitudes to and perceptions of diversity. The participants included twenty-four students in this semester's course—twenty-two were female and two were male. Of these, seventeen were White, six were Hispanic, and one was African American. These demographics reflect those of most teacher preparation programs in the United States today—mostly White and female.

Multicultural Strategies Infused into the Teacher Education Course

The main instructional strategy I employed to integrate multiculturalism into this course was literature circles. Harvey Daniels (2002) defines literature circles as "small, peer-led discussion groups whose members have chosen to read the same story, poem, article, or book" (p. 2). Integrating literature circles into this course provided opportunities for students to engage in conversations about issues related to diversity (e.g., ethnicity, socioeconomic class, gender, special needs, etc.), to think more critically about these issues, and to hear the opinions of others through interactions with their peers.

At the beginning of the semester, I explained the literature circle procedures and gave a short talk on each of the five books related to diverse issues in education. These books included:

- Byrnes, D. A., & Kiger, G. (2005). *Common bonds: Anti-bias teaching in a diverse society*. Olney, MD: Association of Childhood Education International

  This book examines numerous aspects of diversity in schools today. The authors write about various forms of cultural diversity and suggest ways that teachers can build inclusive classroom environments. The common theme that emerges is that while diversity poses difficulties, teachers can create an environment in which differences are recognized and accepted while simultaneously reinforcing a common set of norms and values that bind students together.

- Delpit , L., & Dowdy, J. K. (Eds.). (2002). The skin that we speak: Thoughts on language and culture in the classroom. New York, NY: The New Press.

  This is a collection of thirteen essays by teachers who offer firsthand perspectives on the issue of dialects in the classroom. The authors have gathered personal essays from educators who describe their own struggles to come to terms with the formal language of school and the nonvalidated language of home. Other essays move into the classroom, looking at how different teachers address questions of dialect and how students experience their instruction.

- Gurian, M. (Ed.). (2001). Boys and girls learn differently! A guide for teachers and parents. San Francisco, CA: Jossey-Bass.

  The author and Kathy Stevens argue that from preschool to high school, brain differences between the sexes call for different teaching strategies. Presenting a detailed picture of boys' and girls' neurological, chemical, and hormonal disparities, the authors explain how those differences affect learning.

- Ladson-Billings, G. (2009). Dreamkeepers: Successful teachers of African American children. San Francisco, CA: Jossey-Bass.

  Ladson-Billings integrates scholarly research with stories of eight successful teachers in a predominantly African American school district to illustrate that the "dream" of all teachers and parents—academic success for all children—is alive and can be emulated. The presentation of examples from "intellectually rigorous and challenging classrooms" emphasizes the cultural and social aspects of the issues in education as a whole.

- Sapon-Shevin, M. (2007). *Widening the circle: The power of inclusive classrooms.* Boston, MA: Beacon Press Books.

  The author claims that education must be designed, from the outset, for universal accessibility. Then, rather than try to ignore difference, she argues that teachers should embrace it so that children realize we are all different in different ways. She points out that whatever our particular issue (e.g., Down's syndrome, cerebral palsy, autism, gifted intelligences, etc.), if we work together in an inclusively designed classroom then we learn from one another, which promotes respect among children and social justice in our nation.

These books were selected because they represent current issues related to diversity in classrooms. Students signed up for their first three book choices, forming five groups of four to five students in each group. Each week they read a portion of the book and wrote a one- to two-page response. During class, they met for approximately 15–20 minutes with their literature circle groups to discuss their responses. After meeting for four weeks, each group created an oral book presentation and a handout that was shared with the whole class.

The students' written reflections were collected at the end of each class session so that responses could be analyzed. I used the open coding process (Corbin & Strauss, 2008) to analyze the reflections (n=87). As I read the responses, I looked for patterns that emerged, and grouped them into categories. The categories were organized into the following themes: (a) agreeing with ideas/strategies in the text, (b) making personal connections with the text, (c) finding new insights in the text, (d) having a different perspective from the text, (e) planning to apply information from text in future or current classroom, and (f) questioning/wonderings. Table 2 provides the frequencies, percentages, and illustrative responses for each of the themes.

Table 2. Literature Circle Written Reflection Themes (n=87)

Themes	**Illustrative Responses**	**Frequency**	**Percent**
Agreeing with ideas/ strategies	"I agree with their statements about teaching children to be respectful of sexual orientation and differences that exist in our classroom communities." "I agree that schools don't do enough to prepare children to live harmoniously and equitably with diversity. Although many schools are beginning to incorporate some of the ideas about diversity, several are just skimming the surface."	83	75%
Making personal connections	"I recently subbed in an ESL classroom…there were four students who did not speak English…three were new to the US…they had moved from Burma and one girl was from Africa." "I can relate to the way the African American boys felt. I too have felt intimidated by a White audience and sense that perhaps the way I speak will be confusing."	62	79%
Finding new insights	"I have never thought of it this way, but I do see the differences in materials provided at schools in AISD. Some schools do have better resources and it's most likely based on the socioeconomic status of the families and students at the school." "I was surprised to learn low income children lose ground over the summer while wealthier students gain ground."	37	70%

Themes	Illustrative Responses	Frequency	Percent
Having a different perspective	"As I go farther into this book, I am beginning to consider how falsely positive the author is that all children can learn in an inclusive classroom. Although the idea sounds wonderful, I do not think it is realistic." "I agree with the author that inclusion can be beneficial socially for students with disabilities, but I am still unconvinced that students in inclusion would receive the same benefits from the individualized education that they would receive through special education."	16	37%
Planning to apply something from book in current or future classroom	"A few techniques I want to use in math, science and spatial learning are Venn diagrams, role modeling, and peer tutoring...these three are very useful for both genders...." "'Difference not deficit'...This will be an important point to carry with me into my future classroom."	13	45%
Questioning/ Wondering	"Throughout the book I feel like the teachers believe that standardized tests do not truly measure what the students know. If this is so, why do they still exist?" "Those experiences, along with the book, reminded me of how contentious the subject of language can be. Why is that? And why is it a desire of many people for everyone to talk in the same way?"	13	25%

In addition to literature circles, I infused other teaching methods to achieve the multicultural goals of the course. For example, to increase peer interaction and develop a community of learners, I incorporated cooperative learning activities (Kagan & Kagan, 2009). These included teambuilding and classbuilding activities, as well as numerous Kagan Structures (e.g., RallyRobin, RoundRobin, Quiz-Quiz-Trade, etc.). Since the course focused on classroom management techniques, I also implemented positive discipline procedures such as class meetings (Nelsen, Lott, & Glenn, 2000). Like this chapter's first author, I established a safe environment for discussing difficult issues by creating a social contract with the class at the beginning of the semester.

To develop the social contract, I used procedures outlined in *Capturing Kids Hearts: Participants Manual* (Flippen, 2005). These procedures involved asking the following four questions and recording students' answers on a large sheet of chart paper: (a) How do you want to be treated by the teacher? (b) How do you think the teacher wants to be treated by the students? (c) How should we treat each other? (d) How should we handle problems and/or conflicts that come between us? The students signed the social contract, and it was posted on the classroom wall, where it remained for the duration of the semester. The poster served as a visual reminder of how we had agreed to treat one another during the semester.

Other multicultural strategies included students demonstrating mastery of course content through traditional as well as alternative assessments, such as teaching a culturally responsive lesson in a field-based setting, constructing a comprehensive classroom management plan, creating an annotated bibliography of children's books related to diversity issues, and completing self-reflections of various assignments. When possible, I incorporated choice into the assignments to meet the diverse learning styles of students in my classroom.

Course Outcomes

To evaluate the effectiveness of incorporating the multicultural objectives, I sought formative feedback from students through an open-ended survey at midterm. Using an informal assessment, the Plus/Delta form (Langford, 2004), students were asked to comment on what they felt was going well (Plus) in the course and to make suggestions for changes (Delta). Almost half (47%) of the students commented that they liked seeing lessons and teaching strategies demonstrated in class, and that class activities were relevant to them in their current or future classrooms. Other things they liked about the course included the instructor's teaching style, the teaching materials, and classroom activities that kept them engaged (e.g., cooperative learning, classroom meetings). While 37% of the students suggested more time should be spent on practicing how to write a lesson plan, a few noted that some of the readings were redundant. At the end of the semester, I administered an end-of-course survey that included several multicultural questions. The ten-item survey was adapted from several instruments shared during the Institute. Eight of the survey items asked students to respond using a five-point Likert scale (strongly agree to strongly disagree). Each of these items also included a comments section in which students could write open-ended responses. The last two survey items asked for open-ended responses only. As shown in Table 3, the results of this survey demonstrated positive outcomes on items 1–8. In the comments section, several students indicated that the literature circle discussions provided opportunities to critically examine diversity issues.

Sample responses included:

> "The assigned book I had brought points about diversity issues I hadn't even thought about. The group discussions also provided the opportunity to hear others' analysis of the issues."

> "Reading *Common Bonds* gave [an] excellent overview of diversity issues. Also, all of the diversity presentations helped prepare us for dealing with diversity in the classroom."

Table 3. End-of-Course Survey (n=24)

Item #	Strongly Agree	Agree	Neutral	Disagree	Strongly Disagree
1. This course provided opportunities for me to construct knowledge through social interactions with others.	100%				
2. This course provided opportunities for me to critically examine diversity issues related to education.	91%	8%			
3. This course helped me develop a greater awareness of how to become a more culturally responsive teacher.	95%	4%			
4. The professor used a variety of class activities and assessments (e.g., small-group activities, reflections, whole class presentations, online searches, individual projects, field-based experiences).	100%				
5. This course introduced ideas I had not previously encountered.	78%	21%			
6. I have been able to see connections between the material in this course and real-life situations I might (or presently do) face as a classroom teacher.	95%	4%			
7. The professor allowed students to express their point of view and respected their opinion.	100%				
8. The professor modeled effective teaching practices.	100%				
9. What was the most beneficial part of this course?					
10. Suggestions for improving this course					

With regard to what was the most beneficial aspect of the course, the most frequently occurring responses included the following: (a) cooperative learning strategies, (b) developing the classroom management plan, (c) learning about positive discipline, and (d) the professor's modeling of teaching strategies. As for suggestions to improve the course, 98% of the students either commented that nothing should be changed or left this section blank. One student commented, "There was a lot of overlap between two of the textbooks."

Follow-Up Survey

Since fall 2009 I have taught four sections of this transformed multicultural course. Midterm and end-of-course evaluations from each of these semesters have remained consistently positive. Recently, I sent an email survey to students who had completed the course between fall 2009 and summer 2010 (N=65) to find out if they have implemented any of the strategies learned in CI 5326 in an actual classroom setting. These students were selected because they would have had an opportunity to work in an elementary or middle school classroom through field experiences, student teaching, or as the teacher-of-record. Thirty-five students responded to the survey, for a 53% response rate. Of these, thirty-four (97%) indicated that they had incorporated at least one or more of the multicultural strategies (e.g., cooperative learning, class meetings, positive discipline procedures, social contract, literature circles, children's books related to diversity) in a classroom setting. One of the respondents, who is a first-year teacher, wrote the following:

> I feel that by incorporating these activities [cooperative learning, class meetings, literature circles, children's books related to diversity] into my third grade classroom, my students have become much more tolerant of one another and their social skills have improved dramatically. If you were to ask any of my students to describe our classroom community with one word, they'd all say "family."

Another beginning teacher wrote,

> As a first year teacher, I think that having class meetings and using cooperative learning has tremendously impacted my class. I have a class that is very diverse. Cooperative learning and class meetings have given my class a forum to deal with things that were going on in our classroom and a way to problem solve and fix what we didn't like. There have been a few minor bumps in the road, however, without these tools I have a feeling those minor bumps would have been major potholes.

Some of the respondents who were observing in classrooms or doing their student teaching found they were not able to implement as many of the strategies as they would have liked. For example, one student wrote, "It wasn't possible for me to implement class meetings during field observations and student teaching due to the cooperating teacher's set schedule; otherwise, I would have loved to have held meetings." One respondent, who indicated that she had not had an opportunity to implement any of the strategies during her field experiences, suggested that university students be placed in classrooms where students would be sure to observe these strategies on a regular basis. She wrote, "The teacher I was with did not incorporate anything I had learned in my classes, and even did things that we learned not to do." This comment brings up the importance of placing students in field-based settings that support multicultural teaching practices. I plan to follow up with these teachers once they have their own classrooms to determine if they actually implement the multicultural strategies once they are the teacher-of-record.

Closing Remarks

My objective for attending the Multicultural Institute was to learn more about diversity issues in education today, as well as how to transform curricula in a teacher preparation course. While I know I still have much to learn, I believe I made a start in achieving both of these objectives. Moreover, as a White, female, middle-class teacher with nearly forty years of teaching experience, I believe I learned more about my own cultural identity and how to become a more culturally responsive educator. Each semester, I continue to develop, along with my students (who are mostly White, female, monolingual, and middle-class), as a multicultural educator. While I had previously used many of the same instructional strategies in my courses (e.g., cooperative learning, class meetings, literature circles), the Multicultural Curriculum Transformation and Research Institute helped me view these strategies from a new perspective. I am now more intentional in pointing out how these strategies value the diversity of all students and help build community in the classroom. I focus on how these strategies can help us become more culturally responsive teachers (Gay, 2000).

Moreover, I continue to reflect upon and refine my teaching practices based on the students' feedback and performance, as well as my own professional development in the area of multiculturalism. For example, after reading Eric Jensen's new book *Teaching with Poverty in Mind: What Being Poor Does to Kids' Brains and What Schools Can Do* (2009), I added it as a literature circle choice to help students learn more about the impact of poverty on learning. Ultimately, my hope is that infusing multicultural content and perspectives into my course curriculum will have a positive impact on my students so they will be better prepared to meet the needs of the diverse learners they will most likely teach in their future classrooms.

Final Comments

The two examples of curriculum transformation described in this chapter demonstrate the realities of preparing preservice teachers. These examples align with the literature that states that preparing teachers for the demands of multicultural education is a complex and daunting task (Morey & Kitano, 1997). It is complex because of the dynamic nature of teaching. Thus, it is important that the students have a good understanding about best practices in addition to knowledge of politics, policies regarding diverse populations, and the history of discrimination, prejudice, and related issues.

In summary, *all* children deserve excellence in education. To ensure that *all* our children do indeed receive excellent education, we must demand excellence in multicultural teacher preparation programs (Gardner, 1984). Preservice teachers must believe in the value and potential for greatness of a new generation of students who are racially, socially, ethnically, and culturally different from themselves. To be able to meet this demand, preservice teachers must be not only knowledgeable but also skilled in multicultural education (Gay, 1997). As Ball and Tyson (2011) point out in *Studying Diversity in Teacher Education*, "it is more imperative than ever that teachers be prepared with the attitudes, skills, knowledge, and dispositions necessary to become excellent teachers for students from racial, ethnic, and linguistic backgrounds that differ from their own" (p. 414). Based on the course outcomes after we transformed our syllabi, we believe that the preservice teachers in the two courses described in this chapter were indeed more knowledgeable and skilled in multicultural education.

References

Ball, A. F., & Tyson, C. A. (2011). *Studying diversity in teacher education.* Lanham, MD: Rowman & Littlefield.

Banks, J. A. (2001). *Cultural diversity in education: Foundations, curriculum, and teaching* (4th ed.). Boston, MA: Allyn & Bacon.

Carpenter-LaGattuta, A. (2004). Challenges in multicultural teacher education. *Annual Editions Multicultural Education 2004/2005,* 51–53.

Cochran-Smith, M. (2004). *Walking the road: Race, diversity, and social justice in teacher education.* New York, NY: Teachers College Press.

Cockrell, K. S., Placier, P. L., Cockrell, D. H., & Middleton, J. N. (1999). Coming to terms with "diversity" and "multiculturalism" in teacher education: Learning about our students, changing our practice. *Teaching and Teacher Education, 15* (4), 351–366.

Coopersmith, J. (2009). *Characteristics of public, private, and Bureau of Indian Education elementary and secondary school teachers in the United States: Results from the 2007–08 schools and staffing survey (NCES 2009–324).* Washington, DC: National Center for Education Statistics, Institute of Education Sciences, U.S. Department of Education.

Corbin, J., & Strauss, A. (2008). *Basics of qualitative research* (3rd ed.). Thousand Oaks, CA: Sage.

Cummings, J. (1986). Empowering minority students: A framework for intervention. *Harvard Educational Review, 56* (1), 18–36.

Daniels, H. (2002). *Literature circles.* Portland, ME: Stenhouse.

Darling-Hammond, L., & Bransford, J. (2005). *Preparing teachers for a changing world: What teachers should learn and be able to do.* San Francisco, CA: Jossey-Bass.

Darling-Hammond, L., Wise, A., & Klein, P. (2001). *Who will teach our students?* Paper presented at the Holmes Partnership Annual Conference, Albuquerque, NM.

Flippen, F. (2005). *Capturing kids' hearts: Participant manual.* College Station, TX: Flippen Group.

Gardner, J. W. (1984). *Excellence: Can we be equal and excellent too?* (rev. ed.). New York, NY: W.W. Norton & Company.

Garmon, M. A. (2004). Changing preservice teachers' attitudes/beliefs about diversity. *Journal of Teacher Education, 55,* 201–213.

Gay, G. (1997). Multicultural infusion in teacher education: Foundations and applications. In Morey, A., & Kitano, M. K. (Eds.), *Multicultural course transformation in higher education: A broader truth* (pp. 192–210). Boston, MA: Allyn & Bacon.

———. (2000). *Culturally responsive teaching: Theory, research, & practice.* New York, NY: Teachers College Press.

———. (2010). Acting on beliefs in teacher education for cultural diversity. *Journal of Teacher Education,* 6 (1–2), 143–152.

Gay, G., & Howard, T. (2000). Multicultural education for the 21st century. *The Teacher Educator, 36* (1), 1–16.

Gregorian, V. (2001, August 17). Teacher education must become colleges' central preoccupation. *Chronicle of Higher Education,* B7.

Howard, T. (2010). *Why race and culture matter in schools: Closing the achievement gap in America's classrooms.* New York, NY: Teachers College Press.

Irvine, J. J. (2003). *Educating teachers for diversity: Seeing with a cultural eye.* New York, NY: Teachers College Press.

Jensen, E. (2009). *Teaching with poverty in mind: What being poor does to kids' brains and what schools can do about it.* Alexandria, VA: ASCD.

Kagan, S., & Kagan, M. (2009). *Kagan cooperative learning.* San Clemente, CA: Kagan Publishing.

Krashen, D. S. (1992). *Fundamentals of language education, 1–7.* Torrance, CA: Laredo Publishing.

Ladson-Billings, G. (1999). Preparing teachers for diverse studentpopulations: A critical race theory perspective. *Review of Research in Education, 24,* 211–247.

Langford, D. P. (2004). *Tool time for education: Choosing and implementing quality improvement tools.* Molt, MA: Langford International.

Little, J. W., & Bartlett, L. (March 2010). The teacher workforce and problems of educational equity. *Review of Research in Education, 34* (1), 296–305.

MacDonald, S., Colville-Hall S., & Smolen, L. (2004). Program ownership and the "transformative agenda" in college education: Teachers of teachers working toward a more equitable society. *Annual Editions Multicultural Education 2004/2005,* 18–25.

Morey, A., & Kitano, M. (Eds.). (1997). *Multicultural course transformation in higher education: A broader truth.* Boston, MA: Allyn & Bacon.

Mun Wah, L. (Producer & Director). (1994). *The color of fear* [Motion picture]. United States: Stirfry Seminars.

National Center for Educational Statistics. (2006). *The condition of education.* Washington, DC: Author.

Nelsen, J., Lott, L., & Glenn, S. (2000). *Positive discipline in the classroom: Development, mutual respect, cooperation, and responsibility in your classroom* (3rd ed.). New York, NY: Three Rivers Press.

Nieto, S. (2004). *Affirming diversity: The sociopolitical context of multicultural education* (4th ed.). Boston, MA: Allyn & Bacon.

Pak, S. (2003). *Sumi's first day of school ever.* New York, NY: Viking.

Piquemal, N. A. C., & Kouritzin, S. G. (2003). Angela: A pedagogical story and conversation. *Multicultural Education, 10*(3) 33-42.

Raymond, A. (Producer), & Raymond S. (Producer & Director). (1993). *I am a promise: The children of Stanton Elementary School* [Motion picture]. United States: New Video.

Scarcella, R. C. (1990). *Teaching language minority students in the multicultural classroom.* Englewood Cliffs, NJ: Prentice Hall Regents.

Tatum, B. D. (1994). Teaching White students about racism: The search for White allies and the restoration of hope. *Teachers College Record, 95* (4), 462–476.

Texas Education Agency. (2009). Public education information management systems (PEIMS). Austin, TX: Author.

Villegas, A. M., & Lucas, T. (2002). Preparing culturally responsive teachers—rethinking the curriculum. *Journal of Teacher Education, 53* (1), 20–32.

10

COLLEGE OF EDUCATION

Making Multiculturalism Overt in an Education Graduate Course

Emily J. Summers

This chapter embraces historical, normative, and subjective perspectives as essential parts of embedding multiculturalism within graduate-level teacher education courses. It begins with a brief introductory history of multiculturalism in teacher education and then moves toward a rationale of why we need multicultural education in the field of teacher education. The tone toward the second half of the chapter shifts to my personal experience of the Multicultural Transformation Institute and its influence on graduate teacher education students. I offer findings from my classes both before and after the multicultural curricular change. I conclude with some suggestions for faculty and an overview of where I found my greatest inspiration to begin and continue infusing multiculturalism in my university classes.

A History of Multiculturalism in Teacher Education

The Historical Legacies of Multicultural Education

At the turn of the previous century, Dewey (1902) called for more pluralistic and inclusive settings. Counts (1932) found that critical educational pedagogies worked in opposition to societal hegemony. Throughout the twentieth century, scholars continued to call for educators and teacher educators to make education relevant for all students (Apple, 1992; Counts, 1932; Freire, 1998; Pinar, 1978). We now find ourselves more than a decade into the twenty-first century and despite the continual scholarly notice, the need for multicultural education continues to grow. Colleges of education shoulder the weight of educating this century's teachers, who will either meet this call or continue a trend of inequity within public school settings. Failing to equip teachers with the skills and modeled examples of multicultural coursework propagates a message and a reality of injustice in the U.S. educational system, which *promises* education as a means toward equity. Freire (1985) went further, indicating, "any situation in which humans prevent others from engaging in the process of inquiry is one of violence" (p. 17).

Merely teaching the attitudes and practices of multiculturalism does not ensure protection against unequal conditions in our public schools. Students' rights were generally a byproduct of cultural movements. Cultural studies followed the civil rights movement. Content analysis of gender in textbooks followed the women's rights movement. The Kennedy Administration's family values regarding individuals who were differently abled brought about increased equity for individuals with disabilities within schooling contexts. While schools cannot separate themselves from social and political advancements, as educators we need to take a proactive stance for equity, diversity, and multiculturalism. Students' rights and their inherent diversity cannot continue to be afterthoughts in U.S. public education. Multicultural course reform is a start to reversing this trend of disempowerance in education.

A History of Multicultural Education in Teacher Education

In 1973 the American Association of Colleges of Teacher Education (AACTE) adopted *No One Model American*, which acquainted the mainstream U.S. population with multicultural education. With this, formalized schooling systems began to wake up and take notice of what had been brewing in what was often, but wrongly, considered a well-maintained "melting pot." While authentic multicultural curricular engagement in U.S. public schools generally required more time and pressure, this landmark adoption began the intellectual shift toward at least an acknowledgement of diverse classroom populations and their ongoing needs for equity within educational systems.

More than two decades after AACTE's public embrace of multiculturalism, Banks, in the introductory chapter of the *Handbook of Research in Multicultural Education* (1995), tasked schools with making the institutional changes necessary to allow multicultural curricula to move forward in schools and preservice teacher training programs. He delineated five dimensions of multicultural education, including "content integration, the knowledge construction process, prejudice reduction, an equity pedagogy, and an empowering school culture and social structure" (p. 4). He arrived at these dimensions based on his research, fieldwork in schools, and observations of schooling culture. Banks' five dimensions gave researchers and teacher educators vocabulary and structure to move the conversation and enactment of multiculturalism in our field forward to match the needs of K-16 students. More recently, Grant and

Chapman (2008) compiled a six-volume work on the rich and diverse multicultural history of teacher education that contextually addressed what this short book chapter cannot. The foundational work of Banks and Banks (1995), alongside more contemporary contributions such as the Grant and Chapman series, demonstrated the depth and sequence of teacher education's ongoing struggle. Teacher educators have incorporated these histories into teacher preparation programs, which posited the education that every child deserves as they trained preservice teachers to enter the realities of the U.S. schooling system. Through knowledge of these histories, some of our hopes took hold in U.S. schools. For example, Irvine (2003) found that when universities provided preservice teachers with multicultural teacher education, these educators reduced cultural deficit viewpoints within their own classrooms (Irvine, 2003).

Multicultural Education in Teacher Education: Shifting the Viewpoint

The importance of subjectivity and normativity over centering objectivity

Culture is normatively defined. During the mid- to late 1900s, in response to civil rights movements, schools implemented rapid, albeit shallow, single-group cultural studies (Grant & Sleeter, 2007). Their third-person–plural "they" viewpoint missed the mark of how "we"—first-person plural—reflect on "our" diversity. By shifting our thinking from a third-person orientation toward a first-person positioning, we acknowledge and affirm our engagement in diversity. In 1995 Cochran-Smith asserted that

> Although the American educational system is dysfunctional for large numbers of children who are not part of the racial and language mainstream, there are no universal strategies for teaching children who are culturally and linguistically different from one another, from their teachers, or from students whose interests are already well served by the system. (p. 493)

Have things changed in the decade and a half since this Cochran-Smith quote held true? I think yes and no. Yes—we have begun making differences in how we teach students; however, responsive curriculum cannot be standardized, because it must reflect the normative values of local schools and communities to be authentic and effective. This is why the Multicultural Curriculum Transformation and Research Institute (the Institute) is so powerful. Individual instructors can apply what research has found to work; yet, they can also adapt this knowledge normatively at the course level, based on their own professional, cultural, and community-based knowledge. Further, the Institute comes with a network of colleagues to help apply this more global knowledge intersubjectively so that it will apply individually to each student in the transformed courses.

Personal Experience with the Multicultural Curriculum Institute

My first formal teaching experiences were in Central America, so before attending Texas State's Multicultural Curriculum Transformation and Research Institute, I was already committed to improvement and change. Texas State was my first teaching assignment on a majority-White campus. Even though we have become a Hispanic Serving Institution (HSI) campus, the majority of my Texas State students are White. Further, my field-based teaching campuses have been majority White, middle to upper-middle-class K-12 campuses. Many of my students needed to develop multicultural empathy and expertise, but had no access to highly diverse K-16 or graduate school contexts. The Institute gave me tools to handle this need.

In addition to gaining multicultural teaching tools, I increased my personal understanding of multiculturalism. One of the presenters, Dr. Patricia Larke, spoke to our group from an infused personal and professional perspective. This influenced me to reflect on my own experiences with multiculturalism and privilege. Her talk stirred me to reexamine my Peace Corps experiences from a position of privilege. This reexamination did not lessen the empathy I gained from my developing world experiences, but it did raise questions. I came to understand that while living in the developing world I always had a strong safety net to catch me if things went wrong. I didn't need it, but it was ever-present. My middle-class family's resources, while not immediately accessible to me, were only a bus ride and a phone call away. I was living poor, but I had not always been poor and I could assume that I would not always be poor; my poverty was both chosen and temporary. I could endure shortages and warfare because they were not eternally present in my life story. There were risks, but I always had a timetable of when and how I would exit those experiences. Furthermore, I had a cushion that I brought with me into these developing world experiences: I carried my education and past opportunities with me. I experienced sexism in Central America, but I had had more than two decades of near-equity experiences that spoke against these understandings and protected me from deep damage.

Dr. Larke's words (re)framed my experiences and my understandings. The concept of my Peace Corps experiences as privilege had never occurred to me. I knew that I learned more than I taught while in the Peace Corps. I also knew that I often lived there by the grace of my host country neighbors and friends, as I did not know how to survive beyond a first-world economy of convenience. However, it had never occurred to me that I was able to *serve* because I had a college education, no dependents, no debts, and no immediate economic needs or obligations. My developing world experiences came from a place of privilege. This newfound understanding changed my dedication to multicultural teaching. Multiculturalism was a first-person experience for everyone—even for those of us from majority White, middle-class backgrounds.

Multiculturalism's Powerful Transformation for Students and Teaching

Unmasking the "colorblind" approach

When I surveyed my students about how they teach ethnically/racially diverse students, the most common response involved a "colorblind" approach. I responded to the informational survey by asking, what do we call the absence of all color? Almost immediately, an African American student replied, "not me"! We talked about how in light, white is the presence of all colors and black denotes absence of color, whereas in pigments, we know that white is the absence of all colors and black is the presence of all colors. The "truth" was contextual. Ocular and cultural realities for teachers involve registering and "reading" race, but often we are blindered by what is highly favored or overtly known. What we think is objective is in fact positioned in ways that are not known to us. To recognize what we "know," we must unmask what we have come to understand as blindness in regard to color and culture. The process of recognizing what we know can be challenging, but it is attainable and valuable.

Bell's (1992) work on racial realism can help students to understand race as persistence—it does not go away. As teachers, we do not have the power to undo, nullify, or vanish someone's racial experiences just by saying that we are "colorblind." While teachers may assert the *privilege* to say, believe, and act as if something is true, that does not make it true. Most teachers come to recognize naïve notions of "colorblind" classrooms as an intersectionality of race, privilege, and power, but it can take the entire semester to build this type of understanding. Understanding artificial, teacher-created constructs occurs for some students only after they read multiple firsthand accounts of students' stories and acknowledge the harm that is done to them in the name of perceived neutrality. (Many preservice and in-service students are surprised that education can be anything other than neutral.) Producing teachers who understand students' cultural, ethnic, and racial heritage as assets to learning is a direct result of multicultural infusion. Even with these understandings, some White students struggle to recognize their own heritage. Some students also wrestle with the concept of Whiteness being the (singular) default norm in U.S. schooling to which everyone else must adjust. Understanding the historical and legal contexts of race and privilege assists students' multicultural growth, but preservice teaching students sometimes need field experiences in diverse schools to observe the significance.

Embrace the discomfort; if change were easy it would have happened already! Change often means confronting tradition. This seems obvious, but as a younger female assistant professor, I was absorbed by the gap between my theoretical understandings and their enactment. I wanted change alongside respect for tradition. Any given undergraduate course, regardless of content, will generally teach, refer to, or rely on the fundamentals of creating the lesson plan. Many lesson plan iterations involve adaptations to anticipate special needs. However, as Cochran-Smith (1995) wrote, "implicit in the lesson plan and other similar assignments is the notion that uniform mastery of bits of information and knowledge is the goal of every lesson" (p. 496). Where then does the respect for multiculturalism and knowledge fit within this uniform learning? Transforming a course at the graduate level of teacher education gave me permission to embrace this tension and bring it into the discussions within our classroom community of teacher learners. Asking graduate students to explore how two seemingly conflicting ideals could work in tandem caused various reactions, including a reluctance to engage the divergence.

For the majority of the learners, it took several weeks to establish the mechanisms to approach the topic without feeling as if they were being (in their own words) "disrespectful," "rebellious," or even "anarchist," as one student described it. I used the multicultural course transformation to embed "big multicultural questions" into each semester's course. Instead of taking smaller chunks of information on a weekly basis, we took on three to four core pedagogical questions to examine throughout the semester under a variety of educational contexts. While I think multiculturalism needs to be at all levels of teacher education, I find graduate courses are especially apt places to make the covert overt. In many cases, it was uncomfortable. I tended to let this tension build until it was spoken. I found a key skill in enacting the transformation was to increase my patience and wait time. I had to let my discomfort outwait the students' discomfort.

The longest wait time for reaction to a big multicultural question was almost three minutes; I have yet to find graduate students who will suffer prolonged silence no matter how dreadful they fear the topic may be. In every case, the students realized that our conversational discomfort was a small cost compared to allowing injustices and inequities for early childhood (EC)-12 students to remain unspoken. We focused on shifting our questioning from a third-person standpoint to an inclusive first-person self-inquiry. Students came up with their own questions, as well. What if every teacher (What if we? What if I?) was unwilling to bear a small burden of temporary discomfort in a civilized graduate class? Did we pay for graduate school to affirm what we already know, or to challenge our understandings so that we might be able to improve our teaching?

Findings

My multicultural course reform resulted in (a) increased class diversity, (b) increased willingness to share and take risks, (c) increased student choices, (d) increased scope and quality of students' work products, and (e) increased teacher and student satisfaction.

Increased Diversity. My Philosophical Foundations class has grown from a homogeneous 100% White student enrollment before the course transformation to a more balanced and diverse heterogeneous student enrollment in the most recent data collection, consisting of 30% African American students, 30% Latina/o students, 35% White students, and 5% of students unwilling to disclose their racial/cultural heritage at the start of class. Initially, my Philosophical Foundations class attracted a less diverse group of student than the university's overall demographic profile. Now, my class is more diverse than the university as a whole.

Increased Overtness in Student Choices. Prior to attending the Institute, my syllabus allowed for student choices in assignments. What my syllabus lacked was openness and overtness about why there were choices. I started from an instructional rationale that choice increased students' success and buy-in to assignments. I still believe this is true. What I've grown to realize is that overtly stating that choices allow for diverse cultural expressions permits diverse students to approach the assignments from a culturally infused position. Now, when I go over the choices in the syllabus, I also explain why I offer these choices. I utilize examples from my own cultural experiences, as well as past student assignments that incorporated gender, race, socioeconomics, age, and other equity indicators. As a result, the work has become more personalized, meaningful (to me and to the students), and thoughtful. Discussion topics went from highly objective (e.g., Plato) to inclusive (e.g., Where were Coatlicue, Nana Buluku, and Eve?: Absence in Western Educational Philosophy Foundations); students' papers followed similar paths.

Increased Willingness to Share and Take Risks. As I took risks in infusing my own cultural background and experiences into class discussions, so did my students. Early on, most of the risks were taken in small in-class or online discussion groups, though some risks came in one-on-one emails or discussions between the students and me. Once the students felt affirmed in infusing their own histories into the philosophical content, many were willing to share these examples with the whole class. Two-thirds of the time, this cultural sharing with the whole class occurred in an online discussion. Students reported feeling safer sharing their culture with an electronic time and space buffer. This may have been reactionary, as other students' reactions were significantly more positive in the online forums. Many students who would not make eye contact with fellow students as they shared cultural stories in class responded positively in online forums, where they had time to process the information before responding. I am still working to increase the continuity of positive responses between the online and in-class discussions.

Students' increased risks in sharing cultural content inspired me to take even more teaching risks. Based on the positive online climate for cultural sharing, I am currently teaching a hybrid (50% in-class and 50% online) section of the course. I taught my first 100% online section of the Philosophical Foundations class in summer 2011. My willingness to take risks also influenced my curriculum committee and my department to take risks. I was given a fall and spring course release to develop the online Philosophical Foundations course. Additionally, I was assigned a partner from the university's instructional design team who values diversity in education. Students' voices are being incorporated into the online development by employing a graduate student assistant and requesting volunteer graduate students to help with recording, editing, and curricular content review. This has been an interesting and positive strategy for multicultural course development.

Increased Quality of Student Products. The quality of the students' products has gradually increased since I received training in multicultural course infusion. While I think the overt choices influenced the quality, I also think that the peer feedback has enabled cultural growth across entire learning communities. Before the Institute, I was pleased with my students' learning. In response to what I learned at the Institute, I have changed and increased my goals for students' learning. I now look for end-of-course papers that reflect both academic and diversity quality. To date, I have offered six students a mentoring invitation to present a coauthored paper at a professional conference; five of the six students accepted the challenge. All five student-coauthored papers were accepted to highly esteemed professional conferences, including meetings of the American Educational Research Association, the Popular Culture Association, and the Race, Ethnicity, and Place International Conference. All paper topics centered on diversity in a way that mattered to the student author. Students' coauthored papers included: "The Successes and Limitations of African American Boys with an Incarcerated Parent"; "Perceptions About Future Roles Held by High School Girls Who Did Not Earn a Diploma"; "Overlap and Gap Between Hip-Hop Lyrics and High School Texts' Cultural Understandings of U.S. Presidents"; "An Ethnographic Exploration of the Boondocks' Subcultural Geography"; and "The Backgrounded Multicultural Environments in EC-5 Classrooms."

In contrast to my success in increasing diverse students' varied voices in professional organization presentations, I have had less success in inspiring diverse students to participate more formally in graduate school opportunities. Four of the five students who presented papers at professional conferences were African American (two females, two males) and one was White (female), but my recruitment of diverse graduate student assistants (GRAs/GAs) has been less successful. In part, the barrier seems to lie within the intersectionality of socioeconomics, race, and the culture of higher learning. To be hired as a GRA/GA, a student must be enrolled in nine hours of graduate studies. While I have invited diverse students to apply for these paid opportunities, all but one of the GRA/GA applicants have been White. Likewise, I have found it difficult to recruit diverse students to enroll in the MA program with a thesis. Of my three thesis students to date, two have been White and one has been Chinese American. The ratios for diverse GA/GRA work and thesis enrollment is disproportionately lower than the university's overall student diversity enrollment ratios. I feel that recruiting diverse GAs, GRAs, and thesis students is essential to promote diverse leadership in public EC-16 schooling.

Increased Teacher and Student Satisfaction. Interestingly, increasing the diversity awareness and enactments in my class has also improved my course instructor survey (CIS) ratings. This was not a goal, but it is a measure of both teacher and student satisfaction. I was concerned about cultural backlash, but that has not been my experience. I found that increasing the overt and purposeful multicultural infusion and awareness in my classes benefits everyone. I will end my findings with students' own words on their experiences with a multiculturally infused course, as recorded on end-of-course CIS surveys. I value students' own words, which is why I embedded the students' instructor evaluation comments below exactly as students wrote them. Denzin and Lincoln (1998) assert that "action oriented and clinically oriented qualitative researchers can create spaces for those who are studied (the other) to speak. The evaluator becomes the conduit for making such voices heard" (p. 30); hence, I make ample space for students' words in my multicultural assessment. Some of the comments are not the best samples of students' academic writing; yet, each example is authentic, which is what matters most to me. I teach my class as a learning community; I find that we are all in the process of our academic becoming.

Occasionally, students connect with multiculturally infused teaching in ways that humble me while inspiring me to continue to improve.

24. Comments on the professor's instructional style:

most wonderful and caring professor I've ever had in this university. She genvinaly wanted everyone to do well but also learn the material.

26. Something else that I would like to say to this professor is:

This was the best course I have taken @ Texas State. Thank you.

Student-centeredness lies at the heart of multicultural teaching for me. It also matters to students, who often read the safe and sheltered spaces for multicultural learning and growth as community building and care.

26. Something else that I would like to say to this professor is:

Thank her for caring about how each of us will get the information for this class! She is like the teacher in Freedom Writers, even BETTER!

26. Something else that I would like to say to this professor is:

Dr. Summers – I thoroughly enjoyed this class – your teaching style, your knowledge was insightful + I have learned a great deal this semester. You built a community of learners –

26. Something else that I would like to say to this professor is:

makes the environment a safe place to discuss

24. Comments on the professor's instructional style:

Very unique, adapts to students' needs and lets us express ourselves

26. Something else that I would like to say to this professor is:

Thank you for helping to build relationships in this class, I really enjoyed many, many things about the class

24. Comments on the professor's instructional style:

Outstanding. WOW. Very relaxed, "safe" environment. Dr. Summers is incredibly knowledgeable of the material taught. She treated us as humans, not an entity that gives money. Took the time to actually know us!

24. Comments on the professor's instructional style:

Very diverse with additions of Classic and Pop culture

23. What was most useful about this course?

Professor Insight + presenting concepts from various perspectives

Finally, students often agree that multicultural inclusion and academic rigor go hand-in-hand:

24. Comments on the professor's instructional style:

Fast Paced – Flexible Rigorous

24. Comments on the professor's instructional style:

you are very casual + approachable + personally I like this. you have high expectations but you're also flexible so it's a nice combination.

I directly attribute each of the students' comments above to the training I received and implemented from the Institute. In all ways, it changed my classes and teaching for the better.

Multicultural Strategies Suggestions for Faculty

- Be patient.
- Wholeheartedly believe in the infused multicultural content.
- Use current research from diverse research voices.
- Find a supportive colleague to keep you going past the first few weeks.
- Focus on the required multiculturalism aspects of students' professional duties, while retaining hope of changing minds and hearts. We need to remember that professional standards require adherence in teachers' actions, not their belief systems.
- Keep professional connections across the university. While I have a multitude of support in the College of Education, some colleagues in other departments and colleges face more resistance.
- Start with localized (classroom, course) change, but never forget that multicultural change is a systemic process. Engage the system.
- Model multicultural teaching in addition to teaching students how to do it.
- Explore the multiple reasons *why* multiculturalism matters in addition to teaching *what* it is.
- Address multicultural infusion in the first person (singular and plural) to encourage individual benefit and buy-in to these ideals.
- Strive to narrow the gap between your ideals and your practices.

Where I Found References and Support

Banks' (1995) five dimensions of multicultural education helped me conceptualize the language and landscape of multicultural education. Banks and Banks' (1995; 2006) works were among the first readings I did in this area, and I find that they provide both a firm foundation and encouragement to build on my course constructions. Their explanation of equity pedagogy is what initially drew me to the vocabulary of multiculturalism. According to Banks and Banks (2006), equity pedagogy exists when teachers modify their teaching in ways that will facilitate the academic achievement of students from diverse racial, cultural, and social-class groups (p. 22). For me, this is the alpha and omega of multiculturalism in teacher education, stretching from the novice to the expert ends of the progress continuum. The same simple yet deeply profound challenges are what continue to center my current multicultural instruction. The beauty of Banks and Banks (2006) is that it informs novice teachers of what needs to be accomplished, while prompting a dialogue about the why and how questions for the experienced educator.

References

American Association of Colleges for Teacher Education. (1973). No one model American. *Journal of Teacher Education, 24,* 264.

Apple, M. (1992). Do the standards go far enough? Power, policy, and practice in mathematics education. *Journal for Research in Mathematics Education, 23* (5), 412–431.

Banks, J. A. (1995). Multicultural education: Historical development, dimensions, and practice. In J. A. Banks & C. A. M. Banks (Eds.), *Handbook of research on multicultural education* (pp. 3–24). New York, NY: Macmillan.

Banks, J. A., & Banks, C. A. M. (Eds.). (1995). *Handbook of research on multicultural education.* New York, NY: Macmillan.

———. (2006). *Multicultural education: Issues and perspectives* (6th ed.). New York, NY: John Wiley.

Bell, D. (1992). Racial realism. *Connecticut Law Review,* 24, 363–374.

Cochran-Smith, M. (1995). Color blindness and basket making are not the answers: Confronting the dilemmas of race, culture, and language diversity in teacher education. *American Educational Research Journal, 32* (3), 493–522.

Counts, G. S. (1932). *Dare the school build a new social order?* Carbondale, IL: Southern Illinois University Press.

Denzin, N. K., & Lincoln, Y. S. (Eds.). (1998). *Strategies of qualitative inquiry.* Thousand Oaks, CA: Sage.

Dewey, J. (1902). *The child and the curriculum.* Chicago, IL: University of Chicago Press.

Freire, P. (1985). *The politics of education: Culture, power, and liberation.* South Hadley, MA: Bergin & Garvey.

———. (1998). *Teachers as cultural workers: Letters to those who dare teach.* Boulder, CO: Westview Press.

Grant, C. A., & Chapman, T. K. (Eds.). (2008). *History of multicultural education: Conceptual frameworks and curricular issues.* London, UK: Routledge.

Grant, C. A., & Sleeter, C. E. (2007). *Doing multicultural education for achievement and equity.* New York, NY: Routledge.

Irvine, J. J. (2003). *Educating teachers for a diverse society: Seeing with the cultural eye.* New York, NY: Teachers College Press.

Pinar, W. F. (1978). The reconceptualization of curriculum studies. *Journal of Curriculum Studies, 10* (3), 205–214.

11

COLLEGE OF FINE ARTS AND COMMUNICATIONS

Integrating Multicultural Education into an Instrumental Music Teacher Preparation Course

Mary Ellen Cavitt

History of the Discipline

Throughout human history and across the globe, people have used music to express cultural ideas and values, socioeconomic class, and ethnic and national identities. Ethnomusicology, or the anthropology of music, has long studied music from a cultural or sociological perspective. Although it is often thought of as a study of non-Western musics, ethnomusicology includes the study of Western music and music from all over the world.

In the latter part of the twentieth century, many universities in the United States began implementing "world music" classes to reflect the diversity of their demographics and highlight the distinctions typically observed between Western and non-Western musics. Additionally, these courses attempted to show how particular musics both shape and reflect the cultures of which they are a part. Topics such as music learning and performing, music in ceremony and ritual, and music in cultural context are often explored.

In public schools in the United States, patriotic and folk song collections are frequently taught to promote a sense of cultural identity. In 1994 the National Standards for Arts Education suggested that music classes in the public schools follow nine content standards to specify what students should know and be able to do in music classes. Two of these standards directly asked for a more varied curricular content: (1) "Singing, alone and with others, a varied repertoire of music," and (2) "Performing on instruments, alone and with others, a varied repertoire of music" (MENC, 1994). These standards specifically asked teachers to go beyond their standard repertoire, and as a result, many teachers sought out more culturally diverse music. Another important standard asked that students understand music in relation to history and culture. Six additional standards were suggested as follows:

1. Improvising melodies, variations, and accompaniments;
2. Composing and arranging music within specified guidelines;
3. Reading and notating music;
4. Listening to, analyzing, and describing music;
5. Evaluating music and music performances; and
6. Understanding relationships between music, the other arts, and disciplines outside the arts.

Within each of these content standards, achievement standards were specified to determine learning outcomes at the completion of grades 4, 8, and 12. Several of these achievement standards specifically referenced the importance of studying music of diverse cultures. Listed below are examples of these achievement standards (MENC, 1994):

- Students sing from memory a varied repertoire of songs representing genres and styles from diverse cultures;
- Students perform expressively a varied repertoire of music representing diverse genres and styles;
- Students demonstrate perceptual skills by moving, by answering questions about, and by describing aural examples of music of various styles representing diverse cultures;
- Students identify the sounds of a variety of instruments, including many orchestra and band instruments, and instruments from various cultures, as well as children's voices and male and female adult voices;
- Students identify ways in which the principles and subject matter of other disciplines taught in the school are interrelated with those of music (e.g., foreign languages: singing songs in various languages; language arts: using the expressive elements of music in interpretive readings; mathematics: mathematical basis of values of notes, rests, and time signatures; science: vibration of strings, drum heads, or air columns generating sounds used in music; geography: songs associated with various countries or regions);
- Students identify by genre or style aural examples of music from various historical periods and cultures;
- Students describe in simple terms how elements of music are used in music examples from various cultures of the world;
- Students identify various uses of music in their daily experiences and describe characteristics that make certain music suitable for each use;
- Students identify and describe roles of musicians (e.g., orchestra conductor, folksinger, church organist) in various music settings and cultures;
- Students demonstrate audience behavior appropriate for the context and style of music performed;
- Students analyze the uses of musical elements in aural examples representing diverse genres and cultures;
- Students describe distinguishing characteristics representative of music genres from a variety of cultures; and
- Students compare, in several cultures of the world, functions music serves, roles of musicians, and conditions under which music is typically performed.

Many states and organizations have adopted policies related to the National Standards for Arts Education (e.g., the Kennedy Center's ArtsEdge).

While choral and general music teachers have been relatively successful at implementing a variety of cultures and musics into the curriculum, instrumental music education has lagged behind. At the secondary level, many choral and instrumental ensembles are obliged to use a prescribed music list to select performance repertoire for state-sanctioned festivals and contests. The choral repertoire in general is more representative of diverse cultures than instrumental music. In a recent study (Cavitt, 2010), I explored the cultural identities of composers included in the Texas' state-prescribed music list for wind bands. The goal of the Texas prescribed music list is to represent the best possible wind band repertoire for selection of contest pieces. These lists aid music educators in selecting quality literature, and they are expanded and improved upon regularly. What was evident was that it is a somewhat homogeneous list comprised primarily of White, male, contemporary, and U.S. composers. Much of this homogeneity can be attributed to the increase in popularity of school bands in the United States and the rise of the wind band as a genre in the mid-twentieth century.

University curricula for Western-trained music educators usually dictate that Western art music is the culturally acceptable model. There seems to be a caste system or hierarchy established where Western classical music is ranked above all other musics. The music that is taught in public schools is often largely limited to educational compositions and state-prescribed music lists that usually do not contain music that is considered popular by today's standards. Students who join the band hoping to perform popular music representative of their culture and preferences often are disappointed. School music and the private music of our students may have little in common. The dominant frame of reference for most concert band music is largely Anglo-European, and this culture is reinforced by the use of prescribed music lists.

In addition to music repertoire, instrumentation and the use of Western instruments in orchestra and wind bands limit the authentic performance of diverse musics. Walker (2000) points out that "...band, orchestra, choir, etc., cannot be the activities where multicultural education occurs precisely because they are quintessentially Western in tuning, style, and repertoire" (p. 31). Ensembles that use Western instruments and scales are limited. For example, it would be very difficult for a wind band from the United States to perform a traditional Indian rāja using microtonal intervals. What has resulted is an infusion of non-Western cultural materials and styles into Western traditional forms of music, rather than authentic performances of non-Western music.

Another important consideration is the relationship of instrument selection and gender. Instrument selection may be one of the most consequential decisions made by students in wind bands and school orchestras. Students may be strongly influenced by peers, parents, teachers, and the media in making decisions about which instrument to choose. It is possible that instrument selection may have less to do with which instrument is most suitable than with perception of the appropriateness of the selection with regard to the gender of the student. For more than thirty years, researchers have asked questions about gender stereotyping in music instrument selection. Seminal research began with Abeles and Porter (1978), who sought to determine at what age gender stereotypes are present in young children, and whether adults demonstrate gender stereotypes with regard to instrument selection for their children. Abeles and Porter found that adults associated flute, violin, and clarinet with girls, and drums, trombone, and trumpet with boys. They also found that young children exhibited few gender associations until around the third grade. Additional studies that examined gender perception with regards to instrument selection have been conducted by Abeles (2009), Coffman and Sehmann(1989), Conway (2000), Delzell and Leppla (1992), Eros (2008), Fortney, Boyle, and DeCarbo (1993), Griswold and Chroback (1981), Killian and Satrom (2011), Sinsabaugh (2005), and Zervoudakes and Tanur (1994).

Along with gender, race may be a consideration in music participation and instrument selection. Johnson and Stewart (2004) found that band directors most often help students to make instrument selections using the following methods: (1) student interest, (2) physical interests, (3) counseling, (4) student trials, and (5) instrumentation (in order to balance the instruments of the band). In 2005, Johnson and Stewart found that knowing the race of the student had no significant impact on music educators' instrument recommendations for students, but Bradley (2007) paints a dismal picture of the overall participation in a music program that she defines as typical:

> In my local area public school district, which I believe is not atypical in the U.S.A., ensembles at the elementary level are diverse, since participation in music is required for all students. At K-5 levels, the student population is approximately 51 percent White, 10 percent Asian, and 24 percent African American. Hispanic students comprise 15 percent of all elementary level students, and Native Americans less than 1 percent. However, in middle school the demographics begin to change, and by grade twelve, 70 percent of the total high

> school student enrollment is White. Only 15 percent of the total population of high school students participates in any of the fine arts course offerings. Of this total, 64 percent are White. The picture becomes even more disturbing when other measurements are used. In grade twelve, only 13 percent of students enrolled in fine arts are from low income families, and only 4 percent of high school fine arts students are considered to be special education students, while only 1 percent of students participating in the fine arts in high school are ELL students (English language learners). If we look closely, we may recognize that there is much about our profession that begs examination of its possible role in perpetuating inequities, racial inequities among them. (Bradley, 2007, p. 134)

Elliot (1995/1996) conducted an experiment to investigate the effects of race and gender on musical performance. Eight students (four flutists and four trumpeters) were videotaped performing the same music étude. Each group of flutists and trumpeters consisted of one White male, one White female, one Black male, and one Black female. Each video performance began with a close-up shot of the performer's face and then the camera was pulled to a distance when the performance began. Rather than evaluate the actual performers, the audio portion of the performance was dubbed over and synchronized so that the audio part of each of the four flutists' performances was the same. The same was done for the four trumpeters. Eighty-eight graduate and undergraduate music educators from seven universities assessed the performances of the students (fifty-four males, thirty-four females; forty-seven Whites, thirty-four Blacks, six Asians). Results indicated that although the recordings were identical, Blacks were scored significantly lower than Whites. Elliot stated that low teacher expectations might be cited "as a factor that can impede achievement for students of color" (p. 53). He suggested that anyone devoted to a "bias-free music education" should be required to take part in sensitivity training that addresses racial and gender bias.

Socioeconomic factors have also been investigated in relation to instrumental music education. Fitzpatrick (2006) found that students who participated in instrumental music (regardless of socioeconomic status) outperformed noninstrumental students in every subject and at every grade level she investigated (in fourth-, sixth-, and ninth-grade standardized achievement tests). Lower socioeconomic status (SES) instrumental students even surpassed higher SES noninstrumental students by the ninth grade in all subjects.

Fitzpatrick was not the only researcher to have substantiated the positive relationship of music participation and academic performance. Miksza (2007) studied data from the 1988 National Educational Longitudinal Study to investigate evidence of the impact of music on academic performance in school. He analyzed the records of 5,335 students who either participated in school music programs from eighth through twelfth grade or did not participate at all. Results indicated that reading, math, science, and social studies test scores were significantly better for the music students. He also found that SES correlated with academic success. Even after accounting for SES, in nearly every case, students who participated in music maintained their advantage over nonmusic students. Although these results are correlations, this may be compelling evidence to suggest that removing music from the curriculum when school budgets are cut may be detrimental to students' academic success and may deprive them of the many rewards they gain from music participation.

Schools function as representatives of culture and play an important role in shaping student attitudes toward people with disabilities. The Education for All Handicapped Children Act of 1975 (Public Law 94-142) brought about numerous changes for teachers and students with and without disabilities. The inclusion of students with disabilities in instrumental music classrooms may require alternate instructional strategies or curricular modifications (e.g., editing music or altering instruments or equipment). Careful instrument selections that accentuate the abilities of the student are very important. McCord and Fitzgerald (2006) created an excellent resource with recommendations and cautions for selecting appropriate instruments for students with specific disabilities, and strategies for reading music. Preparing teachers to create a positive learning culture through inclusion, peer tutoring, thoughtful instrument selection, and appropriate musical experiences is an important aspect of training preservice teachers at the university level.

Multicultural music education teaches students to respect, understand, and develop sensitivity to people and music from diverse cultures, abilities, and backgrounds. Teachers must ensure that the music curricula are designed to stress the importance of multicultural music making. We live in a culture that is becoming more diverse each day. Students need to understand that there are many types of musical systems, and different but equally valid ways to make music.

Personal Story about MCTRI Impact

In 2008, I had the opportunity to participate in the Multicultural Curriculum Transformation and Research Institute at Texas State University–San Marcos. I teach instrumental music education to preservice teachers at the university, and had a keen interest in understanding how other professors infuse their courses with culturally, economically, and ethnically diverse issues. I was interested to participate in a discourse that would challenge my belief systems and to learn new ways to structure my curriculum and assessments for a course that prepares students to become band and orchestra directors in the public schools.

As future teachers, my students are charged with educating students from diverse socioeconomic and cultural backgrounds. Most of my students were raised in either a predominantly Hispanic culture or a predominantly White culture, and many return home to teach in the same type of school and culture. At the university, our School of Music provides many opportunities to participate in multicultural ensembles (mariachi, salsa band, and jazz ensembles, for example) and more traditional ensembles (such as orchestra, concert bands, and marching band). In our newest undergraduate catalog, students are now required to take a General Performance Techniques course designed specifically to help future instrumental music teachers learn to teach mariachi and jazz ensembles in the public schools.

Chapter 41 of the Texas Education Code requires school districts that are designated as property-wealthy to share their local tax revenue with school districts that are designated as property-poor (http://www.tea.state.tx.us/portals.aspx?id=6796&menu_id= 645). This requirement, called the "Robin Hood" plan, has a large impact on instrumental music programs throughout the state. Many students from less affluent school districts are provided professional-quality school-owned instruments, while students from moderate to affluent schools are often required to purchase their own instruments. Some of these schools offset the costs of instruments, equipment, uniforms, trips, and additional specialized teachers not provided by the district by assessing student fees that often exceed $300 per student. While many schools insure that all students can participate after joining the band or orchestra regardless of their ability to pay fees, many students may be too intimidated to even consider joining. As graduates from less affluent public high schools (who were provided instruments by their school districts) enter university, many are surprised to learn that the university does not also provide all of the instruments and equipment.

One of my roles at the university is to help place student teachers in public schools for internships. After participating in the Multicultural Institute and serving for many years as a student teacher supervisor, I have come to the realization that I can help break the cycle of university students wanting to teach in public schools that are similar to the schools they attended. Students can be encouraged to accept placement in excellent programs that are different (in socioeconomic, cultural, or racial composition) from those to which they are accustomed. It is imperative that more student teachers are placed with successful mentors at schools with a low socioeconomic profile so that they can be prepared to teach *all* students.

In selecting music for performance with instrumental ensembles, young teachers can be encouraged to go beyond the prescribed music lists and consider multicultural music, music of their students' cultures, and music that is preferred by the student population and viewed as "their" music. Students can help with the process; inexperienced students can be given more choices at the appropriate level of difficulty, and more advanced students may choose concert repertoire, genre, venues, and perhaps even what instrument they prefer to play. Some of the students might be able to compose or arrange music for the ensemble. As students become more involved in the creative process, they will learn to be more independent musicians.

Subsequent to my participation in the Multicultural Institute, I was selected to present a research paper at the 2008 National Symposium on Multicultural Music sponsored by MENC (the National Association for Music Education) and the University of Tennessee, in Knoxville, Tennessee. As stated earlier, the purpose of this paper was to explore the cultural identities of composers included in the Texas state-prescribed music list for wind bands. This paper was published as a chapter in the book *Kaleidoscope of Cultures: A Celebration of Multicultural Research and Practice* (2010), edited by Marvelene Moore. The information gleaned from this research is now part of the curriculum of the course that was transformed as a result of participation in the Multicultural Institute.

The Multicultural Curriculum Transformation and Research Institute at Texas State University was inspirational and thought-provoking. As noted here, it has changed my teaching and the lives of my students by making us more aware of multicultural issues and social injustices that occur in music education classrooms.

Syllabus

The course that I selected to transform was Current Trends in Music II, for instrumental music students (see course syllabus in the Section 4, Chapter 19). Approximately 25% of the course content was multicultural, using a variety of strategies to encourage multiculturalism, instructional strategies, assessment, and classroom dynamics (see assessment instrument in Section 4, Chapter 19). Changes were made to the original syllabus so that the course could be designated as a multicultural perspectives (MP) course (where less than 60% of the course content is multicultural in nature). Selected readings were chosen for the class to supplement the required texts and to reflect cultural diversity. General objectives in the syllabus that focused on multicultural education included the following:

- Analyze and discuss the influence of ethnicity, social class, bilingualism, abilities, disabilities, and gender on human development and music learning.
- Analyze and discuss procedures for the successful administration of school instrumental programs in culturally and socioeconomically diverse communities.

Specific class assignments that focused on multicultural education included the following:

- Complete in-class instrumental teaching presentations/ rehearsals. Teaching will include: sequence of instruction to introduce a new piece of music (chosen to meet the needs of your hypothetically diverse student population), rehearsal targeting goals for improvement, modeling, giving specific individualized feedback, and error correction and behavior modification.
- Create "Grading Criteria" and "Classroom Management Plan" handouts for your hypothetically diverse population of future band or orchestra students. Use models (Internet and others) and base your criteria on principles discussed in class. These handouts will become a part of your portfolio during student teaching and initial job interviews.
- Develop a school music budget based on models and criteria discussed in class. Rationale and justifications must include socioeconomic considerations relevant to proposed student population and the effects of their community on the booster budget and fund raising.
- Assess your intercultural conflict style using the ICS Inventory (Intercultural Conflict Style Inventory) and relate it to teacher-parent conferences and classroom interaction. Small group discussion of your ICS and mock teacher-parent conferences will be presented.

The syllabus also included the following multicultural policy statement:

- Texas State believes that freedom of thought, innovation, and creativity are fundamental characteristics of a community of scholars. To promote such a learning environment, the university has a special responsibility to seek diversity, to instill a global perspective in its students, and to nurture sensitivity, tolerance and mutual respect. Discrimination against or harassment of individuals on the basis of race, color, national origin, religion, sex, sexual orientation, age, or disability are inconsistent with the purposes of the university.

Responses from students

Students were very receptive to the integration of multicultural education into the instrumental music teacher preparation course. Many stated that they preferred considering a hypothetical student population when selecting music for the ensemble. Students enjoyed sharing ideas about instrument selection in regards to student disabilities, lower socioeconomic challenges, and gender stereotypes. After completion of the course, student teacher placements resulted in successful placements and employment for students in low socioeconomic urban school districts. Students seemed to embrace the idea of working with students of varying cultures, races, abilities, and socioeconomic backgrounds. Since the course is approximately 25% multicultural, I have not conducted systematic research in regards to the outcomes or assessment of course goals.

Strategies for other faculty members

Listed below are suggestions I have compiled since teaching this course:

- Prepare future teachers to participate in a diverse society by creating laboratory-teaching opportunities that approximate what they will find in diverse classrooms.
- Ask preservice teachers to consider a hypothetical population of students with varied backgrounds and cultures when selecting music scores.
- Provide appropriate expectations, strategies, and resources for creating a positive learning environment for students with disabilities. Nurture and encourage acceptance of students with disabilities.
- Encourage band and orchestra teachers to hold "blind" music auditions so that the race, gender, and attractiveness of the students are not factors in making decisions.
- Help public school students to create authentic musical experiences that resemble their expectations. Let students make decisions in regards to what music they perform. Help students to construct knowledge and create and compose music that is appealing to them.
- Plan curriculum for the year to include multicultural repertoire. Provide multiple examples of multicultural music for thoughtful reflection and discussion.
- Consider how preservice teachers will navigate religious and holiday music and concerts. (Not all public school students will be able perform religious repertoire or wear uniforms, depending on the personal beliefs of the student or family.)
- Help future teachers understand their school communities by exploring demographics on local and state websites such as the Texas Education Agency Public Education Information Management System (PEIMS) or any other state's Department of Education website.
- Teach future teachers to consider cultural conflict styles to facilitate parent/teacher conferences in public schools.
- Create assignments that require students to plan for and consider the socioeconomic challenges that future students will have to meet. Future band and orchestra directors can create hypothetical budgets that take into consideration students' financial and equipment needs in a typical music program.
- Counsel and encourage future teachers to be placed in internships in lower socioeconomic urban/rural settings.
- Seek additional materials in texts and websites (see Appendix).

Conclusions and Summary

In music education there exists a lack of awareness and acknowledgement of the role that culture plays in our interactions with students, parents, administrators, and audiences. Future music educators must be more responsive to the issues of race, gender, socioeconomic status, abilities, and disabilities in order to accommodate and enable students. As we prepare preservice teachers, we have a social obligation and professional responsibility to urge them to change music education to reflect and include all cultures and all students. Our new music educators must develop musicians of all colors, avoid gender bias in instrument selections, and acknowledge the varied cultures of their students through purposeful programming of concerts. Through the promotion of inherently different but valid ways of making music, we can all benefit. Curricular changes at both the university and public schools are warranted to bring about progress and social justice, and to help students to reach their potential.

References

Abeles, H. (2009). Are musical instrument gender associations changing? *Journal of Research in Music Education, 57* (2), 127–139.

Abeles, H., Porter, S. (1978). The sex-stereotyping of musical instruments. *Journal of Research in Music Education, 26* (2), 65–75.

Bradley, D. (2007). The sounds of silence: Talking race in music education. *Action, Criticism, and Theory for Music Education, 6* (4), 132–162. Retrieved from http://act.maydaygroup.org/articles/Bradley6_4.pdf

Cavitt, M. E. (2010). Cultural identities of composers represented in a state-prescribed concert band repertoire list. In M. Moore (Ed.), *Kaleidoscope of cultures: A celebration of multicultural research and practice: Proceedings of the MENC/University of Tennessee National Symposium on Multicultural Music* (pp. 17–22). Lanham, MD: Rowman & Littlefield.

Coffman, D. D., & Sehmann, K. H. (1989). Music instrument preference: Implications for music educators. *UPDATE: Applications of Research in Music Education, 7* (2), 32–34.

Conway, C. (2000). Gender and musical instrument choice: A phenomenological investigation. *Bulletin of the Council for Research in Music Education, 146,* 1–16.

Delzell, J. K., & Leppla, D. A. (1992). Gender association of musical instruments and preferences of fourth-grade students for selected instruments. *Journal of Research in Music Education, 40* (2), 93–103.

Elliot, C. A. (1995/1996). Race and gender as factors in judgments of music performances. *Bulletin of the Council for Research in Music Education, 127,* 50–56.

Eros, J. (2008). Instrument selection and gender stereotypes: A review of recent literature. *UPDATE: Applications of Research in Music Education, 27* (1), 57–64.

Fortney, P. M., Boyle, J. D., & DeCarbo, N. J. (1993). A study of middle school band students' instrument choices. *Journal of Research in Music Education, 41* (1), 28–39.

Griswold, P. A., & Chroback, D. A. (1981). Sex-role associations of music instruments and occupations by gender and major. *Journal of Research in Music Education, 29* (1), 57–62.

Johnson, C. M., & Stewart, E. E. (2004). Effect of sex identification on instrument assignment by band directors. *Journal of Research in Music Education, 52,* 130–140.

———. (2005). Effect of sex and race identification on instrument assignment by music educators. *Journal of Research in Music Education, 53,* 348–357.

Killian, J., & Satrom, S. (2011). Wind instrument preferences of elementary students based on demonstrator gender. *UPDATE: Applications of Research in Music Education, 29* (2), 13–19.

McCord, K., & Fitzgerald, M. (2006). Children with disabilities playing musical instruments. *Music Educators Journal, 92*, 46–52.

Miksza, P. (2007). Music participation and socioeconomic status as correlates of change: A longitudinal analysis of academic achievement. *Bulletin of the Council for Research in Music Education, 172*, 41–57.

Music Educators National Conference (MENC). (1994). *The school music program: A new vision*. Reston, VA: Author.

National Art Education Association (NAEA). (1994). *The national visual arts standards*. Reston, VA: Author.

Sinsabaugh, K. (2005). Understanding students who cross over gender stereotypes in musical instrument selection. *Dissertation Abstracts International, 66* (05). (UMI No. 3175728).

Walker, R. (2000). Multiculturalism and music re-attached to music education. *Philosophy of Music Education Review, 8* (spring), 31–39.

Zervoudakes, J., & Tanur, J. M. (1994). Gender and musical instruments: Winds of change? *Journal of Research in Music Education, 42*, 58–67.

Additional Texts and Materials

Anderson, W. M., & Shehan Campbell, P. (Eds.). (1996). *Multicultural perspectives in music education* (2nd ed.). Reston, VA: Music Educators National Conference.

Fitzpatrick, K. R. (2006). The effect of instrumental music participation and socioeconomic status on Ohio fourth-, sixth-, and ninth-grade proficiency test performance. *Journal of Research in Music Education, 54*, 73–84.

Gould, E. (2007). *Social justice in music education: The problem of democracy*. New York, NY: Routledge.

Hammel, A. (2011). *Teaching music to students with special needs*. New York, NY: Oxford University Press.

Kelly, S. N. (2009). *Teaching music in American society: A social and cultural understanding of teaching music*. New York, NY: Routledge.

Mixon, K. (2007). *Teaching and reaching all instrumental music students*. Lanham, MD: Rowman & Littlefield.

Oglethorpe, S. (2002). *Instrumental music for dyslexics*. Philadelphia, PA: Whurr.

Shehan Campbell, P. (1991). *Lessons from the world: A cross-cultural guide to music teaching and learning*. New York, NY: Schirmer Books.

———. (1996). *Music in cultural context: Eight views on world music education*. Reston, VA: Music Educators National Conference.

———. (2004). *Teaching music globally: Experiencing music, expressing culture*. New York, NY: Oxford University Press.

———. (2010). *Songs in their heads: Music and its meaning in children's lives* (2nd ed.). New York, NY: Oxford University Press.

Volk, T. M. (2004). *Music, education, and multiculturalism: Foundations and principles*. New York, NY: Oxford University Press.

Wade, B. C. (2004). *Thinking musically: Experiencing music, expressing culture*. New York, NY: Oxford University Press.

12

COLLEGE OF SCIENCE AND ENGINEERING

Culturally Relevant Mathematics

Selina Vásquez Mireles, Sonya R. Rahrovi, and Fernando Vásquez

We are entering a new educational millennium in the United States; political views in education are shifting. For example, one facet that has changed education is the No Child Left Behind Act of 2001 (NCLB). The NCLB is strewn with high accountability standards that have spread nationwide. Some states have only reluctantly moved toward accepting accountability standards set forth by the U.S. government, but Texas was the model state from which NCLB was formulated (McBeath, Reyes, & Ehrlander, 2008).

The importance of understanding the essence of NCLB stems from the embedded policy mandates of high-stakes testing throughout the United States. Texas, however, dealt with high accountability measures before the 1990s (McBeath et al., 2008). More importantly, high-stakes testing in the form of the Texas Assessment of Knowledge and Skills (TAKS) (TEA, 2010) has been incrementally tightened via raising the bar of what is a passable score. High-stakes testing has increased the pressures to pass core courses such as mathematics. As students progress through their academic careers, they are faced with more accountability. Students in Texas are having a much more difficult time passing science and mathematics (TEA, 2010). This is especially true for Hispanics, the population focus of this chapter.

In March 2010 President Obama proposed revisions to NCLB, with an underlying focus on equity. Obama's proposal includes accountability; preparation of college- and career-ready students; great teachers and great leaders; meeting the needs of ELLs and diverse learners; a complete education; successful, safe, and healthy students; and fostering innovation and excellence. In order to create a much more equitable playing field, the Obama administration has suggested making accountability much more flexible, preparing students for careers as well as college, using disaggregated data properly, and creating effective teachers and leaders (NCLB, 2001). Of course, Obama's plan revisits English Language Learners (ELLs) and diverse students. Included in this group are not only Hispanic students who lack sufficient English skills, but also

Native Americans, the homeless, migrants, special groups with disabilities, and neglected children (NCLB, 2001). In addition, Obama's policy suggestions to NCLB include a refocus of literacy with emphases in science, technology, engineering, and mathematics—again, increasing college- and career-readiness skills. Crucial to the proposed changes in NCLB is addressing high-poverty communities and services that support a compendium of communities and families. Afterschool programs will be a crucial factor in supporting families and communities as well. Finally, under the title of Fostering Innovation and Excellence, within NCBL is a new proposed mandate that resembles a manifesto encouraging states and school districts to "race to the top" while increasingly challenging student success (NCLB, 2001). Moreover, one interesting twist is the consideration of public school choice for the public—running counter to the Obama administration's political ideology. In any case, Obama's proposed changes to NCLB appear to be comprehensive with a few underlying themes. Thus, one way of understanding Obama's proposed NCLB changes is by keeping in mind the nucleus of equity, which appears to be strewn throughout the NCLB revisions. It is wise to remember that Obama's NCLB policy changes must be passed by Congress. Generally, the congressional process involves debate, changes in policy, and other dialectical processes that may change the intent of histhe NCLB revisions.

At the same time, we are experiencing vast changes in our demographic population. Vásquez (2006), a culturalist, made an interesting observation when researching the disparities of educational levels among Hispanic men:

> The study of Latino/as has garnered additional attention as the population continues to grow at unprecedented rates. Latinos are observed in large cities such as Houston, Dallas, San Antonio, El Paso, New York, Chicago, and other cities with growing Latino populations. There has been a substantial increase from 1990 to 2000 according to the Institute for Latino Studies at the University of Notre Dame (*Latino population counts: 1990–2000*, 2004). Consequently, demographers have predicated a general swelling of the Latino population, which has not been seen before in the U.S. Yet, the educational levels for Latinos have not met expectations when compared to white Americans (Jasinski, 2000; Valencia, 1991, 2002). (Vásquez, 2006, p. 1)

What is noteworthy here is that Hispanics are taking a backseat in a world that is becoming more and more complex. With complexity comes a need for the attainment of higher level educational skills.

Accountability mandates a need to increase learning for all students. It is forecast that students of Hispanic descent will experience more setbacks as demographics change throughout the United States (Pew Hispanic Center, 2010). There are many theories about why the educational data on Hispanics is so discouraging. The data reported from the TEA (2010) has consistently demonstated that Hispanics are in a downward spiral in the area of mathematics.

A possible solution to poor mathematics scores and mathematics learning in school districts across Texas could include pedagogical methods that contain and involve multiculturalism. Aspects of multiculturalism are great tools for teaching mathematics (Sleeter, 1997). González, Moll, and Amanti (2005) noted that Hispanic students do bring relevant content skills to the classroom, but they exist within a different cultural context. Thus, scaffolding a student's culturally relevant skills with academic areas such as mathematics is crucial in creating learning. Finally, constructivism is a beneficial tool for many mathematics teachers; it allows for the incorporation of cultural and social components of a student's everyday life (Snowman, McCown, & Biehler, 2008). Vital cultural and social relevant pedagogy that will enhance mathematics learning should not be discounted.

History of the Discipline

In this section, we describe the mathematics culture and use it to provide a platform for the infusion of culturally relevant content and instruction. In addition, we present the rationale for focusing on preservice mathematics teachers and developmental mathematics students.

Why Multicultural Education Tenets Are Needed in Mathematics

There is substantial data in the literature to confirm the population shifts throughout the United States—especially in some heavily Hispanic-laden states (Pew Hispanic Center, 2010). Even though there has been a rise in ethnocentrism (Vásquez, 2006) in the last few years because of a general economic slowdown in the United States, the nation must continue to educate its population or face fierce competition from other countries.

Many national concerns rest in our educational system. More specifically, subjects such as mathematics need to be taught to all students. Students of all ages and races continue to struggle with mathematics (TEA, 2010). Data provide a picture of students in general struggling with mathematics across Texas Assessment of Knowledge and Skills (TAKS) scores, and this is particularly true for Hispanics (TEA, 2010).

The TEA has provided data that is difficult to muddle through and not clearly disaggregated, which has is an issue that the Obama revised plan has addressed. In any case, TEA results for the primary 2010 TAKS scores in math for all eleventh-grade high school students throughout Texas indicates that the pass rate was only 85%, while White students had a 97% pass rate (TEA, 2010). Tenth graders who tested in math across Texas high schools had a 69% pass rate, while White students had an 84% pass rate. Ninth-grade Hispanics math test takers throughout Texas had a 65% pass rate in 2010, and White students had an 82% pass rate (TEA, 2010). Hispanics in the eighth grade, too, did not fare as well as White students in math, with 76% passing versus 88%, respectively. For math students in the seventh grade across Texas we see similar patterns, with a 77% pass rate for Hispanics versus 89% for White students (TEA, 2010). The point is clear: Hispanics lag behind White students in math. It is important to note that these percentages are derived from first-time or first-round math TAKS test takers (TEA, 2010).

Expertise in mathematics has been shown to improve one's way of life. However, a lack of mathematics educators has plagued the United States at the same time that the population of the United States is drastically changing as Hispanics become the majority people of color. To increase the expertise of mathematics in the United States, an increase of mathematics teachers is needed, and new pedagogical techniques are needed not only to increase the retention and understanding of mathematics but also to make mathematics relevant to the increasing population of Hispanics.

Mathematics Teachers

The National Council of Mathematics Teachers (NCTM, 2008) follows five foundational principles: curriculum, instruction, and assessment; equity; advocacy; professional development; and research. The vision is "that all students have access to the highest quality mathematics teaching and learning ... [through] a world where everyone is enthused about mathematics, sees the value and beauty of mathematics, and is empowered by the opportunities mathematics affords." Furthermore, NCTM's perspective on equity is to "advance knowledge about, and infuse in every aspect of mathematics education, a culture of equity where everyone is empowered by the opportunities mathematics afford." To achieve equity, teachers must have "high expectations, culturally relevant practices, attitudes that are free of bias, and unprejudiced beliefs [to] expand and maximize the potential for learning" and students must have "access to and engage in challenging, rigorous, and meaningful mathematical experience" (NCTM, 2008).

Stutz (2010) reported that new research indicates that having teachers of color improves the achievement of students of color. He found that "[teachers of color] better understand cultural differences." He further quotes Ed Fuller, an education consultant and associate director of the University Council for Educational Administration at the University of Texas at Austin, that "if you have a predominantly Hispanic or Black student body, studies indicate it is wise to hire teachers who are the same race or ethnicity.... It is important for role modeling and pushing those students to go to college" (Stutz, 2010).

Hispanics

National reports and news articles state that the Hispanic population has become the second largest ethnic group within the United States (U.S. Census Bureau, 2010a). In fact, the U.S. Census Bureau (2010a) states that the estimated Hispanic population on July 1, 2009 was 48.4 million, or 16% of the nation's total population—the nation's largest ethnic or race minority. There was a 3.1% increase in the Hispanic population from July 1, 2008 and July 1, 2009, a total addition of 1.4 million Hispanics, which makes Hispanics the fastest-growing racial/ethnic group. When reviewing the worldwide population of Hispanics, the United States ranks second after Mexico. By July 1, 2050, it is predicted that there will be 132.8 million Hispanics (30% of the nation's population) living in the United States (U.S. Census Bureau, 2010a).

Although the population of public education students is dynamic, there is a steady increase of school-age Hispanic students (Aud et al., 2010; El Nasser & Overberg, 2010). El Nasser and Overberg (2010) reported that "about one out of four five-year-olds will be Hispanic" in the kindergarten class of 2010–2011. In 2009, 26%of children younger than five were Hispanic (U.S. Census Bureau, 2010a). More than 62% of students were students of color in the 2008–2009 school year in Texas (Stutz, 2010). Furthermore, there is an increase in students who do not speak English at home (Aud et al., 2010; El Nasser & Overberg, 2010; U.S. Census Bureau, 2010a). Nationwide, 76% of Hispanics five and older spoke Spanish in 2008 (U.S. Census Bureau, 2010a). El Nasser and Overberg (2010) found that the percentage of five-year-olds who speak English at home is dropping, "from 81% in 2000 to about 78%," and that Spanish speakers at home are increasing, "from 14% to 16%."

Unfortunately, the increase in the nation's Hispanic population does not mean an increase of the Hispanic population in higher education.

The Southern Regional Education Board (2010) states that the "the fastest-growing racial and ethnic groups in the United States today generally have had lower education attainments levels." In a survey of 1,500 Hispanics, the "largest percentage of survey respondents had not completed high school (33 percent)" (AAC&U, 2010). The National Center for Education Statistics (2007) found that "the percentage of 16- to 24-year-olds who were high school status dropouts was higher among Hispanics than among Blacks, Whites, and Asian/Pacific Islanders" in 2005. In addition, the U.S. Census Bureau (2010a) found that while 62% of Hispanics twenty-five and older had at least a high school education in 2009, only 13% of the Hispanic population twenty-five and older had a bachelor's degree or higher in 2009. Some researchers (Lederman, 2010) recommend "another set of metrics that institutional and other leaders can use to measure their own success—or lack of it—in getting students from Latino backgrounds interested in science, technology, engineering, and mathematics (or STEM) disciplines and, ultimately, to degrees"; serving not simply enrolling. Van Horne (2009) found that there are seven barriers encountered by Hispanics entering higher education: (a) competing demands of multiple responsibilities, (b) financial issues, (c) Hispanic cultural beliefs, values, and attitudes toward education, (d) transitioning from high school to college, (e) failing or repeating a course, (f) starting college in developmental courses, and (g) personal attitudes about college. She elaborates that "Latino students often find themselves diverted to developmental college classes based on placement test scores, frequently due to poor English skills or weak foundational college skills" (Van Horne, 2009, p. 4).

Critical Thinkers and Problem Solvers

Mathematics is linked to needed skills in the workforce and higher paying positions (Pepitone, 2009). Jennifer Courter, a research mathematician, was quoted in Needleman (2009) as stating that "[mathematics] is the science of problem-solving"; Steinglass (2010) found that "math is the most selective of cognitive ability" when compared to other majors. Problem-solving skills and cognitive abilities are needed in the workforce according to Ed Koc, director of research at the National Association of Colleges and Employers (NACE), who notes that "math is at the crux of who gets paid... if you have those skills, you are an extremely valuable asset." He continues that "so few grads offer math skills, and those who can are rewarded" (Koc quoted in Pepitone, 2009). The reward comes as an annual income of $94,160 for a mathematician (Needleman, 2009); the median household income for the United States in 2008 was $52,029 (U.S. Census Bureau, 2010b). Pepitone (2009) found that the "top 15 highest-earning college degrees all have one thing in common—math skills." In order to create an "extremely valuable asset" to the workforce (Pepitone, 2009), mathematics education must be equitable for all students. As the NCTM (2008) states, this requires including cultural relevance in mathematics education.

The authors of this chapter focused on two populations: preservice mathematics teachers and developmental mathematics students. By teaching cultural relevance and including cultural relevance in lessons to preservice teachers, the impact on the next generation is increased. The preservice mathematics teachers become agents of change and enter the educational workforce with equity already in mind. The choice to focus on developmental mathematics came from the disproportionate number of Hispanics in developmental mathematics. At the authors' institution, Hispanics are approximately 24% of the developmental mathematics student population (Institutional Research, 2010).

Personal Story about MCTRI Impact

It is students' academic growth that is at stake, and consequently, the state of the nation is the primary motivating factor in transforming mathematics courses for mathematics preservice teachers and developmental mathematics students. More courses in general, and mathematics and science courses in particular, are needed. The institution where this project was launched has only six undergraduate courses in the College of Science that carry the multicultural designation[1] and, proudly, two of these are in mathematics.

There is also a content-specific outcome that inspired this project: the rejuvenation of the interdisciplinary nature of mathematics. It is a popular misconception that mathematics does not involve reading and writing, just the computation of numbers. Yet, the keen skills that mathematics is known to facilitate—such as problem solving and critical thinking—are fostered primarily through the language of mathematics. Thus, it is necessary to provide authentic mathematical experiences to students; this means that diversification of curriculum and pedagogy is imperative. In order to get the most knowledge and skills from studying mathematics, it cannot be studied in a vacuum.

In a similar fashion, there was interest in the hypothesis that science is the natural cultural context for mathematics. The uncoupling of mathematics and science by educational institutions has the potential to produce dissonance that may inhibit our society's mathematical, scientific, and technological advancement. Students enter a science class and learn that *displacement* is the term for *distance* in mathematics class (Mireles, 2009). The development of the correlation model (Mireles, 2009) provides teachers with a mechanism to reunite mathematics and science as it is in the real world. The lessons that adhered to this model were studied for their effectiveness in increasing academic performance in both disciplines.

What Affects—Students, Teaching

Several lessons were created and field-tested in this project. Below are brief descriptions of the lessons. The development of the lessons was informed by the three-part model described in Gutstein, Lipman, Hernandez, and de los Reyes (1997): "The three components are (a) building on students' informal mathematical knowledge and building on students' cultural and experiential knowledge, (b) developing tools of critical mathematical thinking and critical thinking about knowledge in general, and (c) orientations to students' culture and experience" (p. 709). In addition, the three approaches to multicultural education—celebratory, critical, and transformative—described by Bruch, Jehangir, Jacobs, and Ghere (2004) informed the lesson development.

Cell Size and Shape: Measurement, Geometry, Life Science (Preservice)

This lesson focuses on the units of measurement needed to measure cell components and overall cell size. In addition, the lesson investigates the geometry of cell shape. Sickle cell anemia is then discussed, including the populations that are predisposed to the condition and the role it plays in geographic locations that are more likely to have malaria.

Riding the Waves: Trigonometry, Physics, Earth Science (Preservice)

There are many types of waves, such as sound waves, heat waves, ocean waves, and sine waves. This lesson provides students with a platform of wave terminology and the mathematical trigonometric functions that are used to model the curves. Various real-world examples of waves are discussed, including those generated by the 2004 tsunami and Hurricane Katrina in 2005.

Scope and Sequence: Geology, Number Theory, Life Science (Preservice)

The various mathematical sequences such as arithmetic, geometric, and alternating are utilized to facilitate a lesson on inductive reasoning. Geological sequences are investigated, modeled, and used to review historical time periods. In particular, the Fibonacci sequence is studied, and many naturally occurring examples are analyzed, including leaf formations and new cell growth on plants.

Don't Tell Me Moore: Algebra, Physics (Preservice)

The teacher-centered approach to the distance formula is presented and compared to the Moore Method (also known as the Texas Method (Dancis & Davidson, 1970)). The ideas of distance and displacement are reviewed from both a mathematics and science perspective. The lesson provides students with an opportunity to contrast the instructional methods, as well as comment on the classroom culture that is generated through each approach.

Geometry of Dance: Geometry, Algebra (Developmental Mathematics)

Using movie clips of individuals "dancing" (that is, partipating in, for example, football, karate, dance, ice skating, or boxing), students visualize geometric transformations (reflections, translations, and rotations). In particular, the *cumbia*, a traditional Mexican American dance, is shown to provide students with a geometric transformation experience. *Tejano* history (history of Hispanics in Texas) is discussed, and Spanish terms for these movements are highlighted. Students are also asked to extend the idea of geometric transformations to algebraic transformations.

Waiting at the Checkpoint: Queuing Theory, Geometry (Developmental Mathematics)

Many individuals find themselves waiting in lines—at the grocery store, gas station, and cafeteria to name a few. This lesson provides cultural waiting time experiences to students in order to generate authentic data to construct queuing formulas. Scenarios include waiting in lines at the border checkpoints and the "Dollar Dance" in *quinceañeras* (Hispanic girls' sixteenth birthday celebrations) and weddings.

Language of Calculators: Reasoning, Algebra (Developmental Mathematics)

Since technology in general and calculators in particular were launched primarily in the United States, English terms are used to denote functions. These English terms do not always translate well to other languages. For example, a computer *mouse* in English is not referred to as a *ratón* in Spanish. This lesson ties English and Spanish calculator terminology together and uses the calculator language to build mathematical operations. The history of calculators is included, and the influence of Ramón Verea, a Spaniard living in New York, is noted.

Syllabus and Teaching

Both courses sequenced the lessons in a manner that provided a seamless approach to the content. The outlines show how the course includes multicultural aspects. Examples of both courses' outlines are included in Tables 1 and 2 (see Appendix B).

First and foremost in regards to pedagogy is the use of best practices. The predominant learning theory of the time, constructivism, asserts that students learn best through a process that involves their own social and cultural experiences (Snowman et al., 2008). Constructivism is a worldview that utilizes pedagogical methodology that engages a student's way of learning, coupling their background and the curriculum (Snowman et al., 2008). More specifically, constructivism "holds that meaningful learning occurs when people actively try to make sense of the world—when they construct an interpretation of how and why things are—by filtering new ideas and experiences through existing knowledge structures" (Snowman et al., 2008, p. 324). For instance, the preservice students visited local theme parks to 'ride the waves.' Experiencing real-world manifestations of mathematics and science gives new meaning to contextualized problem-solving opportunities.

The pedagogical approaches used in the lessons were aligned to culturally responsive teaching, as defined by Geneva Gay (Gay, 2007; Gay, n.d.). Specifically, there was a concerted effort to identify and utilize students' cultural receptors as opposed to employing the standard mathematics delivery. Several research results contributed to this shift. Phuong-Mai, Terlouw, Pilot, and Elliott (2009) conducted a study that suggests that although cooperative learning is a "best practice," it may need to be adapted for various ethnicities.

Another pedagogical tool of the preservice course was the review of mathematics multicultural research. Examples include Uri Treisman's research on the calculus study habits of different ethnic groups, and Jane Elliott's Blue Eyes/Brown Eyes Exercise (Armendariz & Hasty, 1997; Elliott, 2006;Peters, 1985). Mathematics performance data on various ethnic groups were explored, especially data from the Trends in International Mathematics and Science Study (TIMSS), which evaluates mathematics and science achievement of fourth- and eighth-grade students around the world. The TIMSS report (Gonzales et al., 2009) also provided a platform to discuss similarities and differences in teaching strategies in other nations. In addition, preservice students were asked to work in groups to develop a correlated mathematics and science lesson plan with a multicultural flavor. This assignment required students to research multicultural teaching strategies and allowed them to incorporate their own cultural knowledge in the lesson.

Resistance and Responses—From Colleagues, Students

There were colleagues and students who were in favor of the transformation and there were some who were against it. Some colleagues appreciated the background work and readily employed the lessons in order to transform their classes as well. Other colleagues wished to maintain their autonomy, and felt that these attempts imposed on their academic freedom. One obstacle that surfaced was the anxiety that arose from the lack of background knowledge of the cultural aspects. For example, one instructor who learned the *cumbia* just two days before the lesson felt that the lesson did not have the same authenticity it would have had if it had been taught by an instructor with more practice with the dance. Some faculty believed that culturally relevant teaching meant that they had to customize their lessons to the specific cultures of the students they were teaching at any given time. This misunderstanding made them shy away from the project. Future activities will draw from the lessons learned by Schoem (1993) and other recent professional development activities.

Most students, on the other hand, favored the multicultural transformation. In particular, students identified personally with the cultural aspects of the curriculum and instruction, though the lesson may not have been crafted with that intent. For example, in the geometric transformations lesson, the variety of examples—football, karate, dance, ice skating, and boxing—provided an opportunity for each person to relate to the movements. Veterans in the class quickly noted that a military marching routine is another example of a geometric transformation. Some preliminary results for the Geometry of Dance lesson point to the existence of a "novelty" effect. Students who are far-removed from the cultural aspects tend to find the information more intriguing, and thus, are more likely to perform better. Students who expressed their discontent with the cultural infusion tended to favor more traditional methods of instruction. Holt, in *How Children Fail* (1995), refers to these students as "answer-centered." They are more than likely successful in lecture-style classrooms and are accustomed to memorization of rules and formulas in mathematics. The use of culturally relevant curriculum lends itself to the use of problem-centered curriculum, which is counter to the answer-centered ways. Another interesting outcome worthy of future study occurred when an instructor used the name Pratap Puri, a name common in India, in a word problem. Of the nineteen students taking the exam, five students changed the name to a more common American name such as Jill and John, claiming that the Indian name was a distraction.

Research Results

Culturally relevant lessons were administered to preservice teachers and developmental mathematics students. Each group was administered pre- and post-tests to evaluate the effectiveness of the lessons.

Preservice Mathematics Teachers

In spring 2007, eleven preservice mathematics teachers enrolled in an undergraduate middle-school mathematics teaching course. A comprehensive mathematics pre-test was administered on the first day of class, and a topical science pre-test was administered on the day of each correlated lesson. On the last day of class, a comprehensive mathematics and science post-test was administered. Questions on the pre- and post-tests were identical, and all questions were in a multiple-choice format.

A within-subjects t-test was run to assess the change in content knowledge from pre-test to post-test scores. Statistically significant results were found in both mathematics ($p = 0.004$) and science ($p = 0.005$), indicating gains in both mathematics and science content knowledge. Mathematics test scores improved from a pre-test mean of 91.27 ($SD = 4.31$) to a post-test mean of 96.73 ($SD = 3.93$). Science test scores improved from a pre-test mean of 66.36 ($SD = 11.20$) to a post-test mean of 78.18 ($SD = 11.68$). A student from the class remarked that he had never heard of the Fibonacci sequence prior to this course, and that "its existence in nature and seeing it in the real world helped me to master the concept." The same student also commented that "the exploration of the Fibonacci sequence was particularly interesting because it was coupled with a field trip ... [to an on-campus nature educational location] where a 'hands-on' experience was provided."

These comments indicate that the cultural relevance of correlating mathematics to science that students have some familiarity with aided the conceptual understanding of the mathematics.

Developmental Mathematics Students

In spring 2010, ninety students were taught the Geometry of Dance lesson in a developmental mathematics course. The course is the first in a sequence of two developmental mathematics courses. Students in the developmental mathematics course were administered a pre-test and post-test immediately prior to and after the lesson. The pre- and post-test contained ten identical questions in a multiple-choice format. The lesson plan had five objectives, and two questions on the pre-/post-test were aligned to each objective.

A one-sample t-test was run on the delta between the post- and pre-test scores. The result was statistically significant at $p < 0.001$ (mean = .113, SD = .196), indicating that students' content knowledge of geometric transformations increased.

In a survey administered to the students, 14% of the students who responded to a question asking what they liked best about the lesson remarked on the visual nature of the lesson, citing "the videos" and the "pictures." This visual aid, as well as concrete experiences such as the *cumbia* dance, which is assumed to be familiar to the Tejanos in the population, may be an indication as to why scores increased for this particular objective.

Strategies for Other Faculty Members

There are several strategies that mathematics faculty can use to transform their classes. First and foremost, it should be noted that this is a process, a fun one at that, and it takes time. The easiest way to begin is to ask your students for ideas. A quick survey will allow you to connect with them personally and begin the process of identifying their cultural backgrounds and/or interests. Another way to include culturally relevant material is to have students write a mathematics autobiography. Because popular culture condones the dislike of mathematics, and this is a mathematics class, this is a sure-fire way to "air out" mathematics anxieties and horror stories. It is also a way for an instructor to get some background information, especially prerequisite knowledge and skills, about his/her students. Also, don't reinvent the wheel. Many individuals have developed great multicultural mathematics lessons. Take advantage of the vast resources that are available (see Appendix A). Mathematicians are a colorful group, and their stories provide a nice personal touch to the mathematics being studied. An easy lesson adaptation is to tell a brief story about the mathematician. An analysis by Epstein, Mendick, and Moreau (2010) reveals that popular culture may foster negative images of mathematics and mathematicians, and that this may hinder mathematical advancement. Most ancient cultures had profound mathematical impacts. Utilize their products, such as the calendar and the pyramids, to make mathematical connections. See Troutman and McCoy's (2008) study for effective strategies for incorporating mathematics history and sample lessons.

In addition to the methods noted above, there are four guiding principles that were derived from this project. Each of the principles is described below.

Exploit the Idea That Science Provides the Cultural Disciplinary Context for Math

There is an intuitive notion that mathematics and science complement each other. Traditionally, mathematics looks to science for applied situations, and science turns to mathematics for process. This relationship was extended through the development of the correlation model (Mireles, 2009). By capitalizing on the natural synergy between the two disciplines, additional cultural opportunities present themselves.

Aim for Conceptual Connections

Best practices should always be at the forefront of any instructional endeavor. In mathematics, conceptual understanding is favored over skill attainment. The cultural ties that are made should be substantive and linked to mathematical concepts. This perspective debunks the argument that ethnomathematics is "a watered-down version of 'real mathematics'" (Gutiérrez, 2000).

Frame Concepts in a Real-World Context

Mathematics educators and standards are making a push to authenticate the problems that students are asked to do. Classical word problems, like coin problems and mixture problems, are valued, but real-world contextual situations are more prized. The cultural inclusions should be substantive, and providing a real-world context is more likely to yield substance. In a study by Díez-Palomar, Simic, and Varley (2006), students worked on problems related to school and their neighborhood. Moreover, Appelbaum, Friedler, Ortiz, and Wolff (2009) propose that using problems with an international perspective is a step toward internationalizing university mathematics curriculum.

Diversify the Diversity through Multiple Cultural Ties

Although it should not be forced, there should be an attempt to "get more bang for your buck." Attempt to utilize various cultural connections. For example, a geometric exploration of a traditional piñata includes a discussion of Marco Polo and the sociological impact of his travels. The cultural inclusion of the piñata opens the door to several cultural ties, all within the scope of one lesson (see more references in Appendix A).

Conclusions/Summary

It is clear that mathematics is important to society. The research results presented above showed gains in the content areas of mathematics and science, indicating that cultural factors play a role in academic success. A culturally relevant curriculum can be developed to focus on mathematics knowledge and skills. There are seven examples included in this chapter, as well as resources to support the creation of culturally relevant content and teaching.

Almost all lesson plans can be built within a social constructivists' framework, which ties in culturally relevant mathematics lessons. Research continues to grow in regards to how a constructivist position can enhance all content areas. Mathematics, in particular, appears to be a difficult content area for many Hispanics, so it is imperative that mathematics is culturally relevant (Snowman et al., 2008). To further illustrate, imagine being suddenly let loose in a culture that is foreign to us: Could we survive in a new environment that involves learning a new language, new mannerisms, new knowledge, etc.? Probably not as easily as we would like to, because we have not encompassed the relevant social constructivism embedded within those cultures that would enable us to transfer those survival skills. In contrast, imagine a student who has come from an environment that is sheltered from the mainstream culture. She is intelligent, but cannot grasp all these new cultural features presented to her, much less mathematics material that is situated in the dominant culture.

The U.S. educational infrastructure has not developed a strong structure that serves Hispanics. This can no longer be ignored with the shifting of the demographics in general—for example, the aging baby boomers. Baby boomers are expected to retire in droves without any substantial workforce to continue paying for social security benefits and generating tax revenues; this is just one of the economic realities beginning to loom over us. These undeniable circumstances make Hispanics, as the fastest-growing population in the United States, to maintain the fiscal and monetary soundness of this country. Nevertheless, policy makers, Congress, lobby groups, associations, and others who have a vested interest in planning for our educational future are not preparing for these demographic shifts that will also have dramatic educational implications in the long run. Besides training for an employable workforce, Hispanic students and other students of color require an equitable share of the educational resources in order to maintain a modest standard of living (Acuna, 2003; Vásquez, 2006, p. 2).

Researchers will continue to face Hispanics who do not have a strong European American cultural base, but come with their own funds of knowledge (González, Moll, & Amanti, 2005). In other words, Hispanic students who come to study mathematics may come with valuable skills. They could have learned to count by working the fields with their parents, but they do not recognize numbers because they are not situated in a cornfield. Or, Hispanic students may have learned to cook and sew, which involves quantitative skills, but again, they may not be able to make that crucial link between the traditional mathematics curriculum and their culture. There are ways to scaffold these mathematics lessons with a Hispanic student's cultural background. As demographic data (Murdock et al., 2003) continues to inform us about the upward swing of Hispanics in this country, researchers will be faced with a growing number of research questions (Vásquez, 2006).

Appendix A

References and Resources to Support Course Transformation

Atweh, B., Forgasz, H., & Nebres, B. (Eds.). (2001). *Sociocultural research on mathematics education: An international perspective.* Mahwah, NJ: Lawrence Erlbaum Associates.

This book uses a sociocultural construct to investigate mathematics education research. Various populations are highlighted and their effects on real-world issues inthe mathematics classroom. Issues about gender are also included.

Bazin, M., Tamez, M., & the Exploratorium Teacher Institute. (2002). *Math and science across cultures: Activities and investigations from the Exploratorium.* New York, NY: New Press.

This book provides fourteen activities that integrate mathematics, science, and culture.

Greer, B., Mukhopadhyay, S., Powell, A. B., & Nelson-Barber, S. (Eds.). (2009). *Culturally responsive mathematics education.* New York, NY: Routledge.

This book contains background information as well as information about teaching and learning. Uniquely, the book has a chapter about assessment, includes Latina mothers' perceptions, and addresses the college setting.

Ortiz-Franco, L., Hernandez, N. G., & De La Cruz, Y. (Eds.). (1999). *Changing the faces of mathematics: Perspectives on Latinos.* Reston, VA: National Council of Teachers of Mathematics.

This book provides background information about mathematics issues related to Latinos. Some intervention programs are described.

Rodriguez, A. J., & Kitchen, R. S. (Eds.). (2005). *Preparing mathematics and science teachers for diverse classrooms: Promising strategies for transformative pedagogy.* Mahwah, NJ: Lawrence Erlbaum Associates.

This book provides a theoretical basis and practical strategies to counter resistance to learning to teach for diversity.

Gorski, P. C. (2001). *Multicultural education and the Internet: Intersections and integrations.* New York, NY: McGraw-Hill Higher Education.

This book lists twenty-five sites that are pertinent to mathematics and science issues of inclusion, access, and multicultural teaching principles.

Kitchen, R. S., & Lear, J. M. (2000). Mathematizing Barbie. In W. G. Secada (Ed.), *Changing the faces of mathematics: Perspectives on multiculturalism and gender equity* (pp. 67–73). Reston, VA: National Council of Teachers of Mathematics.

This book chapter describes a lesson about the disproportionate dimensions of Barbie.

Lara-Alecio, R., Irby, B. J., & Morales-Aldana, L. (1998, November). A mathematics lesson from the Mayan civilization. *Teaching Children Mathematics, 5* (3), 154–158.

This article provides a lesson about the mathematics of the Mayans.

McCollough, C., McDonald, J., & Canales, J. (2009, April). *The power of family science learning events: All stakeholders benefit.* Center for Educational Development, Evaluation and Research Yearbook. Corpus Christi, TX: Texas A&M University–Corpus Christi.

This work provides a culturally connected mathematics planning handout.

Appendix B

Table 1. Middle School Mathematics Teaching Outline

Day	Objective
H	*Principles & Standards* Define problem solving *TEKS/TAKS/TExES* Distribute & discuss 6–8 Math TEKS **HW:** Review 6–8 Math TEKS for patterns *Math* Solve Magic Squares problem & reflect (feelings & process)
T	*Principles & Standards* Discuss the NCTM Principles & Standards (Principles; Content & Process Standards) **HW:** Review NCTM Principles (equity, curriculum, teaching, learning, assessment, & technology). Each pair of students will take one of the principles and prepare a brief presentation about it. *TEKS/TAKS/TExES* Discuss the patterns in the 6–8 Math TEKS **HW:** From the 6–8 Math TEKS—Number, Operation, & Quantitative Reasoning Develop a content list *Math* Discuss the Real Number System & its subsets Discuss the Real Number Line **HW:** Demonstrate the derivative of pi, 2^(1/2), e

Day	Objective
H	*Principles & Standards* Present NCTM Principles (1/2) *TEKS/TAKS/TExES* Discuss the 6–8 Math TEKS—Number, Operation, & Quantitative Reasoning content list **HW:** From the 6–8 Math TAKS—"Objective 1: The student will demonstrate an understanding of numbers, operations, and quantitative reasoning"; expand on the content list *Math* Discuss basic axioms (closure, associative, commutative, distributive, identity, inverse) Review the origin and justification of pi, 2^(1/2), e
T	*Principles & Standards* Present NCTM Principles (2/2) Discuss issues surrounding the principles (equity—NCLB; curriculum—New Math, Back to the Basics; teaching—experiential learning, knowing math is doing math; learning—skill & drill; assessment—enhances student learning, alternative methods; technology—negates building of fundamental skills) *TEKS/TAKS/TExES* Discuss the 6–8 Math TEKS/TAKS content list **HW:** From the TExES 4–8 continue to expand on the content list
H	*Principles & Standards* Discuss Number & Operations Standard for Grades 6–8 *TEKS/TAKS/TExES* Discuss the 6–8 Math TEKS/TAKS/TExES content list Have students do TAKS/TExES problems and discuss the connection between objective/domain-competency to problem
T	*Math* Do Fraction/Decimal/Percent (F/D/P) activity **HW:** Find F/D/P models
H	*Math* Present F/D/P models *Fraction Models* Measurement—number line, fraction strips Region or area Part to whole *Decimal Models* Decimal square *Percent Models* 100-unit square
T	**HW:** Find definitions of F/D/P
H	*Math* Finish presentation of F/D/P models Discuss F/D/P definitions and problems *Science* Chemistry
T	*Math* Discuss Ratio & Proportion definitions and problems Do Ratio & Proportion activity **HW**: Find Ratio & Proportion models

Day	Objective
H	*Science* Life Science
T	*Math* Discuss Exponent definitions and problems Do Exponent activity **HW**: Find Exponent models *Science* Life Science
H	*Science* Space
F	Dinosaur Park
T	**Math** Discuss Characterizing Numbers definitions and problems Do Characterizing Numbers activity **HW**: Find Characterizing Numbers models
H	*Science* Physics
T	*Math* Discuss Sequence definitions and problems Do Sequence activity **HW**: Find Sequence models
H	*Science* Earth
F	Aquarena Springs
H	Correlated Lesson—Research
T	Correlated Lesson—Process (template, observation instrument, sample, video)
H	*Principles & Standards* Process: problem solving **HW**: Van De Walle Ch4 p. 59 #1, 2, 3, 6*, 10,11 & #1, 2*
T	*Principles & Standards* Process: reasoning & proof **HW**: T&L Mid Gr Math pp. 21–28 #1–21 ("one" problem per section)
H	*Principles & Standards* Process: communication
T	*Principles & Standards* Process: connections
H	*Principles & Standards* Process: representation **HW**: T&L Mid Gr Math pp.77–91 #1, 9, 18, 19, 21, 25
F	Sea World

Table 2. Developmental Mathematics Outline

Day	Objective
H	Syllabus Definition of algorithm, *Pre-algebra:* Definitions of whole number vs. integers, sets vs. subsets
T	*Pre-algebra* o Order of integers o Operations • Add, Subtract, Multiply, & Divide • Develop algorithms • Address positive and negative numbers
H	*Pre-algebra* o Order of Operations o Estimation/Rounding *Pre-homework*: geometry definitions included in lesson 4.
T	*Geometry*: Go over basic geometry definitions—points, line segments, angles, etc. *Measurement:* Calculate values of missing angles *Pre-homework: polygon definitions/Handout for Day 5*
H	*Geometry:* Polygons/Triangles o Types of Polygons o Triangles • Types • Triangle inequality theorem: How do we know if we have a triangle? (Good exercise with greater than, less than) • Pythagorean Theorem and its converse: How to classify triangles? (no irrational numbers here)
T	*Geometry:* o Polygons—Classifying Quadrilaterals o Going beyond Euclidean Geometry o Geometry of Dance
H	*Measurement* o Linear measurement of geometric, 2D objects o Calculate perimeter and area problems *Pre-homework: statistics definitions/handout for Day 8*
T	*Statistics* o Data Collection o Graphs: bar graphs and stem & leaf plot. Create bar graphs and stem & leaf plots using whole numbers & integers. (Note: pie charts will be included later with irrational numbers)
H	*Probability*: Counting
T	*Probability:* Permutations/combinations o Differences o Tree diagrams

Day	Objective
H	*Intro to Algebra:* Simplify linear expressions o Combine like terms o Distributive property
T	*Intro to Algebra:* o Evaluate expressions o Difference between expressions and equations
H	*Intro to Algebra:* Solve equations o Addition Principle o Multiplication Principle
F	*Measurement*: o Solve for lengths of objects (e.g., boards) o Other word problems
T	*Pre-algebra*: o Definition of rational numbers o Fractions/Simplify fractions o Mixed numbers vs. improper fractions
H	*Pre-algebra:* o Estimation/ordering fractions o Multiply and divide rational numbers
T	*Pre-algebra:* o LCM and LCD o Operations (add and subtract)
H	*Pre-algebra:* o Convert percent, decimal, and fractions o Ratios and proportions
F	*Intro to Algebra:* Solve linear equations with rational numbers in them
T	*Probability:* Calculate probabilities (e.g., drawing a card or rolling a die)
H	*Measurement:* o Checkpoint: Queuing Theory o Define and develop measurement system o Unit analysis/conversions
T	*Statistics:* Averages o Mean, median, and mode o 5 number summary o Graph: Box plot
H	*Geometry/Measurement:* Measures of central tendencies
T	*Pre-algebra:* Irrational numbers and their origins o Definition o Differences between irrationals and rationals o Sets of numbers o Radicals o Square roots, square root property

Day	Objective
H	*Pre-algebra:* Real Number Line o Build number line/ordering o Absolute value
T	*Pre-algebra:* Field properties—An Investigation through the Language of the Calculator
H	*Intro to algebra:* Solve linear equations o Identities: Solutions are all real numbers o No solution
T	*Geometry* o Triangles: Pythagoras & the Pythagorean Theorem o Circles: circumference, area
H	*Measurement/Statistics:* o Calculate circumference, length of arc, area of circle, area of sector o Statistics graphs: pie charts
T	*Measurement:* Similar triangles o 30-60-90 triangles o 45-45-90 triangles
H	*Intro to algebra:* Inequalities

References

Acuna, R. (2003). *U.S. Latino issues.* Westport, CT: Greenwood Press.

Applebaum, P., Friedler, L. M., Ortiz, C. E., & Wolff, E. F. (2009, fall). Internationalizing the university mathematics curriculum. *Journal of Studies in International Education, 13* (3), 365–381.

Armedariz, E. P., & Hasty, L. (1997). Making mathematics instruction inclusive. In A. I. Morey & M. K. Kitano (Eds.), *Multicultural course transformation in higher education: A broader truth* (pp. 126–144). Boston, MA: Allyn & Bacon.

Association of American Colleges and Universities (AAC&U). (2010, September). Facts & figures: Hispanics' views on higher education. *Association of American Colleges and Universities News.* Retrieved from http://www.aacu.org/aacu_news/AACUNews10/september10/facts_figures.cfm

Aud, S., Hussar, W., Planty, M., et al. (2010). *The condition of education 2010* (NCES 2010-028). Washington, DC: National Center for Education Statistics.

Bruch, P. L., Jehangir, R. R., Jacobs, W. R., & Ghere, D. L. (2004, spring). Enabling access: Toward multicultural developmental curricula. *Journal of Developmental Education, 27* (3), 12–19, 41.

Dancis, J., & Davidson, N. (1970). *The Texas method and the small group discovery method.* Retrieved from http://legacyrlmoore.org/reference/dancis_davidson.html

Díez-Palomar, J., Simic, K., & Varley, M. (2006, December). "Math is everywhere": Connecting mathematics to students' lives. *Journal of Mathematics and Culture, 1* (2), 20–36.

Elliott, J. (2006). *Jane Elliott's blue eyes brown eyes exercise.* Retrieved from http://janeelliott.com/index.htm

El Nasser, H., & Overberg, P. (2010, August 27). Kindergartens see more Hispanic, Asian students. *USA Today.* Retrieved from http://www.usatoday.com/news/nation/census/2010-08-27-1Akindergarten27_ST_N.htm

Epstein, D., Mendick, H., & Moreau, M. (2010, February). Imagining the mathematician: Young people talking about popular representations of maths. *Discourse Studies in the Cultural Politics of Education, 31* (1), 45–60. doi: 10.1080/01596300903465419

Gay, Geneva. (2007). [Untitled video.] Retrieved from http://video.google.com/videoplay?docid=-6017529904734532O4#

———. (n.d.). *Goals of culturally relevant pedagogy* [Video]. Teaching Tolerance: A Project of the Southern Poverty Law Center. Retrieved from http://www.tolerance.org/tdsi/asset/goals-culturally-relevant-pedagogy

González, N., Moll, L. C., & Amanti, C. (Eds.). (2005). *Funds of knowledge: Theorizing practices in households, communities, and classrooms.* New York, NY: Routledge.

Gonzales, P., et al. (2009). Highlights from TIMSS 2007: Mathematics and science achievement of U.S. fourth- and eighth-grade students in an international context (NCES 2009-001 revised). Washington, DC: National Center for Education Statistics. Retrieved from http://nces.ed.gov/pubs2009/2009001.pdf

Gutiérrez, R. (2000). Is the multiculturalization of mathematics doing us more harm than good? In R. Mahalingham & C. McCarthy (Eds.), *Multicultural curriculum: New directions for social theory, practice, and policy* (pp. 199–219). New York, NY: Routledge.

Gutstein, E., Lipman, P., Hernandez, P., & de los Reyes, R. (1997). Culturally relevant mathematics teaching in a Mexican American context. *Journal for Research in Mathematics Education, 28* (6), 709–737.

Holt, J. (1995). *How children fail.* Jackson, TN: Da Capo.

Institutional Research, Texas State University. (2010). Retrieved from http://www.ir.txstate.edu

Lederman, D. (2010, January 5). Recalculating Latino STEM success. *Inside Higher Ed.* Retrieved from http://www.insidehighered.com/news/2010/01/05/latino

McBeath, J., Reyes, M., & Ehrlander, M. (2008). *Education reform in the American states.* Charlotte, NC: Information Age.

Mireles, S. V. (2009, September). Balancing the curriculum equation: Understanding mathematics and science correlation components. *Mathematics Teaching in the Middle School, 15* (2), 100–107.

Murdock, S., White, S., Hoque, N. M., et al. (2003). *The new Texas challenge: Population change and the future of Texas.* College Station, TX: Texas A&M University Press.

National Center for Education Statistics. (2007). *Status and trends in the education of racial and ethnic minorities* (NCES 2007-039). Washington, DC: Author. Retrieved from http://nces.ed.gov/pubs2007/minoritytrends/

National Council of Teachers of Mathematics (NCTM). (2008, January). Equity in mathematics education. Retrieved from http://www.nctm.org/about/content.aspx?id=13490

National Council of Teachers of Mathematics (NCTM). (2009, July 15). NCTM foundational priorities. Retrieved from http://www.nctm.org/about/content. aspx?id=172

Needleman, S. E. (2009, January 6). Doing the math to find the good jobs: Mathematicians land top spot in new ranking of best and worst occupations in the U.S. *The Wall Street Journal.* Retrieved from http://online.wsj.com/home-page

Pepitone, J. (2009, July 24). Most lucrative college degrees. *CNNMoney.com.* Retrieved from http://money.cnn.com/2009/07/24/news/economy/highest_starting_salaries/index.htm

Peters, W. (1985). *A class divided* [Television documentary]. PBS *Frontline*. Retrieved from http://www.pbs.org/wgbh/pages/frontline/shows/divided/

Pew Hispanic Center. (2010). Latino population, growth and dispersion [Interactive map]. Retrieved from http://pewhispanic.org/data/maps/

Phuong-Mai, N., Terlouw, C., Pilot, A., & Elliott, J. (2009, December). Cooperative learning that features a culturally appropriate pedagogy. *British Education Research Journal, 35* (6), 857–875.

Schoem, D. (1993). Constructing a teaching assistant training program with a multicultural emphasis. In D. Schoem, L. Frankel, X. Zúniga, & E. A. Lewis (Eds.), *Multicultural teaching in the university* (pp. 272–277). Westport, CT: Praeger.

Sleeter, C. E. (1997). Mathematics, multicultural education, and professional development. *Journal for Research in Mathematics Education, 28* (6), 680–696.

Snowman, J., McCown, R., & Biehler, R. (2008). *Psychology applied to teaching* (12th ed.). Florence, KY: Wadsworth.

Southern Regional Education Board. (2010). *SREB fact book on higher education, 2009*. Retrieved from http://www.sreb.org/page/1123/fact_book_on_higher_education.html

Steinglass, M. (2010, April 21). Are math majors better at reading than English majors? Accumulating Peripherals [Web log]. Retrieved from http://mattsteinglass.wordpress.com/2010/04/21/are-math-majors-better-at-reading-than-english-majors/

Stutz, T. (2010, August 3). Texas needs more minority teachers, experts say. *The Dallas Morning News*. Retrieved from http://www.dallasnews.com/news/education/headlines/20100802-Texas-needs-more-minority-teachers-9353.ece

Texas Education Agency. (2010). Testing and accountability. Retrieved from http://www.tea.state.tx.us/index.aspx?id=2147484910&menu_id=660&menu_id2=795&cid=2147483660

Troutman, J., & McCoy, L. (2008, August). Re-membering mathematics: The effect of culturally relevant lessons in math history on students' attitudes. *Journal of Mathematics and Culture, 3* (1).

U.S. Census Bureau. (2010a). Facts for features: Hispanic heritage month 2010: Sept. 15–Oct. 15. Retrieved from http://www.census.gov/newsroom/releases/archives/facts_for_features_special_editions/cb10-ff17.html.

———. (2010b). State and county quickfacts. Retrieved from http://quickfacts.census.gov/qfd/states/00000.html

Van Horne, K. A. (2009). Against the odds: The success phenomenon of Latino developmental community college students. *Research in Developmental Education, 22* (4).

Vásquez, F. (2006). *Negotiating Chicano masculinities at institutions of higher education: Voices of South Texas Chicano men*. (Unpublished doctoral dissertation). University of Texas at Austin.

13

UNIVERSITY COLLEGE

The Transformation of University Seminar

Stella Silva

The university seminar course has historically been used across the country by institutions of higher education as a freshman orientation course. This course is typically utilized to acquaint incoming freshman with their campus environment and to impact retention, which leads to degree completion. The purpose of this chapter is to demonstrate how the integration of a multicultural perspective in a university seminar course curriculum is valuable for students as well as university seminar instructors. The benefits are reflected in the following:

1. Greater student retention, with an added effort to retain students from underrepresented populations;
2. Recognition of the significant role of the US1100 instructor in supporting student cultural-identity development;
3. Development of a welcoming cultural campus climate; and
4. Increased commitment by the institution to diversity and multiculturalism.

In general, US1100 is a crucial foundational course that sets the tone for incoming freshman students' educational experience and assists students in locating valuable resources on campus that will allow them to be successful. An undergraduate student's interaction with faculty, staff, and peers strongly determines his or her understanding of the culture and functioning of the university. In order to explore the value of the US1100 course, a historical overview of the creation of the course follows.

History of University Seminar

Freshmen orientation classes have traditionally been popular in providing students with information concerning campus resources and climate. In 1888, Boston College hosted the first freshman orientation class, and Reed College was the first institution to offer credit for an orientation course (Bigger, 2005). An effort to assist students in adjusting to their campus environment came in 1972 after a series of riots on the campus of the University of South Carolina. Administrators, trying to find ways to help undergraduate students appreciate the university rather than destroy it, developed a course they called "the first-year experience"

(Bigger, 2005). This course included campus tours, departmental presentations, and information about financial aid and academic resources. From the course, it was concluded that one of the main factors in students' success was the degree to which they perceived faculty members to be genuinely concerned about their welfare. As institutions competed, there was also a great concern for retaining the students they attracted (Bigger, 2005). As accessibility increased for a diverse pool of students, institutions became more aware that the profile of the "freshman" was constantly changing and had come to include nontraditional, older, married, and working students. In addition, specific systems needed to be put into place to meet the needs of students who were not "traditional" freshmen (i.e., recently high school–graduated eighteen-year-olds). On campuses across the country the orientation class had and continues to have many names and various formats, and typically a required, one-hour course offered to all incoming freshmen. Some institutions allow two credit hours per course, others list the course as optional or recommended. As a standard, most first-year seminar courses are one semester in duration and start at college orientation; some programs take it one step further and purchase course text books for students.

University Seminar at Texas State University-San Marcos

At Texas State University, this course is referred to as University Seminar, or US1100, and is housed in University College, formerly known as the College of General Studies, established in 1983. University College was created to provide an academic home for advising undecided majors, as well as an administrative structure for coordination and oversight of the university's general education curriculum. In addition to housing University Seminar, University College has also become the administrative home of the University Honors Program, Student Learning Assistance Center (SLAC), National Student Exchange (NSE), Testing Research-Support and Evaluation Center, Texas Success Initiative Program (TSIP), Athletic Certification, and the Athletic Academic Center.

US1100 has become one of the students' main sources of information that connects them to campus and is designed to smooth the transition to Texas State University for first-year students. Dr. Jeffrey Gordon designed the first university seminar course in 1986 with the goals of instilling practical learning skills, promoting campus life, and advocating campus diversity (Lynch, 2010). Class sizes were small, and instructors were made up of faculty and staff from various disciplines across campus. All instructors were required to have a master's degree and previous teaching experience. The syllabus included very specific information about course objectives, the university's honor code, descriptions of campus activities, and a course agenda. As the program evolved, special sections of the course were developed for students from special populations such as veterans, first-generation students in specific majors, members of the honors program, and residential colleges. Currently, all incoming freshmen at Texas State University are required to take US1100. This provides an opportunity to create an environment where instructors are able to mentor students and answer questions about their first semester (Heathman, 2010). The course is constantly evolving as new and appropriate outcomes emerge, with a formatted syllabus and established guidelines that ensure that all instructors effectively and efficiently serve students. University Seminar is designed to help meet the transitional needs of undergraduate students, as stated in current objectives:

- To facilitate students' adjustment to the challenges of life and learning at Texas State;
- To expand students' understanding of the nature and purposes of a university;
- To identify practical learning skills and concepts that will promote students' academic success;
- To encourage students to explore the connection between university study and life enrichment, lifelong learning, and civic responsibility; and
- To promote respect for diversity issues and concepts.

US1100 course would not be successful without the support of the campus community. With this in mind, there is a campus-wide effort to collectively engage all students in a program with a common theme, which is dubbed the Common Experience. Each year, the chosen text for the Common Experience program is a selected reading for all incoming freshman and the main reading material for all US1100 classes. In addition to providing practical information for students, the Common Experience program promotes a common theme supported by national speakers, events, and activities. It is a yearlong initiative designed to cultivate a common intellectual conversation across the campus and foster a sense of community on campus and in the surrounding community. Some previous subjects from the Common Experience included Hatred, Courage, Protest and Dissent; the Water Planet; Civic Responsibility and the Legacy of LBJ; and the Whole Mind: Crossing Boundaries and Disciplines. The 2011 theme was Sustainability.

Millennial Students

Texas State University is continually adjusting its US1100 courses in order to meet the needs of our current incoming freshmen, who are known as "millennial" students because they were born after 1981. The following description of the millennial student derives from Monaco and Martin (1997). The current student population of "millennials" possesses very specific needs and ways of communicating which, if recognized and addressed, will allow them to be successful. US1100 instructors must take into consideration how these characteristics will significantly impact multicultural and diverse course content. Millennials in the United States are diverse, and 80 million strong, or more than 41% of today's population. These students are the most racially and ethnically diverse generation in U.S. history. One in four grew up in a single-parent household; many grew up with working mothers, blended families, and homes impacted by a divorce rate exceeding 50%. They feel individually and collectively special as a result of strong connections to their parents, who function as their primary role models and major sources of advice as the students attend college (Monaco & Martin, 2007).

Millennials are optimistic, engaged, and highly protected and sheltered by their parents and authority figures, and were rarely left unsupervised by their overindulgent parents. They are motivated, goal-oriented, assertive, and confident; they want to make a difference; are civic-minded and value service learning and volunteerism. They are team-oriented and want to be part of the group; they like to congregate and fear being seen as nonconformist. They are high achievers, and even in elementary school they were expected to earn good grades, work hard, and pursue extracurricular activities. They are focused on achievement, feel pressured to succeed, and are used to filling every hour of the day with scheduled activities (Monaco & Martin, 2007).

These students are conventional and more respectful of adults than any generation in recent memory. They are also accepting of lifestyle and racial and ethnic differences and a wide spectrum of cultures. They need to have immediate feedback, feel a sense of entitlement, lack critical thinking skills, have unrealistic expectations, have a high level of parental involvement, and expect to be handed a how-to guide to succeed in and out of the classroom. They also want to spend less time on tasks and reach success with little effort (Monaco & Martin, 2007). Their strict and structured schedule of extracurricular activities reduced their opportunity to develop independent creative thought and decision-making skills. Their need for direction is in fact a need for someone to tell them the politically correct thing to do or how they should treat each other. Millenials are team-oriented and more comfortable working in groups than individually, particularly on projects. They are confident and highly optimistic but are unclear about how to reach the level of success they are so confident they will attain. They have information at their disposal, through the internet, text messaging, instant messaging, smartphones, telecommunications, and social networking sites, such as YouTube, Twitter, MySpace, and Facebook. Although they are highly skilled in technology, they lack adequate communication skills, simply because they have fewer opportunities for face-to-face encounters due to immediate access to technology. Their unclear path and need for information presents opportunities for teachers to influence their behavior, affect the development of their cultural identity, and encourage critical thinking skills. Their heavy use of technology can benefit a US1100 instructor wanting to include a multicultural perspective because technology provides accessibility to world events and information about how other cultural communities interact with each other.

In order to be successful in reaching these students, educators will need to use progressive and innovative techniques that are inclusive and culturally relevant. Monaco and Martin (2007) cite Howe and Strauss' suggestions for instructional delivery: (1) start with a learning-centered syllabus, (2) provide direction for course assignments, (3) convey behavioral expectations, and (4) outline rules and regulations along with ramifications. The use of technology will allow students to immediately connect with the world around them. Millennial students are at a prime stage for understanding the inclusion of a multicultural perspective and content. Although traditionally a Eurocentric perspective has been used to teach in colleges and universities across the nation, from what we understand about today's learners, it is clear that the role of the educator must change. A text-and-lecture-style model in education is considered a style of the past because it is entrenched in narrow views of history and social realities (Ukpokodu, 2010).

Why Multicultural Education Tenets Are Needed in This Discipline

With changing demographics in the U.S. and an increased number of persons from underrepresented communities, it is imperative that students from all social groups regardless of class, race, ethnicity, sexual orientation, disabilities, and gender attain the knowledge, skills, and competencies necessary to participate in public discourse and civic action with people who differ from themselves. Diversity and multiculturalism are fundamental tenets that should be a part of every institution that is interested in sustainability and long-term economic benefit. As Barceló (2010) states, "If we don't invest in diversity, we perpetuate opportunity and achievement gaps. We put at risk the educational systems that are so central, not only to economic prosperity but also to social and economic justice" (p. 20). Barceló purports that diversity has been a topic that has been discussed for a long time, and that traditional institutional systems, along with traditional leadership models, will not allow institutions to grow. What will allow them to grow is a reimagined academic and cultural space that exists at the intersection of multiple identities, cultures, systems of thought, and knowledge traditions (Barceló, 2010). Barceló's recommendation is that institutions need to move diversity out of planning documents and into the center of the institutions with new and fundamental models for institutional transformation that makes diversity intrinsic to everything we do. This will mean that institutions will need to take a closer look at traditional assumptions, and may need to discard those that hinder the formation of new perspectives (Barceló, 2010).

Incorporating new perspectives can pose challenges for instructors who are willing to include a multicultural perspective in their course content but need assistance with the transformation process. At Texas State University the transformation process is encouraged through the Multicultural Transformation and Research Institute (MCTRI) led by the Center for Multicultural and Gender Studies, which provides resources for university instructors to transform their syllabi and incorporate course content that supports a multicultural perspective. As an instructor at Texas State University, I was privileged to attend the Institute and participate in the process of transforming my syllabus. The following is an account of my experience in summer 2010.

Personal Story about MCTRI Impact

As a student affairs professional and Associate Director in an Office of Multicultural Student Affairs (MSA) as well as a US1100 instructor at Texas State University, I've had many opportunities to receive information about multiculturalism and diversity through professional development workshops and attendance at various conferences and seminars. I found there was always something to learn or a new perspective to consider. My personal challenge was to participate in Texas State's Multicultural Curriculum Transformation and Research Institute during summer 2010 with the goal of completing the Institute with a newly transformed syllabus that I would use in the fall semester of that year. As I thought about the structure of my current syllabus and the need to incorporate a multicultural perspective, I realized that buy-in to the use of a multicultural perspective was part of the process; my own perspective would need to be transformed.

My personal story starts with acknowledgment that my own cultural perspective as a Latina, and the many roles I embrace in my life journey also impact how I see the world. I identify as a person of color from an underrepresented population, a person from a low SES family, a first-generation college student, mother, daughter, member of a familia, sister, aunt, godmother, Christian, and heterosexual woman living in the predominantly Latino city of San Antonio, Texas. All these factors shape who I am and what I value. I never walk away from these identities; I view them as part of my existence, even when one identity dominates another.

In my professional position I consistently challenge myself with new ways of thinking about the students I serve and what I need to do to help them be successful at Texas State University. I try to make a difference in students' lives, but like most instructors and faculty members, I sometimes fail miserably and other times hit the nail right on the head. My decision to attend the Institute was not hard; what was difficult was the knowledge that the inevitable discussions of race, multiculturalism, and diversity would have to take place in order to reach/demonstrate true transformation. I was curious to see who at our predominantly White institution would take the challenge to participate in the Institute. As a person of color, many times I find myself feeling the need to be guarded in discussions but also prepared to say something smart, clever or insightful. The schedule for the Institute was engaging, so I knew that no matter what happened I was going to be a better person simply because of the experience. I also attended the Institute with an African American office mate who relayed to me similar feelings, so I knew I would at least have one ally. I was very impressed by the facilitator's willingness to engage all types of conversation. The material was presented in a very nonthreatening manner, and it appeared that everyone who attended the Institute was willing to make the extra effort to truly transform their syllabus, including faculty from the hard sciences who I observed had difficulty in incorporating multiculturalism into their course work. Everyone appeared to be open to exploring new perspectives. The room was equipped with tables set up in a U-shaped formation which created an inclusive environment conducive to discussion and open communication. The process for the Institute was academically sound, interactive, and nonthreatening, and used an inclusive approach to introducing the integration of multiculturalism as a new perspective for course content.

This process could potentially have been uncomfortable for individuals not familiar with sharing their personal experiences with a group; however, efforts were made to establish a safe zone that ensured everyone the opportunity to share. Some of the many learning opportunities of the Institute included presentations on conflict, teaching styles, cultural assessments, responsive teaching, as well as ways to enrich curriculum through perspectives from women and persons from underrepresented populations. As part of the training, we heard testimonials and assessment examples from past participants of the Institute. In essence, the Multicultural Curriculum Transformation and Research Institute proved to be not only a vehicle for transformation of my syllabus, but also the catalyst for an intrinsic change in my role as an instructor.

Why an Interest in Attending the Institute

I was interested in participating in the Institute and transforming my syllabus because I felt that simply embracing, recognizing, and supporting ethnic and cultural diversity and multiculturalism was not enough. The curriculum in our nation's schools, colleges, and universities should reflect the lives of all of its citizens; yet in many cases continues to embrace a Eurocentric perspective that includes paradigms that provide narrow views of history and social realities (Banks, 1991).

The understanding of and respect for diverse values, traditions, and behaviors comes with the process of transformation. Reaching a higher level of awareness about the existence and expression of differences can improve the quality of life for individuals, ethnic and cultural groups, society as a whole and yes, the lives of University Seminar instructors. The National Conference on Social Studies (NCSS) guidelines suggest that culture changes through the process of innovation: A person (or persons) introduces new ways of thinking or behaving that challenges cultural views, and are accepted by society. For example, as a multicultural educator, knowing that Asian American, African American, Chicano/Latino, and Native American students on campuses across the nation are consistently seen as strangers or foreigners. This is not only disturbing, particularly when their families have lived in the U.S. longer than many European immigrants, or were indigenous prior to the establishment of the U. S. (Takaki, 1991) but also provides an opportunity to challenge cultural views of who is considered a foreigner. Takaki (1991) also recommends that students should have at least a minimal awareness of their own multicultural reality. Students are astute and as their interactions increase and they move through stages of cultural identity development, they start to consider critical questions about why their histories and information about their communities are excluded from the curriculum.

Teaching and How It Affects Students

US1100 classes are the perfect setting for instructors to assist students in understanding how their life perspective fits into the big picture, as college students and their lives in general. In essence, how faculty members present issues of multiculturalism determines whether students embrace the topic and participate in discussion or reject it. Even well-intentioned faculty members should always remember that their interactions have a far-reaching influence on their students (Komarraju, Musulkin & Bhattacharya, 2010). The critical engagement of issues of diversity in the curriculum and in the classroom has a positive impact on student's attitudes toward racial issues, fostering a deeper understanding of diverse perspectives and cognitive development. Ukpokodu proposes that curriculum transformation is not only an academic responsibility but also a moral imperative and social responsibility (Ukpokodu, 2010).

Recognizing the importance of multiculturalism and diversity in students' identity development and intentionally choosing not to include it in the curriculum in any given course does students a disservice and stifles their growth and development as college students. Ukpokodu, citing Conella (1997), supports this belief and questions how we show respect for diversity in terms of the life experiences of the learners. He believes that a real change toward an inclusive society, equity, and social justice can be achieved when students have opportunities to engage in critical curricular and scholarly inquiry and develop a reflective multicultural knowledge base (Ukpokodu, 2010). One way to respect a student's identity is to help them reach their highest level of cultural identity development.

Torres, Jones, and Renn (2009) state that "within student affairs literature, identity is commonly understood as one's personally held beliefs about self in relation to social groups (e.g., race, ethnicity, religion, sexual orientation) and the ways one expresses that relationship" (p. 577). Although the general understanding is that identity is socially constructed and reconstructed as well as situational, societal changes, including changes in the campus environment, are major influences on how one views his own and others' identities. The prime time for exploration of identity development and formation is at the beginning of a student's college careers. At that point, they have temporarily distanced themselves from their familial value system and forging new segments of that value system on campus.

Syllabus and Teaching

The US1100 syllabus is typically a work in progress. Most instructors continually review and evaluate their syllabus each semester in order to be as effective and efficient as possible. The prescribed template for US1100 syllabi includes the following categories:

1. name of course,
2. instructor and University Seminar contact information,
3. course description,
4. course objectives,
5. required Common Experience text,
6. attendance policy,
7. class participation policy,
8. grading scheme,
9. detailed description of assignments,
10. semester course outline, broken down by weeks,
11. weekly outcomes,
12. accessibility statement,
13. academic honesty statement,
14. academic honor code,
15. mission statement of general education,
16. University Seminar statement,
17. University Seminar outcomes, and
18. website information for University Seminar and the Common Experience.

This is the standard format for a US1100 class; although instructors are expected to maintain the standard format of the syllabus, they are given creative license to include various types of information, including the infusion of a multicultural perspective. Since my Institute experience, the additional information in my syllabus now includes a multicultural policy statement and a new cultural stories presentation in which students explore their own families' cultures through interviews with family members. Students are then given an opportunity to share their interviews with the class.

A year later in 2011, using the Common Experience theme of sustainability, I introduced a segment on environmental racism by utilizing technology and scheduling class time for students to view YouTube videos of documentaries about environmental racism produced by college students across the nation. Time was also added to discuss the idea that although the green movement and sustainability appear to be new concepts, indigenous communities have practiced sustainability for thousands of years.

Speakers were invited to present in my class on a variety of topics. I paid close attention to the diversity of speakers and topics, and emphasized the establishment of a safe and inclusive environment for discussion, particularly with unfamiliar or controversial topics. For example, when discussing sexual orientation my goal was to assist freshman who self-identify as gay, lesbian, bisexual, or transgender (LGBTQ), but who have not come out to their friends or family, to know that there was a community at the university that welcomed them. These types of presentations are needed, and as instructors, we need to be confident enough to handle a very dynamic and sometimes controversial discussion session. Topics such as sexual orientation or even race appear to be difficult for some instructors and faculty to discuss, thus creating an uncomfortable classroom environment.

University Seminar courses, as well as courses such as math and science, can be made inclusive by recognizing and including the accomplishments and contributions of persons from underrepresented populations. The unfortunate truth is that many times we justify multiculturalism not as a benefit to humanity, but rather for how it will benefit mainstream culture, by improving the state of the economy or educating a workforce. In addition, Ukpokodu (2010) states that with the growth of a "diverse world and workforce, students will need a range of competencies including cultural understanding and open-mindedness, high order thinking, and relational skills for negotiating and navigating diverse cultural social and political contexts and civic engagements for social change" (p. 27); he adds that "traditional schooling...has not prepared [faculty members] to respond to diverse challenges within their discipline, teaching and student learning" (p. 28).

Resistance and Responses from Colleagues and Students

Working in an office that supports multiculturalism and in my work in multiculturalism and diversity, I've observed that where there is resistance, there is fear—fear of the unknown, fear of having to feel vulnerable, fear of change, or fear of feeling incompetent. Working in this field requires one to be courageous enough to feel vulnerable mostly because it requires self-exploration as one considers a personal path. This is where I feel I have grown and gained wisdom. I have yet to meet a diversity educator who expects participants from the dominant mainstream culture to have all the answers, or know the "politically correct" phrases or answers. My expectation—and I do not attempt to speak for all underrepresented people—is that participants at least try and be informed and exhibit genuine concern and care. Instructors get into trouble when they start to dictate for others, particularly for students, their life experiences. Even well-intentioned instructors will sometimes unintentionally imply that they can identify with a student from a different cultural background, and then take the discussion further by attempting to determine whose "truth" or reality is more valuable or valid. Ukpokodu (2010) reports that there is general resistance from conservative educators who feel that the integration of issues of race, sexual orientation, gender, exceptionality or disabilities, and class only water down the curriculum, and that a Eurocentric perspective represents the facts of American history because it presents a "truth" that should be at the core of the curriculum. The questions that need to be raised concerning this belief system should include, how "truth" meaning one's own reality is determined or in the making of "truth," whose "truth" are we speaking of, as well as who gets to determine what is considered "truth" and is "truth ultimately defined by the academy or rather an individual's experiences. The mere existence of multiple perspectives in the curriculum validates student's experiences. There appear to be many reasons for resistance, however a prominent one is that sometimes faculty members are not grounded in multicultural education; they shy away from the process (Ukpokodu, 2010). Ukpokodu cites Grant's work (1994) and reports that resistance to multicultural curriculum transformation occurs because of misconceptions that (1) it is only for students from underrepresented groups, so if you don't have students of color, there is no need to infuse diversity; (2) it applies only to the arts and humanities and not to mathematics and the hard sciences; and (3) it waters down knowledge and is poor scholarship.

Ukpokodu (2010) adds that one of the reasons for resistance is that many faculty members have a limited knowledge base on diversity as well as how to transform the curriculum to be more inclusive. Including diverse perspectives is not an easy task and sometimes engenders, fear, threat and resistance. Curriculum transformation involves the inclusion of voices that many times have been silenced and marginalized in scholarship and theory. Proponents of curriculum transformation contend that such an initiative promotes balance equity and social justice and reduces marginalization. The question of who determines that "truth," and who decides who gets to be the "meaning makers" enhances student's analytical skills (Sanchez, 1996).

Research Results

At the time this chapter was written, I had recently completed the summer Multicultural Curriculum Transformation and Research Institute with the intent of implementing my transformed curriculum in fall 2010. My transformation included an assessment portion, in which I would ask my class at the end of the semester whether they felt I had satisfactorily integrated concepts of multiculturalism. Since I had not yet collected data from class participants, I instead submitted four questions to University Seminar instructors who taught this course for the better part of ten years. Their experiences were valuable to me in transforming my course. There were many faculty and staff members who taught the University Seminar and transformed syllabi in other disciplines, but there were five veteran staff members who took the initiative to specifically transform their University Seminar syllabus. The following four questions reflect their experiences with the Institute and the transformation of their syllabi.

1. What was the most challenging part of integrating a multicultural perspective into your US1100 syllabus?

   Participant A
   "By far the most challenging part has been the limitation of teaching a one-hour course, now in 50-minute, once a week sessions. Ideally I would like to have at least three to four class periods to explore the 12 cultural attributes (Cushner, K. 2006. *Human diversity in action.* Boston: McGraw Hill) AND engage students in several of the activities, such as 'Who Am I?,' 'Family Tree,' etc. I'm now down to two class periods and an outside 'Comparing Cultures' assignment which integrates some diversity readings, an interview with a person from a different culture, and the Family Tree exercise."

   Participant B
   "I think the most challenging part was remembering all of the information and because I teach a one-hour class, I cannot use all of the information. It was hard to choose what is most important because everything we learned was valuable. Also, I have to think of different mediums to convey this information to freshmen who may not have been exposed to anything like this before."

2. How did participating in the Institute increase your awareness about multiculturalism and or perspectives of other communities other than your own?

   Participant A
   "I had never heard 'culture' defined so broadly as Cushner does using the 12 cultural attributes. Almost all of the diversity workshops I had attended in the past focused primarily on race and ethnicity, which always left me, a Caucasian

woman of European descent, feeling like I had absolutely no 'culture' and nothing to contribute to the conversation."

Participant B
"When participating in this institute, one's awareness of multiculturalism is heightened, and I became even more aware of social justice issues, disability issues and global issues. There are many issues outside the US that affect how we are viewed by other countries. US 1100 can be used as a catalyst to start conversations about these issues."

3. Did you ever experience an "Aha" moment during or after your participation in the Institute? If yes what was it?

Participant A
"The whole concept of 'culturally responsive teaching' was an eye-opener, especially with regard to having students work on and present group projects. Although I can't always accommodate every student's preference, I do give them choices about topics, group mates, the number of students in their group, or style of presentation, etc."

Participant B
"My 'aha' moment was when we discussed different learners and how easy it was to integrate a particular learning style into teaching to include all styles. Also, I have always stated that students need to graduate with having a global perspective; however, I never consciously did anything to help. It was easy for me to change my syllabus to reflect this perspective."

4. What was some feedback from students about your integration of multicultural content and perspective into your syllabus? Please provide a brief description of student's responses.

Participant A
"They love the 'Comparing Cultures' assignment because they have an opportunity to really get to know someone from a different culture than their own. The interviewee can be of any age and can be from out of the USA, or from another state, or from another region in Texas, just as long as they are from a different culture than my student. I prompt them to ask questions about the following:

- Ancestry/nationality/ethnicity
- Languages (including accents or dialects) spoken in their home, town/city & country
- Geography of their town/city &/or country
- Typical housing & transportation in their town/city & country
- Family life including typical size of families, parents' occupations, types of vacations/family outings, etc.
- Educational levels & systems (K-12; college/university; graduate/professional)

- Meals—typical foods & drinks; which meals are more formal or sit-down/family occasions vs. lighter or less formal meals
- Religion including religious holiday traditions in their family as well as in their country/region
- Other holiday celebrations (nonreligious holidays like July 4th in the USA)
- Ask about acceptance/tolerance of different gender roles, sexual preference & social class in their country/state/region only if you are comfortable doing so."

Participant B
"Many choose to interview friends from high school or even relatives, and they always come back saying how much they learned because they never even thought (or gave themselves permission) to ask questions about some of these attributes or areas. The day the assignment is due, each student gets about two minutes to tell us who they interviewed and something unique they learned about their interviewee and their culture. It's really fascinating!

I also try to get into the US 1100 classroom about 5–10 minutes early so I can have music playing from a different culture before each class begins and when they are circulating the roll sheet. Sometimes I ask them to guess where the music or band is from (e.g., Ireland, Cuba, Greece, Middle East, Mexico, Australia), and many students comment on how they like hearing the different styles, instruments, etc."

Participants A and B clearly understand that acknowledging the realities of students not only enriches course content but also enhances the experience for both students and instructors.

Strategies for Other Faculty Members

My experience in the Institute was life changing and transformative. This sentiment was also expressed by many participants including those interviewed in this chapter. With this in mind, I propose recommendations for faculty members who strive to support the integration of multiculturalism into their curriculum.

- Prove your level of commitment to your students about multiculturalism and diversity by integrating it into the syllabus in a sincere and authentic way (it's hard to fool students).
- Enhance your knowledge. Limited knowledge causes discomfort. Although instructors are well-intentioned, if they have not done their homework, they risk giving the wrong impression and being perceived as patronizing.
- Look beyond the monthly celebrations and start by integrating information that is easily attainable and accessible about the contributions of people from underrepresented populations in different academic disciplines, even the hard sciences.
- Accept vulnerability. Accepting responsibility for multicultural curriculum transformation means also being vulnerable for the greater good.
- Embrace the journey. Even if you are uncomfortable with discussing topics such as ethnicity, race, White privilege, sexism, ageism, sexual orientation, or disabilities,

you have to remember that if you have not gone through your own personal journey, you will not know how to help students through theirs.

- Seek understanding at many levels. The need to integrate multicultural information into the curriculum should make us stop and think and ask why is there an absence of information about people from underrepresented populations. Why is this information missing?
- Know that diversity is everyone's responsibility.
- Ask the question, "Who determines the truth and meaning making?" Just because we are experts in our field does not give us the right to invalidate what another person describes as their reality.
- Attend a Multicultural Curriculum Transformation and Research Institute; you will be changing culture one syllabus at a time.

References and Support

Supporting documents for the US1100 course include the University Seminar instructors' guide and other reference materials posted on the Texas State University Seminar website. The Common Experience website is also a vital source, along with the Common Experience annual book selection. The instructors' teaching guide contains class activities, selected readings, event ideas, and class projects, all related to the Common Experience theme. Another supporting document for the University Seminar class is a book focused on successful strategies for achieving success for a student's first year of college called *Your College Experience-Strategies for Success*, ninth edition by Gardner, Jewler, and Barefoot. Topics include but are not limited to, exploring your purpose for attending college, managing your time, understanding emotional intelligence, managing your money and discovering how you learn. Academic and Student Affairs departments across campus also provide various types of materials including brochures, websites, t-shirts, and so on, and there are presentations and workshops on relationships, sexual behavior, date rape, and domestic violence. The Volunteer Connection informs students about community service and volunteer opportunities. Financial Literacy is also a popular presentation as well as activities at the university's local cultural center, nature preserves, and sanctuaries.

Conclusions/Summary

The purpose of the traditional US1100 or University Seminar course is to provide "millennial" students with enough information to impact their retention. The course is also important because it is foundational, and provides an opportunity to affect students' cultural identity development and the campus climate. Transforming the tone of a foundational course allows the instructor, as well as, the institution to inform incoming students about the cultural belief system of the institution. One of the ways to support this belief system is to acknowledge the contributions of persons from underrepresented communities. This relays to students and the faculty, the institution's commitment to multiculturalism and diversity. The University Seminar instructor plays an important role in a student's development and validation, as well as their understanding of the functioning of the university. In addition, the way instructors embrace multiculturalism influences students' critical thinking skills, cultural awareness, and preparations for their future. In essence, diversity is everyone's job. "Truth" should be at the core of the curriculum, not in a traditional sense, but in that it validates individuals' lives and acknowledges the contributions of their people and communities.

References

Banks, J. A. (1991). *Curriculum guidelines for multicultural education.* Retrieved from the NCSS Task Force on Ethnic Studies Curriculum Guidelines website. Retrieved from http://www.socialstudies.org/positions/multicultural

Barceló, N. (2010, April 29). Reimaging diversity in our institutions. *Diverse Issues in Higher Education, 27* (6), 20.

Bigger, J. (2005). Improving the odds for freshman success. NACADA Clearinghouse of Academic Advising Resources. Retrieved from http://www.nacada.ksu.edu/Clearinghouse/AdvisingIssues/First-Year.htm

Cushner, K. (2006). *Human diversity in action.* Boston, MA: McGraw-Hill.

Dochen, C. W., Hodges, R., & Wuestenberg, P. (Eds.). (2008). *Your university experience—The next step, second custom edition for Texas State University–San Marcos.* Boston, MA: Pearson Custom Publishing.

Gleason, P. (2007–2008, winter). Meeting the needs of millennial students. *In Touch Newsletter, 16* (1).

Gordon, J. (1996). *The university in your life.* Boston, MA: McGraw-Hill.

Heathman, C. (2010, February 16). University seminar undergoes makeover. *The University Star.* Retrieved from http://star.txstate.edu/content/university-seminar-undergoes-makeover

Komarraju, M., Musulkin, S., & Bhattacharya, G. (2010, May–June). Role of student-faculty interactions in developing college students' academic self-concept, motivation, and achievement. *ACPA Journal of College Student Development, 51* (3), 333–334.

Lynch, M. (2010, June 3). University seminar. *The University Star.* Retrieved from http://star.txstate.edu/content/university-seminar Jillian Bliss

Monaco, M., & Martin, M. (2007, April–June). The millennial student: A new generation of learners. *Athletic Training Education Journal, 2*, 42–46.

Sanchez, T. R. (1996, January–February). Multiculturalism: Practical considerations for curricular change. *The Clearing House, 69* (3), 171–173.

Takaki, R. (1991, May–June). The content of the curriculum: Two views: The value of multiculturalism. *Liberal Education, 77* (3), 9–10.

Taylor, P. (2008). Higher education curriculum for human and social development: Filling a pail, or lighting a fire? Presentation at the 4th International Conference on

Higher Education, organized by GUNI, Barcelona, , March 31–April 2. the Institute of Development Studies, GUNI Conference.

Torres, V., Jones, S.R., & Renn, K. A. (2009, November–December). Identity development theories in student affairs: Origins, current status, and new approaches. *ACPA Journal of College Student Development, 50* (6), 577.

Ukpokodu, N. O. (2010, winter). How a sustainable campus-wide diversity curriculum fosters academic success. *Multicultural Education, 17* (2), 27–36.

SECTION IV

Guides to Syllabi Change

This section includes course transformation samples from six colleges of Texas State: McCoy College of Business Administration, College of Fine Arts and Communication, College of Science and Engineering, College of Applied Arts, College of Liberal Arts, and University College. Each sample includes a copy of the assessment instrument and a copy of a transformed syllabus. (See detailed discussion about the assessment instrument in Chapter 2.) The multicultural course identification instrument is a standard form for all faculty members who seek multicultural designations for their courses.

14. TEXAS STATE UNIVERSITY–SAN MARCOS
MULTICULTURAL CURRICULUM TRANSFORMATION GUIDE/ASSESSMENT INSTRUMENT

Name of Course: International Marketing—MKT3377
Instructor: Enrique P. Becerra
Department: Marketing Department—McCoy College of Business
Degree:
Degree Program Requirement: **YES** NO

1. Course Description	A study of the international planning and coordination of marketing functions, marketing policies, and the analysis of marketing on an international scope, including environmental and cultural aspects.
2. Course Objectives	**Learning Goals** • To introduce the students to the importance of international trade and its impact on the local economy. • To raise the students' basic awareness of the importance of international marketing and its impact on the local and world economies. • To extend the basic marketing concepts and techniques into the framework of the world marketplace. • To develop understanding and appreciation of different cultures and their influences on consumers' behavior and on business practices. • To tackle ethical and ecological issues in a world with different systems values. • To introduce students to marketing research and the need to use secondary data to make international marketing decisions. • To increase the students' awareness about the importance of relationship building in a business setting.
3. Course Content (60% needed for MC classification)	LEVEL ONE: _ LEVEL TWO: _ LEVEL THREE: X (Check one. Explain.) Course is taught from a cultural perspective—the influence of culture on consumer behavior and its impact on businesses is explored/discussed. Project/assignments require students to compare different cultures.
4. Instructional Strategies	LEVEL ONE: _ LEVEL TWO: _ LEVEL THREE: X (Check one. Explain.) Content is presented in different manners—lecture, videos, projects, and examples.
5. Assessment of Student Knowledge	LEVEL ONE: _ LEVEL TWO: _ LEVEL THREE: X (Check one. Explain.) Students are assessed in different ways—tests (multiple choice, true/false, short essay), written project, and an oral presentation.
6. Classroom Interactions	LEVEL ONE: _ LEVEL TWO: X LEVEL THREE: _ (Check one. Explain.) In-class discussion and/or interaction are encouraged—interactions are kept to the subject at hand—students are encouraged to provide support for their point of view.
7. Course Evaluation	Students demonstrate their understanding of the influence of culture on consumer behavior and its impact on businesses through assignments, particularly through a group country feasibility study project.

Percentage of Multicultural Content: 100%
Multicultural Classification:

MC=multicultural content: courses with 60% of the content multicultural

MP=multicultural perspective: courses using a variety of strategies to encourage multiculturalism, including content, instructional strategies, assessment, and classroom dynamics (when this is the only classification, the content is less than 60%)

Choose the best multicultural classification that describes this course: Circle one. MC MP *MC and MP*

Does this course focus on international diversity, U.S. diversity, women's studies, or a combination of all three? Explain.

This course focuses on the influence of culture on consumer behavior and its impact on businesses, particularly differences among countries, but includes content related to differences within a country's culture.

TEXAS STATE UNIVERSITY–SAN MARCOS

<table>
<tr><td colspan="3">MKT3377.751: International Marketing</td></tr>
<tr><td rowspan="2">Summer II—2006</td><td colspan="2">Class Time: MTWHF 2–3:40 PM</td></tr>
<tr><td colspan="2">McCoy 222</td></tr>
<tr><td colspan="2" rowspan="2">Instructor: Enrique Becerra</td><td>Tel: 512-245-1277 (Voice)</td></tr>
<tr><td>E-mail: eb25@txstate.edu</td></tr>
<tr><td>Office: McCoy 314</td><td colspan="2">Office Hours: MTWHF 1–2:00 PM or by appointment</td></tr>
</table>

Course Description

A study of the international planning and coordination of marketing functions, marketing policies, and the analysis of marketing on an international scope, including environmental and cultural aspects. Exams will be objective, with questions drawn from the text material and lecture material. In-class discussion will involve topics found in the assigned readings and current periodicals. A group project, a country/product analysis, will involve researching and analyzing information to determine entry into a foreign market. Critical-thinking skills and information technology will be utilized to help students understand how to make international marketing decisions. This is a web-assisted class; the Blackboard system will be used.

Course Materials

Required Text: Cateora, P., & Graham, J. (2005). *International marketing* (12th ed.). Boston, MA: Irwin/McGraw-Hill.
Additional Material: Library resources, daily newspaper, current business magazines, etc.

Learning Goals

- To introduce the students to the importance of international trade and its impact on the local economy.
- To raise the students' basic awareness of the importance of international marketing and its impact on the local and world economies.
- To extend the basic marketing concepts and techniques into the framework of the world marketplace.
- To develop understanding and appreciation of different cultures and their influences on consumers' behavior and on business practices.
- To tackle ethical and ecological issues in a world with different systems values.
- To introduce students to marketing research and the need to use secondary data to make international marketing decision.
- To increase the students' awareness about the importance of relationship building in a business setting.

Developmental Skills Enhanced

- Critical Thinking (using critical analysis to relate the process or procedures necessary to implement concepts in the organizational environment—evaluated through group project and in-class discussions).
- Reflective Thinking (reflecting on each concept addressed in lecture—evaluated through examinations, group project, and in-class discussion).
- Ethical Understanding, including understanding of background and cultural diversity and Reasoning (enhanced by readings assigned in textbook and out-of-class research—evaluated through in-class discussion).
- Information Technology Understanding (carried out by lectures illustrating how technology innovations are related to, or influence, or are used to carry out each concept studied; *computer software used in this course will include* Microsoft Word/Excel/PowerPoint and Blackboard, among others; *databases to be used include* World Marketing Data and Statistics and USA Trade Online, among others.
- Real-World Application (carried out by lecture where both domestic and international applications of each concept are provided—evaluated through examinations, group project, and in-class discussion).
- Leadership Skills (carried out by lecture discussions which concentrate on how each concept studied can be used to provide leadership to employees or managers in a company—evaluated through examinations, group project, and in-class discussion).

International Marketing Concepts Covered

International environments, International trade institutions; Cultural Environments; Exporting, Licensing, and Franchising; International Pricing; International Communications; International Distribution Channels, Global Strategic Planning; Marketing Research; International Selling and Sales Management; International Consumer Behavior.

Skills and Knowledge You Are Expected to Bring Into This Course

Effective use of Microsoft Word; effective use of Blackboard technology; ability to read, conceptualize, and apply textbook material and make in-field observations from concepts studied in textbook and lecture; ability to write at junior/senior level, basic knowledge of marketing; basic knowledge of economics, accounting, and finance, including budgeting and forecasting; ability to work in groups.

Prerequisites—MKT3343

Course Policies

A. Instructional Methodology

A lecture/in-class discussion/visual/project exercises format will be used. Unannounced films and/or guest speakers and/or unannounced in-class exercises will be utilized when appropriate. A real-world application approach will be utilized emphasizing markets. In-class participation and discussion will be utilized. Students are expected to contribute from their personal experience and from readings of textbook, current periodicals, newspapers, or television and radio newscasts. *Students are expected to read assigned chapters before coming to class and be prepared to participate. Students should expect to spend no less than three hours of study outside class for every hour of lecture, for a total of no less than nine hours of study outside class.*

B. Attendance

All students are *expected* to attend and participate in the in-class assignments and discussions, as well as to be in the classroom ready to study at the appointed time of the beginning of each class. Attendance is mandatory during project presentations—3 points from the final grade will be deducted for an absence and 1 point for lateness to project presentations.

Any conflict—due to work, job interviews, doctor appointments, etc.—must be cleared with professor **prior** to the class session in question, and a written excuse—from the doctor, company, potential employer, etc.—must be provided to the professor within a day of the class missed.

C. Course Requirements

Assignments

In-class exercises/assignments/discussions will be utilized. All students are expected to participate in these assignments. All students will participate in a group project. Late and or missed assignments are not acceptable.

Examinations

There will be two examinations and one comprehensive final. Examinations will be objective in nature, using a battery of questions including short-essay questions. If required, professor will provide an 882 scantron. *Material covered in the lecture, textbook readings, and in-class discussion and exercises will be covered in the exams.* The comprehensive exam will cover chapters 1–19. Examinations grades will be posted in Blackboard.

Makeup Examinations

No makeup examinations are given. However, family emergency and/or doctor's medical excuse documented in writing and provided by the student missing the exam may be deemed appropriate by professor to warrant a makeup examination. The student missing the examination must let the professor know in advance of missing the exam (if possible—in case of an unexpected health emergency, notification must be received within 24 hours of the exam) by e-mail (eb25@txstate.edu) or by telephone (512-245-1277) about the family/health emergency to be eligible for a makeup examination. Unexcused missed examinations will receive the grade of zero.

Group Assignment

There will be a group assignment. The class will divide into teams consisting of no more than four students per group for a country/product (*consumer product*) feasibility study assignment. The project is ongoing throughout the semester. To facilitate the completion of the project, the assignment has been divided into three sections. However, it is only one assignment.

Please notice that any student dropping the class after the "drop with automatic W" date (July 14, 2006) will receive a failing grade (0 points) for the group assignment.

Each student will select his or her own group. Attention to compatibility as well as to diversity of skills, backgrounds, and/or cultures is encouraged when forming teams. Team problems/issues should be discussed with the professor. However, professor can only try to minimize team problem/issues; solutions to problems/issues should come from within the team. Teams have the right to *"FIRE"* a team member for his/her behavior and/or lack of contribution to the team. The team member fired will receive a grade of F for the group project (parts I—III), including the participation grade. *In order to "FIRE" a team member, the following must take place and be documented:*

1. *The team must address their concerns/dissatisfactions with the team member by putting in writing the behaviors and actions that are detrimental to the team progress, and indicate what must be done within a realistic and specified time frame. A copy of this documentation must be given to the professor at the same time it is given to the team member in question.*

2. *In addition to presenting the written document, the team members must hold a meeting to allow the member in question to ask for clarification and respond to the notification, and to give him/her a chance to rectify the situation. The minutes from this meeting must be forwarded to the professor. The team member in question must make a written response and submit a copy to the professor. However, if the team member in question does not attend the meeting, the team may proceed to "fire" the team member in question after meeting with the professor.*

3. *If the situation is not rectified within the specified time frame, and the team members want to pursue the firing, a meeting with the professor must be scheduled with all parties. However, if the team member in question does not attend the meeting, the team may proceed to "fire" the team member in question after meeting with the professor.*

4. *Should the team decide that a team member, after team and professor consultation, is not contributing to the team in an acceptable manner, the team may "fire" the team member. A firing results in an F for the project (parts I—III), including the participation grade for the fired team member. This option should NOT be taken lightly.*

Teams are strongly encouraged to select a team leader/spokesman and to create rules that team members must abide by.

The group assignment will consist of a country analysis/comparison, a country entry analysis, and a presentation of the findings. It is the responsibility of all team members to turn in the assignment on time. There are NO MAKEUPS for the project. *Teams must turn in the project assignment at the beginning of the class on the due date.*

Communicating ideas is important in marketing. Junior-/senior-level competence in writing is expected. PLEASE check the spelling and grammar of your reports. *Written reports with grammatical errors (spelling, grammar, fractured sentences, etc.) will not be graded until the student/group correct the mistakes. Additionally, 3 points or 30% will be deducted from the report grade if the report has more than ten spelling and/or grammatical mistakes.* Students are *strongly* encouraged to submit the written reports to the writing lab before turning them in to the professor. http://www.txstate.edu/slac/owl.htm

For part I, each team will be required to analyze and compare the macro-level environment (economies, culture, history, legal systems, language, and infrastructure—chapters 1–7) of different countries and the assigned country. Each team will be assigned a different country. Findings will be presented in a six-page double-spaced report, excluding cover page, references, and tables (1-inch margins all around, 12-inch Times New Roman font). A suggested table comparison format is provided in the syllabus. A digital copy (on a CD/diskette/etc.) must be provided to professor.

Part II requires that each team determines the feasibility of marketing *laundry detergent* in the assigned country; an assessment of the U.S. laundry detergent industry, as well as an assessment of the assigned country including market size, market potential, demand drivers, local consumer behaviors, pricing, IMC, and channels, is required, as well as a recommendation for market entry. Findings will be presented in a six-page double-spaced report, excluding cover page, references, and tables (1-inch margins all around, 12-inch Times New Roman font). A digital copy (on a CD/diskette/etc.) must be provided to professor.

Part III requires that each team presents their findings to the classroom. All team members must participate in the presentation. Up to 20 minutes are allotted for each team presentation. Presentations should be made using Microsoft PowerPoint and must be handed in to professor with part II of the project. A digital copy (on a CD/diskette/etc.) must be provided to professor.

Attendance to all presentations is mandatory. Attendance policy will be enforced during presentations.

Participation

Each member of a team will grade all team members, including himself/herself, on their participation on each part of the project. The participation grade sheet is provided in the syllabus (students must make copies). They are due **(hard copy only—no other type**

accepted) in class on the dates on which each part of the project is due. Late participation sheets are not accepted.

A point is deducted from all team members from the grade of the project section for which a participation sheet is not turned in. An additional 2 points are deducted from the grade of the project section for the student(s) not turning in his/her participation grade sheets. There are NO makeups for the participation grade sheets. It is the responsibility of the team members to make sure that the participation grade sheets are turned in on time. *Participation sheets are due on the same date that the project is due.*

Participation grade sheets are confidential but not anonymous. Only the professor will know the grades you give to your team members. Grades for participation will be posted on Blackboard only after the final examination. Participation grades must not be discussed with other team members or with anyone outside class except the professor. Participation grade sheets must be folded and stapled before turning them in.

Participation issues should be discussed with the professor. Do bring any project participation issues to the attention of the professor as soon as possible.

Please notice that any student dropping the class after the "drop with automatic W" date will receive a failing grade (0 points) for the group assignment.

Grade Evaluation

Two exams:	40% of grade
Final:	10% of grade
Group Project:	
Part I:	10% of grade
Part II:	20% of grade
Part III:	10% of grade
Participation:	10% of grade

Please Note

- Three points are deducted from the final grade for each absence recorded (please see absent policy above). Each time a student is tardy, 1 point is deducted from the final grade.
- A point is deducted from all team members from the grade of the project section for which a participation sheet is not turned in. An additional 2 points are deducted from the grade of the project section for the student(s) not turning in his/her participation grade sheets.
- Written reports with grammatical errors (spelling, grammar, fractured sentences, etc.) will not be graded until the student/group correct the mistakes. Additionally, 3 points or 30% will be deducted from project report grade if the report has more than ten spelling and/or grammatical mistakes.
- Professor assigns grades as stated in the syllabus. Grades are earned (obtained) by students, not given by professor. If student requires a certain grade to graduate, etc., student must obtain the points to reach his/her grade requirement. Professor may not deviate from grading policy.

D. Classroom Civility

Please refrain from talking (do raise hand if you want to participate in discussion and/or if you want to ask a question) or leaving during lecture. *Leaving class early is not tolerated; professor will deduct 3 points from student's final grade from leaving early.* Do not eat or drink during class/lecture. All electronic devices, including cellular phones, MP3s, beepers, computers, etc. *MUST BE TURNED OFF* (*students with disabilities, please read section D*). Raise your hand when you would like to participate and or to ask a question. Comments should only be made about the content being discussed (not a participant in the discussion).

E. Other

Grades will be posted on Blackboard. All electronic communications will be sent to the students' Texas State University–San Marcos e-mail address. It is the responsibility of the student to keep up to date with the class. Students are encouraged to check/read their Texas State University–San Marcos e-mail as often as possible.

University/College Policies

A. Drop/Withdrawal

A "W" will be automatically assigned if the drop/withdrawal procedure is completed on or before the drop with automatic "W" date (July 14th). It is the student's responsibility (not the professor's) to make sure s/he has complied with the automatic "W" drop date. Schedule errors in this syllabus do not exempt the student for complying with the university dateline policies. A "W" will be assigned only if the student is passing the course on the date the registrar processes the drop; otherwise, an "F" will be recorded. It is suggested that *students consult the instructor prior to dropping or withdrawing from the class.*

B. Academic Honesty

Submission of any work for a grade for which unauthorized help has been received is termed academic dishonesty and will be grounds for a failing grade in the course. "Unauthorized" is a term used here to designate stealing, copying (with or without permission), collaboration with other individuals, or sharing programming code outside of sanctioned group activities. Students are strongly encouraged to refer to the Texas State student handbook for policies related to academic dishonesty. These policies may be found at http://www.mrp.txstate.edu/studenthandbook/rules.html#academic. *This instructor views any such act as a clear violation of ethical standards and will take appropriate disciplinary and punitive action.*

C. Honor Code

All students are required to abide by the Texas State University honor code. The pledge for students states:

Students at our University recognize that, to insure honest conduct, more is needed than an expectation of academic honesty, and we therefore adopt the practice of affixing the following pledge of honesty to the work we submit for evaluation:

I pledge to uphold the principles of honesty and responsibility at our University.

The complete honor code may be found at http://www.txstate.edu/effective/upps/upps-07-10-01.html under attachment I.

D. Students with Disabilities

A student with a disability may require an accommodation(s) to participate in the course. They must contact the instructor within the first two weeks of the semester. They will be asked to provide documentation from the Office of Disability Services (ODS) at that time. Failure to contact the instructor in a timely manner will delay any accommodations they may be seeking. Ongoing care by a physician does not automatically qualify you as an ODS special needs student. Students are required to file paperwork for accommodations with ODS each semester. Accommodations granted one semester do not automatically carry forward to the next. See UPPS No. 07.11.01 for additional information.

Course Outline

We will adhere as closely as possible to the course outline. However, the professor reserves the right to make changes from time to time.

Monday, July 10	Introduction to Class
Tuesday, July 11	Chapter 1—The Scope and Challenge of Int'l Marketing
Wednesday, January 12	Chapter 2—The Dynamic Environment of Int'l Trade
Thursday, July 13	Chapter 3—The Foundations of Culture
Friday, July 14	Chapter 4—Cultural Dynamics in Assessing Global Markets
Monday, July 17	Chapter 5—Culture, Management Style, and Business Systems
Tuesday, July 18	Chapter 6—The Political Environment
Wednesday, July 19	Chapter 7—The International Legal Environment
Thursday, July 20	Group Project Part I due
Friday, July 21	Recap chapters 1–7—project discussion
Monday, July 24	Exam I—Chapters 1–7
Tuesday, July 25	Chapter 8—Developing a Global Vision—Marketing Research
Wednesday, July 26	Chapters 9–10—Emerging Markets—Multinational Markets Regions and Market Groups
Thursday, July 27	Chapter 11—Global Marketing Management—Planning/Organization
Friday, July 28	Chapters 12–13—Product and Services for Consumers/Businesses
Monday, July 31	Chapter 14—International Marketing Channels
Tuesday, August 1	Exam II—Chapters 8–14
Wednesday, August 2	Chapter 15—Exporting and Logistics
Thursday, August 3	Chapter 18—Pricing for International Markets
Friday, August 4	Chapters 16–19—Integrated Marketing Communications (IMC)—Personal Selling and Sales Management—Negotiating Internationally
Monday, August 7	Chapters 16–19 continuation
Tuesday, August 8	Project Part II and Part III due—Presentations

Wednesday, August 9	Presentations
Thursday, August 10	Final Exam—per University Final Exam Schedule

Participation Grade Sheet

Name: ____________________________
Country Assigned: ____________________________
Project Section (I/II/III) ____________________________

Participation is assessed as follows (*grade yourself last*)

Reliability: Has the team member being punctual with assigned tasks? Grade it from 0 to 10, with 10 being the highest grade and 0 being the lowest grade.

Competence: Has the team member completed the assigned task? Grade it from 0 to 10, with 10 being the highest grade and 0 being the lowest grade.

Excellence: Is the quality of the work performed by the team member up to the standards or expectations outlined by the team? Grade it from 0 to 10, with 10 being the highest grade and 0 being the lowest grade.

Behavior: Has the behavior of the team member met the expectations of the team? Grade it from 0 to 10, with 10 being the highest grade and 0 being the lowest grade.

Total: Total points assigned to team member; maximum 40, minimum 0.

Sample List of Countries for Group Project

Colombia
Argentina
Thailand
Russia
Philippines
Poland
Peru
Vietnam
Romania
South Africa
Egypt
Turkey
Jordan
Pakistan
Algeria

15. TEXAS STATE UNIVERSITY–SAN MARCOS
MULTICULTURAL CURRICULUM TRANSFORMATION GUIDE/ASSESSMENT INSTRUMENT

Name of Course: CIS3317—E-Commerce
Instructor: Kevin Jetton
Department: Computer Information Systems & Quantitative Methods
Degree: Business Elective
Degree Program Requirement: YES **NO**

1. Course Description	Explores the constantly changing world of e-business from an international perspective. This course will emphasize e-business challenges and opportunities in the worldwide marketplace, while focusing on global issues of management, implementation, and integration of IT resources. NOTE: The content of this course has always had an international business/consumer perspective, but added emphasis will be placed on the concept of cultural diversity and multiculturalism throughout the course.
2. Course Objectives	• Students will learn the basic concepts of conducting business electronically. • Students will learn the different forms of e-commerce, including business-to-business, business-to-consumer, and consumer-to-consumer. • Students will learn the technical aspects of online monetary transaction processing and associated security considerations. • Students will learn application development tools for the conceptualization, design, and construction of e-commerce solutions for business. • Students will learn how to formulate Internet strategies for e-commerce applications in the global economy. • Students will learn how to analyze current e-commerce activities, incidents, issues, and future trends from both a globalization and multicultural perspective. • Students will increase their awareness of domestic and global issues as they relate to the cultural diversity of consumers, knowledge workers, and information technology (IT) professionals.
3. Course Content (60% needed for multicultural content classification)	LEVEL ONE: ___ LEVEL TWO: ____LEVEL THREE: X (Check one. Explain.) Major categories/topics of course content (all surrounding e-commerce) include: Internet Revolution (Availability, the Digital Divide, and a Global Reach) Business Models (Business-to-Business, Business-to-Consumer, Consumer-to-Consumer) Infrastructure (Hardware) Website Development (Accessibility) Website Security and Payment Options Marketing (Consumer Demographics and Behaviors) Ethical, Social, and Political Issues (Copyright, Socially Acceptable…) Retailing via the Web Online Services, Content (e-zines), Auctions, and Portals

	Online/Virtual Communities (focus on any group you can think of!) Supply Chain Management & Collaboration Degree of Multicultural Content/Multicultural Perspective: 56% of the chapters & scheduled classes are MC/MP 100% of the projects are MC/MP Each content area, with the exception of the pure technology topics, is presented from a multicultural perspective.
4. Instructional Strategies	LEVEL ONE: ___ LEVEL TWO: ____LEVEL THREE: X (Check one. Explain.) This course is taught in either a medium or large teaching theater, depending on whether it is summer or fall/spring semester, through lecture, demonstration, class discussions, small-group work, and both individual and group projects. The course incorporates a variety of research methods that support student engagement integrating culturally specific instructions. Classroom activities promote analysis, creativity, and application of various topics covered in class. Through the use of Blackboard course materials/resources and specific websites, students are encouraged to create communities of learning. Course projects capitalize on student strengths and experiences, which include opportunities for participation and personal growth. Early in the semester, the first three individual projects focus on the Internet/e-commerce from a multicultural perspective, and small groups will be used to compare and share views. The semester group project will strategically simulate a multicultural project team with the charge to research, analyze, develop, document, and present a working e-commerce website that has a distinct multicultural view/content (with limited functionality as this is not a technical course).
5. Assessment of Student Knowledge	LEVEL ONE: ___ LEVEL TWO: ____LEVEL THREE: X (Check one. Explain.) Tests have always had multiple-choice and short-answer questions to appeal to multiple learning styles. Quizzes will be added to reinforce reading assignments and preparedness for in-class discussions and diverse perspectives. In the past, the reading assignments were assigned written homework tasks, with limited opportunities for feedback and class discussion. Three newly added individual projects will require self-assessment and self-reflection as it relates to e-commerce issues with a multicultural perspective. The semester website creation project will now stress multiculturalism content as well as the makeup of the student project team itself.

6. Classroom Interactions	LEVEL ONE: ___ LEVEL TWO: ____LEVEL THREE: X (Check one. Explain.) "Guidelines for Establishing a Safe Environment for Discussing and Learning About Culturally Sensitive Issues" (Piquemat & Kourizin, 2004) was added to the course syllabus to stress the nature of potentially critical and offensive in-class discussions and topics. The goal of every class session is to facilitate participation from a broad range of student backgrounds and viewpoints through general class discussions and small group discussions. The very nature of the vast variety of websites and their content or focus has always been the focus of the class and a source of debate/discussion/opinions. Every day, some technology issue surfaces in the media (e.g., stolen notebook PC's with sensitive data, hacked information systems, credit/debit cards being compromised, online identity theft, fake websites, chain/fraudulent e-mails, spam, social networking sites such as Facebook and MySpace...). All these make for an interesting semester—it never fails!
7. Course Evaluation	Formal McCoy College of Business course evaluations do not address the multicultural goals of the course. However, course assignments, activities, discussions, and projects demonstrate student accomplishment of the specific multicultural objectives of the course. Pre- and post-multicultural perspective instruments will be used to gauge the initial and subsequent student viewpoints and perspectives as they relate to multiculturalism. Student Multicultural Profile at the beginning of the semester will be done. Semester projects (three individual and one group) all have a multicultural focus. Readings and reflections. Students are allowed to comment positively and negatively on course content, exams, projects, and issues or concerns in writing anonymously at the end of the semester.

Percentage of Multicultural Content: 75%

Multicultural Classification:

Multicultural Content (MC): courses with 60% of the content multicultural

Multicultural Perspectives (MP): courses using a variety of strategies to encourage multiculturalism, including content, instructional strategies, assessment, and classroom dynamics (when this is the only classification, the content is less than 60%)

Multicultural Content and Perspectives (MC and MP): combination of both with 60% content

Choose the best multicultural classification that describes this course: Circle one. MC MP **MC and MP**

Does this course focus on international diversity, U.S. diversity, women's studies, or a combination of all three? Explain.

> The course is an exploration of international diversity as it relates to online retailing/website content and the multicultural mix of consumers, knowledge workers, and the information technology professionals that architect, design, develop, and support the e-commerce websites themselves.

TEXAS STATE UNIVERSITY–SAN MARCOS

CIS 3317—E-Commerce		
Summer II, 2007	Class Time: M–F 8–9:40am	
	McCoy 127	
Instructor: Mr. Kevin Jetton	Tel: 210-275-2062 (cell)	
	E-mail: KJ02@txstate.edu	
Office: McCoy 409	**Office Hours**: Mon–Fri 7–8am and 11:40–12:30pm	

Course Description

Explores the constantly changing world of e-business from an international perspective. This course will emphasize e-business challenges and opportunities in the worldwide marketplace, while focusing on global issues of management, implementation, and integration of IT resources.

Note: The content of this course has always had an international business/consumer perspective, but added emphasis will be placed on the concept of cultural diversity and multiculturalism throughout the course.

Course Materials (Required Textbook)

Laudon, K. C., & Traver, C. (2006). *E-Commerce: Business, technology, society* (3rd ed.). Upper Saddle River, NJ: Pearson Prentice Hall, ISBN: 0-13-173516-0.

Learning Goals (Course Objectives)

Students will learn the basic concepts of conducting business electronically.

Students will learn the different forms of e-commerce, including business-to-business, business-to-consumer, and consumer-to-consumer.

Students will learn the technical aspects of online monetary transaction processing and associated security considerations.

Students will learn application development tools for the conceptualization, design, and construction of e-commerce solutions for business.

Students will learn how to formulate Internet strategies for e-commerce applications in the global economy.

Students will learn how to analyze current e-commerce activities, incidents, issues, and future trends from both a globalization and multicultural perspective.

Students will increase their awareness of domestic and global issues as they relate to the cultural diversity of consumers, knowledge workers, and information technology (IT) professionals.

Prerequisites None

Course Policies

A. Instructional Methodology

Most class sessions will involve extensive discussions of the e-commerce issues raised by the text, readings, and cases. Students will be expected to make substantial contributions to the learning process through participation in class discussion. Students will conduct independent research and analyze global e-commerce practices and issues, and share their findings through class discussions, small groups, homework assignments, readings, and projects.

B. Attendance

Attendance is mandatory and in your best interest in order to do well in the class. It is the student's responsibility to attend class and to obtain lecture information and information regarding assignments and exams, and to receive graded exams and assignments passed back in class. Exams will cover material in the text and classroom discussions that may or may not be dealt with in the text.

C. Course Requirements (Components)

Individual Assignments

There will be three individual assignments (worth 50 points each) that serve as "building assignments" preparing you for the semester group project. These projects will showcase the impact of the Internet and our multicultural global population, workforce, and consumer diversity. Individual research, life experiences, and reflection will be shared in the classroom via small-group discussions, class discussions, and presentations.

These assignments will focus on the "isms" of society as they relate to multiculturalism and the Internet/e-commerce websites.

Project#	Theme/Focus	Description
1	**The Digital Divide**	Access to Computers and the Internet "Haves vs. Have-nots"
2	**Website Content**	Website Words, Pictures, Sounds, Images, Color & Reactions
3	**Project Teams**	Workplace Diversity (getting along and getting the job down)

A handout and in-class discussions will provide all the details for the projects. All assignments are due at the beginning of class on the assigned due date as you walk into class in order to be accepted for full credit. They will be accepted up to **two class days** after the original due date with a late penalty of 20%, and will not be accepted thereafter—no exceptions. An assignment is considered late if it is submitted any time after the start of lecture on the due date, and you MUST submit it in class. Sliding it under my office door or submitting it by e-mail or at the CIS department office will all be considered LATE submissions. Small-group and in-class discussions will be utilized to learn and share our thoughts, issues, and reflections after the assignments have been graded and returned.

Individual Assignment Rubric

Score (On Time)	Score (Late)	A function of completeness, quality, thoughts, examples, effort. and personal reflections/thoughts/perspectives
50	40	Outstanding work, all parts fully completed with personal thoughts/reflections.
40	32	Above average work but slightly lacking in quality, content, and thoughts.
30	24	Average work lacking in quality, content, thoughts, and richness.
20	16	Below average work significantly lacking quality, content, & richness.
10	8	Minimal effort, incomplete, barely attempted the assignment.
0	0	Not submitted at all, or past the late deadline.

*Refer to the semester schedule for homework assignments and due dates. A separate handout and class discussion will cover the assignment's perspective, content, and submission guidelines!

Reading Assignments

There will be ten chapter "mini-case" homework/reading assignments throughout the course, worth 10 points each. To encourage reading and, more importantly, attendance and in-class discussion, rather than having a written assignment, there will be **in-class short quizzes** that focus on the key points from the reading assignment, and also include questions about your opinions on key issues brought out by the reading assignment. Refer to the course schedule for assignments and due dates. The lowest grade will be replaced with a 10 (maximum score), which allows you to miss one or do poorly on one and still get the maximum score.

Examinations

There will be a total of four examinations spread throughout the semester. All exams are closed-book and -notes. They will consist of both multiple-choice and short-answer questions. You **must take all four exams,** and there will be NO opportunities to make up work missed due to unexcused absences from class. Lectures, readings, class activities, demonstrations, and assignments will be the basis for the exams. The examinations must be taken on the scheduled date and time for your section. Students who do not take the exams on the date and time scheduled for their section will receive a grade of zero for those exams. Exams may test all material from assigned readings and lecture and presentations, as well as all items covered by the course homework projects. The instructor will retain all original copies of the exams. Unavoidable absence on any exam must be dealt with **prior** to the exam by notifying the instructor in **writing,** and will be handled on a case-by-case basis. The instructor's discretion will determine what constitutes an emergency

Makeup Examinations

Makeup exams, as a rule, will not be given unless a student has a valid and verifiable excuse (such as medical problems). A student with an approved absence on an exam other than the final will be given a comprehensive makeup exam during the last week of classes in the semester. Students can make up only one missed examination, provided the instructor did approve the absence. For an approved absence in the final exam, the student will be given a comprehensive exam during the final exams week of the following semester. This will remove the "I" from the student's record. A grade of zero will be recorded for all exams missed, including exams for which neither a valid nor verifiable excuse was presented. Usually, only extreme emergencies will qualify for a makeup exam, provided a verifiable reason is submitted within a reasonable period of time. The final decision of whether or not to approve a makeup exam rests with the instructor.

Grade Evaluation

Grades will be determined as follows

Component	Points	%
4 major exams (100 pts each)	400	50.0%
10 mini-case assignments/quizzes (10 pts each)	100	12.5%
3 individual projects (50 pts each) that focus on multicultural issues and perspectives surrounding e-commerce	150	18.75%
Semester group project with a multicultural perspective	150	18.75%
TOTAL	800	100%

Grading scale (of total points, weighted as shown above)

Letter Grade Assignment	
Overall percentage of total points	**Letter Grade**
89.5 and higher	A
79.5–89.4	B
69.5–79.4	C
59.5–69.4	D
Less than 59.5	F

Grade disputes, if any, must be resolved within one week of receiving graded work. All grades become final thereafter.

All grades are final, and extra work will not be an acceptable reason for a change in course grade. All four exams must be taken in order to receive a passing grade for the course.

D. Other

Retention of Graded Material

Students are required to retain all graded assignments for a period of one semester to resolve any grade disputes that may arise. Grade appeals will be entertained only if a student is able to produce all graded assignments for verification. Otherwise, the assigned grade will stand. Grade disputes on individual assignments must be resolved within one week of the date that the graded assignment is returned in class. After that time, the assigned grade becomes final. If you do not pick up your assignments/exams on or close to the day that they are returned in class, you may lose your right to dispute the grade or grading.

Use of Blackboard

Assignments, submission requirements, due dates, and any other announcements related to the class as a whole will be posted to the course site on the Texas State Blackboard website. Students should check the course website on a regular basis, preferably each day, for any new material (projects, assignments, pop quizzes, etc.) that may be posted.

Communication

E-mail is the preferred method for non-face-to-face communications. In such cases, the instructor will communicate with students via your Texas State–assigned e-mail accounts only. The instructor will send e-mails only to your Texas State e-mail account. E-mails sent to the instructor should include the words "CIS 3317" in the subject line. All e-mails to the instructor should be signed at the end with your name and CIS 3317.

Classroom Civility

Students are expected to come to class each day prepared to participate in class discussions and activities. If a class is missed, it is the student's responsibility to get missed assignments, class notes, etc. from a classmate before the next class. It is expected that all students will practice professional behavior during the class. That includes being in class on time, being prepared and attentive, respecting others and their ideas, turning off cell phones, pagers, and other electronic devices, and staying in class until the end (unless you have an emergency or have cleared it in advance with the professor). The instructor may take appropriate disciplinary action against violators of classroom civility, including the removal of offending parties from the class and reporting disruptive students to the dean of the college. Students **must** attend the class section for which they are officially registered and complete all exams, assignments, and other course work in that section. Failure to attend class regularly will result in students missing in-class assignments and explanations. More information regarding classroom responsibilities can be found here:

Students' Responsibilities on Advising and Learning, **found at http://www.business.txstate.edu/advising/policies.htm.**

Guidelines for Establishing a Safe Environment for Discussing and Learning About Culturally Sensitive Issues. The following table, developed by Nathalle A. C. Piquemat and Sandra G. Kourizin (2004), includes the guidelines for establishing a safe environment for discussing and learning about culturally sensitive issues, and **we will all practice/follow them this semester**.

Each person can and should contribute to developing a high level of *trust*.

We must all practice *respect* for ourselves and one another.

We must agree to participate in *open* and *honest* discussion and debate.

Everyone should respect the views of others, even if we do not agree with them.

We should practice positive and productive ways in which we can convey our perspectives, feelings, or disagreements.

Everyone should be willing to make comments or contribute to discussions that will promote cross-cultural learning.

We must *listen* to others, as well as *listen to ourselves,* to continue to support strong and healthy communication.

Everyone should feel comfortable and safe about asking questions of others.

We all need to take time to think and question our own assumptions about others.

It is critical that we all practice being accepted and *nonjudgmental and open-minded.*

We must remember that no one is an expert on all cultures, but we should all be consistently learning new things about others.

It is imperative that we understand that no one person speaks as a representative of the entire ethnic, cultural, or social groups to which they belong.

We can help turn around misinterpretations or misunderstandings.

We recognize that we are all here to learn, and one of the most valuable ways to learn is from each other.

University/ College Policies

Drop/Withdrawal

A "W" will be automatically assigned if the drop/withdrawal procedure is completed **on** or **before 7/13/2007**. If the drop/withdrawal procedure is completed **between 7/14/2007 and 8/2/2007**, a "W" will be assigned only if the student is passing the course on the date the registrar processes the drop. Otherwise, an "F" will be recorded. **It is strongly suggested that students consult the instructor prior to dropping or withdrawing from the class.**

Academic Honesty

Submission of any work for a grade for which unauthorized help has been received is termed academic dishonesty and will be grounds for a failing grade in the course. "Unauthorized" is a term used here to designate stealing, copying (with or without permission), collaboration with other individuals, or sharing programming code outside of sanctioned group activities. Students are strongly encouraged to refer to the Texas State student handbook for policies related to academic dishonesty. These policies may be found at http://www.mrp.txstate.edu/studenthandbook/rules.html#academic. **This instructor views any such act as a clear violation of ethical standards and will take appropriate disciplinary and punitive action.**

Honor Code

All students are required to abide by the Texas State University honor code. The pledge for students states:

Students at our University recognize that, to insure honest conduct, more is needed than an expectation of academic honesty, and we therefore adopt the practice of affixing the following pledge of honesty to the work we submit for evaluation:

I pledge to uphold the principles of honesty and responsibility at our University.

The complete honor code may be found at http://www.txstate.edu/effective/upps/upps-07-10-01.html under attachment I.

Students With Disabilities

A student with a disability may require an accommodation(s) to participate in the course. They must contact the instructor within the first two weeks of the semester. They will be asked to provide documentation from the Office of Disability Services (ODS) at that time. Failure to contact the instructor in a timely manner will delay any accommodations they may be seeking. Ongoing care by a physician does not automatically qualify you as an ODS special needs student. Students are required to file paperwork for accommodations with ODS each semester. Accommodations granted one semester do not automatically carry forward to the next. See UPPS No. 07.11.01 for additional information.

A. Emergency Procedures

In the event that a fire alarm goes off, evacuate the building through the closest exit door in an orderly fashion and move away from the building, until instructed by safety personnel to return to the classroom. In the event of an illness and/or injury during class, notify the professor immediately. All students are to remain seated to allow emergency personnel to access the individual requiring medical attention.

McCoy Hall Policies

Please note that NO FOOD is allowed in any McCoy Hall classroom and drinks in CLOSED CONTAINERS are allowed only in classrooms without power and data connections on the tables. NO FOOD OR DRINKS are allowed in any computer classroom.

Group Project

This project MUST be done in groups of four students. Under no circumstances will groups of five or more students be allowed unless we have an odd number of students in the course, and it will require instructor authorization. In the event that a student drops, the remaining team members will have to carry out the project, much like in the business world when a key employee suddenly resigns.

Your group/team will be creating a website using common FREE website creation tools such as GeoCities by Yahoo or other resources, including those of Texas State University, that you come across. You are also welcome to use Adobe's DreamWeaver or Microsoft's Frontpage or Expression products.

You do not need to be a professional website designer/developer to get an A on this project!

Due Date	What Is Due?
July 20, 2007	Group Name, Team Member Names, and Team Diversity Profile in writing
August 3, 2007	Group Project Notebook (proposal, development details, URL, screen shots)
August 6, 2007	Group Presentations of your website by ALL team members
August 7, 2007	Group Presentations (overflow time if necessary)

*Refer to the next page for details about the semester group project!

Semester Group Project

The Assignment: Develop an e-commerce website for any fictitious business. It is up to your team to decide what business or product(s) (real or fictitious) you would use.
Group Size: Four individuals
Diversity: A mixture of gender and cultural diversity among the team members

The site must have the following features, at a minimum:

1. A background page that lists location of corporate headquarters or equivalent
2. At least two products
3. Business policies for customer transactions, and could include:
    - Complete and easy to understand rate charges if the business provides a service;
    - Shipping policy and charges;
    - Tax policy; and
    - Return policy
4. Privacy Policy
5. Security Statement (or policy)
6. Use at least two images
7. Space for at least one banner advertising (You don't have to put an actual banner.)
8. A webmaster e-mail function on each page
9. No dead-end pages or links
10. A multicultural "perspective" so as to avoid any "isms" through words, pictures/images
11. Allowance for multilingual and multicurrency options

Group Project Grading/Scoring

Your group project website will be "subjectively" evaluated based on its "look and feel" and it content. Be creative and have fun!

Points 150 maximum

50 points for your project notebook
50 points for the website itself (my review of your site)
50 points for in-class presentation by ALL team members

In designing your site, the following aesthetics must be considered:

1. Appropriate use of colors and contrasts
2. Appropriate amount of information on each page—do NOT clutter your pages with too much information
3. Appropriate use of images (so that load time is not too high)
4. Consistent images or logo throughout the site
5. Use of easy navigation features
6. Website look-n-feel
7. Consideration of diversity on the website content

Project Notebook Content

Company Profile
Project Team Member Profile showcasing the Diversity of the Team Members
Project Plan (schedule)
Screenshots of the Web Pages
Individual reflection on what I learned from a MC perspective & the group

Keys to Success for Maximum Points Pretend you are an information technology consulting firm and treat the project a report of your expertise, research, analysis, conclusions, and recommendations for the client that is paying you.

Name of Course: MC 2319 Visual Communication
Instructor: Mr. David Nolan
Department: School of Journalism and Mass Communication
Degree: Mass Communication
Degree Program Requirement: YES NO

1. Course Description	This course studies the principles, theories, and language of visual communication, emphasizing the evaluation and use of images in mass media. Note: This course also explores multicultural perspectives in visual communication concerning race, culture, class, ethnicity, and gender.
2. Course Objectives	This course is designed to help students integrate words and pictures in mass communication from a multicultural perspective. It will help students explore the idea that memorable visual messages with text have the greatest power to inform, educate, and persuade an individual. At the end of the semester, students should be able to: • Look at images created in different media and evaluate them from a multicultural perspective. • Demonstrate basic knowledge in the historical and cultural evolution of visual communication. • Examine their personal, cultural, critical, and ethical perspectives concerning visual communication. • Understand the principles of visual design and be sensitive to issues of race, culture, class, ethnicity, and gender as they relate to design.
3. Course Content (60% needed for MC classification)	LEVEL TWO: ____LEVEL THREE: X (Check one. Explain.) Content covered includes: sense, select, perceive (how we make sense of our world); how light works; the eye, retina, and the brain; color, form, depth, and movement (using an international perspective); sensual and perceptual visual theories (gestalt, constructivism, semiotics, and cognitive theory, and how we culturally make sense of imagery); visual persuasion (explores stereotypes and exploitation through advertising); media stereotyping (explores issues of race, ethnicity, gender, culture, and class); image analysis (analysis and construction of meaning through culturally specific imagery); typography (international perspectives in the use of type); graphic design (exploration of design through a multicultural lens); informational graphics (infographic use culturally and geographically); cartoons (exploration of stereotypes); photography (perspectives on international conflict and poverty); motion pictures (exploration of culturally specific imagery, e.g., Bollywood versus Hollywood); television and video (stereotypes in television programming); computers (international perspectives, issues of access); and the World Wide Web (pornography versus technology, global community). Each content area, with few exceptions, is presented from a multicultural perspective.

4. Instructional Strategies	LEVEL TWO: _X_ LEVEL THREE: ____ (Check one. Explain.) This course is taught in a teaching theater through lecture, demonstration, and discussion. The course also incorporates a variety of research methods that support student engagement, incorporating culturally specific instruction. Classroom activities promote analysis, creativity, and application of various topics covered in class. Through the use of Blackboard course materials, students are encouraged to create communities of learning. Course projects capitalize on student strengths and experiences and include opportunities for participation and personal growth.
5. Assessment of Student Knowledge	LEVEL TWO: ____ LEVEL THREE: _X_ (Check one. Explain.) While the nature of a large lecture course dictates certain assessment methods such as multiple-choice exams, this course incorporates multiple methods of assessment that engage students in authentic forms of self-reflection, evaluation, and change. Visual projects includes: a personal website exploring each student's multicultural lens; a multicultural cartoon analysis that explores issues of race, ethnicity, gender, and social class; and a multicultural poster project that allows students to visually explore specific issues of stereotyping, discrimination, race, age, social class, language, disability, social status, religion, sexuality, health, ethnicity/nationality, or sex/gender. The use of these projects encourages meaning making, synthesis, and application of course content.
6. Classroom Interactions	LEVEL TWO: _X_ LEVEL THREE: ____ (Check one. Explain.) On the first class day and throughout the semester, students are encouraged to participate, confront biases, and ensure respectful interactions with each other. Course standards are explicit, and I communicate the high standards expected in the course on the first day. I implement strategies that promote equity, address oppressive behavior, and ensure various cultures are respected and allowed to participate in their own way. While group activities are limited due to the size of the course, I do encourage interaction by students with various discussion boards that create communities of learning.
7. Course Evaluation	Formal School of Journalism and Mass Communication course evaluations do not address the multicultural goals of the course. However, course assignments, activities, and projects demonstrate student accomplishment of the specific multicultural objectives of the course (i.e., look at images created in different media and evaluate them from a multicultural perspective; demonstrate basic knowledge in the historical and cultural evolution of visual communication; examine their personal, cultural, critical and ethical perspectives concerning visual communication; understand the principles of visual design and be sensitive to issues of race, culture, class, ethnicity and gender as they relate to design). Students are allowed to comment positively and negatively on course content, exams, projects, and issues in writing during the final class day.

Percentage of Multicultural Content: 75%

Multicultural Classification:

MC=multicultural content: courses with 60% of the content multicultural

MP=multicultural perspective: courses using a variety of strategies to encourage multiculturalism, including content, instructional strategies, assessment, and classroom dynamics (when this is the only classification, the content is less than 60%)

Choose the best multicultural classification that describes this course: Circle one. MC MP **MC and MP**

Does this course focus on international diversity, U.S. diversity, women's studies, or a combination of all three? Explain.

The course touches on all three.

TEXAS STATE UNIVERSITY–SAN MARCOS

MC 3319: Visual Communication		
Fall 2011	Campus Schedule: Monday and Wednesday 3:30–4:40 Alkek 250	
Instructor: Mr. David Nolan		Tel: 512-245-9653 E-mail: dnolan@txstate.edu
Office: Old Main 226	**Office Hours**: Mon. & Wed. 10:00–11:00 a.m. and 5:00–6:00 p.m.; Fri. 1:00–2:00 p.m.	

About This Syllabus

This syllabus is your contract with me. By remaining enrolled in the course, you are agreeing that you have read—and that you understand—the terms outlined in this document and that you agree with those terms. If you disagree with the terms outlined in the syllabus, or if you want clarification of any part of the syllabus, then it is your responsibility to get in touch with me to discuss the issue.

Course Description

This course studies the principles, theories, and language of visual communication, emphasizing the evaluation and use of images in mass media. Note: It also teaches you about subconscious influences on your perceptions of reality and your behavior, and the fundamentals of visual literacy, and explores multicultural perspectives in visual media concerning race, culture, class, ethnicity, and gender.

Course Purpose

Allen Ginsberg, poet and author, stated, "Whoever controls the media—the images—controls the culture." We live in a mediated blitzkrieg of imagery. They fill our newspapers, magazines, books, clothing, billboards, computer monitors, television screens, and cell phones as never before in the history of mass communication. Communicating effectively in this visual age of multimedia and mass communication is vital. Visual communication is everywhere today, from electronic media such as web pages and television screens to environmental contexts such as road signs and retail displays. As the National Education Association has pointed out, "Western civilization has become more dependent than ever on visual culture, visual artifacts, and visual communication as a mode of discourse and a means of developing a social and cultural identity." Evidence suggests that people not only communicate visually more than ever, they also communicate better when they communicate visually. Recognizing the importance of visual communication is key to your future success. Since technological advances continue to develop at an unprecedented rate, we need to promote the learning of visual literacies as indispensable to life in the information age. We must recognize the importance of developing visual literacies in order to survive and communicate in this highly complex world. Skills developed in this class include the evaluation of advantages and disadvantages of visual representations, to improve shortcomings, to use them to create and communicate knowledge, and to devise new ways of representing insights. By teaching you to understand and communicate through visuals, this course empowers you with the necessary tools to thrive in this increasingly media-varied environment. In a society where powerful interests employ visual data to persuade, this class shows you how to look beyond the surface to understand deeper levels of meaning and the tactics employed to sway your thinking. Seeing is an avenue to higher-order thinking processes that will help you meet the professional, cultural, and personal challenges of media.

Course Objectives

This course is designed to help you integrate words and pictures in mass communication from a multicultural perspective. It will help you explore the idea that memorable visual messages with text have the greatest power to inform, educate, and persuade an individual. At the end of the semester, you should be able to:

- Demonstrate awareness of the range of visual works in media.
- Demonstrate an understanding of the visual works being studied as expressions of individual or broader human values within a historical, cultural, or social context.
- Articulate an informed critical response to the visual work being studied.
- Demonstrate aesthetic appreciation of the visual works being studied.
- Demonstrate knowledge of the importance of visual communication in defining or exploring a culture.
- Critically study and investigate visual communication in photography, television, computer games, films, comics, advertising, and other visual media.
- Stress a command of media technology and the fundamentals and techniques in visual expression, and the importance of the image as an instrument of expression and communication.
- Create knowledge and techniques of visual communication and the impact and use of key tools of visual communication to express one's own thoughts in the media.
- Examine the intended use of an image in the media.
- Examine the structural and content analysis of media presentations in photography, motion pictures, digital media, video, and graphic design.

Textbook (Required)

Lester, P. M. (2011). *Visual communication: Images with messages* (5th ed.). Belmont, CA: Wadsworth. ISBN-13: 9781439082829. You will need this textbook to pass this course. There is a copy on reserve in the library for this class.

Attendance

School policy permits faculty members to lower a student's final grade for absences or tardiness. Students must attend all classes. Inform me beforehand if possible if you know you will be absent. Your attendance in class is very important in order to pass this course. You get only three preapproved class absences this semester. Use them wisely. After three absences your overall course grade may be lowered.

Student E-Mail

If you have not activated your Texas State e-mail account, go to www.txstate.edu/computing/apps/newuser.html and follow the instructions on the site. You need to have your Texas State e-mail activated as soon as possible for TRACS access.

Contact Info

I keep Monday, Wednesday 10:00–11:00 a.m. and 5:00–6:00 p.m. and Friday 1:00–2:00 p.m. open for drop-in appointments. To request another time, e-mail me. E-mail is the best way to get hold of me outside of class (dnolan@txstate.edu).

Grading

Final grades are based on 1,000 possible total points. Points are tabulated as follows:

1. Test 1 = 300 pts (30%)
2. Test 2 = 300 pts (30%)
3. Final Exam = 300 pts (30%)
4. Poster Project = 50 pts (5%)
5. Visual Journal = 50 pts (5%)
6. Cartoon Extra Credit = 20 pts

This course uses the 10-point grading scale, as follows: A = 90–100; B = 80–89; C = 70–79; D = 60–69; F = 59 or less. If you wish to dispute a grade assigned or a question on an exam, you must do so IN WRITING (e-mail is fine) within 24 hours after the exam, project, or paper has been returned to you. You must include specific reasons why your answer is correct, or why the paper deserves a higher grade. All exams are required and cannot be made up except with a documented excuse approved by the instructor. The three semester exams consist of multiple-choice questions and are "closed-book," covering chapters from the course textbook, subject articles, films, or visuals covered in class, and lecture material that will sometimes be outside of the textbook. The final exam cannot be missed or made up. See the schedule for the final exam day and time.

Academic Honesty

The School of Journalism & Mass Communication commits itself to the preparation of ethical mass media professionals and scholars. Such a mission demands the highest standard of academic honesty and integrity. Violations of academic honesty, including but not limited to plagiarism, unauthorized collaboration, collusion, deception, conflict of interest, and theft, are not tolerated and can lead to severe penalties. Disciplinary actions for violations of the standards for academic honesty are outlined in the Texas State Academic Honesty Statement, printed each year in the Texas State Student Handbook. The policy is also available at: http://www.txstate.edu/effective/upps/upps-07-10-01.html

Disability Support Services

Texas State University seeks to provide reasonable accommodations for all qualified individuals with disabilities. This university will adhere to all applicable federal, state, and local laws, regulations, and guidelines with respect to providing reasonable accommodations as required to afford equal educational opportunity. Students with disabilities who need special accommodations should register with the Office of Disability Services (512-245-3451). If you are a student with a disability certified by ODS and you require accommodation in my class, it is your responsibility to tell me at the beginning of the semester so that accommodation can be provided promptly.

Dropping a Course

You can drop this course by October 24 and receive an automatic W. After October 24 you cannot drop a single course; you must withdraw from all courses. You must drop by September 9 to receive a full refund.

Extra Credit Multicultural Cartoon Analysis

Stereotyped images create false ideals that real people can't hope to live up to, foster low self-esteem for those who don't fit in, and restrict people's ideas of what they're capable of. For this extra credit project, you will explore representations of race, culture, class, ethnicity, and gender by analyzing comics over a five-day period and writing about your observations. This activity leads to greater multicultural awareness of stereotypes in the media and urges you to form more realistic visions of these images as you analyze them.

You will be examining images of men, women, and children in comic strips, evaluating gender, racial, ethnic, religious, and class stereotypes, and providing improved alternatives to the existing representations.

1. Choose one character from a multiframe cartoon series online or in a newspaper, magazine, etc., and track the character over a consecutive five-day period. Collect copies of the comics for the period and turn them in to me on the due date with your paper.
2. Each day summarize the daily storyline for each comic strip and record the issues of gender, race, ethnicity, religion, and/or class that arise from the comic in your journal. Make personal comments as well, relating your own feelings about these issues.

3. At the end of the five-day period evaluate how "fair," "equitable," and "realistic" the comic strip is overall, referring to evidence that you have collected in your daily summaries. Second, perform a "comic character makeover" and explain how you would rewrite your character to make the character more realistic and equitable. Finally, as you examined and revised your comic strip, what did you realize that you didn't notice before about your particular comic strip or comics and cartoons in general?

I will talk about this in class and post a handout on TRACS that will detail the assignment. Total extra credit points possible = 20

First Amendment Poster Project

"Congress shall make no law respecting an establishment of religion, or prohibiting the free exercise thereof; or abridging the freedom of speech, or of the press; or the right of the people peaceably to assemble, and to petition the government for a redress of grievances."

You will work individually and design on a computer an approximately 8.5 x 11-inch full-color poster used to persuade a target audience on the Texas State Common Experience topic of the "First Amendment." I will remain neutral regarding your poster's content. However, I am automatically part of your target audience. If I cannot understand—or if I disagree with the effectiveness of—any part of your poster's design and message, my evaluation of your poster will reflect this.

Purpose: This project affords the student the following opportunities: (1) to consider how visual communication conveys meaning from a cultural perspective; (2) to employ visual communication principles as tools of persuasion; (3) to select appropriate typefaces, fonts, styles, and images; (4) to create effective image and text combinations; (5) to represent (by means of visual design) issues or ideas; (6) to explore and expand technical and aesthetic abilities; (7) to produce representative materials for presentation; and (8) to practice meeting deadlines.

Images: No image is required. However, you can use images if you feel they are a necessary part of the message. This is an educational environment; therefore, you are permitted to use found images as part of your project. However, for this project you are only allowed to use an image without words or slogans already in it, unless they are an integral part of the image (e.g., a photo of a protest march with the protest signs visible). Remember that finding the "right" image takes time, so start early.

Size: The poster must be approximately 8.5 x 11 inches and mounted on 11 x 14-inch black photo-mounting board. It can be either horizontal ("landscape") or vertical ("portrait") format. You can find the proper board at the university bookstore. The bookstore has odd sizes available (e.g., 11 x 13 inch and 10 x 14 inch), and those are also acceptable for this project. No foam core!

Grading: You will be evaluated according to: (1) selection/use of type and image; (2) overall design and creative ability; (3) effectiveness in developing and conveying a concept; (4) craft and technique; (5) effectiveness in attracting and maintaining attention; (6) readability and legibility of both text and images; and (7) professional presentation. In particular, you will lose points for sloppy presentation, typographic errors, spelling, and grammar, for not following instructions, and particularly, for not meeting deadlines.

Submission Guidelines: Make sure you print your full name on the back of the board for identification purposes. The project is due at the beginning of class on the due date listed on the schedule. I will talk about this project in class. See me as soon as possible if you have any questions or concerns.

Total points possible = 50

Visual Journal

You will create and maintain a visual journal for the entire semester. The journal should have at least two entries a week over the semester, starting on the date in the class schedule. When it is turned in you should have a total of twenty-eight entries. Total points possible = 50

What Is Visual Journaling?

Visual journaling has existed throughout history as a process of reflective thinking, and as a recording of image making. Throughout history great thinkers recorded and reflected on their ideas using a variety of visual journaling techniques. Visual journaling is a process that encourages you to get to know yourself on a deeper, intrinsic level. This is an effective way to break down walls of communication by using the visual journaling process as a form of self-exploration and visual communication. Visual journals serve as a record of how we think, which moves us out of the world of reflex and allows us to look beyond the immediate situation and pay closer attention to the process.

Suggestions for Visual Journaling

1. Buy cheap unlined journals, with spirals and black front pages. Leave the covers alone until the end, but there are no rules here and you can do what you like. If you want you can make your own journal or buy a handmade one. You don't have to do a large amount of writing on each page. Use pictures to convey to me what you are thinking about at the time and just make a statement of some type with writing or blocks of text.
2. The first thing you can do is color about ten pages. If the backgrounds are already colored it may be easier to get going. There is something scary about plain white pages to some people, and this may make it easier for you. You can scribble on the pages with crayons or pencil or whatever media you wish to use.
3. It is up to you what you use and how you decorate the background. If you draw then you will know just how much of the background you want to color. If you want to do a lot of writing in the journal, then I would suggest that you color around the top and edges and leave the inside of the page blank. Create your own unique style.
4. When you feel the mood to create, go to the book and choose a page that calls to you.
5. Don't start at the front page at all. This is about creativity and intuition, and learning to see the mediated world around you. Always date the page. This will give you a feel for the rhythm of your life as you look through the journal later on.

6. Now to the collage part. Flick through magazines and just pull out the pages or rip out the pictures that call to you. Sometimes the picture you choose won't convey what you want to say, but it just "feels right." Glue the pictures on the pages and then add the text. You can even cut out letters from a magazine to make up the words.

7. The writing usually comes last. It is a good idea to take your journal with you wherever you go (during lunch, waiting for the bus, traveling) so you can get it out and do the writing when the urge hits you or when an idea pops into your head.

Class Schedule

August			
24 Wednesday	Introduction to the Course / Sense, Select, Perceive		
29 Monday	Light / The Eye, Retina, and the Brain	Chapter 1	Start Visual Journal
31 Wednesday	Color & Form	Chapter 2	
September			
5 Monday	Labor Day Holiday		
7 Wednesday	Depth & Movement		
12 Monday	Gestalt and Constructivist Theory (Sensual Theory)	Chapter 3	
14 Wednesday	Semiotic and Cognitive Theory (Perceptual Theory)		
19 Monday	Visual Propaganda	Chapter 4	
21 Wednesday	Visual Persuasion		
26 Monday	Body Image and the Media		
28 Wednesday	Sexual Imagery and Advertising		
October			
3 Monday	Test 1 (Chapters 1–4)		
5 Wednesday	Stereotypes in Visual Media	Chapter 5	
10 Monday	Visual Analysis	Chapter 6	Cartoon Extra Credit
12 Wednesday	Graphic Title Designs and Saul Bass	Chapter 8	
17 Monday	Graphic Design		
19 Wednesday	Editorial Cartoons & Cartoon Culture	Chapter 10	
24 Monday	Cartooning Technique		
26 Wednesday	Photojournalism	Chapter 11	

31 Monday	Photography Technique		
November			
2 Wednesday	Visual Structure I		Poster Project
7 Monday	Test 2 (Chapters 5–11; 7 & 9 not on test)		
9 Wednesday	Visual Structure II		
14 Monday	Editing the Visual Story		
16 Wednesday	Motion Pictures	Chapter 12	
21 Monday	Motion Picture Technique / The Shot		
23–25 Wed–Fri	Thanksgiving Break		
28 Monday	Computers and Creating Visual Media	Chapter 14	Visual Journal Due
30 Wednesday	Using the Web to Tell Visual Stories	Chapter 15	
December			
5 Monday	Three Visual Screens: Mobile, Web & Television	Chapter 13	
14 Wednesday	Final Exam 2:00–4:30 P.M. (Visual Structure through Chapter 15)		

17. TEXAS STATE UNIVERSITY–SAN MARCOS
MULTICULTURAL CURRICULUM TRANSFORMATION GUIDE/ASSESSMENT INSTRUMENT

Name of Course: MC 13130 Writing for the Mass Media
Instructor: Kym Fox
Department: School of Journalism and Mass Communication
Degree: Mass Communication
Degree Program Requirement: YES NO

1. Course Description	An introduction to the major forms of writing for the mass media: advertising, broadcasting, print journalism, and public relations. *Writing and Reporting News* by Carole Rich was chosen as the text, in part, because it features culturally diverse images and voices.
2. Course Objectives	•Differentiate among the demands of different types of media writing and adjust your writing style and approach based on those demands. •Identify news values and concepts critical to accurate, clear news writing in a multicultural society. •Understand the importance of using culturally diverse sources in the mass media. •Identify appropriate sources of information for various media writing styles and develop a strategy for incorporating diverse sources to accurately reflect the community. •Analyze the role of a culturally diverse workforce within the mass media industry. •Write concisely and accurately in the various media disciplines studied, including print, broadcast, public relations, and advertising. •Construct a basic hard news story with a summary lead and inverted pyramid story organization. •Construct a feature story using appropriate lead and story organization. •Construct a broadcast news story using broadcast conventions. •Construct a news story for the Internet and understand the convergence of various media on the Internet. •Demonstrate skills necessary to construct elements of a multimedia story. •Create a press release using news writing conventions. •Create advertisements following basic copy-writing techniques. •Demonstrate a basic understanding of media law and ethics. •Be conversant in current events.
3. Course Content (60% needed for multicultural content classification)	LEVEL ONE: ___ LEVEL TWO: X LEVEL THREE: ___ (Check one. Explain.) The primary goal of this course is to produce competent writers capable of writing in a variety of mass media styles. To write effectively in each of the styles, the writer must understand the multicultural community in which the media function. In a long semester, one week is devoted to examining the role of culturally diverse sources in news stories. In the mass media, the terms *diversity* and *diverse sources* often take into consideration gender, ethnicity, age, occupation (income), and geography (where you're from). Throughout the rest of the semester,

	students are expected to rely on that foundation to produce accurate news reporting. To reinforce the point, students are specifically evaluated on the incorporation of culturally diverse sources and topics. Further reinforcement is offered weekly through the use of visuals in the classroom. Specific images, both still and video, are chosen because they represent good media practices of using culturally diverse subjects and sources and also represent a multicultural mass media workforce. For example, a broadcast story may be chosen because the anchor is an Asian woman and the news story features the plight of the homeless.
4. Instructional Strategies	LEVEL ONE: ___ LEVEL TWO: ____LEVEL THREE: X (Check one. Explain.) This course is taught in a lecture and laboratory format. The lecture has about 65–75 students with laboratory breakouts of 15–18. In lecture, the students will sit together in laboratory groups to facilitate class discussion and help build a community of learners. During each lecture session, short activities are designated to help the students draw upon personal experiences to analyze and evaluate specific forms of media writing. The traditional lecture is mixed with short video examples whenever possible. Captioning is used in the videos when possible. In laboratory, the community of learners is further encouraged though small groups. Students are encouraged to tackle short exercises together, to draw on the strengths of the various group members. Because writers often do their best work when they are permitted to write about a subject of their choice, I let the students choose most of the topics for their news stores and for their group project. They do "real" reposting, going out to cover events on campus or in the community, rather than writing static facts from a workbook. Peer editing is required on a weekly writing projects, with students encouraged to find new editing partners periodically to experience new perspectives. Laboratory exercises expand upon topics covered in the lecture and promote application of specific material covered.
5. Assessment of Student Knowledge	LEVEL ONE: ___ LEVEL TWO: ____LEVEL THREE: X (Check one. Explain.) Students are assessed primarily through work completed in laboratory or homework turned in during laboratory. As the professor, I teach one laboratory, and graduate assistants conduct the remaining seven laboratories. In an attempt to bring consistency to the assignments, a detailed rubric is utilized on all writing assignments. The students are provided with the rubric, and it is discussed in class prior to the completion of the first assignment. The rubric specifically evaluated the use of culturally diverse sources in each assignment. Although this is a writing-intensive course and, as such, the students do a considerable amount of writing, they are assessed by a variety of means. They are permitted to peer-edit each assignment prior to turning it in. Each writing assignment is evaluated using the coaching method, in which corrections are not made, but suggestions are offered on ways to improve the writing or to point out potential errors and do self-

	evaluations. One group project is conducted each semester, which incorporates service learning. The groups are permitted to choose from a variety of formats for their project, including print, audio, video, or online. The exams are a combination of multiple-choice, true/false, short-answer, short-essay, and a longer writing assignment where students apply specific writing skills.
6. Classroom Interactions	LEVEL ONE: ___ LEVEL TWO: ____LEVEL THREE: X (Check one. Explain.) Classroom interaction can be a challenge at 8 a.m. on a Monday in a room full of 70 students, but we try. To facilitate the interaction and help build the community of learners, the students sit in laboratory groups during lecture. This format lets me call on a specific group of students to start the discussion rather than randomly calling on students and putting them on the spot. In lecture, we sometimes use self-reflection and write our thoughts on a topic before we begin a discussion. In laboratory, students work with partners of their choosing part of the time, and in preassigned groups once the semester is in progress. Much attention is paid to constructing the groups. The goal is for each group to be diverse in media professions (an ad major, a PR major, a broadcast major, etc.) and to be personally diverse in gender, ethnicity, or cultural heritage. The groups are facilitated via the course Blackboard site, where the groups are brought together electronically so they can communicate with ease when they are away from class. Blackboard discussion boards are set up for the groups and for the class as a whole. Students use the Blackboard discussion boards to share writing tips and current events. Group members evaluate each other as well as choose the Most Valuable Group Member, based on what the member brought to the team and how he or she shared individual talents and leadership. In both lecture and laboratory, we occasionally utilize the Muddiest Point or a similar method of inviting students to jot a short note about something that they find confusing or that warrants more discussion.
7. Course Evaluation	The School of Journalism and Mass Communication employs a standard course evaluation throughout the department. It does not address cultural diversity questions specific to any one course. Although I use this evaluation, I also do at least three Blackboard surveys throughout the semester to solicit student input on course material and presentation. It will be appropriate to add a section to the survey regarding cultural diversity. I use instant surveys with fewer than five questions if we have a particularly tough issue in class. This gives students a chance to be heard, anonymously if they so choose. Each writing assignment also is evaluated on the use of culturally diverse sources. The group project is evaluated partly on whether it focuses on an underserved group in the community.

Percentage of Multicultural Content: 20–30%

Multicultural Classification:

Multicultural Content (MC): courses with 60% of the content multicultural

Multicultural Perspectives (MP): courses using a variety of strategies to encourage multiculturalism, including content, instructional strategies, assessment, and classroom dynamics (when this is the only classification, the content is less than 60%)

Multicultural Content and Perspectives (MC and MP): combination of both with 60% content.

Choose the best multicultural classification that describes this course: Circle one. MC **MP** MC and MP

Does this course focus on international diversity, U.S. diversity, women's studies, or a combination of all three? Explain.

This course primarily addresses U.S. diversity because we study American media models and the U.S. mass media industry, but due to our proximity to Mexico, we incorporate a perspective on Mexico as being part of the community.

TEXAS STATE UNIVERSITY–SAN MARCOS

MC 1313: Writing for the Mass Media	
Fall 2011	Campus Schedule: Monday 8–8:50 a.m.; Tuesday 8–8:50 a.m.
Instructor: Kym Fox	Tel: Mobile: 210-508-9364 E-mail: Kfox@txstate.edu
Office: OM 202A	**Office Hours**: M: 11 a.m.–12 p.m.; T–TH: 1–3 p.m. and by appointment
NOTE: If my door is open, you are welcome to stop in anytime.	

Course Description

An introduction to the major forms of writing for the mass media: advertising, broadcasting, print journalism, and public relations. Prerequisite: full major status and typing skills. **Note:** This is the first writing course in the mass communication sequence, and it is writing-intensive. (That means you write A LOT in this class.) It is designed to teach the basics of various media writing styles, with an emphasis on print journalism, but it includes writing for broadcast, the Internet, public relations, and advertising. Students will be expected to sleep with the *Associated Press Style Book*—it's that important. This course is a core requirement in all mass communication sequences. Mass communication majors are required to earn at least a C in this class to continue in the program.

Objectives & Goals

When you have successfully completed this course, you should be able to:

- Differentiate among the demands of different types of media writing and adjust your writing style and approach based on those demands.
- Identify news values and concepts critical to accurate, clear news writing in a multicultural society.
- Understand the importance of using culturally diverse sources in the mass media.
- Identify appropriate sources of information for various media writing styles and develop a strategy for incorporating diverse sources to accurately reflect the community.
- Analyze the role of a culturally diverse workforce within the mass media industry.
- Write concisely and accurately in the various media disciplines studied, including print, broadcast, public relations, and advertising.
- Construct a basic hard news story with a summary lead and inverted pyramid story organization.
- Construct a feature story using appropriate lead and story organization.
- Construct a broadcast news story using broadcast conventions.
- Construct a news story for the Internet and understand the convergence of various media on the Internet.
- Demonstrate skills necessary to construct elements of a multimedia story.
- Create a press release using news writing conventions.
- Create advertisements following basic copy-writing techniques.
- Demonstrate a basic understanding of media law and ethics.
- Be conversant in current events.

Required Text

Harrower, T. (2010). *Inside reporting* (2nd ed.). Boston, MA: McGraw-Hill. ISBN: 13 9780077291525

The Associated Press stylebook. (2010) New York, NY: Associated Press. ISBN 978-0-917360-54-1

(AND don't even *think* of selling it back. You'll need it for several other classes. You may use the electronic version, provided via Alkek databases, but a printed version of the book is preferred for learning AP style.)

Optional but Recommended

Fluker, L. (2010). *Mastering grammar, spelling and punctuation* (1st ed.). Dubuque, IA: Kendall Hunt. ISBN-13: 9780757562693

Kessler, L., & McDonald, L. (Eds.). (2007). *When words collide* (7th ed.). Boston, MA: Wadsworth. ISBN-13: 9780495050254 (An older edition of this book will be less expensive and just as useful.)

Other Required Materials

A dictionary, a thesaurus, a flash drive or other means of transporting your writing projects to the lab computers, and a three-ring binder for your portfolio.

Format

This course will be taught in a lecture and lab format. The weekly lecture will be the basis for the work done in the lab. Attendance at both the lecture and lab is crucial to succeeding in this course. During lecture, you will sit with your lab group to better facilitate class discussion.

TRACS

This course will utilize the TRACS system. Most course handouts and assignments will be posted on TRACS rather than handed out in class.

TRACS Assignments & Assessment Tools

We will use the TRACS assignments tool for most of our class assignments. Please check that area and follow the class calendar provided under the syllabus link in TRACS. We will also use the assessments tool in TRACS for exams and quizzes.

Attendance Policy

The School of Journalism & Mass Communication policy permits faculty members to lower a student's grade for absences or tardiness. You are expected to come to class each week. Graded work will be done during most lecture and lab meetings. This work cannot be made up unless you have arranged an excused absence prior to class as per university policy. In some instances, the lowest grade in a category is dropped. That affords you one absence without harm to your grade. Please come speak with me if you have extenuating circumstances that require you to miss class.

Class Portfolio and Senior Portfolio—Evidence of your work in this class is required for your School of Journalism & Mass Communication Senior Portfolio. You should retain the MC1313 portfolio you submit at the end of the semester for this class so you can use the material for your senior portfolio. Like all good writers, you will want to keep your prose for posterity (or at least until you get finished with this class, because that's how you'll get a grade in here). Keep all your completed writing assignments, both your first version that you turned in AND the rewritten version if that applies to you. Keeping a professional portfolio is important in this career field.

Grading

Grades are available via the TRACS gradebook. All the grading categories, assignments, and weights of grades are visible in the gradebook.

Stories- 30%

This class is all about writing, so much of your grade will be the stories you write. A grading rubric for the stories is posted on TRACS.

Lesser Assignments—10 %

The category consists of smaller assignments primarily done early in the semester and for the portfolio.

The learning modules in TRACs and associated quizzes are a part of this section.

Internet Project—10%

You will be assigned to work in teams of three or four to develop a blog (website) that will be either based on news reporting and journalism or a public relations/advertising-based site. You will publish your project online using words, images, and potentially video. This is a service-learning project that will benefit you and your community. If you select the PR/advertising perspective, an emphasis will be placed on partnerships with culturally diverse and underserved segments of the campus and the community.

Current Events—10%

Staying up on the world's events is crucial to the media professional in every discipline. To succeed in this course, you must stay up to date on local, national, and international current events by reading newspapers, listening to quality news radio (such as NPR or local news radio stations), and watching television news. The Internet also has some valuable news resources. Each week you will have a current events quiz in lecture. Each quiz will be between five and fifteen questions and will include questions from the text reading as well. The quiz is given at the beginning of class. If you miss it, you CANNOT make it up. The lowest current events grade is dropped.

Media Mistakes—Current Events Extra Credit

You may earn extra credit in the current events category by identifying GSP/AP errors in media/PR or advertising examples. Use the TRACS/forum to submit.

Exams—40%

There will be a midterm and final exam. These exams will be a combination of multiple choice, short answer, and writing, as well as AP style and GSP. The final will be comprehensive.

Extra Credit—1 % maximum

Extra credit will be available this semester for specific events relating to mass communication, such as guest speakers on campus. You may submit two extra credit assignments to earn points in this category. Extra credit options: (1) You may complete one online course on NewsU.org and send the course completion via e-mail to your lab instructor; (2) you may attend a mass comm speaker event and submit a one-page, typed synopsis to your lab instructor (you may not double-dip and use an event for which you are receiving credit to attend in this or another class). In addition, any story *written for this course* that is published by a reputable news source (that includes the *University Star*, KTSW, and *Bobcat Update*) will be considered for extra credit. Consult lab instructor for approval.

NOTE: Students who have no more than three unexcused absences are eligible for extra credit. An excused absence requires documentation of an emergency, illness, or school activity.

Assignments

Details of each assignment will be posted on the TRACS site. All assignments are due as per the date on the assignment in the TRACS assignment tool.

Late work

Mass communication is a deadline-driven business, and so is this course. Late assignments will **NOT** be accepted. If you must miss class on the day an assignment is due, you must submit your assignment by the deadline or it will not be accepted. Under rare circumstances, e-mailed assignments will be accepted. These exceptions must be approved by the lab instructor.

Grading

Stories—30 %

Assignments in this category are weighted equally. One grade from this category is dropped if all stories are completed.

NOTE: Story 1 is graded under the Lesser Assignments category and carries less weight.

Story 2–5

A complete breakdown of the grading percentages is posted on TRACS gradebook.

Lesser Assignments—10%

Assignments in this category are weighted equally. A breakdown is available on TRACS gradebook.

Qualities of News, Leads, Story 1—news facts, Portfolio, Learning Module quizzes and other small assignments.

Internet Project—10%

Current Events—10%

The lowest current events grade is dropped.

Exams—40%

All parts weighted equally.

Extra Credit—maximum 1%

E-mail

You MUST have a Texas State e-mail account. The grading program I use and the TRACS system utilizes the Texas State e-mail system. Check your Texas State e-mail account regularly, because I often send notices about internships and scholarships as well as information concerning class.

Academic Dishonesty

The School of Journalism & Mass Communication commits itself to the preparation of ethical mass media professionals and scholars. Such a mission demands the highest standard of academic honesty and integrity. Violations of academic honesty, including but not limited to plagiarism, unauthorized collaboration, collusion, deception, conflict of interest, and theft are not tolerated and can lead to severe penalties. Disciplinary actions are outlined in the Texas State Academic Honesty Statement, printed each year in the Texas State Student Handbook. The policy is also available at www.txstate.edu/effective/ upps/upps-07-10-01.html or www.txstate.edu/swtexan/apolices.html

Students With Special Needs

If you are a student with a disability certified by ODS and you require accommodation in my class, it is your responsibility to tell me at the beginning of the semester so accommodation can be provided promptly. You must notify me by the second week of class if you need accommodation. If your status is pending with ODS, notify me as soon as possible. Contact the ODS office if you have questions, at 245-3451. It is my desire to accommodate students to the best of my ability. ODS certification assists in this endeavor.

Drop Policy

Texas State has a new course drop policy. You can drop this or any course by **Oct. 24, 2011,** and receive an automatic W. **After that date you cannot drop a single course;** you must withdraw from all courses. Please review PPS 4.09 at this website: www.txstate.edu/academicaffairs/pps/pps4/4-09.html

MC1313		**Tuesday/Thursday lecture/lab schedule**
DATE	**CLASS**	**TOPIC & ASSIGNMENTS**
	Lecture	Textbook reading Current events quiz
	Labs	TRACS tools accessed via left column on TRACS Learning modules on TRACS Assignments: Details on TRACS/assignments. Uploaded assignments to TRACS/assignments. Quizzes via TRACS assessments tool Exercises and some peer editing also will be done in lab Forums—Extra Credit AP/GSP forum

Week 1		
Aug. 25	Lab	***Is Writing Important?*** ASSIGN: Syllabus quiz in TRACS/ assessments Practice quiz available to assist with learning TRACS assessments
Week 2		
Aug. 30	Lecture	***What Is News & Who Makes It?*** Chapters 1–2—Topic: Qualities of news Current events quiz 1
Aug. 30	Lab	Topic: What Is AP Style & Why GSP? ...From Citizen J to Pros ASSIGN: Qualities of news TRACS/assignments ASSIGN: AP Style learning module DUE: Syllabus Quiz
Sept. 1	Lab	Leads you know Assign: Basic Leads TRACS/assignments DUE: Qualities of news
Week 3		
Sept. 6	Lecture	***Writing Like a Pro in a Multimedia World*** Chapter 3: News Writing Basics Current events quiz 2
Sept. 6	Lab	**Lead Writing** Leads Workshop & A Basic News Story DUE: Basic leads **DUE 24 hours** before lab as per TRACS/assignments deadline ASSIGN: Basic Leads revision due next lab TRACS/assignments ASSIGN: GSP learning module Assign: Story 1: Basic hard news story TRACS/assignments
Sept. 8	Lab	Basic News Story Working on the Basic News Story DUE: AP Style learning module (including AP Topics Quiz) due 11 p.m. Sept. 8 for all lab sections. DUE: REVISED Basic Leads TRACS/assignments
Week 4		
Sept. 13	Lecture	***Giving Voice to the Voiceless*** Chapter 4: Reporting Basics • Current events quiz 3
Sept. 13	Lab	Topic: Peer editing of Story 1 & The Next Step • Effective use of paraphrases & quotes • How to introduce yourself in an interview • Intro to posting on a blog Assign: Quote Style Learning Module (w/quiz) DUE: Story 1—Basic news story
Sept. 15	Lab	• Topic: Diverse sources exercise Assign: Paraphrase & Quote blog post & STORY 2

Week 5		**Tuesday/Thursday lecture/lab schedule**
Sept. 20	Lecture	Interviewing and good questions: Preparing for a news conference More Chapter 4 basics Current events quiz 4
Sept. 20	Lab	News conference prep & effective interviewing Peer editing Story 2 ASSIGN: GSP learning module DUE: Quote Style Quiz (with learning module) TRACS/assessments Quiz due Sept. 20 for all labs DUE: Story 2
Sept. 22	Lab	Searching online with TX State databases Small groups Assign: Story 3—News conference
Week 6		
Sept. 27	Lecture	A news conference • Story 3—News conference Mandatory attendance. If you miss this news conference you risk a significant point deduction on Story 3. Current events quiz 5
Sept. 27	Lab	Writing the interview Work on Story 3 Midterm review posted
Sept. 29	Lab	Complete Story 3 / Peer edit story 3 in class DUE by end of lab: Story 3 DUE Sept. 29—all lab sections: GPS Common Mistakes Quiz (learning module)
Extra Credit		
Oct. 5 Weds.	**CNN Anchor Soledad O'Brien, 7 p.m. Strahan Coliseum** This is part of the Common Experience. To earn extra credit, write a one-page recap of her presentation, or Tweet about the presentation and copy your Tweets as proof, or shoot video and show it in class. NOTE: If you are in another class for which this is extra credit, submit a different format assignment for each.	
Week 7		
Oct. 4	Lecture	Midterm exam Part 1—News basics/ lecture and textbook
Oct. 4	Lab	Midterm exam Part 2—AP & GSP exam
Oct. 6	Lab	Midterm exam Part 3—writing exam
Week 8		
Oct. 11	Lecture	*Media Convergence* Chapter 8: Online Reporting Current events quiz 6
Oct. 11	Lab	Links, photos and other online extras Assign Story 4—Internet writing

Oct. 13	Lab	Photos and Soundslides And Mass Comm Week prep
Week 9		
Oct. 18	Lecture	**Mass Comm Week**—No lecture this week. You are expected to attend Mass Comm Week events and complete Story 4. Full schedule at TxStateMCWeek blog.
Oct. 18	Lab	Mass Comm Week—check lab instructor for assigned MCWeek session and meeting place.
Oct. 20	Lab	Mass Comm Week—check lab instructor for assigned MCWeek session and meeting place. DUE: Story 4 Post to class blog and copy of text to TRACS/Assignments
Week 10		**Tuesday/Thursday lecture/lab schedule**
Oct. 25	Lecture	*More Media Convergence & Broadcast* Chapter 8: Online Reporting Current events quiz 7
Oct. 25	Lab	Workshop Web writing & Broadcast style Peer evaluation Story 4
Oct. 27	Lab	Writing as we speak Broadcast words
Week 11		
Nov. 1	Lecture	*The Impact of News 24/7: Broadcast* Chapters 9: Broadcast Journalism Current events quiz 8
Nov. 1	Lab	Broadcast writing exercises Assign: Story 5—Optional Story (to drop another story grade)
Nov. 3	Lab	Broadcast writing Broadcast exercise (graded writing)
Week 12		
Nov. 8	Lecture	*Being an Advocate* Chapter 10: Public Relations Current events quiz 9
Nov. 8	Lab	Writing Press Releases Exercise: Press release writing style Assign Internet project / TRACS/assignments
Nov. 10	Lab	Planning a successful project Internet project group work Assign group tasks, review deadlines DUE Nov. 10—all labs: Story 5—Optional Story (Since this is an optional story, it is due for all labs at the same time)
Week 13		

Nov. 15	Lecture	Chapters 7: The Law & Ethics • Current events quiz 10 • Final Exam Review available
Nov. 15	Lab	Internet Project GROUP WORK DUE: Internet Project blog URL (present to class)
Nov. 17	Lab	Internet Project GROUP WORK Due: Internet Project blog / About Us / About Project posts (present to class)
Week 14		
Nov. 22	Lecture	Ethics in Mass Comm Chapter 7 • Current events quiz 11 (LAST ONE) PORTFOLIOS due in lecture to lab instructor
Nov. 22	Lab	GROUP PRESENTATIONS
Nov. 24	Lab	Thanksgiving Enjoy your break
Week 15		
Nov. 29	Lecture	Final Exam Part 1 ** Media Writing (text & lecture)
Nov. 29	Lab	Final Exam Part 2 ** Comprehensive—and AP & GSP exam 2
Dec. 1	Lab	Final exam Part 3** Writing a Story LAST DAY to submit to the AP & GSP extra credit forum
Final exam note		**Tuesday/Thursday lecture/lab schedule**
		****NOTE**: Because the Media Writing course is structured in a once-a-week lecture and twice-a-week lab format, our final exam falls during the last week of classes. We have no other final exam during the regular finals week.

18. TEXAS STATE UNIVERSITY–SAN MARCOS
MULTICULTURAL CURRICULUM TRANSFORMATION GUIDE/ASSESSMENT INSTRUMENT

Name of Course: MU2313—Introduction to Fine Arts
Instructor: Richard Hall
Department: School of Music
Degree: All (Part of the core curriculum)
Degree Program Requirement: YES NO

1. Course Description	A study of the interrelation of music with art, dance, and theater. (A chronological survey of artistic styles, media, and genres from antiquity to the contemporary, with special emphasis on the Western arts, taking into account the influence of various world cultures.)
2. Course Objectives	At the end of this course, the students will: • Be aware of a wide variety of works in the arts and humanities. • Be able to present and explain the historical, social, and cultural context in which a given work of art was created; articulate the meaning/meanings of a given work of art within a historical, social, and cultural context; present and explain the given works of art in the context of an individual artist's career, aesthetic convictions, and/or personal history with regards to race, culture, class, ethnicity, and gender. • Be able to articulate the elements that make up works in the various artistic disciplines; comprehend historical, social, and cultural influences upon critical procedures and values applied to the arts. • Be able to apply the principles of critical and aesthetic judgment incorporating different perspectives. • Comprehend the concept of aesthetic principles, articulate the elements that make up works in the various artistic disciplines, and define principles within the artistic discipline. • Comprehend the influence of philosophy and its impact on various arts across cultures and within cultures, and comprehend the relationships between literature and arts across cultures. • Be able to engage as a diverse audience in the creative process or interpretive performance, and comprehend the physical and intellectual demands required of the writer or visual or performing artist. Throughout the semester, the students will be quizzed and tested on various works of art, musical pieces, and architectural structures that they have never seen before (even in class). Using applied knowledge, the students will identify the artist and/or style of the work, have a general idea of the cultural, historical, and empirical influences on the work and/or the artist, and list these influences as well as characteristics that contribute to the work and/or style.

3. Course Content (60% needed for multicultural content classification)	LEVEL ONE: ___ LEVEL TWO: ___LEVEL THREE: X (Check one. Explain.) The very nature of the course makes the content 100% multicultural. There is not a class session in which the influence of world cultures or the effects of diversity on an artist (race, culture, class, ethnicity, gender, etc.) is not discussed. Special emphasis will be given to several specific world styles that have influenced certain artist/composers, e.g., Navajo sand painting, African tribal mask, Indonesian Javanese gamelan music, African music, Jewish art, Muslim art and architecture, Spanish and Mexican painters, the music of India, Chinese art, women artists. The impact these world styles have on our current culture and art styles will also be discussed.
4. Instructional Strategies	LEVEL ONE: ___ LEVEL TWO: X LEVEL THREE: ____ (Check one. Explain.) Most of the class is lecture-based. However, class discussion is used, particularly with regards to social issues dealing with the arts, e.g., downloading music, certain countries suppressing the arts. Informal surveys dealing with these issues will be utilized and discussed in class (Should someone be able to download music for free without the consent of the artist? Why or why not?) Also, interactive flash quizzes on TRACS help the students review exam material. Classroom Performance System (CPS) quizzes will be used to present some new information and/or to measure the comprehension of earlier material.
5. Assessment of Student Knowledge	LEVEL ONE: ___ LEVEL TWO: ____LEVEL THREE: X (Check one. Explain.) Exams will consist of fill-in-the-blank questions utilizing a word bank. Many questions will entail analyzing works/pieces that have never been seen in class (inference learning). Written critiques dealing with art exhibits, music performances, architectural structures, and world styles will also be assigned (the world exploration critique being an Internet assignment). Students are given a choice as to the art museum or musical performance to attend, hence many students will go to events in their local areas, exposing them the social implications of the arts in their communities. The CPS electronic-remote system is also used for short pop quizzes to access student understanding of the material and for informal and formal surveys measuring student input on the material. Extra credit is offered for engagement with other artistic events throughout the community.
6. Classroom Interactions	LEVEL ONE: ___ LEVEL TWO: X LEVEL THREE: ____ (Check one. Explain.) Classroom interaction is difficult in a large class setting. However, throughout the semester there will be some class discussion focusing on historical, political, philosophical, and cultural issues that are relevant to the works discussed in class and how these issues have affected the arts today. CPS quizzes will also be used not only as a way to measure student learning, but also to help the students become more active participants in the large classroom environment. Students are also encouraged to attend musical events/art museums with fellow classmates and discuss their experiences, both past and present. Hopefully, this will cause the students to reflect on the impact that the arts have on their communities.

7. Course Evaluation	Precourse evaluations through TRACS will be used to assess the students' past experiences relevant to the course (e.g., how many know how to read music, how many have never been to an art museum, etc.) and to measure the students' expectations for the course. CPS surveys throughout the semester as well as an end-of-course evaluation on TRACS will be used to measure the students' thoughts on the multicultural content and coverage of current artistic issues, and to see if the expectations presented by students at the beginning of the semester were met.

Percentage of Multicultural Content: 100%

Multicultural Classification:

Multicultural Content (MC): courses with 60% of the content multicultural

Multicultural Perspectives (MP): courses using a variety of strategies to encourage multiculturalism, including content, instructional strategies, assessment, and classroom dynamics (when this is the only classification, the content is less than 60%)

Multicultural Content and Perspectives (MC and MP): combination of both with 60% content

Choose the best multicultural classification that describes this course: Circle one.
MC MP **MC and MP**

Does this course focus on international diversity, U.S. diversity, women's studies, or a combination of all three? Explain.

The course content is strongly focused on the diverse issues that influenced artists and the evolution of the arts in relation to race, culture, class, ethnicity, and gender on both a national and global scale.

TEXAS STATE UNIVERSITY–SAN MARCOS

Music 2313—Hall—Intro to Fine Arts		
Fall 2007	Campus Schedule: Monday 8–8:50 a.m.; Tuesday 8–8:50 a.m.	
Instructor: Richard Hall	Tel: 245-2651	
	E-mail: richardhall@txstate.edu	
Office: MUS 212	**Office Hours**: MW 11 a.m.–12 p.m. or by appointment	

Course Description

A study of the interrelation of music with art, dance, and theater. (A chronological survey of artistic styles, media, and genres from antiquity to the contemporary, with special emphasis on the Western arts, taking into account the influence of various world cultures.)

Course Objectives

At the end of this course, the students will:

- Be aware of a wide variety of works in the arts and humanities.
- Be able to present and explain the historical, social, and cultural contexts in which a given work of art was created; articulate the meaning/meanings of a given work of art within historical, social, and cultural contexts; present and explain the given works of art in the context of an individual artist's career, aesthetic convictions, and/or personal history with regards to race, culture, class, ethnicity, and gender.
- Be able to articulate the elements that make up works in the various artistic disciplines; comprehend historical, social, and cultural influences upon critical procedures and values applied to the arts.
- Be able to apply the principles of critical and aesthetic judgment, incorporating different perspectives.
- Comprehend the concept of aesthetic principles, articulate the elements which make up works in the various artistic disciplines, and define principles within the artistic discipline.
- Comprehend the influence of philosophy and its impact on various arts across cultures and within cultures, and comprehend the relationships between literature and arts across cultures.
- Be able to engage as a diverse audience in the creative process or interpretive performance, and comprehend the physical and intellectual demands required of the writer or visual or performing artist.

Throughout the semester, the students will be quizzed and tested on various works of art, musical pieces, and architectural structures that they have never seen before (even in class). Using applied knowledge, the students will identify the artist and/or style of the work, have a general idea of the cultural, historical, and empirical influences on the work and/or the artist, and list these influences, as well as characteristics that contribute to the work and/or style.

Required Text

Sporre, D. (2008). *The creative impulse: An introduction to the arts* (w/CD insert) (7th ed.). Upper Saddle River, NJ: Prentice Hall.

Required Material

CPS *RF Receiver for Higher Ed,* made by eInstruction. ISBN: 1881483649

Attendance

In order to experience the full scope of this course, students must attend all class lectures. There are no excused absences. Attendance will be counted through pop quizzes given at the beginning and/or the end of class during the semester using CPS–RF remotes. Please be on time to class. Students who expect to miss class must arrange to receive the missed material from fellow colleagues. **No makeups for missed exams—no exceptions.**

Grading

Four Exams	300 points (100 pts. each, lowest is dropped)
Five Art/Music/World critiques	100 points (20 pts. each)
Quizzes (13)	100 points
Final Exam	100 points (required)
Total	600 points

Grading Scale (for final grade)

600–540 pts = A; 539–480 pts = B; 479–420 pts = C; 419–360 pts = D; 359–0 pts = F

Grades will be sent only through a Texas State e-mail account.

Homework, Tests, and Exams

Homework primarily consists of reading, listening, and viewing assignments associated with certain text and audio/ visual examples as well as attendance at live performances/exhibits. Some assignments may consist of computer usage (TRACS, PowerPoint, Flash). All university students have access to various labs on campus. Additional assignments or extra credit may be announced when appropriate. The exams of this course will be fill-in-the-blank (with a word bank), entailing visual and aural recognition of assigned works, as well as detailed knowledge of works discussed in class. Academic dishonesty **will not** be tolerated. Any offense could result in failing the course or serious disciplinary actions from the university. (Consult your student handbook for additional information.)

Music 2313.0001—Hall—Intro to Fine Arts—Syllabus—Fall 2007 Schedule

Week 1 8/22	Syllabus Elements of Art
Week 2 8/27, 8/29	Ancient World, Archaic Greece, Greek Classicism **Chs. 1, 2, 3**
Week 3 9/3, 9/5	**Mon.—Classes do not meet** Roman Period, Judaism, Byzantium **(Jewish Music)** **Chs. 4, 5, 6**, Review
Week 4 9/10, 9/12	**Mon. Exam 1 (Chs. 1–6)** Early Mid Ages, High Mid Ages **Chs. 7, 8 (Muslim Art)**
Week 5 9/17, 9/19	High Mid Ages, Early Ren., **(Chinese Art)** **Chs. 8, 9** ***Mon.—Critique 1 Due***
Week 6 9/24, 9/26	High Ren., Mannerism **Ch. 10 (Music of India)** Northern Renaissance, Reformation **Ch. 11** Review
Week 7 10/1, 10/3	**Mon. Exam 2 (Chs. 7–11)** Baroque **Ch. 12 (Spanish, Mexican Art)**

Week 8 10/8, 10/10	Classical Period (Enlightenment) **(Indonesian Music)** **Ch. 13** ***Mon.—Critique 2 Due***
Week 9 10/15, 10/17	Review **Wed. Exam 3 (Chs. 12–13)** Romantic Age, **Ch . 14 (Women Artists)**
Week 10 10/22, 10/24	Romantic, Realism, Impressionism **(Japanese Art)** **Chs. 14, 15** ***Wed.—Critique 3 Due*** *Mon.—Last day to drop (w/"W")*
Week 11 10/29, 10/31	Post-Impressionism, Modernism **Chs. 15, 16 (African Art)** Review
Week 12 11/5, 11/7	**Mon. Exam 4 (Chs. 14–16)** Post-Modernism **Ch. 17 (Native American Art)**
Week 13 11/12, 11/14	20th-Century Music, Art & Architecture ***Wed.—Critique 4 Due***
Week 14 11/19, 11/21	20th-Century Music, Art & Architecture **(African Music)**
Week 15 11/26, 11/28	20th-Century Music, Art & Architecture ***Wed.—Critique 5 Due***
Week 16 12/3	Final exam review **(All Extra Credit Is Due)**

The instructor reserves the right to modify the schedule as he sees fit.

Final Exam Dates

MU2313-0001 Wednesday, Dec. 5th, 8:00AM–10:30AM

Drop/Withdraw

Effective Fall 2007, the Automatic "W" and Drop Deadline have changed. Refer to the course schedule.

Class Discussions

The course will, at times, engage discussions on a wide variety of topics dealing with the arts around which there are a range of diverse perspectives and opinions. All students are allowed to share their viewpoints and ask questions; respectful dialogue is essential. No personal attacks will be tolerated. Civility is an expected component of participation. Students are also asked to be open and respectful of the information and works presented.

Students with special needs (as documented by the Office of Disability Services) should identify themselves at the beginning of the semester.

Music 2313.0001 Fall 2007—Hall

Critiques

You will be required to turn in **five** critiques (one from each category) on various fine art performances and exhibits.

Critiques:

1 **Professional Music Performance** A performance or concert of serious music by an internationally recognized professional group (Austin Symphony, Austin Lyric Opera, Austin Broadway Series, Dallas Symphony, Houston Symphony) or a faculty member or featured guest artist of Texas State. Critique all works performed.

2 **Student Music Performance** A performance or concert of serious music by a student or group of students from Texas State University School of Music. Critique all works performed.

3 **Professional Art Exhibit** A visit to a professional art gallery (Austin Museum of Art, Mexi-Arte Museum–Austin, Blanton, Umlauf Sculpture Garden & Museum–Austin, San Antonio Museum of Art, McNay–San Antonio) viewing a special collection or the general collection. Critique at least seven works.

4 **Texas State Art Exhibit** A visit to a student/faculty/featured artist exhibit at the **Atrium Mitte** Complex at Texas State. (**No other gallery on campus will count.**) Critique at least five works.

5 **World Art Exploration** You will critique two art pieces and/or musical pieces from several world genres (Jewish, Muslim, Chinese, India, Spanish-Mexican, Indonesian, Japanese, Native American, African). These works will be found on websites that will be provided to you later in class (& posted on TRACS).

Not all concerts/museums are acceptable. If the performance group/museum is not listed above, your critique may not count. Check with the instructor if you are not sure about an event. You **may not** use an exhibit/performance in which you participate or a convocation performance. All performances/exhibits/events must be attended/visited during the Spring 2006 semester.

- Critiques must be typed and no less than 500 words, no more than 700 words.
- Include a cover page that contains Name, Class Time, Section number, and Type of Critique.
- Critiques must be stapled.
- A copy of the program must be stapled to the back of the critique. **No exceptions**. (Consists of a small booklet/pamphlet/handout listing all performers/works performed, a museum brochure explaining the exhibit(s), a postcard featuring guest/faculty artist in the case of **Atrium Mitte** exhibit)
- Critiques **will not** be accepted by e-mail.
- Critiques are due at the **beginning** of class; critiques turned in after class are late. (Critiques will **not** be accepted early.)
- Critiques may be done in any order.
- Keep a hold of your critiques that are given back. If a discrepancy occurs with your grade, you can then prove me wrong.

- Critiques should give a sense of the artistic experience. Be constructive, studious, and professional. Give positive and negative points of the performance/exhibit (be specific).

Not Typed	Wrong length (500–700 words)	Not Stapled	No Typed Cover page	No Program	Late (One class session)	Content (Spelling, Grammar, etc.)
-20 points	-15 points	-5 points	-5 points	-10 points	-10 points	Down to -20 points

Some examples of questions to ask while attending a performance/exhibit

Music

- Date/ location of performance? Who are the performers?
- Titles of the pieces? Composers? Dates written?
- What can you say about the contrast during the work?
- What cultural influences are contained in the work?
- What is your subjective experience of the work? What mood does it convey? Does this work remind you of anything?
- How does it relate to others we have studied in class? How is it different?

Art Exhibit (Painting, Sculpture, etc.)

- Date/ location of exhibit? Who are the artists?
- Titles of works? Dates completed? Medium? (oil, watercolor, bronze, marble)
- What is the subject of the work?
- Describe specific artistic details. (brushstroke, focal point, texture)
- What can you say about the contrast of the work? (color, line, space)
- What cultural influences are contained in the work?
- What do YOU think the artist is trying to say?
- **How does it relate to others we have studied in class? How is it different?**

Theater/Dance

- Date/ location of performance? Who are the performers?
- Titles of the piece/pieces? Director? Dates written?
- Briefly describe the plot, characters, choreography, sets, costumes, etc.
- What can you say about the contrast during the work?
- What cultural influences are contained in the work?
- **How does it relate to others we have studied in class? How is it different?**

When making points, be specific.

Extra Critiques:

You may also do the following extra critiques for added credit.

- Any **one** performance by the Texas State Theater or Dance Department 12 pts.
    - www.finearts.txstate.edu/theatre/index.html
- Austin Lyric Opera's production of *Opera's Greatest Hits* 12 pts.
    - Nov. 2, 3, 4.
    - www.AustinLyricOpera.org
- Something on campus 12 pts.
    - place
    - date
- A visit to the Harry Ransom Center at UT in Austin 12 pts.
    - www.hrc.utexas.edu/home.html
- A second World Art Exploration 12 pts.

Extra critique events may not be used for regular critiques. All critique guidelines do apply.

Due Dates: 1st Critique—Sept. 17, 2nd Critique—Oct. 8, 3rd Critique—Oct. 24, 4th Critique—Nov. 14, 5th Critique—Nov. 28.

10 pts will be deducted if a critique is late. Any critique turned in after the due date is late. Critiques will only be accepted one class session after the due date.

19. TEXAS STATE UNIVERSITY–SAN MARCOS
MULTICULTURAL CURRICULUM TRANSFORMATION GUIDE/ASSESSMENT INSTRUMENT

Name of Course: MU 3269—Current Trends in Music II
Instructor: Mary Ellen Cavitt
Department: Music
Degree: Bachelor of Music
Degree: Program Requirement: YES NO

1. Course Description	This course is designed to introduce you to the fundamental principles of effective instrumental music instruction and to provide opportunities for you to practice applying those principles in your own teaching. All of you are talented, skilled musicians and intelligent, well-educated people. Your decision to pursue music education as a career reflects your interest in music as an art form and your commitment to the education and well-being of all children. I hope that throughout the semester you will be challenged to examine carefully your own expectations, hopes, and biases regarding a professional life in teaching. The ultimate goal of the course is that you acquire a basic understanding of the fundamental principles of our discipline, a realistic perspective of your own strengths and weaknesses as developing professionals, and a compelling interest in learning about and confronting the challenges that lie before you in the remainder of your undergraduate education and in your future professional lives.
2. Course Objectives	• Stimulate thinking concerning the role of music and music instruction in the lives of all children, and the responsibilities of teachers in setting and accomplishing appropriate instructional goals. • Organize, synthesize, and apply knowledge and skills related to music and human learning. • Develop personal teaching skills by applying fundamental principles of effective instruction in guided experiences. • Analyze and discuss the influence of ethnicity, social class, bilingualism, abilities, disabilities, and gender on human development and music learning. • Demonstrate knowledge of basic psycho-acoustic principles as they apply to the teaching of instrumental music. • Analyze and discuss general techniques of student measurement and evaluation to instrumental music classes. • Apply philosophical/psychological principles and organization theory in developing models of instrumental music curricula. • Demonstrate basic pedagogical knowledge on all common brass, woodwind, percussion, and string instruments. • Analyze and discuss procedures for the successful administration of school instrumental programs in culturally and socioeconomically diverse communities.

3. Course Content (60% needed for multicultural content classification)	LEVEL ONE: ___ LEVEL TWO: _X__LEVEL THREE: ____ (Check one. Explain.) The majority of the course content is related to instructional strategies, teaching skills, and music pedagogy. Approximately 25% of the content will be multicultural. Specifically, students will be directed to (1) consider music of diverse cultures to motivate and challenge students, and (2) analyze how their students' diverse socioeconomic statuses, cultures, abilities, and genders will affect music teaching and administration.
4. Instructional Strategies	LEVEL ONE: ___ LEVEL TWO: ____LEVEL THREE: __X_ (Check one. Explain.) In addition to lecturing, discussing, engaging students in constructing knowledge, and building critical thinking skills, students will form peer-teaching ensembles. This will encourage transfer of lecture information into active learning. Students will have multiple opportunities to select music from diverse perspectives, create lesson plans, teach, and rehearse ensembles independently.
5. Assessment of Student Knowledge	LEVEL ONE: ___ LEVEL TWO: ____LEVEL THREE: _X__ (Check one. Explain.) In addition to traditional papers and exams, I will use alternative assessments that focus on student growth as future teachers: action-oriented teaching projects using multicultural music, and self-assessment and reflection related to the course. For example, students will engage in teaching projects (with videotaped self-reflections and self-assessments) and develop assessment criteria and classroom management and administrative tasks for their future music classrooms. I will use frequent low-magnitude assessments rather than infrequent high-magnitude assessments. Additionally, students will receive feedback from their peers. Some of the skill-based assignments are designed so that students can reach a level of mastery. Because of this, they are given multiple opportunities to retest (or re-teach) and receive additional feedback and evaluation. The emphasis is on creating successful future teachers. Student teaching will be videotaped, and self-assessed, peer-assessed, and teacher-assessed.
6. Classroom Interactions	LEVEL ONE: ___ LEVEL TWO: ____LEVEL THREE: _X__ (Check one. Explain.) A small part of the semester will include lecture and discussion. I will keep data on participation rates to make sure that I am aware of my biases and responsiveness to students of varying abilities, races, and genders. I want to make sure that I don't unintentionally interact with a particular subset of my students. I will also ask students to practice giving peer feedback (and I will assess their peer assessments). Throughout the semester, students will take the information presented in lectures and transfer it into practice. Students will be systematically placed in groups/ensembles that promote equity and support cross-group interactions. Each student will have multiple opportunities to serve in the role of teacher for the small group music ensembles.
7. Course Evaluation	Our departmental course evaluations are standardized, but I will create separate written evaluations to measure accomplishment of multicultural goals. Throughout the semester we will dialogue about the effectiveness and appropriateness of the selected multicultural material. Data collected regarding classroom interaction will influence course evaluation.

Percentage of Multicultural Content: 25%

Multicultural Classification

Multicultural Content (MC): courses with 60% of the content multicultural

Multicultural Perspectives (MP): courses using a variety of strategies to encourage multiculturalism, including content, instructional strategies, assessment, and classroom dynamics (when this is the only classification, the content is less than 60%)

Multicultural Content and Perspectives (MC and MP): combination of both with 60% content

Choose the best multicultural classification that describes this course: Circle one. MC **MP** MC and MP

Does this course focus on international diversity, U.S. diversity, women's studies, or a combination of all three? Explain: This course will focus on a combination of all three (international, U.S., and women) because the music will be representative of a variety of cultures and composed by both males and females.

TEXAS STATE UNIVERSITY–SAN MARCOS

Syllabus: MU 3269—Current Trends in Music II		
Spring 2009		
Instructor: Dr. Mary Ellen Cavitt	Tel: 245-8450 E-mail: M.E.Cavitt@txstate.edu	
Office:	**Office Hours**: MW F TTH	12:30–1:45 PM 12:30–1:45 PM 10–11 and by appointment

Description

This course is designed to introduce you to the fundamental principles of effective instrumental music instruction, and to provide opportunities for you to practice applying those principles in your own teaching. All of you are talented, skilled musicians and intelligent, well-educated people. Your decision to pursue music education as a career reflects your interest in music as an art form and your commitment to the education and well-being of all children. I hope that throughout the semester you will be challenged to examine carefully your own expectations, hopes, and biases regarding a professional life in teaching. The ultimate goal of the course is that you acquire a basic understanding of the fundamental principles of our discipline, a realistic perspective of your own strengths and weaknesses as developing professionals, and a compelling interest in learning about and confronting the challenges that lie before you in the remainder of your undergraduate education and in your future professional lives.

General Objectives

- Stimulate thinking concerning the role of music and music instruction in the lives of all children, and the responsibilities of teachers in setting and accomplishing appropriate instructional goals.
- Organize, synthesize, and apply knowledge and skills related to music and human learning.
- Develop personal teaching skills by applying fundamental principles of effective instruction in guided experiences.
- Analyze and discuss the influence of ethnicity, social class, bilingualism, abilities, disabilities, and gender on human development and music learning.
- Demonstrate knowledge of basic psycho-acoustic principles as they apply to the teaching of instrumental music.
- Analyze and discuss general techniques of student measurement and evaluation to instrumental music classes.
- Apply philosophical/psychological principles and organization theory in developing models of instrumental music curricula.
- Demonstrate basic pedagogical knowledge on all common brass, woodwind, percussion, and string instruments.
- Analyze and discuss procedures for the successful administration of school instrumental programs in culturally and socioeconomically diverse communities.

Materials

Required Texts

Duke, R. A. (2005). Intelligent music teaching: Essays on the core principles of effective instruction. Austin, TX: Learning and Behavior Resources.

Jurrens, J. (1991). Tuning the band and raising pitch consciousness. San Antonio, TX: RBC Music.

Selected Readings have been chosen to supplement the required texts and to reflect cultural diversity:

Abril, C. R. (2006). Music that represents culture: Selecting music with integrity. *Music Educators Journal, 93* (1), 38–45.

Colwell, R. J., & Goolsby, T. (2002). *The teaching of instrumental music* (3rd ed.). Englewood Cliffs, NJ: Prentice Hall.

Kohut, D. L. (1996). *Instrumental music pedagogy*. Champaign, IL: Stipes Publishing.

Henniger, J. C. (1999). Ethnically diverse sixth graders' preference for music of different cultures. *Texas Music Education Research,* 37–42.

Madsen, C. K., & Madsen, C. C. (1983). *Teaching/discipline: A positive approach for educational development* (4th ed.). Raleigh, NC: Contemporary Publishing Company.

McCord, K., & Fitzgerald, M. (2006). Children with disabilities playing musical instruments. *Music Educators Journal, 92* (4), 46–52.

Mixon, K. (2007). *Reaching and teaching all instrumental students.* Lanham, MD: Rowman & Littlefield Education.

Wade, B. C. (2004). *Thinking musically: Experiencing music, expressing culture.* New York: Oxford University Press.

Additional Materials

You are strongly advised to apply for membership in MENC to receive *Music Educator's Journal*, and to subscribe to *Instrumentalist* magazine. Readings may be assigned from these and other sources.

Binder / Notebook
Each student must provide a three-ring, hardcover binder for notes and handouts.

Texas State student e-mail account

At least four mini DV videos

Specific Objectives

- Read essays and selected readings dealing with principles of effective instruction in instrumental music, and submit brief summaries outlining the main points of each essay.
- Design an instructional sequence and present a teaching demonstration concerning one aspect of instrumental pedagogy (secondary instrument); participate in pedagogical demonstrations and group observations.
- Complete in-class instrumental teaching presentations/ rehearsals. Teaching will include: sequence of instruction to introduce a new piece of music (chosen to meet the needs of your hypothetically diverse student population), rehearsal targeting goals for improvement, modeling, giving specific individualized feedback, and error correction and behavior modification. Meet specified criteria relating to teaching and performance. Complete self-evaluation forms (provided) on videotaped instruction.
- Create "Grading Criteria" and "Classroom Management Plan" handouts for your hypothetically diverse population of future band or orchestra students. Use models (Internet and others) and base your criteria on principles discussed in class. These handouts will become a part of your portfolio during student teaching and initial job interviews.
- Develop a school music budget based on models and criteria discussed in class. Rationale and justifications must include socioeconomic considerations relevant to proposed student population, and the effects of their community on the booster budget and fund-raising.
- Assess your intercultural conflict style using the ICS Inventory and relate it to teacher-parent conferences and classroom interaction. Small group discussion of your ICS and mock teacher-parent conferences will be presented.
- Class Discussions/Demonstrations. Logical comments, thoughts, and questions. Miss no more than three scheduled classes for any reason. Each absence beyond three will result in a grade reduction of one letter. If you arrive after roll has been taken, it is your responsibility to meet with the instructor after class to make sure that your attendance is documented. Two late arrivals will be treated as one absence.

- Students will have the opportunity to participate in laboratory teaching ensemble and apply the principles discussed in class. Attendance at the laboratory is optional; not attending will have no deleterious effect on your grade. The lab ensemble will function better if we have more people there to participate!

Attendance Policy

Miss no more than three scheduled classes for any reason. Each absence beyond three will result in a grade reduction of one letter.

Late Arrivals

If you arrive after roll has been taken, it is your responsibility to meet with the instructor after class to make sure that your attendance is documented. In the field of education, promptness is not a courtesy; it is an obligation. Class will begin promptly at 12:30 p.m. Students entering class after 12:30 will be marked as late. Two late arrivals will be treated as one absence. Students entering class after 12:45 p.m. will be marked as absent. This policy also applies to students leaving class early.

Grade Criteria

Written assignments/quizzes	30%
Teaching/Presentations/Projects	35%
Written exams/tests	20%
Final exam	10%
Notebook & grade checklist	5%

All assignments must be turned in on time to receive full credit. Assignments turned in within two weeks after the due date will receive a deduction of 50 points. Assignments that are received more than two weeks past the due date will not receive credit.

All assignments are due during the next class unless otherwise indicated. No incompletes will be given. Instructor reserves the right to raise a course grade in exceptional circumstances.

* Teaching Lab Ensemble (Friday 12:30–2:00 PM) is highly recommended for those students wishing to implement principles discussed in class.

Notes: Any assignment(s) may be changed with my prior approval. Do not engage in busywork if you know the material. All assignments must be completed and submitted on the printed due dates in order to receive credit. No incomplete grades will be given for any reason. Instructor reserves the right to raise a course grade in exceptional circumstances.

By accepting admission to Texas State University, each student makes a commitment to understand, support, and abide by the Academic Honor Code, without compromise or exception. Violations of academic integrity will not be tolerated. This class will be conducted in strict observance of the Honor Code. Refer to your Student Handbook for details: http://www.mrp.txstate.edu/studenthandbook/rules.html

Multicultural Policy Statement

Texas State believes that freedom of thought, innovation, and creativity are fundamental characteristics of a community of scholars. To promote such a learning environment, the university has a special responsibility to seek diversity, to instill a global perspective in its students, and to nurture sensitivity, tolerance, and mutual respect. Discrimination against or harassment of individuals on the basis of race, color, national origin, religion, sex, sexual orientation, age, or disability are inconsistent with the purposes of the university.

Please Note: Reasonable accommodations for students with disabilities may be arranged by contacting the instructor of this course on an individual basis. This syllabus can be made available in an alternate format upon request.

20. TEXAS STATE UNIVERSITY–SAN MARCOS
MULTICULTURAL CURRICULUM TRANSFORMATION GUIDE/ASSESSMENT INSTRUMENT

Name of Class: PHYS 1310 Elementary Physics I
Instructor: H.C. Galloway
Department: Physics
Degree:
Degree Program Requirement: YES NO

1. Course Description	A non-mathematical survey of mechanics, properties of matter, heat, and sound. These topics are described in a conceptual way with applications relating to the world around us.
2. Course Objectives	• Relate physics to your own environment, including your own background experiences and cultural identification. • Understand and identify physical principles and quantities such as motion, force, acceleration, velocity, work, and energy. • Identify heat transfer and its relationship to energy. • Understand the physical properties of matter. • Develop problem-solving skills to evaluate physics problems relating to everyday situations.
3. Course Content	LEVEL TWO: X LEVEL THREE: ____ (Check one. Explain.) I encourage students to investigate their attitudes and personal experiences about the physical world. Examples will be drawn from a wide variety of experiences, and presented using a wide variety of pictures and graphics to give students a sense that all of them can learn and use physical theories to understand their world. We will also directly discuss why this particular view of scientific endeavors and theories is used, and historically why the viewpoints found in physics are mostly European and male.
4. Instructional Strategies	LEVEL TWO: X LEVEL THREE: ____ (Check one. Explain.) Students are given an opportunity to discuss in small groups and to engage the instructor in discussion. Homework is on an interactive website, and class communication is carried out through both electronic and verbal access. Students use inquiry-type worksheets and exercises to build up concepts, and work with peers to assess their level of knowledge.
5. Assessment of Student Knowledge	LEVEL TWO: X LEVEL THREE: ____ (Check one. Explain.) Standard exams comprise a significant component of the grading, but exam questions will be a variety of short-answer and essay-type questions rather than solely multiple-choice. Homework is online and multiple-choice and numerical problems provide instant feedback. Essay questions will be graded daily. In-class group work will also count towards a grade, and will be graded weekly on a participation basis.

6. Classroom Interactions	LEVEL TWO: X LEVEL THREE: ____ (Check one. Explain.) Students will daily work in groups. I will allow the students to choose their own groups, and will also assign groups to ensure students work with a more diverse set of groups. Some assignments will allow students to bring examples from their own lives to share with others.
7. Course Evaluation	Standard course evaluation. I am proposing to physics department that we add questions about multicultural perspectives to our course evaluation.

Percentage of Multicultural Content: 5–10%

Multicultural Classification

MC=multicultural designation: classes with 60% of the content multicultural

MP=multicultural perspective: classes using a variety of strategies to encourage multiculturalism, including content, instructional strategies, assessment, and classroom dynamics

Choose the multicultural classification that describes this class: Circle one. MC **MP** MC and MP

Does this class focus incorporate global diversity or U.S. diversity or a combination of both? Explain.

Examples used in course are taken from both U.S. and global diversity. Multicultural perspectives are primarily targeting U.S. diversity.

TEXAS STATE UNIVERSITY–SAN MARCOS

PHY 1310—Elementary Physics		
Summer I 2005		
Instructor: Dr. Heather Galloway	Tel: 512 245 7916	
	E-mail: galloway@txstate.edu	
Office: RFM 3205	**Office Hours**: MTWTh 9–10 AM or by appointment	

Textbook

Hewitt, P. (2002). *Conceptual physics* (9th ed.). Boston, MA: Addison Wesley. ISBN 0-321-05202-1. Previous editions of the textbook may be used, as your homework assignment will be on WebAssign. However, you will be responsible for figuring out which sections correspond for reading assignments.

Course Description

A non-mathematical survey of mechanics, properties of matter, heat, and sound. These topics are described in a conceptual way, with applications relating to the world around us.

Educational Beliefs

Physics is a description of the way the world works. It affects all of us, whether we think about it or not. By learning to actively use the ideas of classical physics, students should be able to more accurately describe and predict the physical world. Although physics is considered a difficult subject, I believe that all students are capable of learning the material if they actively engage the content and break the task down into small enough steps. To encourage this type of learning, I will provide opportunities in class for group work and activities. Please remain on task during these activities. At the end of group work time, I will lead a discussion to help us all summarize.

Course Objectives

- Relate physics to your own environment, including your own background experiences and cultural identification.
- Understand and identify physical principles and quantities such as motion, force, acceleration, velocity, work, and energy.
- Identify heat transfer and its relationship to energy.
- Understand the physical properties of matter.
- Develop problem-solving skills to evaluate physics problems relating to everyday situations.

Grading

Semester Exams	50%
Final Exam	20%
Homework (WebAssign)	20%
Physics Journal	10%

A=90–100, B=80–89.9, C=70–79.9, D=65–69.9, F<65

Homework

Assignments will be due approximately daily at midnight on WebAssign, an online homework service. Approximately two homework assignments will be dropped. This will cover problems such as Internet access, computer issues, or other emergencies. No extensions will be granted. Homework will be completed using the Internet service WebAssign, but is taken from problems out of your textbook.

Your username for WebAssign is your user ID from computing services. For example, Xavier Quintano's user ID might be something like XQ1234. The institution is txstate (lowercase). Your password is your Texas State student number printed on your ID (six digit number). You should change your password to something else.

You must go to the bookstore and purchase a WebAssign card or pay online to have access to this service. You need to use your Texas State e-mail for correspondence. The URL for WebAssign is http://www.webassign.net/, and the student login page should be bookmarked as http://webassign.net/student.html.

Physics Journal

This will consist of approximately daily assignments. Each day I will post what material should be in your journal on the class website. Please put these materials into a bradded folder or a report cover. Journals will be turned in each Friday. I will grade them during the exam, and you can pick them up after the exam.

Semester Exams

There will be four exams during the semester covering material from lectures and material in the text. These exams will be every Friday during the semester (6/10, 6/17, 6/24, and 7/1) except the last week. when there is a final. No makeup exams. The exam will be given during the second half of the class period and will take approximately 50 minutes. Exams will be short-answer and problems-type questions similar to those in your homework assignments.

Comprehensive Final—The final exam for this class is July 8, 2005 from 10:30 a.m. to 12:30 p.m. It will cover material from the entire semester. Your final will replace your lowest semester exam grade, and will serve as your makeup exam if you have missed an exam for any reason.

Drop/Withdrawal

You may drop a class until June 10, 2005 with an automatic "W." After that time, you may receive an "F" or a "W" if you drop the course. I will give a grade of "W" if you drop no later than one day after the first exams are graded, but you must come by and discuss it with me. The final deadline to drop a class is on June 30, 2005.

Attendance Policy—Attendance will not be taken. However, in-class work will be part of your physics journal, and you will be responsible for completing any tasks you miss and getting notes from another student for any classes you miss. Some class information will be posted online, but beyond those materials, I will not provide class notes.

Disability Support Services

Texas State University seeks to provide reasonable accommodations for all qualified individuals with disabilities. This university will adhere to all applicable federal, state, and local laws, regulations, and guidelines with respect to providing reasonable accommodations as required to afford equal educational opportunity. It is the student's responsibility to register with Disability Support Services and to contact the faculty member by the third day of class for a previously identified disability to arrange appropriate accommodations.

Academic Honesty Policy

Learning and teaching take place best in an atmosphere of intellectual fair-minded openness. All members of the academic community are responsible for supporting freedom and openness through rigorous personal standards of honesty and fairness. Plagiarism and other forms of academic dishonesty undermine the very purpose of the university and diminish the value of an education. Specific sanctions for academic dishonesty are outlined in Texas State Student Handbook.

Tentative Schedule items in bold correspond to worksheets that are to be included as part of your physics journal; this will be updated on website each week.

Date	Topic/Activities	Homework
6/6	Ch. 1—syllabus, nature of science, course policies, **physics ice breaker, force concept map**	HW 1 due (optional assignment to understand web assign Read Ch. 2, Appendix A, C, and D
6/7	Ch. 2—**Newton's 1st Law,** Inertia,	HW 2 due, read Ch. 3
6/8	Ch. 3—**Linear Motion**	HW 3 due, read Ch. 4 &5
6/9	Ch. 4—Newton's 2nd Law, in class practice on vectors, **Practicum Ch. 1–5** discuss, Ch. 5—Newton's Third Law	HW 4 due, read Ch. 5
6/10	Exam 1 over Ch. 1–4, Journal pages 1–5 due	HW 5 due, read Ch. 6
6/13	Ch. 5—Review Newton's 3rd Law, Ch. 6—**Momentum**	HW 6 due, read Ch. 7
6/14	Ch. 7—**Energy**	HW 7 due, read Ch. 8
6/15	Ch. 8—**Rotational Motion**	HW 8 due, read Ch. 9
6/16	Ch. 9—Gravity, **Ch. 9&10 worksheet**, discuss **Practicum Ch 6–10,** Ch. 10—Projectile and Satellite Motion	HW 9 due, read Ch. 10
6/17	Exam 2 over Ch. 5–9, Journal pages 6–10 due	HW 10 due, read Ch. 11
6/20	Ch. 11—Atomic Nature of Matter	HW 11 due, read Ch. 12
6/21	Ch. 12—Solids	HW 12 due, read Ch. 13
6/22	Ch. 13—Liquids	HW 13 due, read Ch. 14
6/23	Ch. 14—Gases and Plasmas	HW 14 due, read Ch. 15
6/24	Ch. 15—Temperature, Heat and Expansion, Exam 3 over Ch. 10–14	HW 15 due, read Ch. 16
6/27	Ch. 16—Heat Transfer	HW 16 due, read Ch. 17
6/28	Ch. 17—Change of Phase	HW 17 due, read Ch. 18
6/29	Ch. 18—Thermodynamics	HW 18 due, read Ch. 19
6/30	Ch. 19—Vibrations and Waves	HW 19 due, read Ch. 20
7/1	Ch. 20—Sound, Exam 4 over Ch. 15–19	HW 20 due, read Ch. 21
7/4	Independence Day	No class
7/5	Ch. 21—Musical Sounds	HW 21 due
7/6	Review	
7/7	Review	
7/8	Final—10:30 AM–12:30 PM	

21.TEXAS STATE UNIVERSITY–SAN MARCOS

MULTICULTURAL CURRICULUM TRANSFORMATION GUIDE/ASSESSMENT INSTRUMENT

Name of Course: CHEM 4385/5385 Metabolism
Instructor: Linette Watkins
Department: Chemistry & Biochemistry
Degree: Biochemistry and Chemistry minor
Degree Program Requirement: YES NO Biochemistry major

1. Course Description	A study of the biodegradation and biosynthesis of carbohydrates, lipids, amino acids, proteins, and nucleic acids. Prerequisites: A grade of "C" or better in CHEM 2342

2. Course Objectives	**Cognitive Goals**
	• Acquire and master the vocabulary of metabolism
	• Organize information
	• Expand chemistry process skills
	  o Improve problem-solving skills using methodology
	  o Analyze and interpret data from text and primary journal articles
	  o Improve visualization and modeling skills
	• Develop the ability to ask questions, examine assumptions, and solve problems
	• Apply knowledge to new and different situations
	• Develop the ability to select appropriate actions and/or tools
	• Understand the big picture
	Affective Goals
	• Obtain a belief in one's ability to learn and apply the material
	• Advance intellectual tolerance and integrity
	• Set personal goals for improvement and ask for help
	Social Goals
	• Work cooperatively and demonstrate commitment to a group
	• Listen to and learn from peers
	• Value others
	Lifelong Learning Goals
	• Become self-directed: Initiate the learning process
	• Become self-reflective: Review goals, purposes, outcomes, new learning, etc.
	• Become a self-assessor: Assess one's own progress for strengths, areas for improvement, and insights into your learning process to continuously improve
	Measurable Outcomes: Upon successfully completing this course the student should:
	1. Have a working vocabulary of metabolic terms (can give a definition, use terms in context, apply the term to a new context).
	2. Be able to identify/explain the metabolic fate of proteins, carbohydrates, and lipids.
	3. Be able to predict/explain the behavior of biomolecules/biochemical systems by applying chemical principles to these systems.
	4. Be able to explain and interpret data generated from application of biochemical techniques.
	5. Be able to transform written descriptions of quantitative behaviors of biomolecules into graphical representations, and vice versa.

	6. Be able to understand, interpret, and formulate models that represent the current understanding of a metabolic system. 7. Be able to interpret experimental data and relate the interpretation to the current knowledge of metabolic systems. 8. Be able to use a methodology to read and interpret a scientific research article, and be able to articulate its contents in written and oral formats. 9. Be able to use a problem-solving methodology to solve problems involving metabolism of biomolecules and utilizing biochemical techniques. 10. Be able to work cooperatively in teams to identify a problem, formulate a plan, and accomplish a task. 11. Be able to do quality assessments of the performance of others and her/himself.
3. Course Content (60% needed for multicultural content classification)	LEVEL ONE: ___ LEVEL TWO: X LEVEL THREE: ___ (Check one. Explain.) The course does not have 60% multicultural content as it is focused on scientific concepts. Throughout the semester, the students are engaged in synthesis of information, evaluating the mechanism by which knowledge was discovered in the field, and learning concepts and applying them to new problems. Contrasting viewpoints that evolved during the discovery process are provided when available.
4. Instructional Strategies	LEVEL ONE: ___ LEVEL TWO: ___ LEVEL THREE: X (Check one. Explain.) Each 80-minute class period will have the general schedule outlined below. 10 min Quiz on preclass assignments and readings 15 min Mini-lecture 45 min In-class group activity with reporting 10 min Class closure, group assessment, and review of assignments Instructional strategies will be student-centered, guided inquiry using the following activities from the *Foundations of Biochemistry* workbook. • Understanding the Rate Determining Step in a Metabolic Pathway • Understanding Metabolically Far From Equilibrium Reaction • High Energy Compound • Enzymes in Glycolysis • Regulation of Glycolysis and Gluconeogenesis • Metabolic and Hormonal Control in Glycolysis and Gluconeogenesis • Regulation of Glycogen Storage and Breakdown • Glycolysis and Gluconeogenesis Problem Solving • Glycolysis and Gluconeogenesis Problem Solving, Part 2 • Pentose Phosphate Pathway • Exploring Pyruvate Dehydrogenase and the Citric Acid Cycle • Exploring the Citric Acid Cycle • Electron Transport • Oxidative Phosphorylation • Fatty Acid Degradation and Glucose Synthesis • Understanding Fatty Acid Biosynthesis • The Urea Cycle and the Effects of Protein Degradation • Integrated Metabolism The strategy used in the *Foundation* workbook is POGIL (Process Oriented Guided Inquiry Learning). POGIL is a National Science Foundation–funded

	initiative that "seeks to simultaneously teach content and key process skills such as the ability to think analytically and work effectively as part of a collaborative team" (www.pogil.org). POGIL seeks not to relay information for students to memorize, but to teach them to work together to construct knowledge and develop learning skills.
5. Assessment of Student Knowledge	LEVEL ONE: ___ LEVEL TWO: ___LEVEL THREE: X (Check one. Explain.) **Types of Assessment Tools** 1. **Written Exams**: Three in-class written exams and a cumulative written final exam will be completed by all students individually. Exams will focus on problem-solving, applying factual knowledge to more complex problems. Each chapter has a list of specific objectives that should be used as study tools. These learning objectives are directly correlated to the material covered on the exams. 2. **Assignments and Activities:** Since students learn in many different ways, a wide variety of teaching and learning tools will be used, both in and out of the classroom. Some of these will be graded based on completion or participation, while others will be graded based on performance. Some will be completed individually, while others will be completed working as a group. The type of activity will be clearly indicated when it is assigned. The list below is a fairly comprehensive list of the types of assignments and activities that students should expect this semester. • **Assignments**: Completion of a preclass assignment will be required prior to each in-class activity. No late assignments will be accepted. Because the goal of assignments is to prepare you to be a productive participant in group activities, all assignments must be completed prior to coming to class, and will be evaluated based on completeness. Assignments will be listed and posted on TRACS before their due dates. The amount of time needed to complete assignments varies, so PLAN AHEAD. • **Reading Logs or Chapter Notes**: The success of in-class group activities requires that all members come prepared. Therefore, it is essential that you produce a reading log or chapter notes on chapters associated with a given activity BEFORE coming to class. The use of textbooks will not be allowed for in-class quizzes, but reading logs and notes may be used. Refer to the current assignment schedule for chapter sections associated with given activities. • **In-class Activities:** On most class days, group in-class activities will be carried out. Grades will be assigned for participation in these activities. • **Skill Exercises**: A set of skill exercises that assess your understanding of a given topic will be due on the class period following most in-class activities. Unlike assignments, which are scored based on completion only, skill exercises will be collected and graded for correctness. Skill exercises will be posted on TRACS. You are responsible for downloading and completing them after each activity. • **Problem-solving Activities**: Several times during the semester you will apply your group problem-solving skills in class for points. • **Quizzes**: Individual quizzes will be given at the beginning of every class. Some group quizzes may also be given.

	• **Student Presentations**: We will read excerpts from at least three original research papers this semester, interpret results, and predict future experimental results. Students will also work in groups to present amino acid degradation and biosynthesis pathways. • **Bioinformatic Gene Annotation**: The Department of Energy's Joint Genome Institute (JGI) has sequenced the genomes of several microbes and paired with twenty schools in the nation, including Texas State, so that students can have the opportunity to perform gene annotation analysis. Texas State has adopted *Cellulomonas flavigena* 134, DSM 20109 for annotation by our students. Students will be introduced to gene annotation modules designed by the JGI called IMG-ACT and undergo exploratory annotations as part of this course and in courses throughout the biochemistry curriculum. • **Self-assessments**: Students will be required to catalog their reflections about the course, their teams, themselves, and progress on their personal goals. Self-assessments will be completed periodically during the semester. The self-assessments will be the data used to monitor students' growth as learners. A description of the self-assessment process is posted on TRACS.
6. Classroom Interactions	LEVEL ONE: ___ LEVEL TWO: ____LEVEL THREE: X (Check one. Explain.) All group work is performed with defined roles for each group member. The roles are rotated daily, and each role and description is listed below. In the first week of classes, each student in the group evaluates his/her own learning style and academic strengths and weaknesses, and compares it to the other group members' learning styles, strengths, and weaknesses. The goal is for all students to recognize the potential contribution of each of the group members, and any potential for conflict due to different learning styles. **Team Manager** 1. Communicates team questions to instructors. 2. Keeps the process enjoyable and rewarding for team members. 3. Makes sure each team member has a role and is performing that role. 4. Ensures that all team members can articulate what has been learned. 5. Manages time, stress, and conflict, keeping members focused. 6. Actively participates and contributes to the team. **Recorder** 1. Records group roles and instructions at the beginning of a task. 2. Documents group decisions and discoveries legibly and accurately. 3. Controls the information flow, articulating concepts in alternative forms when necessary. 4. Prepares reports that can be used for discussion purposes; integrates and synthesizes discoveries about new concepts. 5. Actively participates and contributes to the team. **Spokesperson** 1. Speaks on behalf of the team when called upon to do so. 2. Asks questions posed by the team and/or requests clarification. 3. Makes oral presentations to the class on behalf of the team. 4. Collaborates with the Recorder in maintaining the team's notes.

	5. Actively participates and contributes to the team. **Reflector** 1. Makes observations about the team's performance and interactions. 2. Records strengths, areas for improvement, and insights in a "Reflector's Report." 3. Reports periodically to the group (and possibly others) from the Reflector's Report, rephrasing evaluations in a positive and constructive manner. 4. Collaborates with the Recorder in maintaining the team's notes. 5. Actively participates and contributes to the team
7. Course Evaluation	Current course evaluation questions are determined by the department using the IDEA assessment. A revision of this form will be undertaken in the coming year. Questions similar to those proposed by Jack Meacham will be proposed for the revised assessment. If they are not adopted, a separate assessment tool will be administered in the classroom.

Percentage of Multicultural Content: 10%

Multicultural Classification

Multicultural Content (MC): courses with 60% of the content multicultural

Multicultural Perspectives (MP): courses using a variety of strategies to encourage multiculturalism, including content, instructional strategies, assessment, and classroom dynamics (when this is the only classification, the content is less than 60%)

Multicultural Content and Perspectives (MC and MP): combination of both with 60% content

Choose the best multicultural classification that describes this course: Circle one. MC **MP** MC and MP

Does this course focus on international diversity, U.S. diversity, women's studies, or a combination of all three? Explain. **All three**. Scientific discovery described in the course includes research conducted in the U.S. and internationally by men and women biochemists. Material will be presented with more deliberate emphasis on the discoverers.

TEXAS STATE UNIVERSITY–SAN MARCOS

CHEM 4385—Metabolism		
Spring 2011		
Instructor: Dr. Linette M. Watkins		Tel: 245-3125 E-mail: LW09@txstate.edu
Office: CENT 403	**Office Hours**: T/R 12:30–2PM, M/W 11–12 appointment	

Course Description

A study of the biodegradation and biosynthesis of carbohydrates, lipids, amino acids, proteins and nucleic acids. Prerequisites: A grade of "C" or better in CHEM 2342

Required Textbooks

Berg, J., Tymoczko, J., & Stryer, L. (2007). *Biochemistry* (6th ed.). New York, NY: W. H. Freeman.

Loertscher, J., & Minderhout, V. (2009). *Foundations of biochemistry*. Lisle, IL: Pacific Crest.

Recommended Text

Hames, D., & Hooper, N. (2005). *BIOS Instant notes biochemistry* (3rd ed.). New York, NY: Taylor & Francis.

Course Goals

Cognitive Goals

- Acquire and master the vocabulary of metabolism
- Organize information
- Expand chemistry process skills
  - Improve problem-solving skills using methodology
  - Analyze and interpret data from text and primary journal articles
  - Improve visualization and modeling skills
- Develop the ability to ask questions, examine assumptions, and solve problems
- Apply knowledge to new and different situations
- Develop the ability to select appropriate actions and/or tools
- Understand the big picture

Affective Goals

- Obtain a belief in one's ability to learn and apply the material
- Advance intellectual tolerance and integrity
- Set personal goals for improvement and ask for help

Social Goals

- Work cooperatively and demonstrate commitment to a group
- Listen to and learn from peers
- Value others

Lifelong Learning Goals

- Become self-directed: Initiate the learning process
- Become self-reflective: Review goals, purposes, outcomes, new learning, etc.
- Become a self-assessor: Assess one's own progress for strengths, areas for improvement, and insights into your learning process to continuously improve

Measurable Outcomes: Upon successfully completing this course the student should:

- Have a working vocabulary of metabolic terms (can give a definition, use terms in context, apply the term to a new context)
- Be able to identify/explain the metabolic fate of proteins, carbohydrates, and lipids
- Be able to predict/explain the behavior of biomolecules/biochemical systems by applying chemical principles to these systems
- Be able to explain and interpret data generated from application of biochemical techniques
- Be able to transform written descriptions of quantitative behaviors of biomolecules into graphical representations, and vice versa
- Be able to understand, interpret, and formulate models that represent the current understanding of a metabolic system
- Be able to interpret experimental data and relate the interpretation to the current knowledge of metabolic systems
- Be able to use a methodology to read and interpret a scientific research article, and be able to articulate its contents in written and oral formats
- Be able to use a problem-solving methodology to solve problems involving metabolism of biomolecules and utilizing biochemical techniques
- Be able to work cooperatively in teams to identify a problem, formulate a plan, and accomplish a task
- Be able to do quality assessments of the performance of others and her-/himself

Grading

Written Exams: Three in-class written exams and a cumulative written final exam will be completed by all students individually. Exams will focus on problem-solving, applying factual knowledge to more complex problems. Each chapter has a list of specific objectives that should be used as study tools. These learning objectives are directly correlated to the material covered on the exams. There will be three in-class exams. Each exam will be worth 100 pts. There will be no makeup exams. The final exam will be cumulative, and worth 200 pts.

Assignments and Activities: Since students learn in many different ways, a wide variety of teaching and learning tools will be used, both in and out of the classroom. Some of these will be graded based on completion or participation, while others will be graded based on performance. Some will be completed individually, while others will be completed working as a group. The type of activity will be clearly indicated when it is assigned. The list below is a fairly comprehensive list of the types of assignments and activities that students should expect this semester. The total number of points available from these activities is 100 points.

Assignments: Completion of a preclass assignment will be required prior to each in-class activity. No late assignments will be accepted. Because the goal of assignments is to prepare you to be a productive participant in group activities, all assignments must be completed prior to coming to class, and will be evaluated based on completeness. Assignments will be listed and posted on TRACS before their due dates. The amount of time needed to complete assignments varies, so PLAN AHEAD.

Reading Logs or Chapter Notes: The success of in-class group activities requires that all members come prepared. Therefore, it is essential that you produce a reading log or chapter notes on chapters associated with a given activity BEFORE coming to class. The use of textbooks will not be allowed for in-class quizzes, but reading logs and notes may be used. Refer to the current assignment schedule for chapter sections associated with given activities.

In-class Activities: On most class days, group in-class activities will be carried out. Grades will be assigned for participation in these activities.

Skill Exercises: A set of skill exercises that assesses your understanding of a given topic will be due on the class period following most in-class activities. Unlike assignments, which are scored based on completion only, skill exercises will be collected and graded for correctness. Skill exercises will be posted on TRACS. You are responsible for downloading and completing them after each activity.

Problem-solving Activities: Several times during the semester you will apply your group problem-solving skills in class for points.

Quizzes: Individual quizzes will be given at the beginning of every class. Some group quizzes may also be given.

Student Presentations: We will read excerpts from at least three original research papers this semester, interpret results, and predict future experimental results. Students will also work in groups to present amino acid degradation and biosynthesis pathways.

Bioinformatic Gene Annotation: The Department of Energy's Joint Genome Institute (JGI) has sequenced the genomes of several microbes and paired up with twenty schools in the nation, including Texas State, so that students can have the opportunity to perform gene annotation analysis. Texas State has adopted *Cellulomonas flavigena* 134, DSM 20109 for annotation by our students. Students will be introduced to gene annotation modules designed by the JGI called IMG-ACT and undergo exploratory annotations as part of this course and in courses throughout the biochemistry curriculum.

Self-assessments: Students will be required to catalog their reflections about the course, their team, themselves, and progress on their personal goals. Self-assessments will be completed periodically during the semester. The self-assessments will be the data used to monitor students' growth as learners. A description of the self-assessment process is posted on TRACS.

Exam schedule

Thursday, February 17	Exam 1	Chapters 14–16
Tuesday, March 29	Exam 2	Chapters 17–21

Tuesday, April 26	Exam 3	Chapters 22–27
Tuesday, May 10, 8 AM	FINAL EXAM	Chapters 14–27

Attendance Policy

Exams: Students with excused absences will be allowed to substitute the score from their final exam for the score of one missed exam. Absences must be approved prior to missing the exam. Doctors' notes will be required for all excused absences. Unexcused absences will result in a zero.

Class: Since class preparation and participation is essential for effective learning, students should come to class on time and prepared. Students tardy for or missing more than two classes will begin losing points in their class participation grade.

TRACS: A TRACS site is required for this course. In order to access the site, you must have a valid Texas State University username and password.

Drop Policy: The deadline for dropping this class is Thursday, March 24 at 5 p.m. All students who drop by this deadline will receive a "W" in the class. The deadline for withdrawing from all of your classes is Thursday, April 21 at 5 p.m. For additional information about dropping a course or withdrawing from the university, see your catalog, the Schedule of Classes, or the registrar's webpage.

Academic Honesty Statement: Learning and teaching take place best in an atmosphere of intellectual fair-minded openness. All members of the academic community are responsible for supporting freedom and openness through rigorous personal standards of honesty and fairness. Plagiarism and other forms of academic dishonesty undermine the very purpose of Texas State and diminish the value of an education. Specific sanctions for academic dishonesty are outlined in the Student Handbook. Violation of the honor code in any way will result in one letter grade decrease in a student's overall class grade.

Special Needs Information: Students with special needs (as documented by the Office of Disability Services) should identify themselves at the beginning of the semester.

Topics to be covered over the course of the semester:

Topic	Chapter in Berg text	Section in Foundations text
Introduction to team learning*		None
Metabolism	15	Understanding the Rate Determining Step in a Metabolic Pathway
	15	Understanding Metabolically Far From Equilibrium Reaction
	16	High Energy Compound
Glycolysis	16	Enzymes in Glycolysis
Gluconeogenesis	16	Regulation of Glycolysis and Gluconeogenesis
Signal transduction	14/16	Metabolic and Hormonal Control in Glycolysis and Gluconeogenesis

	16	Glycolysis and Gluconeogenesis Problem Solving
	16	Glycolysis and Gluconeogenesis Problem Solving, Part 2
Exam 1	14–16	
Citric Acid Cycle	17	Exploring Pyruvate Dehydrogenase and the Citric Acid Cycle
	17	Exploring the Citric Acid Cycle
Electron Transport	18	Electron Transport
Oxidative Phosphorylation*	18	Oxidative Phosphorylation
Light Reactions of Photosynthesis	19	None
	19	None
Dark Reactions of Photosynthesis	20	Pentose Phosphate Pathway
Glycogen metabolism	21	Regulation of Glycogen Storage and Breakdown
Exam 2	17–21	
Fatty acid metabolism*	22	Fatty Acid Degradation and Glucose Synthesis
	22	Understanding Fatty Acid Biosynthesis
Protein breakdown	23	The Urea Cycle and the Effects of Protein Degradation
Amino acid synthesis	24	None
Membrane lipid synthesis	25	None
Nucleotide metabolism	26	None
Integrated metabolism*	27	Integrated Metabolism
Exam 3	22–27	
Review for final	14–27	

- contains multicultural content

Note: The above syllabus was created in collaboration with Jenny Loertscher and Vicky Minderhout from Seattle University.

22. TEXAS STATE UNIVERSITY–SAN MARCOS

MULTICULTURAL CURRICULUM TRANSFORMATION GUIDE/ASSESSMENT INSTRUMENT

Name of Course: CJ 4309D—Race, Ethnicity, and Criminal Justice
Instructor: Scott Bowman, Ph.D.
Department: Criminal Justice
Degree: B.S. **Degree Program Requirement:** YES **NO**

1. Course Description	This course is an examination of the relationship between race/ethnicity and the criminal justice system. Although this is a criminal justice course, you will also find that it includes a discourse in history, political science, sociology, and economics. This is attributable to the contemporary complexities of how race/ethnicity is constructed (and deconstructed), as well as intersectionalities of gender, age, and socioeconomic status. Therefore, we will spend a considerable portion of the course simply examining the way(s) in which race/ethnicity is formed, determining whether race (and ethnicity) matters, and examining other concepts that may better strengthen this examination. During the remainder of the semester, we will specifically examine various components of the criminal justice system and the outcomes that are produced along racial/ethnic lines. Systems such as the police, the courts, sentencing, and the death penalty will be examined in considering how race/ethnicity creates disproportionate outcomes. In addition, we will also consider how gender, race, age, and other demographics further expand the outcomes. During the final part of the semester, we will consider variables that are external to the criminal justice system, yet have a direct influence on its practices, such as historiography, the media, politics, and racial attitudes. To be successful in this course you will need to dedicate yourself to regular attendance in class. You will need to do readings on time, to actively participate in the development of ideas both during class and in small group discussions, and to allow enough time to think through your writing assignments. I sincerely want you all to do well in this course, and you are encouraged to drop by during our office hours or make an appointment if you have questions or concerns.
2. Course Objectives	**Structural Course Objectives** • mastery of key theoretical concepts of race, ethnicity, privilege, power, and criminal behavior • recognititon of the intersectionalities of class, gender, geographic location, etc. • development of critical thinking, listening, and writing skills—ability to apply theoretical concepts of race, ethnicity, and justice to the larger society • engagement in discussions and critical writing assignments

	Shared Course Objectives **Multicultural Policy Statement** Texas State believes that freedom of thought, innovation, and creativity are fundamental characteristics of a community of scholars. To promote such a learning environment, the university has a special responsibility to seek diversity, to instill a global perspective in its students, and to nurture sensitivity, tolerance, and mutual respect. Discrimination against or harassment of individuals on the basis of race, color, national origin, religion, sex, sexual orientation, age, or disability are inconsistent with the purposes of the university. Therefore, the shared objectives of the course will provide and/or expect that: • **each** individual has the welcomed opportunity to speak on any (course-related) issue—without interruption; • all individuals are free to speak without the repercussion of personal attack—*especially when sharing a personal narrative*; • individuals take moment(s) throughout the semester to use their "sociological imagination" (Mills)—allowing themselves to imagine themselves from the perspective of others; • individuals recognize that the discourse of race is truly not an independent discourse, and that the subject(s) of class, gender, age, geographic location, etc. should also be freely incorporated into the discussion; • individuals recognize that, despite their particular affiliations in any group, no individual (including the instructor) "speaks for" or is "an expert" on a particular group based simply on their affiliation, nor should they (including me) feel responsible to do so; • that *you challenge yourself and your classmates throughout the course.*
3. Course Content (60% needed for multicultural content classification)	LEVEL ONE: ___ LEVEL TWO: ___LEVEL THREE: X (Check one. Explain.) The *entire* course content is centered on race/ethnicity with significant supplemental content that addresses socioeconomic status and gender. Although it is presented as a "race/ethnicity" course, the intersectionality of these demographics is an inescapable discourse.
4. Instructional Strategies	LEVEL ONE: ___ LEVEL TWO: ___LEVEL THREE: X (Check one. Explain.) The foundation for the instructional strategies of this course is centered on (a) challenging the way(s) in which race/ethnicity is constructed, (b) presenting more useful tools for examining disparities within the criminal justice system (e.g., privilege, covering, racial formation), and (c) considering the disparity/discrimination argument carefully from both perspectives. These strategies will be introduced to the students; however, it will ultimately be up to them to discuss, debate, incorporate, and amend their own viewpoints (as a direct part of the class dialogue and structure). This is essential to this course and this department, as students are presumed to be entering the labor force as practitioners.

5. Assessment of Student Knowledge	LEVEL ONE: ___ LEVEL TWO: ___LEVEL THREE: X (Check one. Explain.) Throughout the course, there will be numerous opportunities to assess their acquired knowledge, as well as their personal interpretations of the information. Included in this process will be a series of in-class assignments (some individual, some group) that are self-reflective in nature and incorporate elements of the course, two group projects that will be directly centered around race/ethnicity and particular forms of criminal justice and/or social elements that potentially increase the likelihood of finding oneself in the criminal justice system, and a final paper that will directly involve (at least) an incorporation of race/ethnicity and (more likely) an inclusion of socioeconomic status and gender. In addition, there are tools to be used (e.g., http://www.pbs.org/race/002_SortingPeople/002_00-home.htm) that both assess and advance student knowledge on the subject.
6. Classroom Interactions	LEVEL ONE: ___ LEVEL TWO: ___LEVEL THREE: X (Check one. Explain.) As stated in the syllabus, there are "ground rules" that orchestrate classroom interactions. The course itself is largely discourse-centered. Since much of the dialogue on race/ethnicity and the criminal justice system lends to a "disparity/discrimination" debate, participants will be encouraged to discuss these issues during class. They will be presented with the statistical outcomes of race/ethnicity within the criminal justice system and be left to *respectfully* construct explanations for these outcomes. In addition, these explanations will inevitably incorporate socioeconomics and gender.
7. Course Evaluation	Students will fill out "pre-test" and "post-test" evaluations that not only measure their growth in the discourse of multiculturalism, but also provide opportunities for an assessment of the overall course from a multiculturalism perspective.

Percentage of Multicultural Content: 100%

Multicultural Classification:

Multicultural Content (MC): courses with 60% of the content multicultural

Multicultural Perspectives (MP): courses using a variety of strategies to encourage multiculturalism, including content, instructional strategies, assessment, and classroom dynamics (when this is the only classification, the content is less than 60%)

Multicultural Content and Perspectives (MC and MP): combination of both with 60% content

Choose the best multicultural classification that describes this course: Circle one.
MC MP **MC and MP**

Does this course focus on international diversity, U.S. diversity, women's studies, or a combination of all three? Explain.

This course focuses primarily on U.S. racial and ethnic diversity; however, it also heavily incorporates components of women's studies, wealth distribution and poverty studies, and ageism studies. Although there is certainly room for international diversity, its inclusion will be revisited at a later date—due primarily to the complexities of constructing "race and ethnicity" on a global level.

TEXAS STATE UNIVERSITY–SAN MARCOS

CJ 4309D: Race, Ethnicity and Criminal Justice		
Fall 2008	Campus Schedule: 12:30–1:45 p.m. (T/TH)	
Instructor: Dr. Scott Bowman	Tel: 512-245-3584 E-mail: scott.bowman @txstate.edu	
Office: Hines #1	**Office Hours**: M: 11 a.m.–12 p.m.; T–TH: 1–3	

Course Description

This course is an examination of the relationship between race/ethnicity and the criminal justice system. Although this is a criminal justice course, you will also find that it includes a discourse in history, political science, sociology, and economics. This is attributable to the contemporary complexities of how race/ethnicity is constructed (and deconstructed), as well as intersectionalities of gender, age, and socioeconomic status. Therefore, we will spend a considerable portion of the course simply examining the way(s) in which race/ethnicity is formed, determining whether race (and ethnicity) matters, and examining other concepts that may better strengthen this examination.

During the remainder of the semester, we will specifically examine various components of the criminal justice system and the outcomes that are produced along racial/ethnic lines. Systems such as the police, the courts, sentencing, and the death penalty will be examined in considering how race/ethnicity creates disproportionate outcomes. In addition, we will also consider how gender, race, age, and other demographics further expand the outcomes. During the final part of the semester, we will consider variables that are external to the criminal justice system yet have a direct influence on its practices, such as historiography, the media, politics, and racial attitudes

To be successful in this course you will need to dedicate yourself to regular attendance in class. You will need to do readings on time, to actively participate in the development of ideas both during class and in small group discussions, and to allow enough time to think through your writing assignments. I sincerely want you all to do well in this course, and you are encouraged to drop by during our office hours or make an appointment if you have questions or concerns.

Course Objectives

Structural Course Objectives

- mastery of key theoretical concepts of race, ethnicity, privilege, power, and criminal behavior
- recognition of the intersectionalities of class, gender, geographic location, etc.

- development of critical thinking, listening, and writing skills
- development of the ability to apply theoretical concepts of race, ethnicity, and justice to the larger society
- engagement in discussions and critical writing assignments

Shared Course Objectives

Multicultural Policy Statement

Texas State believes that freedom of thought, innovation, and creativity are fundamental characteristics of a community of scholars. To promote such a learning environment, the university has a special responsibility to seek diversity, to instill a global perspective in its students, and to nurture sensitivity, tolerance, and mutual respect. Discrimination against or harassment of individuals on the basis of race, color, national origin, religion, sex, sexual orientation, age, or disability are inconsistent with the purposes of the university.

Therefore, the shared objectives of the course will provide and/or expect that:

- each individual has the welcomed opportunity to speak on any (course related) issue—without interruption;
- all individuals are free to speak without the repercussion of personal attack—*especially when sharing a personal narrative*;
- individuals take moment(s) throughout the semester to use their "sociological imagination" (Mills)—allowing themselves to imagine themselves from the perspective of others;
- individuals recognize that the discourse of race is truly not an independent discourse and that the subject(s) of class, gender, age, geographic location, etc. should also be freely incorporated into the discussion;
- individuals recognize that, despite their particular affiliations in any group, no individual (including the instructor) "speaks for" or is "an expert" on a particular group based simply on their affiliation, nor should they (including me) feel responsible to do so; and
- that students challenge themselves and their classmates throughout the course.

Course Materials

The two texts listed below are required for this semester:

Walker, S., Spohn, C., & DeLone, M. (2000). *The color of justice: Race, ethnicity and crime in America* (2nd ed.). Belmont, CA: Wadsworth Thompson Learning.

Beckett, K., & Sasson, T. (2000). *The politics of injustice: Crime and punishment in America.* Thousand Oak, CA: Pine Forge.

Additional handouts (provided)

The texts are available for purchase at the Texas State Bookstore. You are also responsible for and may be tested on any other materials shown or discussed in class, such as handouts, films, websites, etc.

TRACS

This is Texas State's online source for class information. In addition to the above texts, students should have an e-mail account and be able to access Blackboard. For example, I will post additional information on assignments, general information, website links for class, and test study guides on TRACS. You can also use it to check your grades throughout the semester. For help with your e-mail account or computer questions, please speak to me via telephone or e-mail or during office hours.

Course Requirements

First and foremost... please turn cell phones off or to vibrate when you enter class. I understand that there are times when you will need to take telephone calls during class; feel free to excuse yourself during class. However, ringing phones and pagers are a distraction to both the lecturer and your classmates.

Attendance: You are all adults. There will not be any formal attendance policy. HOWEVER, there will be a series of unannounced in-class discussions and/or in-class papers that will be given throughout the semester. There will be no makeups for these, except in the case of a documented medical excuse or documented family emergency.*

NOTE: These quizzes are designed primarily as an informal attendance policy and will not be too difficult, but they are worth a significant portion of your grade. If you miss them, it could become the difference between letter grades. The in-class papers and discussions are designed to help you think about the issues in the readings, to encourage active participation in class, and to help you with the exams. Class will start (and end) promptly each day.

*Students who miss class due to athletic or other university events are required to follow official TEXAS STATE policies if they wish to make up assignments, tests, etc. Those who fail to do so will not be accommodated.

In-class Papers/In-class Group Discussions: As previously mentioned, there will be a series of unannounced discussions and/or writing assignments that are given throughout the semester. Rest assured that content in these assignments counts more than grammar! Papers and quizzes are designed to get you reading and to facilitate class discussion. If you do the readings, you will be prepared.

Group Assignments: There will be three small-group projects during the semester. They will not be overly comprehensive; however, they will require you to critically apply theoretical elements to practical, applicable circumstances.

Tests: There will be two tests during the semester, consisting of various types of questions (e.g., multiple-choice, true/false, short-essay) developed from the readings, assignments, lectures, and films in class. I will allow for a makeup exam only with documented medical excuse or documented family emergency. If you read the material, take good notes, and attend classes regularly, you should be in great shape for the exams.

Final Paper: The final exam will be a "group project" final paper to be turned in on the last day of class. The paper will be approximately **twelve to fifteen pages** long. More information will be provided during the semester regarding the specifics of the paper.

Plagiarism: You cannot hear the plagiarism message enough. It is a serious offense at this university and will not be tolerated. Quoted and paraphrased passages must be cited appropriately in your written work. Copying sentences or whole sections of another's work from websites or other materials is considered plagiarism and will be grounds for disciplinary action, if not dismissal, from the university. This is not limited to research papers—this is also relevant in the presentation of homework assignments, etc.

Also, and along these lines, please make sure to familiarize yourself with the Academic Integrity Policy as outlined in the most current Texas State Student Handbook. This policy not only deals with issues such as plagiarism and other behaviors considered to be violations of academic integrity, but also provides guidelines regarding the various sanctions that accompany these types of actions.

Grades: Total

Five In-class Writing Assignments @ 10pts ea	50
Test 1 @ 100 pts	100
Test 2 @ 100 pts	100
Three Group Projects @ 25pts ea	75
Final Paper @ 125 pts	125
Total 450 points	

Grading Scale

450–402 A

401–358 B

357–313 C

312–268 D

267 & below E

Grade disputes must be submitted in writing one week after the grade is given, with clear and substantial arguments for changing the grade.

Written and oral communication will be evaluated in the following way:

A: Outstanding. Superior. Written work is presented at the college level, using Standard English and an acceptable style guide. Meets all course expectations promptly. Shows clear grasp of concepts and participates regularly and enthusiastically in class and group discussions.

B: Very Good. Clearly above average. Written work is presented at the college level using Standard English and an acceptable style guide, with only few minor flaws. Meets course expectations promptly. Shows adequate grasp of concepts and participates regularly and enthusiastically in class and group discussions.

C: Good. Average. Written work is presented at the college level using Standard English and an acceptable style guide, with many minor flaws. Shows a reasonable grasp of concepts and participates in class and group discussions.

D: Below expectations. Writing is marred by major mechanical problems. Does not meet course expectations promptly. Fails to participate regularly in class and group discussion.

E: Far below expectations. Written work consistently falls below college level, even when revised. Fails to report to Writing Center or seek other appropriate help. Consistently late in meeting course expectations, and fails to participate in class and group discussions.

Note: Should you require accommodation from Disability Resources, you must register with that office to receive those services.

SEMESTER COURSE OUTLINE

Aug 28th

Course introduction & overview of syllabus
Introduction to ideologies of race/ethnicity

Sept 2nd and 4th

Film—*Race: The Power of Illusion* (part I)
Handouts—The Social Construction of Race

Sept 9th and 11th

Handouts—Privilege
Handouts—Covering

Sept 16th and 18th

Handouts—Five Faces of Oppression

"The Color of Justice"
Chapter 1—Race, Ethnicity, and Crime

Sept 23rd and 25th

Chapter 2—Victims and Offenders
Chapter 3—Race, Ethnicity, Social Structure, and Crime

Sept 30th and Oct 2nd

Handout—Forty Acres and a Mule: Historical and Contemporary Obstacles to Black Property Accumulation
Film—*Race: The Power of Illusion* (part III)

Oct 7th and 9th

Chapter 4—Justice on the Street
Film

Oct 14th and 16th

Chapter 5—The Courts
Chapter 6—Justice on the Bench

Oct 21st and 23rd

Film
Exam #1

Oct 28th and 30th

Chapter 7—Race and Sentencing
Chapter 8—The Color of Death

Nov 4th and 6th

Chapter 9—Corrections—A Picture in Black and White
Chapter 10—Minority Youth and Crime

Nov 11th and 13th

"The Politics of Injustice"
Chapter 1—Criminal Justice Expansion
Chapter 2—Crime in the United States
Chapter 3—Murder, American Style

Nov 18th and 20th

Chapter 4—The Politics of Crime
Chapter 5—Crime in the Media

Nov 25th and 27th

Film
NO CLASS—THANKSGIVING

Dec 2nd and 4th

Handout—Race and Public Opinion
Chapter 6— Crime and Public Opinion

(Week of) Dec. 8th

Exam #2
Final Papers Due

23. TEXAS STATE UNIVERSITY–SAN MARCOS

MULTICULTURAL CURRICULUM TRANSFORMATION GUIDE/ASSESSMENT INSTRUMENT

Name of Course: English 3311 (Advanced Writing)
Instructor: Nancy Effinger Wilson
Department: English
Degree: English **Degree Program Requirement: YES** NO

1. Course Description	Study and practice of advanced expository writing, with focus on achieving clarity and readability.
2. Course Objectives	• Read and discuss expository writing samples that reflect the rich diversity of human communicative practice; • Learn to read critically the texts that shape/coerce how we see ourselves and others as individuals and as groups; • Experiment with various aspects of writing—process, language, writing style, perspective, organization, medium, content—in order to enlarge the accepted definition of "good writing"; • Learn to write effectively given diverse audiences and purposes, and using various media.
3. Course Content (60% needed for multicultural content classification)	LEVEL ONE: __ LEVEL TWO: __ LEVEL THREE: X Expository Readings: bell hooks' *Teaching to Transgress*; Gloria Anzaldúa's *Borderlands*; Geneva Smitherman's *Word from the Mother*; Victor Villanueva's *Bootstraps*; Sara Suleri's *Meatless Days*; Kenji Yoshino's "The Pressure to Cover"; Jack Kerouac's *Lonesome Traveler*; Strunk & White's *Elements of Style.* Websites: NPR StoryCorps (http://www.storycorps.org); Smithsonian Center for Folklife and Cultural Heritage and *Talk Story* newsletter (http://folklife.si.edu/center/talk.aspx); *The Speech Accent Archive* (http://accent.gmu.edu/); the CIA *World Factbook* (https://www.cia.gov/library/publications/the-world-factbook); United Nations (http://www.un.org); *BBC News* (http://news.bbc.co.uk); *Al Jazeera English* (http://english.aljazeera.net). Writing Assignments: (1) Compile material for a literacy narrative by collecting three or four stories from your own family, schooling, church, and the media that have shaped your idea of self (personally, culturally, academically, etc.). You must replicate these stories using the original language/dialect. Braid/weave into these stories your personal reflections of how each story has impacted your identity, then and now. Consider using graphics and artifacts in the final product. (2) Read and discuss texts that define good writing (Strunk and White) and other texts that problematize "good writing": Edited American English (Anzaldúa and Smitherman); linear, "male" organization (Suleri and Kerouac); adversarial "Western" perspective (Toulmin argument model); and possibly narratives from #1. Prepare

	a personal manifesto outlining your own view of "good writing." You will share these with the class to develop new paradigms for "good" writing. (3) Read and discuss Villanueva, Rodriguez, and Yoshino in preparation for writing a similar "coming of age" literacy narrative using the material collected in assignment #1 and informed by assignment #2. You will include your own grading rubric informed by the class' definition(s) of good writing. (4) Create a PowerPoint slideshow of images promoting a particular organization, culture, community, and profession. (5) In small groups, share #4 and select one PowerPoint (master narrative) to deconstruct in order to reveal the subtext of the earlier PowerPoint. Prepare an accompanying two-page group report of how group identity (in general and in these cases, in particular) is shaped via master narratives and the media. Share via a group presentation. (6) At the beginning of class, you will receive honorary citizenship in a country other than your own. Once a week you will post in blog form news stories and other information about that country, preferably from a non-U.S. source. You will be paired with another student and read that person's blog weekly. Your final blog entry will be an analysis of the experience, especially in terms of temporarily decentering/enlarging your national citizenship. (7) You will submit 1–6, with revisions, as a final e-portfolio/portfolio with a three-page analysis that connects the pieces in some way and includes five "action items" for your future.
4. Instructional strategies	LEVEL ONE: ___ LEVEL TWO: ___ LEVEL THREE: X I will make a concerted effort to create a learning atmosphere that makes all students comfortable in contributing their unique perspectives to the class discussion. Out-of-class assignments are designed to build on critical thinking, writing, and revising skills. In my own interactions with students in class and outside of class (presentations, leading discussion, creating assignments, grading), I will accommodate a variety of learning, writing, and thinking styles.
5. Assessment of student knowledge	LEVEL ONE: ___ LEVEL TWO: ___ LEVEL THREE: X Because I believe the best writing reflects higher-order thinking, I will place writing/presentation content at the forefront of my course and in my assessment of student writing. However, I also acknowledge that assessing writing quality is highly contextual and subjective. For this reason, as a class we will develop a variety of grading rubrics for evaluating writing quality. For every writing/presentation assignment, the student will be required to state targeted audience and purpose (context) and self-evaluate using one of our created grading rubrics. I will also use a class-generated grading rubric, in addition to my marginal comments/suggestions. For all projects, students will have opportunities to receive feedback from their classmates and me.

6. Classroom interactions	LEVEL ONE: __ LEVEL TWO: __ LEVEL THREE: X Since this is a small writing course, the majority of our class time will involve active learning and sharing—class discussions, small-group discussion, small-group collaborative writing/presenting projects, peer-review workshops, individual and group presentations, and in-class writing opportunities at various stages of the writing process. Class participation and writing/reading assignments have been designed to promote the interrogation of "master narratives" in order to create critical consciousness and potentially transformative behavior. I have included this statement on the course syllabus: "We will all be tactful and supportive of each other in our in-class and out-of-class interactions with one another."
7. Course evaluation	Our class discussions and writing assignments are directly linked to the multicultural goals of this class and the broader multicultural goals of this university. In addition, I will add specific questions to the English Department course evaluation in order to assess student response to the course content, assignments, and my teaching of the course.

Percentage of Multicultural Content: 90%

Multicultural Classification:

MC=multicultural content: courses with 60% of the content multicultural

MP=multicultural perspective: courses using a variety of strategies to encourage multiculturalism, including content, instructional strategies, assessment, and classroom dynamics (when this is the only classification, the content is less than 60%)

Choose the best multicultural classification that describes this course: MC and MP

Does this course focus on international diversity, U.S diversity, women's studies, or a combination of all three? All three.

Explain: Through writing assignments and class readings/discussions, we will be examining writing styles that diverge from Edited American English (women's language, world Englishes, English dialects) and organizational strategies that differ from those associated with "Western" models.

TEXAS STATE UNIVERSITY–SAN MARCOS

English 3311: Advanced Writing		
Spring 2009	Campus Schedule: Monday 8–8:50 a.m.; Tuesday 8–8:50 a.m.	
Instructor: Nancy Wilson	Tel: 245-7660 E-mail: nw05@txstate.edu	
Office: Flowers Hall G09	**Office Hours**: TTH 10–11 and by appointment	

Required Texts

Gloria Anzaldúa's *Borderlands*

Sara Suleri's *Meatless Days*

Thomas Cahill's *How the Irish Saved Civilization*

Strunk & White's *Elements of Style*

Course Objectives/Goals

- Read and discuss expository writing samples that reflect the rich diversity of human communication.
- Learn to read critically the texts that shape/coerce how we see others and ourselves as individuals and as groups.
- Experiment with various aspects of writing—process, language, writing style, perspective, organization, and medium, content—in order to enlarge the accepted definition of "good writing."
- Learn to write effectively given diverse audiences, purposes, and using various media.

Course Description

Because I believe the best writing reflects higher-order thinking, I will place writing/presentation content at the forefront of this course and in my assessment of your writing/presentations. The majority of our class time will involve active learning including group work, student presentations, and in-class writing opportunities at various stages of the writing process. I will make a concerted effort to create a learning atmosphere that makes all students comfortable in contributing their unique perspectives to the class discussion and that accommodates a variety of learning, writing, and thinking styles. Out-of-class assignments are designed to build on critical thinking, writing, and revising skills. For all projects, you will have opportunities to receive feedback from your classmates and me. We will all be tactful and supportive of each other in our in-class and out-of-class interactions with one another.

Writing Assignments

1. (1) Compile material for a literacy narrative by collecting three or four stories from your own family, schooling, church, and the media that have shaped your idea of self (personally, culturally, academically, etc.). You must replicate these stories using the original language/dialect. Braid/weave into these stories your personal reflections of how each story has impacted your identity, then and now. Consider using graphics and artifacts in the final product.
2. (2) Read and discuss texts that define good writing (Strunk and White) and other texts that problematize "good writing": Edited American English (Anzaldúa and Smitherman); linear, "male" organization (Suleri); adversarial "Western" perspective (Cahill and Toulmin argument model); and possibly narratives from #1. Prepare a personal manifesto outlining your own view of "good writing." You will share these with the class to develop new paradigms for "good" writing.

3. (3) Read and discuss Villanueva, Rodriguez, and Yoshino in preparation for writing a similar "coming of age" literacy narrative using the material collected in assignment #1 and informed by assignment #2. You will include your own grading rubric informed by the class' definition(s) of good writing.
4. (4) Create a PowerPoint slideshow of images promoting a particular organization, culture, community, and profession.
5. (5) In small groups, share #4 and select one PowerPoint (master narrative) to deconstruct in order to reveal the subtext of the earlier PowerPoint. Prepare an accompanying two-page group report of how group identity (in general and in these cases in particular) is shaped via master narratives and the media. Share via a group presentation.
6. (6) At the beginning of class, you will receive honorary citizenship in a country other than your own. Once a week you will post in blog form news stories and other information about that country, preferably from a non-U.S. source. You will be paired with another student and read that person's blog weekly. Your final blog entry will be an analysis of the experience, especially in terms of temporarily decentering/enlarging your national citizenship.
7. (7) You will submit 1–6, with revisions, as a final e-portfolio/portfolio with a three-page analysis that connects the pieces in some way and includes five "action items" for your future.

Grades

Assignment #1:	10%
Assignment #2:	15%
Assignment #3:	15%
Assignment #4:	10%
Assignment #5:	10%
Assignment #6 (blog):	10%
Assignment #6 (discussion):	5%
Assignment #7 (portfolio):	15%
*GSP Post-test:	10%

*Must pass the GSP Post-test in order to pass the class.

Due Dates

If you must submit work late, you must notify me prior to the due date.

Attendance

Because we do most of our work in class, you should not miss any classes at all. If you accumulate more than three absences, I will lower your grade in the course by a full letter grade; after four absences, your grade drops two letter grades, and so on. If you miss a workshop day, the grade for that assignment will be docked.

Cheating/Plagiarism

I shouldn't need to mention this, but if you cheat on an exam or assignment, you will fail the course.

Students With Special Needs

Students who have special needs/disabilities (as documented by the Office of Disability Services) should notify me immediately in order to discuss any special accommodations that may need to be made.

Good luck in the course!

ENGLISH 3311 SYLLABUS

January 15 Introduction to the course. Overview of the writing process.

January 17 Grammar/Spelling/Punctuation pre-test. Receive your honorary citizenship in another country and your blog space on TRACS. Visit websites featured on TRACS under "Resources for Assignment #6."

January 22 Bring Strunk & White to class. Discuss GSP pre-tests. Receive assignment #1: Qualitative research and connections for a literacy narrative. Visit websites featured on TRACS under "Resources for Assignment #1."

January 24 Discuss Suleri's *Meatless Days.*

January 29 Discuss Cahill's *How the Irish Saved Civilization.*

January 31 Discuss Suleri, Cahill, Smitherman, and Toulmin. Receive assignment #2: Personal manifesto of "good writing."

February 5 Bring to class your stories for assignment #1. Writing workshop.

February 7 Bring to class draft of assignment #1. Peer-editing workshop.

February 12 Assignment #1 due. Discuss assignment #2. Drafting workshop.

February 14 Discuss Villanueva and Rodriguez.

February 19 Discuss Yoshino, Villanueva, and Rodriguez. Receive assignment #3: Literacy Narrative.

February 21 Assignment #2 draft due. Peer-editing workshop.

February 26 Assignment #2 due. Groups assigned to select best manifestos. Begin developing grading rubrics.

February 28 Continue working on grading rubrics. Select three for the class.

March 4 Assignment #3 draft due. Peer-editing workshop.

March 6 Assignment #3 due. Receive assignment #4: master narrative PowerPoint.

March 11 & 13 Spring Break

March 18 Meet in library to work on assignment #4. Subjects for assignment #4 due to me by end of class.

March 20 Groups assigned for assignment #5. Writing workshop for assignment #4.

March 25 Assignment #4 due. Group work for assignment #5.

March 27 Group work for assignment #5.

April 1 Group presentations of assignment #5.

April 3 Group presentations of assignment #5.

April 8 Assignment #5 due. Discuss assignment #6.

April 10 Pairs present on assignment #6. Assignment #7: portfolio.

April 15 1:1 Conferences. Bring all graded assignments with you to our meeting.

April 17 1:1 Conferences. Bring all graded assignments with you to our meeting.

April 22 Discuss assignment #6 and prepare for GSP post-test.

April 24 GSP post-test. Portfolios (assignment #7) due.

Final exam: Make-up GSP post-test.

24. TEXAS STATE UNIVERSITY–SAN MARCOS

MULTICULTURAL CURRICULUM TRANSFORMATION GUIDE/ASSESSMENT INSTRUMENT

Name of Course: Medical Sociology 3363
Instructor: Gloria P. Martinez-Ramos
Department: Sociology
Degree:
Degree Program Requirement: YES NO

1. Course Description	The purpose of this course is to introduce to you a broad range of theoretical frameworks that examine how health, illness, and quality of life are socially constructed using a multicultural perspective.
2. Course Objectives	In this course, students will do the following: • Learn basic and advanced concepts and theories about medical sociology regarding social epidemiology, access to health care, doctor-patient interaction, illness narratives and survivorship, and equity in health care delivery in the United States and internationally. • Critically examine diverse worldviews and perspectives concerning how social inequality (advantages and disadvantages) based on race, ethnicity, class, gender, sexuality, and ability impacts health, illness, and well-being. • Analyze narratives or stories of individual social identities that are shaped by their health, illness, and healing to develop an appreciation for the lived experiences of people who are different from themselves. • Practice oral and written critical thinking and writing skills with an awareness of how health issues are shaped and framed into research questions. • Engage in cooperative group learning to create a class website that explores social change and social movements in health care for individual patients/consumers, practitioners, community, and the environment.
3. Course Content (60% needed for MC classification)	LEVEL ONE: ___ LEVEL TWO: X LEVEL THREE: ___ (Check one. Explain.) I encourage students to critically examine (both in writing and orally, in class discussion) the theoretical frameworks and measurement and operations of analysis of the research material that is presented in class. In addition, the curriculum includes research written by women, as well as by racial- and ethnic-minority and feminist scholars who challenge the dominant epistemologies in medical sociology. This course takes a systems of inequality approach, which stresses interlocking systems of inequality—especially those based on race, class, ethnicity, gender, sexuality, age, and geographic space that produce dimensions of privilege and disadvantage that impact health, illness, disease, and well-being. Students will be challenged and transformed by being exposed directly to the privilege and disadvantage that affects their own and other people's well-being from a sociological standpoint.

4. Instructional Strategies	LEVEL ONE: ___ LEVEL TWO: X LEVEL THREE: ____ (Check one. Explain.) As an inspirational teacher, my goal is to convey the excitement and value of sociological intellectual inquiry and build upon students' previous learning by incorporating their diverse experiences into the classroom. Central to my pedagogical goals is to bridge teaching and learning with open and constructive dialogue. I aim to achieve clarity in the classroom by, for example, providing a brief statement of the thesis or argument; outlining the main points; providing concrete examples (at least one for every major point or important concept); and restating the same argument in different ways. Sociological theory is regularly presented in the form of a short lecture followed by a small-group discussion, in which students are compelled to defend (and thus clarify) in groups with their peers, their views on competing interpretations. Peer-group dialogue is an important when I teach sociological theory because it fosters active learning, leadership, creativity, and in-depth constructive feedback. Students create the group discussion question every week and select one week to lead a group dialogue with five other students in class. In my teaching I have found that group discussions are invaluable to students learning sociological theory and research methods because they are exposed to multiple interpretations and perspectives from their fellow students. I am aware that there are problems with lectures; for example, they are less effective in provoking critical thinking and problem-solving; students frequently forget lecture material; it is a more passive way of learning; and it doesn't tap into other forms of learning such as visual or group interactions. In order to address this issue, I regularly alternate lectures with discussions or other teaching activities, such as: (1) I pose a question, ask students to write individually on it for a minute, ask students to pair up to discuss the question, then bring it back to the larger group; (2) I give an example of a case study and ask students to solve, then discuss their approaches and address any issues; and (3) I present movies, documentaries, and video clips that addresses a social problem in health care. Critical-response writing provides an opportunity for students think about, share, and communicate something that is related to the topics covered in the course that matters to them. It is a great way to ignite new energy for students to address social issues from a sociological point of view and think, "What else can I make of this?" This is a useful strategy to help students think sociologically in more complex and concrete ways. When the course is over, I like students to leave with a nuanced understanding of social issues about health, illness, and medicine in their community and in our society, an appreciation of using the sociological imagination, and an increased self-awareness of the role and responsibilities of the individual in a diverse global society.

5. Assessment of Student Knowledge	LEVEL ONE: ___ LEVEL TWO: X LEVEL THREE: ___ (Check one. Explain.) Critical-response papers are required for this class, and half of the papers must cover a multicultural topic from the readings. (Writing) Each student will create his or her own discussion questions, and is required to facilitate a 1-hour group discussion. (Participation) Students will create a website that compiles information about groups and organizations that address issues introduced in the class with multicultural content. (Participation)
6. Classroom Interactions	LEVEL ONE: ___ LEVEL TWO: X LEVEL THREE: ___ (Check one. Explain.) Efforts will be made to address culturally consonant equity in class participation; to confront biases as they arise, and ensure respectful interactions; and to encourage explicit communication of high standards and ability affirmation. Ground rules for class discussion are created by the students in the class.
7. Course Evaluation	The student course evaluation includes the following statements/questions: "I became more interested in multicultural issues in medical sociology. Explain why." "What has the teacher done that has helped you learn?" "What have you done to help other students in the course to learn?"

Percentage of Multicultural Content: 75%

Multicultural Classification:

MC=multicultural content: courses with 60% of the content multicultural

MP=multicultural perspective: courses using a variety of strategies to encourage multiculturalism, including content, instructional strategies, assessment, and classroom dynamics (when this is the only classification, the content is less than 60%)

Choose the best multicultural classification that describes this course:

Circle one. MC MP **MC and MP**

Does this course focus on international diversity, U.S. diversity, women's studies, or a combination of all three? Explain.

The content of this course focuses on a combination of U.S. diversity, women's studies, and international diversity.

TEXAS STATE UNIVERSITY–SAN MARCOS

Sociology 3363: Medical Sociology		
Instructor: Dr. Gloria P. Martínez-Ramos		Tel: 245-2470 E-mail: gm21@txstate.edu
Office: Derrick M20	**Office Hours**: MW 3:30 to 4:30pm	

General Course Description

This course focuses on the social determinants and social contexts of human health, illness, and disease. The purpose of this course is to introduce to you a broad range of theoretical frameworks related to health, illness, and medicine. In addition, this course examines how health, illness, and quality of life are socially constructed. Issues such as how race, ethnicity, class, age, neighborhood, and family structure shape health disparities, illness experience, health status, and social movements in health will be covered. **This class has been designated Multicultural Content (MC) and Multicultural Perspectives (MP) by the Multicultural Curriculum Transformation Project at Texas State University, which means that this course includes 60% or more multicultural content and teaching strategies.**

Learning Objectives

- Students will learn basic and advanced concepts and theories about medical sociology, social epidemiology, health care policy, doctor-patient interaction, illness narratives and survivorship, and equity in health care delivery in the United States and internationally.
- Students will examine how social inequality based on race, ethnicity, class, gender, sexuality, and ability shapes people's health, illness, and well-being.
- Students will critically read, analyze, and discuss scholarly books, research articles, narratives, films, and documentaries about people's experiences with health and illness, and develop questions related to medical sociology.
- This class is a writing-intensive class. Students will read and write critical analysis, summaries, book reviews, and compare-and-contrast papers on issues introduced in the readings; share and discuss their writing in class; and write an independent research paper as part of their final exam.

Required Texts

Brown, P. (2008). *Perspectives in medical sociology* (4th ed.). Long Grove, IL: Waveland Press.

Earley, P. (2006). *Crazy: A father's search through America's mental health madness.* New York, NY: Berkley Books.

White, A. A., III. (2011). *Seeing patients: Unconscious bias in health care.* Cambridge, MA: Harvard University Press.

Sulik, G. A. (2011). Pink ribbon blues: How breast cancer culture undermines women's health. New York, NY: Oxford University Press.

Journal of Health and Social Behavior. Fall 2010 supplemental issue dedicated to the 50th anniversary of the journal and of the Medical Sociology Section of the American Sociological Association. Available on TRACS.

Films and documentaries will be used for writing assignments and to support lectures. Additional reading and writing resources available on TRACS.

Library Reserve code is: girlscout

Attendance and Participation

All ideas will be held up to be examined intellectually with civility. You will be presented with a variety of thoughts about these topics, and it is up to you to decide where you stand on the various issues. The role of the instructor is to help students facilitate critical inquiry in the learning process at both individual and group levels, and to foster respect for all learners in the classroom. Your group activities will be part of your participation grade. Group activities will involve sharing your analysis and interpretations of assigned readings in class. When you are in class, I expect that students will have their **cell phones and pagers off.** Be prepared for class.

Attention and courtesy: Just as I will not be inattentive or impolite to you, I will not tolerate inattention, incivility, or vulgarity, either to me or to other students. When I am speaking to you and the rest of the class, I expect to have your undivided attention. When another student is speaking, I expect you to give him or her your undivided attention. If you disagree with something that is said in class, you will be given the chance to express your disagreement politely.

Promptness/Staying the entire class period: You should arrive to class on time. If you are going to be more than 5 minutes late, do not come to class—it disrupts everyone. You should stay in class until it is over unless you have made prior arrangements with me. Do not get up and leave during a class session unless you are ill or have spoken with me prior to the class meeting.

Attention to the course material during our class meetings: Do not read newspapers, magazines, or any other material during this class meeting unless it pertains to what we're doing. Do not sleep during class. If you are going to sleep, don't come to class. Everyone will contribute, sharing the responsibility in making our class a positive experience. It is your responsibility to find out about any missed course material, including announcements and handouts given at any time during the class meeting.

Late Work

Timely completion of your assignments is imperative. Your papers are due before the class begins, if you turn in your paper after class then it will be considered a day late. If you have a death in the family (with documentation) or a medical emergency with a doctor's note, I will consider your request for an extension. Otherwise, your grade will be docked 10 percentage points for every day that the assignment is late. Incomplete group work will receive a zero. Makeup exams will be given only in the event of a medical or other serious emergency, which must be documented.

Writing Assignments

It is expected that you write five, four-page-long writing assignments based on assigned questions from the assigned readings. The papers are due before class begins. The paper must be typed in 12-point font and double-spaced (excluding bibliography). A cover page and bibliography and a total of four pages are necessary. Citations using the American Sociological Association style are required. The Writing Resource Packet has examples of the ASA style. Points will be docked if your paper is not submitted in the correct format. If you do not receive a grade, you must rewrite the paper with suggested improvements from the instructor or the teaching assistant and resubmit the paper to get a grade. Rewritten papers must be turned it at the following class meeting.

The papers will be evaluated on your organization and format, insights and ideas, integration of research articles, and grammar and mechanics.

Writing guidelines:

- Essays must have an introduction, body, and conclusion.
- They must be typed and double-spaced with a 1-inch margin.
- Students must turn in hard copies of all assignments in this course.
- If you turn in papers to the sociology office before the due date, make sure that you write my name on the front of the paper so that the office staff members know that the paper is for me. It is up to you to ensure that the paper makes it into my mailbox.
- Make two copies of your assignment and back up all of your documents.
- Make sure the printing is legible.
- If you need writing assistance, contact the Writing Center at G09 (512) 245-3018 or http://writingcenter.english.txstate.edu. The instructor will provide a Writing Resource Packet from the Writing Center.

Exams

All exams are take-home writing exams. Exams focus on lectures, readings, films, and documentaries. If you need special accommodation for your exams, please let me know two weeks before the exam date. You will be docked 25 points after your exam has been graded if you turn in a late exam.

Office Hours

I will be available to you outside of class should you desire help, clarification, etc. Feel free to drop by during my office hours. I might have to change my office hours one or two times during the semester, but I will let you know in advance. If you need to contact me, you may do one of the following: send me an e-mail message (best way to contact me), leave a message on my office phone voice mail, or, of course, drop by my office during office hours. I will return student phone calls only in the case of emergencies. If you need to meet with me outside of my office hours, I am happy to set up an appointment with you.

Grading: weighted percentage of the total grade of 100%

Your grade is based on the following:

Writing Assignments 40%

The highest four scores from the five assignments will be recorded. Each assignment is worth 10 percentage points.

Midterm Exam 30%

Final Exam 30%

Your percent grade in each criterion is multiplied by the weighted percentage listed above, and at the end of the semester all of those points are added to calculate your final grade. For example, if you get a 90% on the Midterm Exam, your weighted percentage points is calculated as 90 X .30=27 percentage points. At the end of the semester all of your weighted percentage points are added to make up your final percent grade. I do not give incompletes in this class. You must drop before the deadline to receive the automatic "W." If you do not feel that you can finish the requirements of this course, then you should drop the course according to the Texas State University–San Marcos guidelines. If you need to earn a certain grade in this course (e.g., to maintain a scholarship, to graduate, or to maintain your academic status for athletics or otherwise), then it is your responsibility to earn that grade.

Final Grade

A	=	(90–100)
B	=	(80– 89)
C	=	(70–79)
D	=	(60–69)
F	=	(50–59)

Students With Special Needs

Students with special needs as documented by the Office of Disability Services should identify themselves at the beginning of the term. The Department of Sociology is dedicated to providing these students with necessary academic adjustments and auxiliary aids to facilitate their participation and performance in the classroom. Please indicate special needs on your student index card.

Academic Dishonesty

"Academic dishonesty" includes a variety of violations. It refers to acts such as cheating on a test or committing plagiarism when writing a paper. The Sociology Department holds that it is the responsibility of each student to know what constitutes academic dishonesty. A lack of understanding of the term is no excuse when academic dishonesty is at issue. Similarly, a student may not be excused from a current violation because he/she committed a similar act in the past and was not charged with a violation of university policy. Any student who is accused of academic dishonesty has the right to challenge the accusation, but the challenge must be submitted in writing and in accordance with Texas State University–San Marcos policy. University statements regarding academic dishonesty can be found at the following websites:

http://www.txstate.edu/effective/upps/upps-07-10-01.html

http://www.mrp.txstate.edu:16080/studenthandbook/rules.html#academic
(Texas State Handbook)

http://www.txstate.edu/effective/upps/upps-07-10-01.html
(Academic Honesty, UPPS No. 07.10.01

The complete statement on the policy of the Department of Sociology regarding academic dishonesty (including plagiarism) is available on the departmental website, www.soci.txstate.edu. I reserve the right to ask students to change seats during exams if I see any suspicious behavior, even if it is unintentional. If I ask you to move to another seat during an exam, it does not mean that I am accusing you of academic dishonesty. However, if you appear to be looking at another student's exam, if you are not covering your answer with a sheet of paper, or if someone else can see your answers, then I will ask you to move. I do not give out grades over the phone or via e-mail, in order to protect student confidentiality.

Teaching Philosophy

My goal is to convey the excitement and value of sociological intellectual inquiry and to build upon students' previous learning by incorporating their diverse experiences into the classroom. Central to my pedagogical goals is to bridge teaching and learning with open and constructive dialogue. I aim to achieve clarity in the classroom by, for example, providing a brief statement of the thesis or argument; outlining the main points; providing concrete examples (at least one for every major point or important concept); and restating the same argument in different ways. Critical-response writing provides an opportunity for students to think about, share, and communicate something that is related to the topics covered in the course that matters to them. This is a useful strategy to help students think sociologically in a more complex and concrete ways. When the course is over, I like students to leave with a nuanced understanding of social issues about health, illness, and medicine in their community and in our society, an appreciation of using the sociological imagination, and an increased self-awareness of the role and responsibilities of the individual in a diverse global society.

Electronic Devices in Classroom Policy Department of Sociology

The absence of unnecessary distractions and interruptions being essential for an effective learning environment, the Department of Sociology requires that each and every student adhere to the following rules regarding the use of electronic devices in the classroom. These guidelines constitute department policy, and the student's receipt and acceptance of a course syllabus containing a course instructor's rules on the use of electronic devices shall constitute acceptance of this policy.

Definition

Electronic device includes cell phones (including smartphones), computers (laptops, notebooks, netbooks, and handhelds), MP3 and other digital audio and video players (including DVD players), and analog and digital audio and video recording devices (still and movie cameras).

1. A student may not use an electronic device during class time without the express permission of the instructor. Use of cell/smartphones during class time is always prohibited, as is leaving the room to answer or make a call.

2. A student with a diagnosed disability must present to the course instructor the appropriate paperwork from the Office of Disability Services in order to work out an accommodation for the use of otherwise prohibited electronic devices.
3. In all cases, when permission has been granted by an instructor for the use of an electronic device in the classroom, the student shall employ such device solely in a manner appropriate to the course work, avoiding distractions or interruptions to fellow students or the instructor, including leaving the room to use such device.
4. The course instructor has the discretion to grant either individual or a blanket approval or prohibition of the use of one or more types of electronic devices in the classroom.
5. The course instructor reserves the right to withdraw previously granted approval for the use of an electronic device, on an individual or blanket basis, if in the instructor's best judgment continued use of such device detracts from the effectiveness of the classroom-learning environment.
6. The course instructor shall include in each course syllabus a statement establishing under what conditions electronic devices may be used in the classroom, and the manner in which a violation of the instructor's rules of use of such devices shall be addressed. In case of a change in status of an electronic device in the course of the semester, the instructor will update the course syllabus as appropriate.
7. A student violating an instructor's classroom policy or individual instructions on the use electronic devices in the classroom shall be subject to any or all of the following actions:

    - Confiscation of the device by the instructor for the remainder of the class period
    - Dismissal from the class for the day on which the offense occurs
    - Referral of the student to the Office of Student Justice for disciplinary action under the Code of Student Conduct

Spring 2011 Semester Schedule

January 19 W, 24 M, 26W, 31 M, February 2W (Writing Assignment 1 Due) Feb 7–14

Introduction to Medical Sociology

Katherine J. Rosich and Janet R. Hankin. "Executive Summary: What Do We Know? Key Findings from 50 Years of Medical Sociology" (TRACS)

C. Phelan, Bruce G. Link, and Parisa Tehranifar. "Social Conditions as Fundamental Causes of Health Inequalities: Theory, Evidence, and Policy Implications" (TRACS)

Debra Umberson and Jennifer Karas Montez. "Social Relationships and Health: A Flashpoint for Health Policy" (TRACS)

Eric R. Wright and Brea L. Perry. "Medical Sociology and Health Services Research: Past Accomplishments and Future Policy Challenges" (TRACS)

Carol A. Boyer, Stefan Timmermans, and Hyeyoung Oh. "The Continued Social Transformation of the Medical Profession" (TRACS)

Dennis D. Waskul and Hillip Vannini. "Introduction: The Body in Symbolic Interaction" (TRACS)

February 16, 21 M, 23 W, 28 M, March 2 W, 7 M, 9 W (Midterm Exam)

Social Determinants of Health

David R. Williams and Michelle Sternthal. "Understanding Racial-ethnic Disparities in Health: Sociological Contributions" (TRACS)

David R. Williams. "Race, SES, and Health: The Added Effects of Racism and Discrimination"

Judith Lorber and Lisa Jean Moore. "Women Get Sicker but Men Die Quicker: Social Epidemiology"

Sally Macintyre, Anne Ellaway, and Steven Cummins. "Place Effects on Health"

Mirowsky, J. and C. Ross. "Neighborhood Disadvantage, Disorder, and Health" (TRACS)

Peggy A. Thoits. "Stress and Health: Major Findings and Policy Implications" (TRACS)

Leonard I. Pearlin and Carol S. Aneshensel. "Stress, Coping, and Social Supports"

David Kotelchuck. "Worker Health and Safety at the Beginning of a New Century"

Kate W. Strully. "Job Loss and Health in the U.S." (TRACS)

John Mirowsky and C. Ross. "Creative Work and Health" (TRACS)

Spring Break March 13–20

March 21 M, 23 W, 28 M, 30 W, April 4 M (Writing Assignment 3)

Social Construction of Health and Illness

Elliot G. Mishler. "Ch 1 Viewpoint: Critical perspective on the biomedical model" and "Ch 6 The Social Construction of Illness" (TRACS)

Phil Brown. "Naming and Framing: The Social Construction of Diagnosis and Illness"

Gareth Williams. "The Genesis of Chronic Illness: Narrative Reconstruction"

Eliot Freidson. "The Social Organization of Illness"

Peter Conrad and Kristin K. Barker. "The Social Construction of Illness: Key Insights and Policy Implications" (TRACS)

Sandra S. Stantonfile. "Alzheimer's Disease: A Family Affair and a Growing Social Problem" (Released April 2001). file:///Users/gm21/Desktop/alzheimer%27s%20world%20statistics_files/overview.php.html

Freund, Peter. "The Expressive Body: A Common Ground for the Sociology of Emotions and Health and Illness" (TRACS)

Help Seeking and Access to Health Care

David Mechanic and Donna D. McAlpine. "Sociology of Health Care Reform: Building on Research and Analysis to Improve Health Care" (TRACS)

David Mechanic and Sharon Meyer. "Concepts of Trust among Patients with Serious Illness"

Coker et al. "Perceived Racial/Ethnic Discrimination among 5th Grade Students and Its Association with Mental Health" (TRACS)

Karen E. Lutfey. "Examining Critical Health Policy Issues within and beyond the Clinical Encounter: Patient-Provider Relationships and Help-Seeking Behaviors"

(TRACS)

Book: *Crazy: A Father's Search through America's Mental Health Madness,* by Pete Earley

April 6 W, 11 M, 13 W, 18M, (Writing Assignment 4)

Health Care and Doctor-Patient Interactions

Peter Conrad. "The Shifting Engines of Medicalization"

James Jones. "The Tuskegee Syphilis Experiment"

Karen A. Lyman. "Infantilization: The Medical Model of Care"

Pills, Power. "People: Sociological Understandings of the Pharmaceutical Industry (Joan Busfield)"

Joan Cassell. "The Gender of Care"

Daniel Chambliss. "Nurses' Role: Caring, Professionalism, and Subordination"

Book: *Seeing Patients: Unconscious Bias in Health Care,* by Augustus A. White III

April 20 W, 25 M, 27 W, 2 M (Writing Assignment 5)

Health Social Movements

Phil Brown, Stephen Zavestoski, Sabrina McCormick, Brian Mayer, Rachel Morello-Frosch, and Rebecca Altman. "Embodied Health Movements: New Approaches to Social Movements in Health"

Steven Epstein. "Democracy, Expertise, and AIDS Treatment Activism"

Penn Loh and Jodi Sugerman-Brozan. "Environmental Justice Organizing for Environmental Health: Case Study on Asthma and Diesel Exhaust in Roxbury, Massachusetts"

Melanie R. Wasserman, Deborah E. Bender, Shoou-Yih Lee, Joseph P. Morrissey, Ted Mouw, and Edward C. Norton. "Social Support among Latina Immigrant Women: Bridge Persons as Mediators of Cervical Cancer Screening" (TRACS)

Book: *Pink Ribbon Blues: How Breast Cancer Culture Undermines Women's Health,* by Gayle Sulik

Final Exam May 9th 4:30pm

25. TEXAS STATE UNIVERSITY–SAN MARCOS

MULTICULTURAL CURRICULUM TRANSFORMATION GUIDE/ASSESSMENT INSTRUMENT

Name of Course: History 1310: History of the United States to 1877
Instructor: Dr. Rebecca Montgomery
Department: History
Degree: B.A.
Degree Program Requirement: Yes No

1. Course Description	This course is a general survey of the history of the United States from the beginning of European settlement through the end of Reconstruction. It examines the historical events of colonization, the Revolution, nation-building, and the Civil War within a global context and from diverse cultural perspectives. Much of the course content will focus on the significance of gender, race, and ethnicity in the development of American identity, culture, and institutions. It also will explore the relationship between social difference and social power, and how subordinate groups have worked to expand American concepts of freedom and liberty.
2. Course Objectives	Students will gain a basic understanding of the historical context of America's place in the world and of the origins and nature of historical change. They will develop analytical skills through written work, including the interpretation of historical documents. They also will gain an appreciation for the ways in which history is a dynamic process involving both conflict and collaboration among diverse groups. Viewing history from multiple perspectives will provide students with a more accurate and complete understanding of the nation's past, enhance critical thinking skills, and impart the cultural knowledge necessary for success in a diverse world.
3. Course Content	LEVEL ONE: ___ LEVEL TWO: ___ LEVEL THREE: X Focus is on the unique, multicultural origins of the U.S. in comparison to other nations. The central theme (extensively developed in the survey textbook by Eric Foner) is changing concepts of freedom and liberty. This includes how liberty for European Americans comes at the expense of freedom for American Indians and African Americans, and how liberty for men comes at the expense of freedom for women, as well as how subordinate groups have constantly tried to widen concepts of freedom and liberty to realize their radical democratic potential. Lectures also examine class difference and the significance of ethnicity and race for class identity in the U.S.
4. Instructional Strategies	LEVEL ONE: ___ LEVEL TWO: X LEVEL THREE: ___ This course is taught in a teaching theater with a class size averaging between 320 and 350 students, which limits choices of instructional strategies. However, I use pictures and voices of diverse groups to stimulate thought and discussion, and encourage students to make connections between the past and present. Discussion is facilitated

	with the use of microphones, and students are rewarded for verbal contributions through their classroom participation grade. Also, each large section has three supplemental instruction leaders, undergraduates who attend classes and hold discussion and study sessions. This sort of "peer tutoring" definitely encourages peer learning. In the future, I plan to create learning communities by dividing classes into small groups and adding online discussion requirements.
5. Assessment of Student Knowledge	LEVEL ONE: ___ LEVEL TWO: ___ LEVEL THREE: X This is a writing-intensive course, meaning written work must comprise 70% of the final grade. All in-class essays require students to look at the world from diverse perspectives, either by writing a persuasive essay from the perspective of a particular demographic group or by analyzing historical documents written on the same topic or event by persons from diverse backgrounds. Since this is a first-semester course, the goal is to advance students' reading, writing, and critical thinking skills while not unduly penalizing them for the skills deficits they bring to college. In addition to essays, exams include multiple-choice (30%) and short-answer questions (30%) that test both factual knowledge and understanding of the larger significance of events. Students get credit for individual improvement, meaning that if they bomb the first test but then make steady improvement, the first exam is weighted less. And although adherence to formal writing standards is encouraged, students are not required to conform to one writing style, but get some credit for creativity as well as for more fact-based narratives.
6. Classroom Interactions	LEVEL ONE: ___ LEVEL TWO: X LEVEL THREE: ___ Again, the teaching theater limits opportunities for interaction. However, my teaching philosophy, which is included in the syllabus as follows, will be discussed on the first day of class: "The multicultural approach to teaching and learning models a truly democratic society by acknowledging and valuing the experiences of all social groups. This approach requires teachers and students to question their own assumptions and to consider the perspectives of others in a nonjudgmental and open-minded way. This means that the multicultural course is democratic in process as well as in content; since a respectful environment is necessary for open and honest dialog, mutual respect must be the foundation of all classroom discussion and interaction."
7. Course Evaluations	The department's standard student evaluation form will be modified to include the following question: "What are three things that you have learned in this course?" I also intend to develop a questionnaire that will measure the extent to which the multicultural objectives have been met.

Percentage of Multicultural Content 85%

Multicultural Classification

Multicultural Content (MC): courses with 60% of the content multicultural

Multicultural Perspectives (MP): courses using a variety of strategies to encourage multiculturalism, including content, instructional strategies, assessment, and classroom dynamics

Multicultural Content and Perspectives (MC and MP): combination of both with 60% content

The multicultural classification that best describes this course is: MC and MP

It focuses on a combination of U.S. diversity and women's studies.

Explanation

The lectures alone contain 85% multicultural content (20.5 out of 24 lectures), and the survey text assigned for the course integrates diverse perspectives in addition to providing a multicultural narrative of historical change. The textbook theme of changing concepts of freedom and liberty, which also is integrated into lecture and classroom discussion, does not just "paste on" the multicultural content, but shows how it is integrally related to the development of American social, economic, political, and legal institutions—it transforms the whole analytical framework of American history. As discussed above, appreciation and respect for the significance of cultural diversity also is encouraged through guidelines for classroom interaction, instructional strategies, and assessment tools.

TEXAS STATE UNIVERSITY–SAN MARCOS

HISTORY 1310: History of the U.S. to 1877		
Instructor: Dr. Rebecca Montgomery	Tel: (512) 245-2116	
	E-mail: rm53@txstate.edu	
Office: Taylor-Murphy 227	**Office Hours**: T/H 9:30am–12:00pm and by appointment	

Course Syllabus

Course Description

This course is a general survey of the history of the United States from the beginning of European settlement through the end of Reconstruction. It will examine the historical events of colonization, the Revolution, nation-building, and the Civil War within a global context and from diverse cultural perspectives. Much of the course content will focus on the significance of gender, race, and ethnicity in the development of American identity, culture, and institutions. It also will explore the relationship between social difference and social power, and how subordinate groups have worked to expand American concepts of freedom and liberty.

Course Objectives

Students will gain a basic understanding of the historical context of America's place in the world and of the origins and nature of historical change. They will develop analytical skills through written work, including the interpretation of historical documents. They also will gain an appreciation for the ways in which history is a dynamic process involving both conflict and collaboration among diverse groups. Viewing history from multiple perspectives will provide students with a more accurate and complete understanding of the nation's past, enhance critical thinking skills, and impart the cultural knowledge necessary for success in a diverse world.

Teaching Philosophy

The multicultural approach to teaching and learning models a truly democratic society by acknowledging and valuing the experiences of all social groups. This approach requires teachers and students to question their own assumptions and to consider the perspectives of others in a nonjudgmental and open-minded way. This means that the multicultural course is democratic in process as well as in content; since a respectful environment is necessary for open and honest dialog, mutual respect must be the foundation of all classroom discussion and interaction.

Course Requirements

Attendance at class meetings. Lectures and discussion are required components of the course, and students whose work schedules or personal obligations prevent regular attendance should enroll in a section with more convenient meeting times. Beginning with the fourth one, each absence will result in a 10-point reduction in the classroom participation portion of the final grade.

Completion of reading assignments. All students must read the following required books. It is best to stay current with textbook readings in order to have some context for the related lectures.

A. Foner, E. (2008). *Give me liberty! An American history*, vol. 1. New York, NY: W. W. Norton.

B. Perdue, T., & Green, M. (2004). *The Cherokee removal: A brief history with documents.* New York, NY: St. Martins.

Completion of writing assignment. All students will write an in-class essay on the assigned book *The Cherokee Removal*. The essay will require interpretation of selected documents from the second part of the book, and will be written in class on the date indicated on the attached semester schedule. A study guide for the book will be handed out in class.

Examinations. There will be two midterm exams and one final exam. Exams will consist of an objective section (multiple-choice), a short-answer section, and an essay question. Students will receive a study guide for each exam one week in advance. Exams will cover both textbook and lecture material.

Makeup Policy: Makeup exams are allowed only in cases of *documented* unavoidable events that prevent attendance on exam day. **Please Note**: Students who are unable to attend the regular exam session must notify the professor by e-mail or phone within 48 hours and provide documentation of their emergency. Students who do not give such notification and provide documentation will not be allowed to make up the missed exam. All makeup exams will be administered during IA office hours in the last week of regular class (the first week in December) unless some other prior arrangement has been made.

Fulfillment of Individual Responsibilities. Each student has individual responsibilities that go beyond simply showing up for class and reading the assigned books.

a. **Mutual Courtesy and Respect**—Students have a responsibility to maintain an effective learning environment by avoiding behavior that interferes with the ability of others to hear and concentrate. For example: (1) address comments to the entire class rather than just to adjacent students; (2) on those rare occasions when arriving late or leaving early is unavoidable, minimize the disruption by notifying the professor or IA in advance; (3) be sure to turn off all cell phones and beepers before class starts. Disruptive behavior is prohibited by Section 2.02 of the Texas State University Code of Student Conduct and is subject to disciplinary action.

b. **Academic Calendar and Course Information**—Students also have a responsibility to be familiar with the key dates on the academic calendar (such as deadlines for dropping the course, and the first and last days of class) in addition to course-specific information such as midterm and final exam dates and all other course requirements as outlined in the syllabus. Dates and deadlines are marked on the attached semester schedule, but will not always be announced in class. All course handouts are posted on TRACS, which can be accessed from the Texas State home page link. Links to the academic calendar and the final exams schedule are on the Registrar's home page, which can be accessed from the "current student" pull-down menu on the Texas State home page.

Grades

Final grades will be determined as follows:

First Exam	25%	90–100	A
Second Exam	30%	80–89	B
Final Exam	30%	70–79	C
In-class Essay	10%	60–69	D
Participation	5%	Below 60	F

Note: October 27 is the last day to drop a class.

Student Resources

- **The Professor**—Please see me during office hours or e-mail me if you have any questions or problems concerning your performance in the course or the nature of course requirements. E-mails sent during the week will receive a response within

24 hours, and those sent on the weekend will receive a response within 48 hours. But do not underestimate the importance of talking to professors face-to-face!

- **Supplemental Instructors** (SIs)—SIs are undergraduate tutors who attend all lectures and have study sessions in the Student Learning Assistance Center (SLAC) on a weekly basis. I strongly urge you to attend these sessions, as students who attend them receive a final grade that is on average at least half a letter grade higher than students who do not.
- **Instructional Assistants** (IAs)—IAs are graduate students who grade most of the written assignments. They attend lectures and hold regular office hours, and along with the SIs are valuable sources of information on how best to study and prepare for exams.
- **History Tutors**—SLAC has a history tutor available during all hours of operation. Check the SLAC website for the names and hours of the history tutors for this semester.
- **Miscellaneous—forming study group with other students is** a strategy that also can be very helpful. Other sources of assistance include the Writing Lab in Flowers Hall.

(Students with disabilities or other special needs or concerns should notify the professor at the beginning of the semester.)

Cheating/Plagiarism Policy

Cheating violates university policy and undercuts the purposes and value of higher education. Cheating includes any attempt to defraud, deceive, or mislead the instructor in arriving at an honest grade assessment, and may include copying answers from other students or using unauthorized notes during tests. Plagiarism is a particular form of cheating that involves presenting as one's own the ideas or work of another, and may include using another person's ideas without proper attribution or submitting another person's work as one's own. Cheating and plagiarism violations always result in a grade of zero for the assignment involved, and may also result in a failing grade for the course. See the Student Handbook for university policies and procedures regarding violations of the Academic Honor Code.

Alkek Rules and Emergency Protocol

No tobacco products or food or open drink containers; only nonspill mugs with tops and bottles with a screw-top cap are allowed. Do not place feet on seat backs. Enter and exit through the assigned doorways. Lost and Found items are kept in the Teaching Theater office. In the case of fire or an alarm, evacuate through the closest exit door in an orderly fashion and move away from the building, unless instructed by safety personnel to do otherwise. In the event of an illness or injury during class, notify the IA or professor immediately and remain seated to provide access to the individual requiring attention.

SEMESTER SCHEDULE

Note: Students will have prior notification of any necessary changes in the semester schedule.

Date	Topics	Textbook Readings
Aug. 28	Introduction and Overview	
Sep. 2	A Collision of Cultures	Chap. 1
Sep. 4	Establishing English Colonies in the South	Chap. 1 & 2
Sep. 9	The Emergence of Chattel Slavery	Chap. 2
Sep. 11	Puritanism and the Northern Colonies	Chap. 2
Sep. 16	Successes and Failures in Indian Policy	
Sep. 18	Economic Change and Northern Society	Chap. 3
Sep. 23	Race and Social Hierarchy in the South	Chap. 4
Sep. 25	Political & Intellectual Origins of Revolution	Chap. 5
Sep. 30	**First Exam (lecture notes and chapters 1–5)**	
Oct. 2	The Revolution in Social Perspective, Part I	Chap. 6
Oct. 7	The Revolution in Social Perspective, Part II	Chap. 6
Oct. 9	Reconciling Centralized Power with Liberty	Chap. 7
Oct. 14	The Jeffersonian Ideal and Federal Policy	Chap. 8
Oct. 16	Commerce and Conflict in the Early Republic	Chap. 8
Oct. 21	The Market Revolution & the Middle Class	Chap. 9
Oct. 23	Early Industrialization and the Worker	Chap. 9
Oct. 28	Defining Democracy in Jacksonian America	Chap. 10
Oct. 30	**Second Exam (lecture notes and chapters 6–10)**	
Nov. 4	Slavery, the Family, and Southern Society	Chap. 11
Nov. 6	Social Change and Social Reform	Chap. 12
Nov. 11	**Essay exam on *The Cherokee Removal***	
Nov. 13	The Politics of Abolitionism	Chap. 12
Nov. 18	Manifest Destiny and the Western Frontier	Chap. 13
Nov. 20	Intensification of Sectional Conflict	Chap. 13
Nov. 25	The Racial Politics of War	Chap. 13 & 14
Nov. 27	No Class: Thanksgiving Holiday	
Dec. 2	Redefining Citizenship	Chap. 14
Dec. 4	The Successes and Failures of Reconstruction	Chap. 15
Dec.?	**Final Exam (lecture notes and chapters 11–15)**	

26. TEXAS STATE UNIVERSITY–SAN MARCOS
MULTICULTURAL CURRICULUM TRANSFORMATION GUIDE/ASSESSMENT INSTRUMENT

Name of Course: US 1100: University Seminar (for Science Majors)
Instructor: Debra Feakes
Department: University Seminar
Degree: Core Requirement
Degree Program Requirement: YES NO

1. Course Description	University Seminar is an introduction to the nature and aims of university education, with special emphasis on the value of broad learning. (This section of the course is offered for chemistry and biochemistry majors.)
2. Course Objectives	The objectives of the US1100 course are: • To facilitate students' adjustment to the challenges of life and learning at Texas State University–San Marcos • To expand students' understanding of the nature and purpose of the university • To identify practical learning skills and concepts that will promote students' academic success • To encourage students to explore the connections between university study and life enrichment, lifelong learning, and civic responsibility • To promote respect for diversity issues and concepts
3. Course Content (60% needed for multicultural content classification)	LEVEL ONE: ___ LEVEL TWO: _LEVEL THREE: _*X* (Check one. Explain.) The course content includes several projects that promote cultural learning related to scientific knowledge, e.g., making contact with a diverse group of science educators through correspondence and interviews, and case studies of the backgrounds of a diverse group of scientists.
4. Instructional Strategies	LEVEL ONE: ___ LEVEL TWO: ___LEVEL THREE: X (Check one. Explain.) The instructional strategies include facilitating full-group discussion, small-group discussion, online and onsite self-reflection, and extra-credit field trips. The size of the class (average of thirty students) and the projects supports a variety of approaches to enhancing knowledge related to the course objectives. Students have many opportunities to integrate their prior knowledge with course content and ideas of others.
5. Assessment of Student Knowledge	LEVEL ONE: ___ LEVEL TWO: ___ LEVEL THREE: X (Check one. Explain.) Students are provided with a variety of assessment measures as well as a choice in several of the daily projects and extra-credit opportunities.
6. Classroom Interactions	The students interact during each class session with the instructor and each other. The course involves discussion, group discussions, oral presentations, and self-reflection, with emphasis on respect and balanced participation.
7. Course Evaluation	The standard course feedback form provided by the department is the key tool for evaluating student response to multicultural activities and goals.

Percentage of Multicultural Content: 60%

Multicultural Classification

Multicultural Content (MC): courses with 60% of the content multicultural

Multicultural Perspectives (MP): courses using a variety of strategies to encourage multiculturalism, including content, instructional strategies, assessment, and classroom dynamics (when this is the only classification, the content is less than 60%)

Multicultural Content and Perspectives (MC and MP): combination of both with 60% content

Choose the best multicultural classification that describes this course: Circle one. MC MP **MC and MP** Multicultural perspectives are integrated throughout the course content areas and prioritized in pedagogical strategies.

Does this course focus on international diversity, U.S. diversity, women's studies, or a combination of all three? Explain. **All three**. Scientific discovery and participation explored in the course includes research conducted in the U.S. and internationally by men and women biochemists. Material will be presented with deliberate emphasis on the science makers.

TEXAS STATE UNIVERSITY–SAN MARCOS

US 1100: University Seminar		
Fall 2004		
Instructor: Dr. Debra A. Feakes	Tel: (512) 245-7609 E-mail: df10@txstate.edu	
Office: Chemistry Building, Room 319	**Office Hours**: Wednesday, 2–2:50 pm	
Any variation to these hours will be announced in class. If you cannot come to the posted office hours, you may schedule an appointment to meet with me.		

Required Materials

Ferrett, S. K. (2003). Peak performance, success in college and beyond (4th ed.). New York, NY: McGraw-Hill.

Description

"University seminar is an introduction to the nature and aims of university education, with special emphasis on the value of broad learning" (p. 96, 2004–2006 Catalogue).

Objectives

The objectives of the US1100 course are:

- To facilitate students' adjustment to the challenges of life and learning at Texas State University–San Marcos
- To expand students' understanding of the nature and purpose of the university
- To identify practical learning skills and concepts that will promote students' academic success
- To encourage students to explore the connections between university study and life enrichment, lifelong learning, and civic responsibility
- To promote respect for diversity issues and concepts

Grading

The following grade weighting will be utilized to determine your final grade. Grades will be assigned on a standard grading scale.

Participation/Attendance	35%
Homework	40%
In-class Presentations	10%
Journal	15%
Total	100%

Academic Honesty Statement

"Learning and teaching take place best in an atmosphere of intellectual fair-minded openness. All members of the academic community are responsible for supporting freedom and openness through rigorous personal standards of honesty and fairness. Plagiarism and other forms of academic dishonesty undermine the very purpose of Texas State and diminish the value of an education. Specific sanctions for academic dishonesty are outlined in the student handbook" (p. 56, 2004–2006 Catalogue).

Special Needs Information

Students with special needs (as documented by the Office of Disability Services) should identify themselves at the beginning of the semester.

Attendance

You are expected to be on time for class and attend every session. A significant portion of your grade is dependent on class participation. Therefore, failure to attend can have significant consequences. No distinction will be made between excused and unexcused absences; however, if you are unavoidably detained, please contact me immediately. If you are absent, it is your responsibility to obtain any missed information, assignments, or handouts.

Blackboard

A Blackboard site will be used for this course. In order to access the site, you must have a valid Texas State University username and password. Please check the Blackboard site regularly for announcements and postings.

Journal

Each of you will keep an "electronic journal" throughout the semester. This journal will constitute 15% of your final grade. Each week, in addition to answering that week's Blackboard topic question, I would like you to address the following:

How was your week?

What caused you the most concern this week? How did you address that concern?

What gave you the most happiness this week?

What did you try new this week?

At the end of each week, you will submit your responses to me. Details of the process will be given in class.

Extra Credit

Extra credit, worth a total of 5%, can be added to your grade based on attendance at two "cultural events" on or off campus. If the event is ticketed (for example, a play or a concert), simply bring the tickets to me. If the event is not ticketed (for example, a lecture series), bring a program of the event or a one-page typed summary of the event. Current information regarding events will be distributed throughout the semester and posted on Blackboard.

Course Outline

The following is an outline of the course. Items are subject to change throughout the semester as needed.

Date	Discussion Topic
August 25	Class Introduction and Goals Exercise **HW:** Talk to two adults that attended college. What did they get from their college experience and what advice do they have?
September 1	Educational Resources, Learning Styles **HW:** Document your entire week. Identify what times are you most effective or least effective. What could you do to improve your schedule?
September 8	Time Management (Chap. 3) **HW:** Bring a picture of a scientist to the next class. You can draw the picture, cut it out from a newspaper or magazine, or take a photo.
September 15	Diversity (Chap. 11) **HW:** Interview one of the chemistry professors (if you are a major in the Department of Chemistry and Biochemistry) or one of the biology professors (if you are a major in the Biology Department).
September 22	"Night" and the "Periodic Table" (Chap. 5) **HW:** Write to a professor at a college or university in one of the following categories and "interview" him or her: (a) an

	underrepresented country (in terms of science), (b) a traditionally Hispanic-serving institution, (c) a tribal college, or (d) a traditionally African American–serving institution
September 29	Case Studies Discussion **HW:** Pick one of the scientists on the list provided and research his or her background and contributions
October 6	History of Science "Revisited" Presentations **HW:** Locate a code of ethics from another academic institution, organization, company, or government entity and bring it to class.
October 13	Ethics (Chaps. 2 and 14) **HW:** Sign up for academic advising.
October 20	Career Development and Advising (Chap. 14) **HW:** Write down three volunteer activities that you would look like to become involved with.
October 27	Civic Responsibility (Chap. 12) **HW:** Identify somebody in a career that you would like to pursue, and ask them how they achieved their goals.
November 3	Developing Good Habits (Chap. 13) **HW:** Look at your classes for next semester. What will you have to do to succeed? Complete a worksheet for each course.
November 10	What is Science? **HW:** Working in groups, select two ongoing scientific debates for discussion. E-mail the topics to me.
November 17	Debate Topic Selection **HW:** Working in groups, gather the information necessary for the debate.
December 1	Scientific Debate (Chap. 9)

Drop Policy

The automatic "W" deadline is Tuesday, 13 September. After this date, you may drop the course with a "W" only *if*:

- you request the drop from the professor in person *and*
- you have been an active participant in and out of the class *and*
- you follow the appropriate administrative procedures for dropping a course. The drop/withdrawal deadline for this course is Monday, 21 November.

REFERENCES

Abbas, A., & Erni, J. N. (Eds.). (2005). *Internationalizing cultural studies.* Malden, MA: Blackwell.

Adams, J. Q., Niss, J. F., & Suarez, C. (Eds.). (1998). *Multicultural education: Strategies for implementation in colleges and universities.* Macomb, IL: Western Illinois University Foundation.

Adams, M. (1997). *Teaching diversity and social justice.* New York, NY: Routledge.

Allen, D. (Ed.). (1998). *Assessing student learning: From grading to understanding.* New York, NY: Teachers College Press.

Angelo, A. T. (1993). *Classroom assessment techniques: A handbook for college teachers.* San Francisco, CA: Jossey-Bass.

Augsburger, D. W. (1995). *Conflict mediation across cultures: Pathways and patterns.* Louisville, KY: Westminster/John Knox Press.

Avruch, K. (1998). *Culture & conflict resolution.* Washington, DC: USIP Press.

Banks, J. A. (1996a). *Multicultural education series.* New York, NY: Teachers College Press.

Banks, J. A. (Ed.). (1996b). *Multicultural education transformation knowledge and action: Historical and contemporary perspectives.* New York, NY: Teachers College Press.

Banks, J. A. (2004). *Diversity and citizenship education.* San Francisco, CA: Jossey-Bass.

Banks, J. A., & Banks, C. (Eds.). (2004). *Handbook of research on multicultural education.* San Francisco, CA: Jossey-Bass.

Banks, J. A., & Banks, C. A. M. (Eds.). (2005). *Multicultural education: Issues and perspectives.* Hoboken, NJ: John Wiley & Sons.

Branch, J., Cohn, R. E., & Mullennix, J. (Eds.). (2007). *Diversity across the curriculum: A guide for faculty in higher education classroom.* San Francisco, CA: Jossey-Bass.

Broussard, S., Cummings, J., Johnson, J., Levi, K., & Bailey-Perry, M. (2006). *Cultural and educational excellence revisited: Knowing, doing, being, and becoming as though saving the African American child matters.* Portland, OR: Inkwater Press.

Brown, M. C. (Ed.). (2007). *Still not equal: Expanding educational opportunity in society.* New York, NY: Peter Lang.

Chen, J., Horsch, P., DeMoss, K., & Wagner, S. (2004). *Effective partnering for school change: Improving early childhood education in urban classrooms.* New York, NY: Teachers College Press.

Cohen, R. (1997). *Negotiating across cultures: International communication in an interdependent world.* Washington, DC: USIP Press.

Colangelo, N., Dustin, D., & Foxely, C. (1979). *Multicultural nonsexist education: A human relations approach* (2nd ed.). Dubuque, IA: Kendall/ Hunt.

Cox, T. (1993). *Cultural diversity in organizations: Theory, research and practice.* San Francisco, CA: Berrett-Koehler.

Cushner, K. (2006). *Human diversity in action: Developing multicultural competencies for the classroom* (3rd ed.). Boston, MA: McGraw-Hill.

Dana, R. H. (1993). *Multicultural assessment perspectives for professional psychology.* Boston, MA: Allyn & Bacon.

Davidman, L., & Davidman, P. (1997). *Teaching with a multicultural perspective: A practical guide* (2nd ed.). New York, NY: Longman.

Dilworth, M. (Ed.). (1992). *Diversity in teacher education: New expectations.* San Francisco, CA: Jossey-Bass Publishers.

Duarte, E. M., & Smith, S. (2000). *Foundational perspectives in multicultural education.* New York, NY: Longman.

Farr, S. (2010). *Teaching as leadership.* San Francisco, CA: Jossey-Bass.

Foote, D., Frost, M., Hynes-Berry, M., Johnson, J. W., Miller, B. C., & Perkins, B. P. (1993). *Responding to literature: Multicultural perspectives.* Evanston, IL: McDougal, Littell.

Fullan, M. (1999). *Change forces: The sequel.* Philadelphia, PA: Falmer Press/Taylor & Francis.

Garcia, G., et al. (2002). *Assessing campus diversity initiatives: A guide for campus practitioners.* Washington, DC: Association of American Colleges and Universities.

Gardner, H. (1993). *Frames of mind: Theory of multiple intelligences.* New York, NY: Basic Books.

Gay, G. (2000). *Culturally responsive teaching.* New York, NY: Teachers College Press.

Gollnick, D. M., & Chinn, P. C. (2005). *Multicultural education in a pluralistic society & exploring diversity package* (7th ed.). Upper Saddle River, NJ: Prentice Hall.

Gorski, P. (2005). *Multicultural education and the internet: Intersections and integrations* (2nd ed.). Boston, MA: McGraw-Hill.

Grant, C. A. (Ed.). (1999). *Proceedings of the National Association for Multicultural Education.* Mahwah, NJ: Lawrence Erlbaum.

Greene, M. (1991). Retrieving the language of compassion: The education professor in search of community. *Teachers College Record, 92* (4), 541-555.

———. (1993). Diversity and inclusion: Toward a curriculum for human beings. *Teachers College Record, 95* (2), 211–221.

Grossman, H. (1995). *Teaching in a diverse society.* Boston, MA: Allyn & Bacon.

Gurung. A. R., & Prieto R. L. (2009). *Getting culture: Incorporating diversity across the curriculum.* Sterling, VA: Stylus.

Hale, J. (2001). *Learning while Black: Creating education excellence for African American children.* Baltimore, MD: Johns Hopkins University Press.

Hammer, M. R. (2005). The intercultural conflict style inventory: A conceptual framework and measure of intercultural conflict approaches. *International Journal of Intercultural Research,* 29, 675–695.

Harris, P., & Morgan, R. (1991). *Managing cultural differences: High performance strategies for new world of business: Capitalize on international markets: Improve communications with foreign nationals and U.S. minorities: Master business protocol and cross-cultural courtesy* (3rd ed.). Houston, TX: Gulf.

Hernandez, N. (1989). *Multicultural education: A teacher's guide to linking context, process, and content* (2nd ed.). Upper Saddle River, NJ: Merrill Prentice Hall.

Herold, M. E. (2003). *Issues in Latino education: Race, school culture, and the politics of academic success.* Boston, MA: Allyn & Bacon.

Hines, S. M. (Ed.). (2003). *Multicultural science education: Theory, practice, and promise.* New York, NY: Peter Lang.

Howard, G. (1999). *We can't teach what we don't know: White teachers, multiracial schools.* New York, NY: Teachers College Press.

Irvine, J. J. (2003). *Educating teachers for diversity.* New York, NY: Teachers College Press.

Kelley, R. D. G. (1994). *Race rebels: Culture, politics, and the black working class.* New York, NY: The Free Press.

Kenton, S. B., & Valentine, D. (1997). *Crosstalk: Leader's guide: Communicating in a multicultural workplace.* Upper Saddle River, NJ: Prentice Hall.

Kincheloe, J., Slattery, P., & Steinberg, S. (2000). *Contextualizing teaching: Introduction to education and educational foundations.* New York, NY: Longman.

Kivel, P. (2002). *Uprooting racism: How white people can work for racial justice.* Scarborough, Canada: New Society.

Kunjufu, J. (1989). *Critical issues in education African American youth.* Chicago, IL: African American Images.

Leistyna, P. (2005). *Cultural studies: From theory to action.* Oxford, UK: Blackwell.

Levi, J. A., & Stevens D. D. (2005). *Introduction to rubrics: An assessment tool to save grading time, convey effective feedback and promote student learning.* Herndon, VA: Stylus.

Lutzker, M. (1995). *Multiculturalism in the college curriculum: A handbook of strategies and resources for faculty.* Westport, CT: Greenwood Press.

Magala, S. (2005). *Cross-cultural competence.* New York, NY: Routledge.

Maternal and Child Health Bureau. (1998a). *Oppression: Cultural diversity curriculum for social workers and health practitioners.* Austin, TX: National Maternal and Child Health Resource Center on Cultural Competence and the Centers for Minority Health Initiatives and Cultural Competency at the Texas Department of Health.

———. (1998b). *Persons with disabilities: Cultural diversity curriculum for social workers and health practitioners.* Austin, TX: National Maternal and Child Health Resource Center on Cultural Competence and the Centers for Minority Health Initiatives and Cultural Competency at the Texas Department of Health.

Mazel, E. (1998). *"And don't call me racist!": A treasury of quotes on the past, present, and future of the color line in America.* Lexington, MA: Argonaut Press.

McCarthy, C., & Crichlow, W. (1993). *Race, identity, and representation in education.* New York, NY: Routledge.

McDiarmid, G., & Williamson, K. (1992). *A case of innovative mathematics: Teaching in a multicultural classroom.* Fairbanks, AK: University of Alaska Fairbanks, Center for Cross-Cultural Studies.

McLaren, P. (2003). *Life in schools: An introduction to critical pedagogy in the foundations of education* (4th ed.). Boston, MA: Allyn & Bacon.

McLemore, S., & Romo, H. (1998). *Racial and ethnic relations in America.* Boston, MA: Allyn & Bacon.

Morey, A. I., & Kitano, M. (1997). *Multicultural course transformation in higher education: A broader truth.* Boston, MA: Allyn & Bacon.

Moule, J. (2011). *Cultural competence: A primer for educators* (2nd ed.). Belmont, CA: Wadsworth Press.

Nieto, S. (2003). *What keeps teachers going?* New York, NY: Teachers College Press.

Noel, J. (2000). *Developing multicultural education.* Guilford, CT: Dushkin/McGraw-Hill.

O'Grady, C. R. (2000). *Integrating service learning and multicultural education in colleges and universities.* Hillsdale, NJ: Lawrence Erlbaum.

Pang, V. (2001). *Multicultural education: A caring, centered, reflective approach.* Boston, MA: McGraw-Hill.

Phillion, J. (2005). *Narrative and experience in multicultural education.* Thousand Oaks, CA: Sage.

Reid, C. (2004). *The wounds of exclusion: Poverty, women's health, and social justice.* Edmonton, Canada: Qual Institute Press.

Rhodes, R. (1994). *Nurturing learning in Native American students.* Hotevilla, AZ: Sonwai Books.

Schoem, D. (1995). *Multicultural teaching in the university.* Westport, CT: Praeger.

Schoem, D., Frankel, L., Zuniga, X., & Lewis, E. A. (Eds.). (1993). *Multicultural teaching in the university.* Westport, CT: Praeger.

Schultz, F. (2004). *Annual editions: Multicultural education.* Guilford, CT: McGraw-Hill.

Simons, G., Abramms, B., Hopkins, L., & Johnson, D. (1996). *Cultural diversity fieldbook: Fresh visions and breakthrough strategies for revitalizing the workplace.* Princeton, NJ: Peterson's/Pacesetter Books.

Solomon, M. (1990). *Working with difficult people: Hundreds of office-proven strategies and techniques to get cooperation and respect from tyrants, connivers, badmouthers and other difficult people you must work with everyday.* Englewood Cliffs, NJ: Prentice Hall.

Sutcliffe, B. (2001). *100 ways of seeing an unequal world.* London: Zed Books.

Tatum, B. (1997). *Why are all the black kids sitting together in the cafeteria? And other conversations about race.* New York, NY: Basic Books.

Teaching Tolerance Project. (1997). *Starting small: Teaching tolerance in preschool and the early grades.* Montgomery, AL: Southern Poverty Law Center.

Timpson, W. M. (2003). *Teaching diversity: Challenges and complexities, identities, and integrity.* Madison, WI: Atwood.

———. (2006). *147 practical tips for teaching diversity*. Madison, WI: Atwood.

Trentacosta, J. (Ed.). (1997). *Multicultural and gender equity in the mathematics classroom.* Reston, VA: National Council of Teachers of Mathematics.

Watkins, W., Lewis, J., & Chou, V. (2001). *Race and education: The roles of history and society in education African American students.* Boston, MA: Allyn & Bacon.

Webster, Y. (1997). *Against the multicultural agenda: A critical thinking alternative.* Westport, CT: Praeger.

Woodson, C. G. (1998). *The education of the Negro.* Brooklyn, NY: A&B Publishers Group.

ABOUT THE CONTRIBUTORS

Enrique Becerra is an associate professor of marketing at Texas State University–San Marcos. He received his Ph.D. from Florida Atlantic University. His primary interests are consumer behavior and advertising. His research concentrates on the effects of culture, ethnicity, and/or self-concept on advertising and/or behavior, including on- and offline advertising and consumer behavior. His work has been accepted for publication in the *Journal of the Academy of Marketing Science,* the *Journal of Business Research,* the *Journal of Advertising Research,* the *European Journal of Marketing,* and the *Journal of Electronic Commerce Research,* among others.

Scott Bowman is an assistant professor of criminal justice at Texas State University–San Marcos. He received his Ph.D. from Arizona State University in justice studies. His work has been published in the *Journal of African-American Studies* and *The Journal of Consumer Education.*

Mary Ellen Cavitt is a professor of music education and the director of graduate studies in music at Texas State University–San Marcos. She received her Ph.D. in music education from The University of Texas at Austin. She is the editor of the *Texas Music Education Research Journal,* the Texas Music Educators Association Region 18 college division chair, and past chair for the Instructional Strategies Research Interest Group for the Music Educators National Conference (MENC), National Association for Music Education. She recently received the 2011 Texas State University Alumni Teaching Award of Honor and the 2011 Presidential Award for Excellence in Teaching for the College of Fine Arts and Communications.

Barbara Davis is a professor of curriculum and instruction at Texas State University–San Marcos. She received her Ed.D. from Texas Tech University. Her work has been published in the United States as well as internationally. In 2001 she received the Southwest Texas Presidential Award for Excellence in Teaching. She received the Texas State Alumni Association's Teaching Award of Honor in 2010. Her work has appeared in *Childhood Education, Phi Delta Kappan,* and the *Journal of Research in Childhood Education.*

Maria G. De la Colina is an associate professor in the Department of Curriculum and Instruction at Texas State University–San Marcos. She received her Ph.D. from Texas A&M University, and specializes in second language acquisition, bilingualism, and multiculturalism. Her main areas of research are in bilingual/ESL education PK–12, second language acquisition, and multicultural education. Her work has been published in the United States as well as internationally, including in the *Journal of Latinos in Education,* the *National Forum Journal for Teacher Education–Electronic, Revista Educación y Ciencia, the Journal of Border Educational Research,* and the *Journal of Educational Administration.*

Debra Feakes is an associate professor of chemistry and biochemistry at Texas State University–San Marcos. She received her Ph.D. from Utah State University and her post-doc from the University of California at Los Angeles. Her research interests are in main group inorganic chemistry. Her work has been published in numerous journals, including the *Journal of Chemistry Education* and the *Journal of Inorganic Biochemistry.* She received the 2011 Presidential Award for Excellence in Service at the professor/associate level.

Kym Fox is a senior lecturer in journalism at Texas State University–San Marcos. She received her M.A. from the University of the Incarnate Word. As a reporter, she has won awards for her coverage of child abuse and juvenile justice, as well as state honors for news and feature writing. She is on the national board of the Society of Professional Journalists, the oldest and largest journalism organization in the United States.

Heather Galloway is the director of the University Honors Program and a professor in physics at Texas State University–San Marcos. She teaches a wide range of classes, including University Seminar, Freshman Physics, Quantum Mechanics, Honors Thesis, and Building a Greener Future: One Home at a Time. Her research and professional activities now focus on science education. Her work has appeared in the *Journal of Vacuum Science & Technology, Polymer Journal,* and the *Journal of the American Chemical Society.*

Richard Hall is a senior lecturer of music at Texas State University–San Marcos. He received an M.M. in composition from Texas State University. Richard's music has been performed at several regional, national, and international conferences. He has published software and book reviews for the *South Central Music Bulletin,* where he is also the music graphics editor. He has scored two independent films, and assists with the Texas Mysterium for Modern Music Ensemble. His work has appeared in the *South Central Music Bulletin.*

Catherine Hawkins, LCSW, is a professor of social work at Texas State University. She holds a MSW and received her Ph.D. from The University of Texas at Austin. Her main areas of interest and research are in direct practice, issues of sustainability and human trafficking, and spirituality in social work and international social work. She has led study abroad groups to Mexico and Cambodia, and was a visiting professor at the Madras School of Social Work in Chennai, Tamil Nadu, India in Fall 2006. Her work has appeared in the *Journal of Research on Women and Gender* and *Critical Social Work.*

Kevin Jetton is a lecturer in computer information systems and quantitative methods at Texas State University–San Marcos. He received his MBA from The University of Texas at San Antonio. He is an information technology educator, consultant, and professional association leader, as well as a Boy Scout leader and a meeting/conference/event planner. He is a 2007 graduate of the Multicultural Curriculum Transformation and Research Institute.

Patricia Larke is a professor of education at Texas A&M University–College Station. She received her Ed.D. from the University of Missouri–Columbia. She has published multicultural education articles in journals such as *Action in Teacher Education, Excellence and Equity, National Forum of Multicultural Issues Journal,* and has presented more than 200 papers at state, regional, and national multicultural education and research conferences. She is coeditor of the *Journal of the Texas Alliance of Black School Educators.* Her areas of interest are multicultural education, international education, culturally responsive teaching in higher education, and education of African-American girls. From 2005 to 2010, she presented on culturally responsive teaching at the Multicultural Curriculum Transformation and Research Institute at Texas State University–San Marcos. She is the former president of the Texas chapter of the National Association for Multicultural Education, and currently serves on its board of directors. In 2010 she received the Texas Chapter National Association for Multicultural Education (NAME) Career Achievement Award.

Sandra Mayo is the director of multicultural and gender studies and associate professor of theatre at Texas State University–San Marcos. She received her Ph.D. from Syracuse University. She chairs the Women and Gender Research Collaborative and is on the board of directors and the editorial board of the peer-reviewed, online *Journal of Research on Women and Gender,* both under the auspices of the Center for Multicultural and Gender Studies. She leads the Multicultural Curriculum Transformation and Research Institute and has presented multicultural curriculum transformation workshops at colleges and universities in the United States and in Africa. Her scholarship includes numerous conference presentations and publications on theatre and multiculturalism. Her most recent publications include two edited books on the plays of Sterling Houston—*Myth, Magic, and Farce: Four Multicultural Plays* (2006) and *High Yello Rose and Other Texas Plays* (2009). She has published in the *Journal of Case Studies in Education, Texas Theatre Journal, Theatre Journal, Middle Atlantic Writer's Association Journal, Black Stream (Journal of the Black Theatre Association of ATHE), Texas Books in Review,* and *Blacks in New York Life and History.* She currently serves on the board of directors of the Texas chapter of the National Association for Multicultural Education.

Audrey McKinney is an associate professor of philosophy at Texas State University–San Marcos. She received her Ph.D. from the University of Pennsylvania. She is on the editorial board of the *Journal of Research on Women and Gender.* She is also the director of the New Mexico/West Texas Philosophical Society. She coedited *New and Old World Philosophy* (2000). She has reviewed many articles, journals, books, and textbooks. Her work has appeared in *The Journal of the British Society for Phenomenology.*

Selina Vasquez Mireles is a professor of mathematics at Texas State University–San Marcos. Her main research interest is in mathematics education. She is the director of the Center for Mathematics Readiness. Her work has been published in the *Journal of Mathematic Science and Mathematics Education, The Texas Science Teacher, Texas College Mathematics Journal, School Science and Mathematics,* and *Mathematics Teaching in the Middle School.* Her most recent article, "Developmental Mathematics Program: A Model for Change," was published in 2010 in the *Journal of College Reading and Learning.*

Rebecca Montgomery is an associate professor of history at Texas State University–San Marcos. She received her Ph.D. from the University of Missouri–Columbia. Her research and teaching interests lie primarily in the Gilded Age and Progressive Era United States, with emphasis on gender, race, and education in the New South. She is also interested in the history of rural women. Her current book project is a biography of the educational reformer Celeste Parrish.

Andrew Nance is a practicing architect and assistant professor of interior design at Texas State University–San Marcos. He received his M.A. from The University of Texas at Arlington. He has taught both architecture and interior design at several institutions including the University of Colorado at Boulder, The University of Texas at Arlington, The University of Texas at San Antonio, and San Antonio College. His current research involves the integration of technology and sustainability in design pedagogy, as well as the processes and theories present in the design process. His work has been included in *Ubiquitous Learning: An International Journal.*

David Nolan is a senior lecturer of mass communication for the School of Journalism and Mass Communication at Texas State University–San Marcos. He received n M.A. from

Texas State University, and is currently working on a Ph.D. in adult, professional, and community education from the College of Education at Texas State. He is the associate editor of the *Southwestern Mass Communication Journal* (SWMCJ), a judge for numerous national press association contests, and guest speaker and lecturer at workshops and classrooms around Texas. He is a member of the National Press Photographers Association, Association for Education in Journalism and Mass Communication, and the Texas Photographic Society. One of his most recent honors was the 2006 Friends of Fine Arts and Communication Excellence in Service Award from Texas State.

Christine Norton, LCSW, is an assistant professor of social work at Texas State University. She received her Ph.D. from Loyola University of Chicago. Her areas of practice, research, and interest are in adolescent development, treatment and empowerment, wilderness and adventure therapy, youth mentoring, juvenile justice, alternative sentencing and restorative justice, experiential education, and international social work. She has more than fifteen years experience working with high-risk youth in a variety of settings, including therapeutic wilderness programs, juvenile justice, schools, and mentoring organizations. She recently received a $90,000 grant to develop a program to work with alumni of foster care who are now college students in Texas.

Sonya Rahrovi is the senior grant coordinator for multiple programs, such as Mix It Up and FOCUS: Fundamentals of Conceptual Understanding & Success, housed in the Department of Mathematics at Texas State University–San Marcos.

Gloria Martinez Ramos is an assistant professor of sociology at Texas State University–San Marcos. She received her Ph.D. from the University of Michigan–Ann Arbor. Her main interest areas are social stratification, race, class, and gender, sociology of health, illness and aging, Latino sociology, and qualitative research methodology. Her work has appeared in *The Journal of Health Care for the Poor and Underserved, Journal of Latinos in Education, Camino Real Estudios de las Hispanidades Norteamericanas,* and *Sociological Focus—Special Issue on Race and Ethnic Health Disparities.*

Stella Silva is the associate director of multicultural student affairs at Texas State University. She received her Ph.D. from The University of Texas at Austin in educational administration/ higher education, and a graduate portfolio certification in Mexican American studies. She has fourteen years of professional work experience in the areas of multiculturalism, diversity, and social justice, and she participated in the 2010 People's Institute, Undoing Racism. She is the founding advisor for Latinas Unidas (a Latina student empowerment group), a member of the Admissions Standards Committee at Texas State University, and a 2010 graduate of the Texas State Multicultural Curriculum Transformation and Research Institute. She received the Texas State Mariel M. Muir Excellence in Mentoring Award in 2006, and has been a University Seminar instructor for more than ten years.

Emily Summers is an assistant professor in the Department of Curriculum & Instruction at Texas State University–San Marcos. She received her Ph.D. from University of Houston. Her primary research interest is the ethnographic examination of educational contexts. Her scholarship emphasizes issues of equity in education, as well as the intersections of formal and informal cultures in constructing students' educative experiences. Her work has appeared in *Contemporary Issues in Technology and Teacher Educa-*

tion Journal, the *National Forum of Multicultural Issues Journal, and* the *Journal of Education, Informatics and Cybernetics.*

Mary Tijerina, LMSW, is an associate professor in social work at Texas State University–San Marcos. She received her Ph.D. from The University of Texas at Austin. Her main areas of research are in programs and strategies that help people with fetal alcohol syndrome or chemical addiction problems, and people of color who suffer health problems. In the past, she served as the bachelor of social work coordinator, and most recently as the master of social work coordinator. She is very involved in the Hogg Foundation Bilingual Scholarship program, as well as university programs aimed to assist first-generation college students. Her work has been included in *Advances in Social Work,* the *Journal of Social Work Education, Special Issue: Practice Perspectives with Racial and Ethnic Minorities,* and *Professional Development: The International Journal of Continuing Social Work Education.*

Raphael Travis, Jr., LCSW, is an assistant professor of social work at Texas State University. He received his Ph.D. from the University of California–Los Angeles. He blends experiences from direct social work practice and public health research in his current work. Ongoing projects examine the principles of positive youth development as they relate to out-of-school time programs, juvenile justice and reentry, and hip-hop culture. Each aspect of his research seeks to better understand positive influences on young people's health and well-being over the course of their life. Particular attention is given to multicultural populations. His publications can be found in the *Journal of Community Practice,* the *Journal of Human Behavior in the Social Environment,* and the *Journal of Ethnic & Cultural Diversity in Social Work.*

Keila Tyner is an assistant professor in of family and consumers science at Texas State University–San Marcos. She received her Ph.D. from Iowa State University, and teaches fashion merchandising. She has published in the *Journal of Family and Economic Issues,* and the *Clothing and Textiles Research Journal.*

Fernando Vasquez is a lecturer in curriculum and instruction at Texas State University–San Marcos. He received his Ph.D. from The University of Texas at Austin and his M.I.S. from the University of North Texas. He teaches Foundations of Bilingual and ESL Education and Materials for Teaching ESL in the Content Areas at Texas State.

Linette Watkins is an associate professor in the Department of Chemistry and Biochemistry at Texas State University–San Marcos. She received her Ph.D. from the University of Notre Dame. Her main research interests are examining the ways that bacterial enzymes can be used to remove sulfur from petroleum to make cleaner burning fuels.

Nancy Wilson is a professor of English at Texas State University–San Marcos. She received her Ph.D. from The University of Texas at San Antonio. She is the director of the Writing Center. Her main areas of interests are writing center theory and practice, rhetoric and composition, and world literature. Her work has appeared in *Kairos: A Journal of Rhetoric, Technology, and Pedagogy.*

Walter Wright is an associate professor in the Legal Studies Program at Texas State University–San Marcos. He holds an LL.M. in international legal studies from New York University. His areas of interest are in mediation, alternative dispute resolution, commercial transactions and employment law. His work has been published in numerous books and journals in the United States, several Latin American countries, and China, and includes *Prologue for Oscar Di María* and *Los Métodos Alternativos y los Infortunios Laborales.* In 2009 he received the Susanne C. Adams Award from the Texas Association of Mediators.

Ani Yazedjian is an associate professor of family and consumer sciences at Texas State University–San Marcos. She currently serves as the special assistant to the provost for International Student Services. She received her Ph.D. from the University of Illinois at Urbana–Champaign. Her main research interests focus on college students' adjustment and achievement, young adults' sexuality and contraceptive use, adolescent identity development, and adolescent parents' romantic relationships. She has also served as a program evaluator for a number of different programs. She has published in the *Journal of Education Research, The College Student Affairs Journal, The Journal of the First-Year Experience and Students in Transition,* and *Marriage and Family Review.*

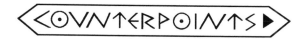

COUNTERPOINTS

Studies in the Postmodern Theory of Education

General Editor
Shirley R. Steinberg

Counterpoints publishes the most compelling and imaginative books being written in education today. Grounded on the theoretical advances in criticalism, feminism, and postmodernism in the last two decades of the twentieth century, Counterpoints engages the meaning of these innovations in various forms of educational expression. Committed to the proposition that theoretical literature should be accessible to a variety of audiences, the series insists that its authors avoid esoteric and jargonistic languages that transform educational scholarship into an elite discourse for the initiated. Scholarly work matters only to the degree it affects consciousness and practice at multiple sites. Counterpoints' editorial policy is based on these principles and the ability of scholars to break new ground, to open new conversations, to go where educators have never gone before.

For additional information about this series or for the submission of manuscripts, please contact:

Shirley R. Steinberg
c/o Peter Lang Publishing, Inc.
29 Broadway, 18th floor
New York, New York 10006

To order other books in this series, please contact our Customer Service Department:

(800) 770-LANG (within the U.S.)
(212) 647-7706 (outside the U.S.)
(212) 647-7707 FAX

Or browse online by series:

www.peterlang.com